EARLY CHURCH RECORDS of Alexandria City and Fairfax County, Virginia

F. Edward Wright
and
Wesley E. Pippenger

HERITAGE BOOKS
2012

HERITAGE BOOKS
AN IMPRINT OF HERITAGE BOOKS, INC.

Books, CDs, and more—Worldwide

For our listing of thousands of titles see our website
at
www.HeritageBooks.com

Published 2012 by
HERITAGE BOOKS, INC.
Publishing Division
100 Railroad Ave. #104
Westminster, Maryland 21157

Copyright © 1996

All rights reserved. No part of this book may be reproduced or transmitted in any form or by any means, electronic or mechanical, including photocopying, recording or by any information storage and retrieval system without written permission from the author, except for the inclusion of brief quotations in a review.

International Standard Book Numbers
Paperbound: 978-1-58549-329-6
Clothbound: 978-0-7884-3406-8

TABLE OF CONTENTS

INTRODUCTION iv

ALEXANDRIA MONTHLY MEETING 1
    Alexandria Monthly Meeting Minutes, 1802-1827 1
    Account Book For Friends 37
    Records of Marriage Certificates 38
    Certificates of Removal 39
    Membership 44

CHRIST (EPISCOPAL) CHURCH, FAIRFAX PARISH 54
    Extracts from the Vestry Book 54
    Pews in the Gallery 82
    Plat of Christ Church Burial Ground (Wilkes Street) 85
    Names of Burial Plot Owners, 1812 86
    Rectors of Fairfax Parish 87
    Vestrymen of Christ Church 88
    Record of Burial Permits, Christ Church Churchyard 89
    Extracts From Tombstone Inscriptions 94

TRURO PARISH 98
    Extracts From the Vestry Book 98

FIRST PRESBYTERIAN CHURCH 117
    Register of Baptisms, Marriage, and Funerals 117

INDEX 153

INTRODUCTION

SOCIETY OF FRIENDS (QUAKERS)

The minutes of the Alexandria Monthly Meeting begin on 9th month 23rd 1802, as created by Phineas Janney. The Meeting consisted of only one preparative meeting. In 1807, a second meeting was added in the City of Washington. The primary record used here is "No. 1, Record of the Minutes of Alexandria Monthly Meeting, Commencing 9th Month 23rd 1802, P. Janney" to 12th month 1827, by Robert H. Miller, recorder. The subsequent minute book used is "Record of the Minutes of Alexandria Monthly Meeting, Commencing 1st Month 24th 1828, Robert H. Miller, Recorder." These were taken from microfilm copies from the Maryland State Archives, Special Collections, reels 567 and 569.

EPISCOPAL CHURCH

In 1732, Truro Parish was formed when Hamilton Parish of Prince William County was divided, shortly after the founding of that county. When Fairfax County was formed in 1742, from Prince William County, the boundaries of Hamilton and Truro parishes were slightly changed. The town of Alexandria was established in 1749. Truro Parish was divided in 1765, and the boundaries of Fairfax Parish were ultimately established relative to a line between Dogue Creek near Mount Vernon, and Difficult Run. When Alexandria was incorporated as a city in 1779, it was included in Fairfax Parish.

Unfortunately the oldest of registers of baptisms, marriages and burials for Truro or Fairfax parishes have not survived. The extant register begins in 1828. The source used here is the first vestry book of Christ Church, Fairfax Parish, 1765-1843. We have extracted from the minutes information which relates to orphans who were bound out, names of needy persons, names of person buried, and a few other items which may prove of genealogical value. Only a few baptisms were recorded in the minutes, they being records of some of the vestrymen. A transcript of the earliest vestry book was made in 1914 by Mary Gregory Powell, historian, Mount Vernon Chapter, Daughters of the American Revolution. At that time she also made an account of the legible tombstone inscriptions in the churchyard on Washington Street. This transcript and the original record are available on microfilm at Alexandria Library's Lloyd House.

The minutes of Truro Parish end in 1785. They have been transcribed in full by the Pohick Bicentennial Executive Committee. Copies are available at Pohick Church, Lorton, Virginia. In 1907, Rev. Philip Slaughter published, *The History of Truro Parish in Virginia*, in which he drew heavily on these minutes. One should consult this book for details on the historical background of this parish and its many prominent parishioners. The original record is in the collection of the Library of Congress, Washington, D.C. A photocopy of the Truro Parish Vestry Book is held by The Library of Virginia.

PRESBYTERIAN CHURCH

The Presbyterian Church of Alexandria became the First Presbyterian Church of Alexandria in 1817, with formation of the Second Presbyterian Church out of the Alexandria congregation. The primary record used here is "Record of Baptisms, Marriages, and Funerals During the Ministry of the Rev. Doct. James Muir in the [First] Presbyterian Church of Alexandria, D.C." The original transcript is kept by the church at 316 S. Royal St. A photostat of the register was made in 1929 and is catalogued as accession number 20078 in The Library of Virginia. A microfilm copy is available from the Library.

Wesley E. Pippenger
Arlington, Virginia

F. Edward Wright
Westminster, Maryland
1996

ALEXANDRIA MONTHLY MEETING
Alexandria Monthly Meeting Minutes, 1802-1827

23/9/1802. Committee appointed to consider request of Friends of Alexandria to have liberty of holding a Monthly Meeting (MM) at Alexandria, that their meeting to be held on the fifth day preceding the fourth seventh day in each month and to be distinguished by the name of Alexandria MM. Signed Jacob McKay, John Hirst, Israel Janney, John McPherson, James Trayhern. John Butcher, John Janney, Thomas Matthews and Philip Wanton are appointed to propose a suitable person to act as clerk of the Meeting.

[16/8/1802. A meeting to be held at Alexandria was approved. James Mendenhall, David Lupton, Isaac Steer, Reuben Schooley, John Haines, John Hirst, Mahlon Taylor and Goldsmith Chandley [Chandlee] to attend the first meeting. Extracted from the minutes of Fairfax Quarterly meeting].

21/10/1802. Thomas Matthews was appointed to serve as clerk. A letter from a committee of Waterford MM in Ireland stated that Samuel Hutchinson had some time ago removed from thence and they received information of his settling in that town and had married contrary to rules of the Society. Elisha Janney, Edward Stabler and William Hartshorn are appointed to obtain information of his place of abode if found to reside within the limits of the Meeting. Elizabeth Cole, Hannah Jackson and Joseph Turner now attending.

25/11/1802. The committee reported that Samuel Hutchinson is not now resident in this place and they have not obtained his whereabouts. Frequent complaints of the neglect in attendance of week day meetings. [Extracted from the minutes of Fairfax Quarterly Meeting held at Hopewell, 14th of the 11th mo. 1802].

Property holdings information:
1. One-half acre lying on Queen Street (and known as the Burying Ground) was purchased from Thomas West for which a deed was taken on behalf of the Society in the name of William Hartshorn, John Butcher, John Saunders, John Sutton and Aaron Hewes, dated 8th of the 5th mo. 1784.
2. A lot on the west side of St. Asaph (on which the meeting house now stands) conveyed for the use of Friends by Benjamin Shreve to William Hartshorn, John Butcher, John Saunders, John Sutton and Aaron Hewes by deed dated in the 4th mo. 1785 and recorded in the county court of Fairfax.
3. A corner half-acre lot (purchased for the purpose of building a meeting house on) situated on the south side of [Wolfe] and west side of St. Asaph, by deed in name of William Hartshorn, Jr., Philip Wanton, Elisha Janney and John Janney, recorded in the Corporation Court of Alexandria, 1798.

John Janney, Treasurer. Philip Wanton, Aaron Hewes and Mordecai Miller were appointed a committee for superintending the affairs of the Burying Ground. John Janney and Aquila Janney, overseers; Jonathan Butcher appointed to the concerns of the lot on the corner of [Wolfe] and St. Asaph streets and the receiver of the rents from the two tenements thereon. Signed Thomas Matthews and Edward Stabler.

23/12/1802. The case of Samuel Hutchinson to be forwarded to the Waterford MM. A certificate produced for George Laurence, Judith his wife, and their son, William, from Nantucket MM for the Northern District dated first of 9th mo. last. Crooked

Run MM reported that Lydia Horner formerly Fosset [Fawcett] had married contrary to discipline to a man not in membership. Thirty copies of the General Epistle from Friends at their last yearly meeting held in London being received one of them read.

20/1/1803. A certificate produced for James Coffin Laurance, Jadedah his wife and their two children, Benjamin and Sally from Nantucket MM held for the Northern District dated 1st 9th mo. 1802, transferred by indorsement from Fairfax Monthly meeting. Proposal for altering hour of meeting from ten to eleven o'clock agreed to. William Hartshorn, Edward Stabler and Philip Wanton appointed to settle treasurers accounts also to consider what sum may be proper to raise for use of the meeting the ensuing year.

24/2/1803. Thomas Shreve produced a certificate from Chesterfield MM dated 8th of the present month. The clerk has sent a copy of the minutes on case of Lydia Horner to Crooked Run MM. George Drinker, Elisha Janney and Aaron Hewes are appointed to raise sum for treasurer. Sarah Vasse produced a certificate from Northern District Philadelphia MM dated 27th of 7th mo. 1802, directed at Fairfax MM.

24/3/1803. Ann Shreve produced a certificate from Indian Spring MM held at Sandy Spring dated 17th of 12th mo. 1802. A certificate produced for Isachar Scholfield from Indian Spring MM dated 17th of the 9th mo. 1802, addressed to Fairfax MM. Minute from Quarterly Meeting, the substance including communication from committee on Indian affairs, object of which is raising additional funds for effecting the Benevolent Intentions of Friends towards the Indian Natives.

21/4/1803. A certificate was produced from Nantucket MM for Charles Spence Lawrance and Mary Lawrence [sic], children of George Lawrence, dec., dated 2nd of 7th mo. 1801, addressed to Baltimore MM and transferred to this meeting. A certificate produced for William Lownes, son of James, from White Oak Swamp MM dated 3rd of last mo. 1803. Samuel Heston produced a certificate from Baltimore MM dated 10th of 2nd mo. last. This meeting informed that Dawson Fisher, an orphan member, is living with a family not in profession with the Society, whereas compensation is claimed for his past maintenance, and a suitable place for him amongst Friends is to be procured.

26/5/1803. William Hartshorne and Susannah Shreve appear to declare their intention of marriage, Susannah is desired to produce her father's consent. Lydia Green produced a certificate from Baltimore MM dated 10th of 3rd mo. last. A sum of $125 collected and paid to the Treasurer; a sum of $137.25 collected for the benefit of the Indian natives. Proposition to appoint friend Mary Stabler to the station of an Elder of the Meeting, subject to remain under consideration. Application being made for a certificate for Tacy McPherson (wife of Isaac) and the younger branches of their family to Baltimore MM, vizt. Jane and Elizabeth, Isaac's daughters by former wife, and Hesther, Mary, Anne and Wm., children of Tacy, all in their minority. Request for certificate for Ann Coates to Baltimore MM; William Kenworthy and Elisha Janney appinted to assist women friends in preparing one.

23/6/1803. Marriage of William Hartshorne and Susannah Shreve: having expressed the continuance of their intention of marriage, with each other, to which no obstruction appearing, Susannah having obtained her parents consent; they are left at liberty to solemnize their said marriage agreeable to the good order used among friends. John Butcher and John Janney are appointed to attend the solemnization thereof, report to the next meeting and return the marriage certificate. David Smedley produced a certificate from Hopewell MM dated 4th day of 4th mo. last. Flemming Bates produced a certificate from White Oak Swamp MM held 5th of the 3rd mo. last. A certificate for Edith Scholfield dated 4th of 8th mo. 1802, from Concord MM. William Laurence has married contrary to discipline with a woman not in membership. Mary Stabler is appointed elder. A certificate for Tacy McPherson and children to Baltimore MM is approved. A certificate granted for Ann Coates to Baltimore MM. William Kenworthy was appointed to keep a record in a suitable book of certificates of removal from this meeting. Philip Wanton appointed to keep a record of marriage certificates as well as births and burials.

21/7/1803. Marriage of William Hartshorne and Susannah Shreve conducted. The committee reported that Dawson Fisher has been removed from the place of his former residence and placed with the family of Benjamin Steer, a member of the Fairfax MM. Discussion of a more eligible situate for a Burying Place; the lot at present occupied for that purpose being a desirable object to friends generally, friends George Drinker, Philip Wanton, and William Hartshorne are desired to attend to the matter and report terms for new piece of ground, and whether the present ground can be sold on terms that will justify the disposal of it reserving that part already appropriated to the purpose of interment with an outlet to the street. A sum of $138.25 has been collected for the benefit of the Indian natives.

25/8/1803. A certificate granted for Dawson Fisher to Fairfax MM. Jacob Janney produced a certificate from Baltimore MM dated 14th of last mo.

22/9/1803. Fleming Bates requests a certificate to Cedar Creek MM for the purpose of marriage with Unity Crew, a member of that Meeting.

20/10/1803. John Janney is appointed to serve as clerk is absent at present meeting. A certificate granted for Fleming Bates to Cedar Creek MM to marry Unity Crew. This meeting being small in consequence of the sickly state of the Town [a yellow fever epidemic was rampant there].

10/11/1803. Moses Janney produced a certificate from MM of Baltimore dated 14th of the 7th mo. last. Thomas Matthews informs Meeting that the time of his appointment to act as Clerk is now expired.

24/11/1803. A certificate produced for Amos Gibson from Goose Creek MM held 29th of the 8th mo. last. William Hartshorne and William Yates appointed to attend the Quarterly Meeting; John Butcher informs that the situation of part of his family prevented his attending. Wm. Kenworthy is nominated to serve as clerk of Meeting, but he not being present. Proposed to have some alteration made in the stove pipe belonging to our Meeting House, and its inclosure.

22/12/1803. A half-acre lot may be had at the corner of Franklin and St. Asaph streets for $150; authorized to proceed and purchase it for use as burying ground, the present grounds cannot now be sold to advantage. William Kenworthy appointed to serve as clerk. Monies to be raised by the MM constitute a proportion of 3/6 in the Pound.

26/1/1804. Cost for burying ground lot is now $250. A certificate produced for Lydia Horner from Crooked Run MM dated 5th of 11th mo. last.

23/2/1804. Legal proceedings are necessary by grantor before he can make a clear conveyance. Treasury's account finds balance on hand as £10.8.11½. Phineas Janney to provide a suitable book to record the treasurer records. Edward Stabler replaces Aquila Janney as overseer for 1 year.

22/3/1804. Indisposition of David Smedley's wife prevented his attending the last meeting. The meeting informed that William Lawrence has never returned, he has not been heard from since he sailed from the West Indies, it is believed that he is lost on his way home, wherefore the case is closed. A certificate for Hannah Jackson produced from Northern District Philadelphia dated 21st last month.

26/4/1804. Will request Quarterly Meeting permission to grant ministers and elders the privilege of holding select monthly meeting separate from that of Fairfax, at the fourth hour in the afternoon on the 7th day preceding the select Quarterly Meeting. A certificate for Unity Bates produced from Cedar Creek MM, Hanover County, Va., dated 14th instant.

21/6/1804. A certificate for Isaac Jackson, Jr. from New Garden MM, Chester Co., Pa., dated 2nd instant.

26/7/1804. Isachar Scholfield requests a certificate to Indian Spring MM for himself and family. The committee appointed to procure a burying ground have informed the meeting that because of the late law of the Corporation prohibiting interments within its limits, in ground not before appropriated to that purpose, they have since given up the lot they had contracted for. Request approved to hold select monthly meeting.

23/8/1804. A certificate produced for Samuel Burrows Bidgood from Philadelphia MM held 25th of 5th mo. last. Isaac Jackson requests certificate to New Garden MM in Pa. Catharine Pugh requests a certificate for herself and children to New Garden MM.

20/9/1804. A certificate for William Matthews from Buckingham MM, Bucks Co., Pa. dated 6th of last mo. A certificate for Isaac Jackson Jr. granted to New Garden MM, Pa. Complaint is brought against Benjamin Shreve, Jr. for marrying contrary to discipline with a woman not in membership.

25/10/1804. A certificate granted for Isachar Sholfield, his wife, Edith and their son, Thomas to Indian Spring MM. A certificate granted for Catharine Pugh and her children, Isaac and Sarah and one for Hannah Jackson granted to New Garden MM. Edward Stabler laid before the Meeting for sympathy and concurrence his prospect of proceeding to North Carolina to accompany beloved friend Ann Alexander and her companion in the course of a religious visit through the southern states; he being an elder in good esteem.

22/11/1804. William Kenworthy's term as clerk is expired.

20/12/1804. William Kenworthy to be reappointed a clerk. Complaint against Philip Wanton for the intemperal use of spirituous liquors and not complying with his contracts. Jonathan Butcher produced an acknowledgment condemning his paying a militia fine, dated in Alexandria, 12th mo. 19th 1804.

24/1/1805. Benjamin Shreve, Jr. disowned for marrying contrary to discipline to a woman not of our society. Wm. Yates is absent. James Coffin Laurence requests certificate for himself and family to Nantucket MM for the Northern District.

21/2/1805. A certificate from Fairfax MM for Robert Gover dated 25th of 8th mo. last. A certificate for James Coffin Laurence granted for himself and his family to Nantucket MM for the Northern District. Complaint against Henry Woodrow reported for marrying contrary to discipline with a woman not of our society and neglecting meeting. Edward Stabler reappointed as overseer and John Janney as treasurer for another year.

21/3/1805. Controversy about membership in the Fairfax Quarterly Meeting is closed, and it is agreed that friends continue to belong that meeting. Sarah Matthews' husband announces she is now on a visit to her relations and friends in and near Philadelphia; she being a minister in good esteem. Amos Gibson requests a certificate of removal to Fairfax MM.

25/4/1805. Amos Gibson granted a certificate to Fairfax MM. Complaint against William Gore for marrying contrary to discipline to a woman not of our society and also for hiring enslaved persons. Benjamin Mason reported by Baltimore MM that he has married contrary to discipline to a woman not of our society.

23/5/1805. Testimony against Henry Woodrow will be prepared. Sarah Matthews produced a certificate from the yearly meeting of ministers and elders held in Philadelphia, from the 13th to the 19th of last mo.

20/6/1805. Henry Woodrow informs meeting of his intent to appeal his case. Further consideration regarding spirituous liquors.

25/7/1805. Elisha Talbott produced a certificate from Baltimore MM dated 13th of last mo., accepted. More discussion on spirituous liquors, and that each individual is to exercise a religious care to avoid being in any way instrumental in extending the mischiefs of an article so destructive to the health and happiness of man. Complaint against Moses Janney for marrying contrary to discipline to a woman not in our society. William Kenworthy informed the meeting that because of his wife's declining health he will leave his station in the MM.

22/8/1805. John Janney to serve as clerk the ensuing year. Henry Woodrow, residing at a considerable distance [from the Meeting], is reported for not attending meetings and marrying a woman not a Friend; he by birth had a right of membership with the Friends, but for years past absented himself.

26/9/1805. Certificate for Wm. P. Richardson from Fairfax MM, has the original; Thomas Matthews is appointed to apply to him for it.

24/10/1805. Certificate for Wm. P. Richardson, dated at Fairfax MM, 1st mo. 26th 1805, he having resided for some years in this place. Certificate for John Wilson from Philadelphia MM for the Northern District, dated 25th of 6th mo. 1805.

21/11/1805. Moses Janney acknowledges his faults and advises that his attendance at the next meeting is expected. Friend Wm. Crotch from Great Britain visiting.

26/12/1805. Certificate from Baltimore MM for Levis Janney and wife and their son Benjamin, minor, dated 10th of 10th mo. Wm. P. Richardson's certificate is returned to Fairfax MM. Thomas Matthews requests certificate for himself, wife [Sarah] and two children, Charles and Caleb Bentley, to Philadelphia MM for the Middle District. Certificate requested for Wm. Matthews to the same monthly meeting. Wm. Kenworthy requests a certificate for himself and wife [Rebeckah] to Dunnings Creek MM in Pennsylvania.

23/1/1806. Contact made with Philip Wanton who appeared sensible of his tsransgressions. A certificate for Thomas and Sarah Matthews with their two minor children Charles and Caleb Bentley to Philadelphia MM for the Middle District was produced. Also one for William Matthews to the same MM. A certificate for William and Rebeckah Kenworthy directed to Dunnings Creek MM in Pa. was produced. Proposal for Mary Janney and John Janney to the station of Elders is concurred.

20/2/1806. Testimony prepared by Edward Stabler on behalf of the Friends, called Quakers, against William Gore for his marriage with a person not of the Society and for hiring slaves from those who held them in bondage. Balance on hand in treasury of £12.1.2½. A certificate is requested for Lydia Green to White Oak Swamp MM in Va. Baltimore MM, 9th of last mo., informs that Elizabeth Janney, Jr., requests to be disowned.

20/3/1806. Certificate requested for Aaron Hewes, Jr. (a minor) to join him to White Oak Swamp MM in Va. Women Friends request assistance to unite with them in a visit to Mary Martin (late Woodrow) on account of her accomplishing her marriage contrary to discipline. Certificate of Wm. P. Richardson accepted from Fairfax MM; however he is charged with having attended military services, acting as the manager of a lottery and attending the marriage of a young couple from among Friends of one who was a member of the Society. Elizabeth Janney expressed a preference that a certificate be forwarded for her to Baltimore MM.

24/4/1806. Philip Wanton has frequently given way to the intemperate use of intoxicating liquors which has (as we apprehend) been one and perhaps the principle cause of his having disreputably failed in trade to the injury of many. He is disowned.

22/5/1806. The case of Martha Jones, formerly Matthews, having accomplished her marriage contrary to our discipline with a man not in membership, for some time past under the care of Women Friends; the committee is left at liberty to request the assistance of Goose Creek MM if necessary. A certificate is requested for Robert Hartshorne to New York MM. Mary Martin expresses her sorrow for a breach of discipline in accomplishment of her marriage, and desires to retain her right of membership; acknowledgement is accepted.

26/6/1806. Certificate for Robert Hartshorne is approved. Thomas Shreve and Jacob Janney are appointed to open a subscription for members for raising funds to benefit the Indian natives. A certificate is produced for Elizabeth Janney from Baltimore MM. A certificate is requested by Ruth Janney for herself and children to Hopewell MM.

24/7/1806. $61 has been subscribed for the benefit of the Indian natives, to be collected and forwarded to the Quarterly Meeting. A certificate is requested for Jona. Butcher, Jr. to Hopewell MM to enable him to accomplish marriage with Phebe Ross, a member of that meeting. Elisha [Talbott] and Sarah Saunders declare intention to marry. Meeting clerk's term to expire.

21/8/1806. Inquiry into Elisha Talbott's marriage engagements, appears nothing to prevent his proceeding for him and Sarah Saunders. Certificate to be prepared for Jonathan Butcher to Hopewell MM. Thomas Matthews, Jr. has removed from among us without a certificate. A certificate is requested for Jonathan Scholfield to Fairfax MM in order to accomplish marriage with a member thereof. It is reported that William P. Richardson has in addition to the other charges, lately accomplished marriage contrary to discipline.

25/9/1806. Marriage of Elisha Talbott and Sarah Saunders has not been accomplished owing to the indisposition of Sarah Saunders. Committee proposes and appoints John Janney for clerk and Phineas Janney for recorder.

23/10/1806. Marriage of Elisha Talbott and Sarah Saunders accomplished. Testimony against Wm. P. Richardson to be prepared. Levis Janney requests a certificate for himself, wife [Mary] and son Benjamin to Baltimore MM; Elizabeth Janney requests a certificate to the same monthly meeting. Certificate for Mary Shotwell from Philadelphia MM, dated 29th of the 8th mo. last.

20/11/1806. Certificate from Indian Spring MM, the 19th of the 9th mo. 1806, for Richard H. Litle. Marriage certificate of Elisha Talbott and Sarah Saunders now produced and recorded. A certificate of removal is requested for William Yeates, Jr., to Indian Spring MM.

25/12/1806. A certificate of removal for Thomas Matthews, Jr. to Philadelphia MM for the Middle District. A certificate for Phebe Butcher from Hopewell MM, dated 1st of the 12th mo. 1806. A letter received from Goose Creek MM informing that a visit had been paid to Martha Jones; she desires to retain her membership [disowned 23/7/1807]. Rebeckah Miller proposed for the station of Elder.

22/1/1807. Propose to replace Edward Stabler with Thomas Shreve as overseer. Certificate of removal is requested to Baltimore MM for John Shreve. Certificate requested for Mahlon Scholfield, son of John and Rachel of Prince George's Co., Md., to Hopewell MM in order that he may proceed in marriage with a member thereof [Ann Neill, dau. of Lewis and Rachel Neill].

26/2/1807. Subject of appointing overseers of solid attention; Thomas Shreve and John Janney stand appointed until further direction. A certificate for Wm. Hopkins from Baltimore MM, the 12th of this mo. Certificate prepared for Mahlon Scholfield. A certificate for Eleanor Scholfield from Fairfax MM, 24th of the 1st mo. 1807, received.

26/3/1807. A certificate from Hopewell MM for Wm. H. Brown, dated 5th of the 1st mo. 1807.

23/4/1807. A certificate is requested for Jacob Janney to Indian Spring MM to enable him to proceed in marriage with a member thereof.

25/6/1807. A certificate for Evan Taylor from Wilmington MM, Del., dated 5th mo. 7th 1807. A complaint from preparative meeting against Joseph Janney for engaging in a personal contest with another person, which he acknowledges. A certificate from Hopewell MM for Ann Scholfield, dated 5th mo. 4th 1807. Informed that Wm. Lownes has removed within the verge of White Oak Swamp MM in Va. and has been in the practice of performing military duty [disowned].

23/7/1807. A complaint is made against Wm. Hopkins for joining a military company, which he does not deny [disowned]. Testimony against Martha Jones (late Matthews) having accomplished a marriage with a man not of our religious Society.

20/8/1807. A certificate is requested for Deborah Stabler to Indian Spring MM for herself and her two [minor] children, Caleb and Henry.

24/9/1807. Edward Stabler to accompany friend Mary [Mitchel] in paying a religious visit to the families of friends belonging to the Baltimore MM. Subject of enclosing more of the burying ground was presented, George Drinker, Thomas Shreve and Wm. Hartshorne are appointed to consider matter.

22/10/1807. Testimony against Wm. Lownes presented. Committee about enclosing burying ground agree that it would be the best for the present to extend the fences which now stand on the east and west sides of the enclosed ground to the north line of the lot; work approved and is to be done. A certificate is requested for Samuel Heston to Baltimore MM for Western District. A certificate is requested for Charles Spencer Laurence (a minor) to Nantucket MM.

26/11/1807. Term for clerk is to expire. Titles of property belonging to the Meeting being under consideration.

24/12/1807. John Janney appointed clerk. A certificate from Hopewell MM for Wm. Jolliffe, his wife Rebecca and their three children, Mary, John and Elizabeth, dated 7th of 9th mo. 1807.

21/1/1808. Informed that John Wilson, a member of this meeting, has removed within the limits of Philadelphia MM for Northern District without a certificate. Philip Wanton having been appointed some years past to keep a record of births and burials, Elisha Talbott is appointed to call on him for the book. Informed that Andrew Scholfield requests to be reunited to Friends, having been disowned some years ago by Fairfax MM [accepted]. A certificate for Hannah Janney from Indian Spring MM, dated 12th of the 12th mo. 1807.

Alexandria Monthly Meeting 9

25/2/1808. The book of births and burials being now produced, George Drinker appointed to keep the records for the ensuing year. Mordecai Miller and Elisha Talbott appointed to apportion, collect and pay to the Treasurer $50 for the expenditures of the ensuing year.

24/3/1808. A certificate for Anthony Gover from Fairfax MM, dated 23rd of 5th mo. 1807. Edward Stabler believes Andrew Scholfield desires to be reinstated. A certificate was requested for Jesse Talbott to Indian Spring MM in order that he may accomplish marriage with Hannah Litle, Jr., a member of that meeting.

21/7/1808. Informed that Elizabeth Scholfield has requested to be received into membership. Judith Janney has requested to be reinstated in membership, she having been disowned by a Nantucket MM.

23/6/1808. Edward Stabler and Mary Hartshorne appear at the meeting and declare their intention of marriage, consent of parents being had.

25/8/1808. Testimony against William Hopkins read, and he is disowned. Marriage of Edward Stabler and Mary Hartshorne accomplished, and certificate is returned. Friends appointed to united with woman friends find no obstruction to Elizabeth Scholfield being received into membership, and also believe it would be right to reinstate Judith Janney.

20/10/1808. A certificate for John Shreve from Baltimore MM for Western District, dated 11th of the 5th mo. 1808. Moses Janney requests that his son Isaac and his stepson George Lawrence, Jr., minors, be admitted as members [received]. Subject of appointment of Edward Stabler as a minister and concurred; the clerk directed to furnish the Quarterly meeting of ministers and elders with a copy of the minutes.

24/11/1808. A certificate for Hannah [Talbott] from Indian Spring MM, dated 16th of the 9th mo. 1808.

22/12/1808. John Janney appointed as clerk and Jonathan Butcher as recorder.

23/2/1809. A committee is to visit Rebecca Paton, late Butcher, who has accomplished her marriage contrary to discipline.

23/3/1809. Minute from Quarterly meeting approving appointment of Edward Stabler as minister. Subject of building a new meeting house and disposing of the one occupied, being opened and considered; Mordecai Miller, Elisha Talbott, Edward Stabler, Andrew Scholfield and John Janney appointed to make a report of this at the next meeting. William Yeates appointed in place of Phineas Janney to the committee having the care of the meeting house.

20/4/1809. A certificate from Hopewell MM for Jonathan Ross, dated 7th of the 11th mo. 1808. A committee proposes a new meeting house of 36 x 60 feet, two stories high for the purpose of erecting galleries at a future period will be a suitable size; estimated cost, excluding galleries, to be $2,500; volunteer subscriptions have been obtained for $1,748.33 sufficient to erect building and enclose it. Certificate from Nantucket MM, dated 3 mo. 2 1809, for Judith Janney received.

25/5/1809. Through the preparative meeting, Ulysses Kinsey has applied to be admitted as a member. Proposition through Edward Stabler of uniting the monthly meetings of Pipe Creek, Indian Spring and Alexandria in a separate Quarter.

22/6/1809. Quarterly meeting proceed to be constituted by the three monthly meetings of Pipe Creek, Indian Spring and Alexandria would be proper, to be held at Sandy Spring on the 5th day after the first seventh day in the second, fifth, eighth and eleventh months, to be called the Sandy Spring Quarterly meeting. A letter was received from two Friends of the monthly meeting held at Weyanoke in Va. requesting assistance in visiting Aaron Hewes, Jr., on the subject of accomplishing his marriage contrary to our discipline. A certificate from Fairfax MM, held 25th of 3rd mo. 1809, for Mary Ross (formerly Janney), wife of David Ross. Rebecca Lloyd has made application to be reinstated as a member of our society [reinstated].

20/7/1809. Increased pleasure in the Christian testimony against the use of, trading in, or distilling spiritous liquors, as the importation of them has (we believe) nearly ceased.

24/8/1809. A certificate for William Yeates, Jr. from Indian Spring MM, dated 19th of the 5th mo. 1809. A certificate from Hopewell MM for David Ross, dated 1st of the 5th mo. 1809. A certificate for Oliver Wilson from Baltimore MM for Eastern District.

21/9/1809. Consent to reinstate Rebecca Lloyd. Informed that Elisha Janney has failed in business and it is feared his estate will not be sufficient to pay his debts.

26/10/1809. Report on Elisha Janney presented; he is exhonerated from any fraudelent intentions. Janney believes himself possessed of sufficient [resources] to pay all of his creditors when partial distribution is made. The causes of his failure were the embarrassments of trade and the diminished value of produce consequent on the embargo, and afterwards the loss of his mill by fire; fictitious capital. Elisha Janney is released from the station of an elder. Samuel B. Bidgood requested a certificate to Baltimore MM for Western District.

23/11/1809. Pattison Hartshorne, Jr., requested by a friend, a certificate to New York MM.

21/12/1809. It is reported that Ulysses Kinsey has removed from Alexandria. Elisha Janney apologizes to Society for his indiscretions. A certificate was requested for Peter Saunders to Hopewell MM in order that he marry Hannah McPherson, a member thereof.

25/1/1810. A certificate for Daniel McPherson, Elizabeth his wife and their three children: Rebecca, Mary-Ann and Samuel, from Hopewell MM, dated 4th of 12th mo. 1809. Propose Thomas Shreve to the station of elder; concurred. John Janney is appointed clerk. Elisha Janney requested a certificate for himself, his wife Mary, and eight of their children: Ruth, Albina, John, Mary, Anna, James, Aquila and Cornelia, to Fairfax MM.

Alexandria Monthly Meeting   11

22/3/1810. Committee appointed for building of a new meeting house reports that nearly all money subscribed has been collected and appropriated towards the building; the building may be ready for use in the 6th mo. next if additional funds can be raised; that $1,000 will be sufficient to put it in a situation to be occupied with comfort.

26/4/1810. The preparative reports that William Hartshorne has failed in trade and it is feared his estate will not prove sufficient to meet all his engagements. [26th 7 mo. 1810: It is later stated that he sustained a considerable loss by having produce on hand at the time the late embargo took place.] Edward Stabler has for some time attended the yearly meeting in Va. in conjunction with his sister-in-law Deborah Stabler of attending further religious services within the limits of Cedar Creek MM. A certificate for Hannah Saunders from Hopewell MM, dated the 2nd inst.

24/5/1810. Elisha Talbott was appointed to inform Andrew Scholfield a reason will be expected for his non attendance. [He furnished a reason at the next meeting.] A certificate for Aaron Hewes, Jr., from Weyanoke MM in Va., dated 7th of the 4th mo. 1810. Informed that Oliver Wilson has accomplished his marriage contrary to our discipline.

26/7/1810. Committee has visited William Hartshorne regarding his ability to meet all his engagements. It does not appear likely there will be sufficient to meet all his engagements unless his real estate sell nearer to his estimate of the value thereof than can reasonably be calculated on. The deficiency may we apprehend be chiefly attributed to his having labored under difficulties and the payment of heavy interest for several years, to the embarrassment on trade for two or three years past, and to a considerable loss sustained by produce on hand at the time the late embargo took place. His property real and personal (with the exception of his wife's) which was not mortgaged previous to the time he stopped payment as also the residue if any of that which was mortgaged has been conveyed to a trustee to be applied to the payment of his debts in equal proportions upon the creditors signing a discharge, reserving to himself the right of receiving the portion or dividend of those who refuse.

23/8/1810. A certificate for George S. Hough from Fairfax MM, dated 27th of 6th mo. 1810. A certificate for William H. Brown was requested to Hopewell MM in order that he may accomplish his marriage with Martha Wilson. The new meeting house is in a situation to be conveniently used, it was agreed to commence holding meetings therein on next first day.

20/9/1810. Friends Jonathan Hunn from Mother Kiln MM in Del. and Ann Mifflin and Sarah Lane from Philadelphia attended the meeting and produced certificates.

22/11/1810. A certificate was requested for Richard H. Litle to Indian Spring MM in order that he may accomplish marriage with Elizabeth [Talbott], a member of that meeting. A certificate of removal was requested for Jesse [Talbott], his wife Hannah and their son John Litle [Talbott], to Baltimore MM for Western District.

20/12/1810. A certificate for Grace Shreve from Upper Springfield MM, N.J., dated 9th mo. 5th 1810. A certificate was requested for Moses Janney, his wife Judith and their two children: Isaac R. Janney and Oliver Janney, to Fairfax MM.

24/1/1811. Women Friends requested assistance in preparing a certificate for Mary Shotwell to Philadelphia MM.

21/2/1811. John Janney appointed as clerk.

21/3/1811. A certificate for Mary Buchanan from New Garden MM, Pa., dated 10th of the 1st mo. 1811.

23/4/1811. A certificate for John Morgan from Fairfax MM, dated 28th of the 11th mo. 1810.

23/5/1811. A certificate for Elizabeth Litle from Indian Spring MM, dated 19th of 4th mo. last. was received.

20/6/1811. A certificate for David Lupton, Jr., his wife Ann and their dau. Rachel, from Hopewell MM, dated 9th of the 5th mo. 1811. A few lines received from Fairfax MM on account of Moses Janney's affairs not being entirely settled to satisfaction. A certificate for Martha Brown from Hopewell MM, dated 4th of the 4th mo. last. Update on new meeting house, that a new subscription was opened $1,085 subscribed and paid, that cost including stoves has been about $3,680, and to settle accounts more funds will be required. Excessive expenses have been partly occasioned by putting up the frame for the youth's galleries, the cost of new benches, two large stoves, and other requisites not taken into the former calculation. Approved to collect $900 from members.

22/8/1811. A certificate for William Thomas from Philadelphia MM, dated 25th of the 7th mo. last. A certificate requested for Robert Gover to Fairfax MM. Susannah Carr has requested to be admitted a member of our Society.

24/10/1811. Phineas Janney and Sarah Hartshorne appear and declare their intention of marriage.

21/11/1811. A certificate for Gerard Plummer, his wife Mary, and their son Philip, from Indian Spring MM, dated 10th mo. 25th 1811. A certificate for Edward Stabler, Jr., from Indian Spring MM. George Drinker reports no objection to proposed marriage of Phineas Janney and Sarah Hartshorne. George S. Hough and Susannah B. Carr appear to declare their intention of marriage. Appointment of Ann Shreve to the station of an elder was approved by the Quarterly meeting.

26/12/1811. Marriage of Phineas Janney and Sarah Hartshorne accomplished, a certificate recorded. A certificate for John Morgan to Fairfax MM was requested. A certificate of removal for William Yeates, Jr., was requested to Indian Spring MM. Certificates for Sarah and Elizabeth Peach from Indian Spring MM, dated 15th of last mo.

23/1/1812. Marriage of Geo. S. Hough and Susan B. Carr accomplished. A certificate for William Yeates, Jr., to Indian Spring MM. Elisha C. Dick has requested to be united in membership with Friends. Term of clerk has expired. John Janney, Phineas Janney, Andrew Scholfield and Mordecai Miller were appointed to investigate the titles to the real property of Friends belonging to this meeting and report any case is

Alexandria Monthly Meeting 13

necessary in respect to them.

20/2/1812. A certificate for Isaiah Hopkins from Indian Spring MM, dated 1st mo. 17, 1812. Elisha C. Dick approved as new member. Richard H. Litle proposed as new clerk, concurred. A certificate for Mary Grubb from Short Creek MM, Ohio, held 12th mo. 24, 1811.

26/3/1812. Committee to review property titles found the titles sufficiently secure for the present. Subject of releasing present overseers was proposed. John Janney, Edward Stabler, William Jolliffe, Mordecai Miller and Aaron Hewes appointed to make any further improvements to the meeting house and lot.

23/4/1812. Propose that Elisha Talbott and Daniel McPherson fill stations of overseers. A certificate was requested for William Thomas to Philadelphia MM for Northern District.

21/5/1812. A certificate for Lewis [Neill], Jr., from Hopewell MM, dated 14th of this mo. A certificate was requested for Joseph Janney to Indian Spring MM to enable him to marry Elizabeth Hopkins, a member of that meeting.

20/8/1812. A certificate was requested for Fleming Bates and [wife Unity and their five minor children] family to Cedar Creek MM.

24/9/1812. Informed that Mary Wiley formerly Lawrence, has accomplished marriage contrary to discipline, with a man not in membership [disowned]. A certificate for Warwick Price Miller was requested to Philadelphia MM.

22/10/1812. Testimony against Mary Wiley, declared no longer a member until she may become qualified to be reunited to the Society. Mahlon Scholfield appointed to keeping records of births and deaths in place of George Drinker who requested to be released.

26/11/1812. A certificate for Elizabeth Janney from Indian Spring MM, dated 23rd of the 10th mo. A certificate for Rachel Judge from Baltimore MM for the Eastern District, dated 12th instant. Certificate requested for William R. Wanton, a minor, to Baltimore MM for the Western District.

24/12/1812. Discussion of imposition of military fines and exactions.

21/1/1813. David Wilson and Hannah Irwin appear and declare their intention of taking each other in marriage, the former being a member of Hopewell MM.

25/2/1813. A certificate for Thomas Wilson and his wife Mary, with their minor children: Rebecca, Enoch and Thomas, from Hopewell MM, dated 4th of this mo. Also certificates for David Wilson, Catharine Wilson and Samuel Wilson from the same monthly meeting, same date. A certificate for Mary Buchanan to Hopewell MM. Certificate of removal for David Wilson accepted. Term for clerk has expired.

25/3/1813. A certificate for Martha Ellison, a minor, from Philadelphia MM for Northern District, dated 24th of the 11th mo. 1812. A certificate for Charles Litle, minor, from Indian Spring MM, dated 15th of the 1st mo. last. Marriage of David Wilson [a member of Hopewell MM] and Hannah Irwin accomplished. Richard H. Litle appointed as clerk for the ensuing year. Additional work on the meeting house's galleries approved.

22/4/1813. A certificate for John Hughs, a minor, from Indian Spring MM, dated 19th of 2nd mo. A certificate for Abijah Janney from Goose Creek MM, dated 1st instant. Committee appointed by Pipe Creek, Alexandria and Indian Spring MMs to confer further on proposition for establishing a new Quarterly Meeting, signed 4th mo. 7th 1813 by Thomas Wood, Jane Hibbard, Thomas Shreve, Ann Scholfield, Roger Brooke and Edith Scholfield. Informed that Evan P. Taylor has accomplished his marriage contrary to discipline with a woman not in membership with Friends. A certificate for Mary Peach from Indian Spring MM, dated 2 mo. 19.

20/5/1813. A certificate for Thomas H. Howland from New Bedford MM, dated 4th mo. 22nd 1813. A certificate for William Kenworthy and his wife Rebecca from Baltimore MM for Western District, dated 4th mo. 7th. Horatio Scott has requested to become a member of our Society.

24/6/1813. Committee has interviewed Evan P. Taylor who expressed a desire of retaining his right of membership. Friend Ann Ferris has presented a certificate from Wilmington MM with endorsement by Concord Quarterly Meeting concurring with her prospect of visiting some or all the meetings belonging to Baltimore yearly. Sarah Ferris and John Ferris produced certificates from Wilmington MM approving their accompanying Ann Ferris in her religious visit. Committee that was appointed to consider propriety of establishing an afternoon meeting for worship makes report.

26/8/1813. Rachel Smedley has requested to be received into membership. Informed that Rachel Waugh, formerly Judge, has accomplished her marriage contrary to discipline with a man not in membership with us; previous admonition and care having been suitably extended.

23/9/1813. Letter of apology from Evan P. Taylor; Elisha C. Dick appointed to inform Taylor of his acceptance. Testimony against Rachel Waugh, disowned.

21/10/1813. It is reported that Jonathan Ross has appeared in the ranks for the performance of military duty and furnished a substitute upon a late requisition from the Government [disowned]. Also a report that John Shreve had performed a tour of military duty and had attended a militia muster [disowned]. Also that a substitute had been hired for Joseph Janney for the performance of a tour of military duty. Samuel Shreve and Rachel Smedley appeared and declared their intention of taking each other in marriage.

23/12/1813. Testimony against Jonathan Ross, disowned. Testimony against John Shreve, declared no longer a member because of military duty. Sum of $460 to complete the meeting house's gallery has been collected; that the work has been completed with exception of benches for the west end for which additional money is needed. The old meeting house is in a suffering condition. Marriage of Samuel Shreve and Rachel Smedley accomplished.

Alexandria Monthly Meeting

24/2/1814. Joseph Janney permitted a militia substitute to be employed in the late requisition of government. William Yeates requested a certificate to Fairfax MM in order to accomplish marriage with Sarah Cavin, a member of that meeting.

24/3/1814. Term for clerk has expired. A change is overseers is considered.

21/4/1814. Present overseers are to be released and that Abijah Janney, William Kenworthy and Richard H. Litle be appointed to succeed them.

26/5/1814. A certificate was requested for David Saunders to Baltimore MM for Western District. Andrew Scholfield was appointed a member of the committee which has in charge the care of the Burial Ground in place of a former member dec.

23/6/1814. A certificate for Jonathan and Elizabeth Janney and their three minor children: Anna, Isaac and Richd. F. Janney, from Baltimore MM for Western District, dated 11th of last mo. Lydia Horner has requested that her children: Elizabeth, Thomas F., Martha B., Lydia Ann and Isaac Horner be admitted into membership, their father not being a member of the Society.

21/7/1814. A committee appointed to visit the family of John Horner, Jr. in relation to the admission of his children as members; he concurs with his wife's request; the children were received along with a younger son John born since last meeting. A certificate for Samuel McPherson and his wife Mary from Hopewell MM, dated 9th of 6 mo. last. A certificate for Thomas Neill and his wife Mary from Hopewell MM, dated 9th of 6 mo. last. A list of Friends who suffered an amount of sufferings under the requisitions of the courts martial in 1813:

Sufferers Names	Amt. demanded	Amt. taken
Phineas Janney	14.75	15.
Mahlon Scholfield	61.75	61.75
Jona. Scholfield	61.75	73.20
David Lupton	64.75	64.75
Peter Saunders	64.75	64.75
Geo. S. Hough	60.--	60.
Dl. McPherson	64.	64.
Thomas Shreve	13.	13.75
Oliver Wilson	54.50	59.40
Evan P. Taylor	76.76	76.76
Jacob Janney	10.	10.
	546.1	563.36

Edward Stabler, Jr.	Imprisonment
Saml. Shreve	Imprisonment

13 sufferers, 2 imprisonments, 11 loss of property

Friends Esther Griffith and Hannah Field of Purchase MM in N.Y. attended this meeting and produced a certificate of concurrence from their meeting with their prospect of visiting the southern and western states. John Cromwell produced a certificate of concurrence from the same monthly meeting on his accompanying them.

25/8/1814. The confused state of the Town in consequence of the vicinity of the British army occasioning the absence of many of our members and no business appearing that would suffer by delay the meeting adjourned until 5th day 8th of next month.

8/9/1814. Informed that Peter Hartshorne has accomplished his marriage in a way not conformable to our discipline and with a woman not in membership with us. A certificate for William R. Wanton from Baltimore MM for Western District, dated 10th of the 8th mo. Certificates for Sarah Ann Hewes and Deborah Hewes to Crosswicks MM, N.J.

22/9/1814. In the case of Peter Hartshorne, it was determined that he resides within the limits of Baltimore MM for Western District; their aid will be requested [disowned].

20/10/1814. Mary Wilson, clerk at this time. A certificate for Jane and Letitia Heston from Baltimore MM for Western District, dated 10th of the 8th mo. last. A certificate for Sarah Yeates from Fairfax MM, dated 31st of the 8th mo. last. A certificate from Baltimore MM for Western District for Joseph Heston, his wife Ann, who has died since the date of certificate (7/9/1814) and their two minor children: William and Charles and a minor grandson Joseph H. Wright.

24/11/1814. Subjects of schools, ardent spirits, and those of the African race which may be in Friends' families discussed.

22/12/1814. Concern over decline in attendance of meetings. A certificate for Thomas V. Huck from Indian Spring MM, dated 16th of 7th mo. last. Andrew Scholfield was appointed as one of the committee in the case of Peter Hartshorne, in place of David Lupton, Jr., dec.

26/1/1815. Lengthy insertion about education. Importance of education of offspring, acquisition of literary and scientific knowledge; select schools superintended by committees of the Society. Scarcity of suitable teachers, education under the patronage of the yearly meeting of Baltimore and similar to that at Ackworth in England, to Weston and nine partners in America. A certificate for Sarah Janney to Fairfax MM.

23/3/1815. Religious testimony against war. A certificate was requested for Thomas F. Horner, minor, to Plainfield MM, Ohio.

20/4/1815. A certificate was requested for Aaron Hewes and his wife Mary, to Philadelphia MM for Western District. A certificate was requested for Aaron Hewes, Jr. to Philadelphia MM for Western District. A certificate for Micajah Welding from Indian Spring MM, dated 16 of 12th mo. last. Women Friends have an inquiry whether any further care should be extended in the case of Rebecca Leslie who has been under dealings by the Women's Meeting for marrying contrary to discipline.

Alexandria Monthly Meeting 17

25/5/1815. Since last meeting Aaron Hewes, Jr. has accomplished marriage with a woman not in membership with us [disowned]. Richard H. Litle appointed as clerk for the ensuing year. Certificates for Sarah P. and Mary Ann C. Hewes to Philadelphia MM for Western District. John Janney, Andrew Scholfield, Phineas Janney, and William Hartshorne were appointed a committee to enquire whether it may be practicable to change our place of interment.

20/7/1815. Horatio Scott has accomplished marriage contrary to discipline with a woman not in membership [disowned]. Discussion of a proposed school. The marshal has deferred the collection of most of the penalties which had been imposed regarding military requisitions.

24/8/1815. Application has been made to the [Alexandria] Common Council for permission to change the situation of the Burying ground to another within the limits of the Corporation, on which permission was not granted, and that at present it does not appear probable that it can be obtained. Consideration of putting a new enclosure around the present place of interment. A certificate was requested for Charles Litle, minor, to Baltimore MM for Western District.

21/9/1815. Enclosure to burial ground estimated to cost $280, will report when work is completed. Testimony against Horatio Scott. A certificate was requested for William Jolliffe, his wife Rebecca, and their minor children: Mary, John, Elizabeth, William and Joseph, to Hopewell MM. A certificate was requested for Anthony P. Gover to Fairfax MM in order that he may marry Sarah Janney of that meeting.

26/10/1815. Communication from Indian Spring MM informing that the friends composing Washington preparative meeting desire to be incorporated with this meeting. A certificate from Fairfax MM, dated 27th of last mo., for James Russell, his wife Susan, and their four minor children: John Thomas, Joseph Janney, Hannah Ann and Rebecca. A certificate was requested for William Kenworthy and his wife Rebecca to Goose Creek MM. A school to be kept under the direction of this monthly meeting for the education of females; Rachel Painter, teacher, $500 per annum.

23/11/1815. A certificate was requested for Isaiah Hopkins to Indian Spring MM.

21/12/1815. A certificate for Alban G. Smith from Philadelphia MM for the Southern District, dated 27th of 9th mo. last. Certificate for Rebecca Neill and her dau. Mary, from Hopewell MM, dated 9th 11mo. last. A certificate for Lydia Neill from the same monthly meeting. Lewis Neill has married in a manner contrary to discipline with a woman not in membership with us [disowned]. A certificate was requested for William R. Wanton, minor, to Baltimore MM for Western District.

25/1/1816. A certificate for John Swayne and his wife Sarah from Fairfax MM, dated 29th 11 mo. last. Balance of treasury account $61.24, of which a sum will be required to defray expense of a new fence around the Burying Ground.

22/2/1816. A certificate for Hannah Janney from Fairfax MM, dated 2nd of last 8 mo. A certificate for Rachel Painter from Concord MM, Pa., dated 30th of the 11 mo. last. Certificate from Hannah Litle (a minister) from Indian Spring MM, dated the 15th

12 mo. last. The committee appointed in the first month 1814 to superintend the finishing the galleries to the meeting house reported that the work was done and paid for. Elisha Talbott and Andrew Scholfield were appointed to examine the record book of births and deaths and report whether they appear to have been accurately recorded.

21/3/1816. Certificate from Maria Perkins from Fairfax MM, dated 30th 1 mo. last.

25/4/1816. Friends are prohibited from hiring slaves from those who hold them. The committee appointed to examine the record book of births & deaths reported that there appeared to be some differences in the records and their correction would be attended with difficulty. They therefore recommended the appointment of a committee to aid the recorder in obtaining the information necessary. A certificate for Abijah Janney (ch. by his 1st wife Jane (McPherson)): Samuel M., Asa M., Hannah, Anna, Richard Mott, Hannah M. and Tamson - from Goose Creek MM, Loudoun Co., Va., dated 28th of last mo. [Corrections have been annotated in such a manner as to make it difficult to ensure I have an accurate interpretation - Ed.] A certificate for Joel Wright from Baltimore MM for Western District, dated 10th instant. A certificate for Joshua Baker from Fairfax MM, dated 31st of last mo. Joseph Rinker has requested to be received into membership.

23/5/1816. Catharine Moon has requested to be received as a member. A certificate for Samuel Peach from Baltimore MM for Western District, dated 10th last mo. A certificate for Sarah Janney from Hopewell MM, dated 4th of last mo.

25/7/1816. A list of subscribers in amount of $3,152 has been obtained toward establishment of a school. Abijah Janney requests to be released from the station of an overseer.

22/8/1816. A certificate for James Pharr and his wife Elizabeth from Buckingham MM, Pa., dated 5th inst. It is reported that John Swayne has assaulted a man with whom he had some difference and which he does not deny; disowned. A certificate for Sarah Gover from Fairfax MM. A certificate for Rebecca Leslie to Fairfax MM approved.

26/9/1816. A certificate for John Morgan, his wife Eliza and their infant son Joseph, from Fairfax MM, dated 29th of 5 mo. last. At the request of Hopewell MM the women Friends will visit Margaret Wood who has married contrary to discipline.

24/10/1816. A certificate to be prepared for John Hewes, minor, to Indian Spring MM.

21/11/1816. A certificate was requested for Nathaniel Ellicott, his wife Elizabeth and their four minor children: Nathaniel, Mary, Jonathan and Andrew, to Baltimore MM for Western District.

26/12/1816. It is reported that Thomas Irwin, Jr., has taken an oath before a military court, has frequently attended balls and the theatre, frequently absented himself from meetings and his deportment in many respects has been inconsistent with the order of our Society [disowned]. A certificate was requested for Edwd. Stabler, Jr. to

Alexandria Monthly Meeting 19

Baltimore MM for Western District. Expenses of $118.71 for articles in possession of the meeting, viz. one stove and pipe, benches, desks, four chairs, one atlas of maps, one load of wood ready cut for the use of the school, and one partition in the school room; salary of the tutoress. Certificate requested for Edward Stabler, Jr. to Baltimore MM for the Western District.

23/1/1817. A certificate for Abram Howland, minor, from New Bedford MM, Mass., dated 24th of 10th mo. last. A certificate was requested for John A. Ellicott to Baltimore MM for Western District. A certificate for Deborah Morgan, minor, from Fairfax MM, dated 2nd of the 10th mo. last.

20/2/1817. A certificate was requested for Jno. Janney to Frankford MM in order to marry Ann Shoemaker, a member thereof. A certificate was requested for Abijah Janney in order to marry Mary (Mitchell) widow of John Ellicott, Jr., a member of Baltimore MM for Western District. A certificate was requested for Samuel McPherson and his wife Mary to Fairfax MM. Richard H. Litle has a prospect of removing from within the limits of this monthly meeting and requests to be released from the station of clerk. A certificate for Hannah Ellicott to Baltimore MM for Western District.

20/3/1817. Thomas Irwin, Jr. late a member of the Society of Friends, has violated our testimony by taking an oath before a military court. Only one of the trustees is now living to whom the lot upon which the old meeting house now stands, and also the lot occupied as a burying ground. John Janney, Elisha C. Dick, Edward Stabler and Phineas Janney are appointed a committee to obtain a conveyance of the property.

24/4/1817. A certificate for Thomas Swayne from Hopewell MM, dated 9th of the 1st mo. last. A certificate was requested for Micajah Welding to Indian Spring MM.

22/5/1817. A certificate for Margaret Wood from Hopewell MM, dated 10th of the 4th mo. 1817.

26/6/1817. A complaint that Jonathan Scholfield has failed to pay a debt, a long time due and has not called a general meeting of his creditors as advised by the overseers of this meeting [disowned]. A request was made by Fairfax MM to visit with Nancy (Ann) Eaches for having accomplished marriage contrary to our discipline. A certificate for Rebecca Swayne and her two minor children, Joshua and Noah, from Hopewell MM.

26/6/1817. Committe for burial ground and lot conveyances reports that a deed has been made, dated 4th mo. 24th 1817, to John Janney, Edward Stabler, Phineas Janney, George S. Hough and Jonathan Janney, as trustees on behalf of the monthly meeting. A certificate for Rebecca Swayne and her two minor children, Joshua and Noah, from Hopewell MM, dated the 6th of the 3rd mo. last.

24/7/1817. A certificate for Israel Janney, Jr., from Baltimore MM for Western District, dated 6th mo. 6th last. A certificate for Mary (Mitchell-Ellicott) Janney from Baltimore MM for Western District, dated 11th of 7th mo. last. A certificate for Ann (Shoemaker) Janney, 2nd w. of John, from Frankford MM, Pa., dated 27th day of the 6th mo. last.

25/9/1817. A certificate for Benjamin W. Powell from Baltimore MM for Western District, dated 8th of 8th mo. last.

20/11/1817. A list of members of Washington Preparative Meeting: William Morgan, an Elder; Sarah Morgan, an overseer; William Morgan, Jr.; Miranda Morgan; Thomas Morgan; Jane Morgan; Arnold Boone; Hannah Boone; Hannah Shoemaker Boone; Elizabeth Boone; Mary Spencer Boone; Thomas Spencer; Alice Spencer; Mary Ann Spencer; Sarah Hall; Sarah Odle Hall; Thomas Samuel Hall; Mary Robertson; Samuel Brooke; Elizabeth Brooke; Samuel Hutchinson; John Barcroft; William Yeates, Jr., an overseer; Hannah Yeates; Elizabeth Yeates; Henry Yeates; William Patterson; Beulah Patterson; Rachel Scholfield; Joseph L. Scholfield; Mary (Russell) Scholfield, an overseer; Joseph Scholfield, Jr.; Hannah Schofield; Thomas Levering, an overseer; Rachel Ann Levering; Levi Underhill; John Hughes; William A. Scott; George Scott; Ann Scott; Ann Elgar; Elizabeth Elgar; Margaret Elgar.

Alban G. Smith has accomplished marriage with a woman not in membership and contrary to discipline [disowned]. A certificate for Hannah Pope from Baltimore MM for Eastern District, dated 11 mo. 6th 1817. A certificate for Jno. Rawlings from Wytham MM, county of Essex, Great Britain, dated the 4th of the 5th mo. last.

25/12/1817. A certificate for John McPherson and his wife Hannah from Hopewell MM, dated 6th of the 11th mo. last. Also a certificate for John McPherson, Jr. and Rebecca McPherson from the same meeting, same date. Also for Hannah H. Hopkins and Deborah Hopkins from Indian Spring MM. A certificate was requested for Jacob Janney, his wife Hannah and four minor children [Philip, Lewis, Mary and Henry] to Indian Spring MM. A certificate for Mary Grubb to Short Creek MM, Ohio. A certificate for Caleb Stabler, minor, from Indian Spring MM, dated 20th of 6th mo. last. Committee appointed to superintend the Alexandria female school provided written report.

22/1/1818. A communication from Little Falls MM stating that Susanna Hurdle, formerly Mason, had accomplished her marriage contrary to discipline and requested this meeting to treat with her. Elizabeth Mattingly has requested to be received into membership. John Hughes has accomplished marriage with a woman not in membership and contrary to discipline [disowned]. Danl. McPherson some year ago was very active in originating and bringing into operation and conducting an institution in this place known as the Merchants Bank which was managed so incorrectly as to fail for a very large amount, and involved a great number of innocent persons in heavy losses; he extended his engagements in business beyond the limits of prudence.

26/2/1818. A certificate for Danl. Haines, his wife Beulah and their three minor children: Maria, Rebecca and Susan, from Hopewell MM, dated 5th of 6 mo. last. Also one from Fairfax MM for John Ball, his wife Susanna and their three minor children: Elizabeth, Joseph Parkins and William James, dated 26th of 11th mo. last. A certificate for Ann Eaches from Fairfax MM, dated 28th of last mo. Peter Saunders some years ago was very active in the Merchants Bank [similar text with Danl. McPherson, above].

26/3/1818. A certificate for Thomas Rutter from Philadelphia MM for Southern District, dated 22nd of last mo. Abner Pope and Maria Parkins to marry, he being a member of another meeting. Term for which clerk was appointed has expired.

23/4/1818. A certificate for William Temple from Philadelphia MM for Northern District, dated 24 of 2 mo. last. Also a certificate for Robinson Hough, minor, from the same monthly meeting, dated 27th of 1st mo. last.

21/5/1818. Marriage of Abner Pope [with written consent of his parents] and Maria Parkins accomplished. Levi Underhill and Elizabeth Mattingly appear and declare intention of marriage, having consent of parents.

25/6/1818. A certificate for Thomas M. Bond, minor, from Fairfax MM, dated 29th of 4th mo. last.

23/7/1818. Hannah Litle, a minister, departed this life on the 5th of the 11th no. 1817, in the 60th year of her age. There are three schools taught by members of our society, two of which are under the direction of this meeting. A certificate for William R. Foulke from Indian Spring MM, dated 20th of 3rd mo. last. Marriage of Levi Underhill and Elizabeth Mattingly accomplished. William H. Brown has committed a breach of an implied contract by selling a quantity of flour to James Patton and afterwards refusing to deliver a considerable portion thereof. [Disowned. For more details see minutes of 24/9/1818.] A certificate for Maria Pope to Baltimore MM for Western District. A communication received from Philadelphia MM through the clerk of Indian Spring MM, that Ann Parker, late Collins, had accomplished marriage contrary to our discipline with a person not in membership with us. Martha Ellison has joined the Baptist Society.

20/8/1818. Peter Saunders states he regrets having anything to do with the Merchants Bank of Alexandria; however he is not conscious of being instrumental in its downfall; his case is discontinued. A certificate for Hannah Janney, minor, from Goose Creek MM, dated 30th of the 4th mo. last. A certificate was requested for Israel Janney Jr. to Philadelphia MM for Northern District in order to marry Elizabeth Warder, dau. of John and Ann Warder of that meeting. Also a certificate for William Stabler to Chesterfield MM, N.J., to marry Deborah Hewes, a member of that meeting.

24/9/1818. The committee in the case of Daniel McPherson (who acknowledged imprudence) accepts the correctness of his attitude and that he has learned through his errors.

22/10/1818. Thomas V. Huck and Mary Neill appeared and expresssed intentions of marriage with each other.

26/11/1818. A certificate for Isaiah B. Hughes from Pipe Creek MM, dated 13th of 6th mo. last. Also one from Baltimore MM for Western District, dated 6th of 11th mo. 1818, for John Litle, his wife Sarah and their son Robert Sinclair Litle, a minor. A minute was received from the Quarterly Meeting of Friends held at the Western Branch, Isle of Wight County, Va., dated 6th of 11th mo. last, expressive of their satisfaction with the religious visit of Edward Stabler. A certificate for Susanna H. Hurdle from Little Falls MM, dated 4th of 8th mo. last.

24/12/1818. A certificate for James Moore, Jr., from Fairfax MM, dated 28th of 10th mo. last. Marriage of Thos. V. Huck and Mary Neill accomplished.

21/1/1819. A certificate for Joshua Riley from Baltimore MM for Western District. Also one for Geo. Shoemaker from Gwyned MM, Pa., dated 31st of 12th mo. last. It is reported that James Shaw has been in habits of intemperance with a consequent neglect of his business [disowned].

25/2/1819. A certificate for Deborah H. Stabler, wife of Wm. Stabler, formerly Hewes, from Chesterfield MM, N.J., dated 2nd inst. Also one for Elizabeth W. Janney from Philadelphia MM for Northern District, dated 29th of 12th mo. last.

25/3/1819. A certificate for Isaac B. Beall from Indian Spring MM, dated 15th of 1st mo. last. Tace Shoemaker requests to be reinstated as a member [granted]. Rachel Waugh has made a similar application [denied].

22/4/1819. Report of school committee. A certificate for Hannah Ross from Hopewell MM, dated 9th of 7th mo. last. A certificate for Elizabeth Shaw to Buckingham MM, Pa. Stephen Wilson and Hannah Pope appeared and declared their intentions of marriage with each other, the former being a member of another mo. meeting.

20/5/1819. Letter written to Horsham MM, Pa. of the result in the case of Tace Shoemaker. A certificate for Stephen Wilson from Goose Creek MM, dated 29th of 4th mo. last, expressing his clearness of marriage engagements other than with Hannah Pope. A certificate for Gideon Davis, his wife Nancy [Hughes] and their five minor children: Herephila, Rodney, Morgan, Levi and Martha, from Indian Spring MM, dated 19th of 3rd mo. last.

24/6/1819. Marriage of Stephen Wilson and Hannah Pope accomplished. A certificate for Amos Gilbert from Indian Spring MM, Md., dated 16th of 4th mo. last. Also one from Concord MM, Pa., for Hannah James Churchman, dated 3rd inst. Informed that Daniel McPherson has recently taken the benefit of the insolvent law [disowned].

22/7/1819. A certificate for Hannah Wilson to Goose Creek MM. Also for Margaret Wood to Hopewell MM; likewise one for Susannah H. Hurdle to Baltimore MM for Western District. The necessities of the poor have been generally attended to. Certificate for Thomas Canby from Indian Spring MM, dated 18th of 4th mo. last, and one from the same meeting for Margaret Farr, dated 6th mo. 18, 1819.

24/8/1819. The Quarterly Meeting rules that Alexandria MM was too hasty in its action regarding Wm. H. Brown and does not confirm the proceedings. Certificate for Tace Shoemaker from Horsham MM, dated 28th of last mo. A certificate was requested for Wm. Temple to Sadsbury MM, Pa.

23/9/1819. Elisha C. Dick receives a gift in the ministry. A certificate for Geo. Janney, his wife Susanna, and their six minor children: Ruth, Hannah, Jacob, Isaiah, Esther, Susanna and George, from Fairfax MM, dated 28th of 7th mo. last. A certificate for Wm. Morgan, minor, to Philadelphia MM in Green Street.

21/10/1819. A certificate for Mary Sutton and her dau. Rebecca, minor, from Chesterfield MM, county of Darby, Great Britain, dated 13th of the 4th mo. last.

23/12/1819. Establishment of boarding school mentioned. A certificate for Martha B. Horner, minor, to Plainfield MM, Ohio. The certificate for Susanna H. Hurdle to Baltimore MM for Western District was endorsed and returned with information that she had settled again in the limits of this meeting. A certificate for James Sutton from Chesterfield MM, Great Britain, dated 2nd mo. 10 1818, directed to Radnor MM, Pa., endorsed to Indian Spring MM and by them to this meeting.

20/1/1820. John E. Carey, with his parents to consent, and Ann H. Irwin appeared with their intention to marry.

24/2/1820. A certificate for John E. Carey from Baltimore MM. Amos Griffith produced a certificate of concurrence from Westland MM, Pa., to accompany James Hallock on a religious visit to the southward and eastward, from Marlborough MM, N.Y. A certificate for Saml. Sutton the younger from Chesterfield MM, Great Britain, dated 12th of the 5th mo. 1818, directed to Radnor MM and endorsed and forwarded to this meeting. Informed that Isaac B. Bean has removed from the verge of this into the verge of Fairfax MM [a certificate was sent].

23/3/1820. Marriage of John E. Carey accomplished. Certificate produced for Isaac B. Bean to Fairfax MM.

25/5/1820. A certificate for Thos. Gilpin from Baltimore MM for Western District, dated 7th of 7th mo. last. Certificate for Phoebe Sutton from Burlington MM and it appearing that she has returned to the limits of Burlington. Certificate for Sarah Corbett and her minor dau. Martha, from Hardshaw East MM held at Warrington, Great Britain, dated 10th of 2nd mo. last. Certificate for Rebecca Russell from Wilmington MM, dated 4th mo. 28, 1820. A certificate for Mary Sutton and her dau. Rebecca, directed to Chesterfield MM, county of Darby, Great Britain.

22/6/1810. A certificate for William Ellison from Philadelphia MM for Southern District, dated 26th of 4th mo. last.

21/7/1820. Miami MM communicates that Thomas Neill, a member of this meeting had commenced a suit at law against a member of Society and has been using strong drink to excess [disowned - a copy of the testimony sent to Miami]. Nomination of Elisha C. Dick as minister.

24/8/1820. A certificate was requested for Daniel Haines and three minor daus. to Hopewell MM.

21/9/1820. William Canby [with the consent of his parents] and Sarah Janney appeared to declare intentions to marry, he being a member of another monthly meeting. A certificate for Mary Neill to Miami MM, Ohio.

26/10/1820. A certificate was requested for John McPherson and wife to Indian Spring MM. A certificate was requested for William H. Miller to Fairfax MM in order to marry Amy Ann Philips of that meeting.

23/11/1820. Marriage of William Canby and Sarah Janney accomplished. A certificate for Rebecca McPherson to Indian Spring MM. Certificate for John McPherson and wife Hannah to Indian Spring MM was produced. Certificate for Rebecca McPherson to Indian Spring MM prepared. A certificate was requested for Thomas and Joshua Swayne to Fairfax MM. A certificate for Lydia Horner and her four minor children: Elizabeth, Lydia Ann, Isaac and John, to Plainfield MM, Belmont Co., Ohio.

21/12/1821. The affairs of Daniel Haines in an unsettled state and he is making preparation to take the benefit of the insolvency law. The overseers report that David Ross has been for a considerable time past in the practice of drinking ardent spirits to a degree that has been reproachful to himself and our religious society [disowned]. A certificate for Rebecca Swayne to Fairfax MM. A certificate for Isaac Lambourn and Mahlen Scott, from Salem and Short Creek MM, Ohio, neither of whom it appears has set the with the limits of this meeting; certificates to be returned.

25/1/1821. William H. Brown accused of being in a dispute with some persons who were formerly his tenants and assaulting one of them. A certificate for Sarah Canby to Indian Spring MM.

22/2/1821. A certificate for Samuel Myers, Paulina his wife and their three minor children: Sarah, Mary and Hannah, dated 10th of last mo. A certificate for Daniel Haines and his three minor daus.: Maria, Rebecca and Susan to Hopewell MM. Testimony of Thomas Neill presented. A certificate was requested for Jesse S. Wilson to Goose Creek MM.

22/3/1821. Informed that Thomas Gilpin had frequented a house of lewd and ill fame and had left Washington secretly with what effects he had without paying his debts.

26/4/1821. A certificate for Samuel Rawlings from Chattens MM in the county of Cambridge, Old England, dated 9th of 1st mo. last. Propose Geo. S. Hough as clerk. Testimony produced against Thos. Gilpin. A certificate was requested for Wm. H. Brown, his wife Martha and their three minor children to Hopewell MM. A certificate for Amy Ann Miller from Fairfax MM, dated 28th of last mo. Samuel Hutchinson with the concurrence of his wife, requests that their two sons, Thos. and John, both minors, might be received as members.

24/5/1821. Nomination of George S. Hough as clerk confirmed. A certificate for Mary Bender, widow, and her dau. Juliana Bender, from Philadelphia MM for Southern District, dated 1 mo. 24, 1821. A certificate was requested for Jos. Canby and Amos Gilbert, minor, to Indian Spring MM. Reported that Evan P. Taylor has been in the practice of using ardent spirits immoderately, frequenting a tavern and associating with unprofitable company which we apprehend has led to the derangement of his business and want of punctuality; has neglected religious meetings [disowned].

21/6/1821. A certificate for Robert Rawlings from Grace Church Street MM, London, dated 4th mo. 10th 1820; also one from Chattens MM, Cambridge Co., Great Britain, for John Rawlings, his wife Mary and their two children: Mary and James; also one for Josiah Bender from Philadelphia MM for Southern District. Reported that John Rawlings, Jr., has been in the practice of retailing ardent spirits and is unwilling to relinquish the same. Thomas Canby has removed within the limits of Indian Spring MM.

26/7/1821. A certificate was requested for Thos. Shreve and five minor children: Elizabeth, Margaret, Grace, Thomas and Mary, to Chesterfield MM, N.J. George Shoemaker, having requested a certificate to Gwynedd MM, Pa. in order to marry Elizabeth Lukens of that meeting.

23/8/1821. A certificate for Thomas Shreve, a minister, to Chesterfield MM, N.J., for he and his five minor children, viz. Elizabeth, Margaret, Grace, Thos. and Mary. A certificate for Jane Heston to Baltimore MM for Western District.

20/9/1821. Committee considers a certificate granted by this meeting on 9th mo. 1819 for William Morgan, Jr. to Green Street MM, Philadelphia, certificate aught not to have been cancelled. A certificate from Fairfax MM, dated 30th of 5th mo. last, for Jos. Steer, Sarah his wife and their six minor children. Mary M., Phineas J., James M., Isaac H., Lydia Ann and Phoebe M., from Fairfax MM. Informed that Miranda Guy, late Morgan, has accomplished marriage contrary to our discipline with a person not in membership with us. Geo. Janney has removed within the limits of another meeting; his wife and children to appear at next meeting.

20/12/1821. A certificate was requested for Israel Janney and his wife Elizabeth and their two minor children: Caroline W. and Charles W., to Philadelphia MM for Northern District. A certificate was requested for Joel Wright and Charles Heston, minors, to Baltimore MM for Western District. Also one for Thomas Morgan, minor, to the same meeting. A certificate for Abagail Shoemaker from Frankford MM, Pa., dated 26th of 10th mo. last; also one from same meeting for Abigail Shoemaker Jr.

24/1/1822. A certificate for George Janney, his wife Susannah and their six minor children: Jacob, Esther, Isaiah, Susan, George and Sarah, to Indian Spring MM. Committee appointed to examine minute records found that the minutes recorded up to 1st mo. 1818 and that they had agreed to propose Geo. S. Hough as clerk. Jonathan Butcher requested through a friend to be released from station of recorder. Committee regarding titles to Friends meeting house and burial grounds was continued. A certificate for Ruth Hannah Janney to Indian Spring MM.

21/2/1822. Committee proposes Caleb Stabler as recorder for a term of two years. A certificate for Abner Pope, his wife Maria and two minor children: Edward and Mary Ann, from Baltimore MM for Western District, dated 12 mo. 7 1821. Mention of Fair Hill Boarding School. Joseph Janney has accomplished marriage contrary to the order of Society with the sister of his former wife. Hannah Janney, late Hopkins, has accomplished marriage contrary to the rules of society with a man who was husband of her sister, dec'd. [disowned].

21/3/1822. Report by committee on real estate find occupancy of Alexandria Preparative Meeting a lot on which their present meeting house stands, a lot on which their old meeting house stands and which is now used as a school house, and one other lot which is used by said preparative meeting as a burial ground and within the limits; and occupancy of Washington Preparative Meeting, a lot upon which their meeting house stands, and another lot used by them as a burial ground. Deeds to properties are vested in trustees as follows: W.T. Alexander and wife to [William] Hartshorne and others, recorded in the clerk's office in Alexandria, Nov. 1798, Liber H, fol. 650; Aaron Hewes to John Janney and others, recorded at the clerk's office in Alexandria, May 1817, Liber D2, folio 375; Thos. Monroe to William Morgan and others, recorded in the clerk's office, Washington, Liber T No. 19, folios 349, 350; Jonathan Shoemaker to Samuel Lukens and others, recorded in Washington, Liber T No. 19, folio 114, 115 and 116. A certificate for Susannah H. Hurdle to Indian Spring MM. Samuel Sutton, Jr., has lived intimately with a female by whom it is said he has a child and has left the District in company with her [disowned].

25/4/1822. Samuel Sutton, Jr. has been quilty of criminal conduct calculated to bring disgrace upon [the] Society. Samuel Wilson has accomplished marriage contrary to discipline with a woman not in membership with us [disowned]. A certificate for Mahlon Hough from Fairfax MM, dated 27th last mo. Also one from Concord MM, Pa. for Pennell Palmer, dated 28th of last mo.

23/5/1822. Dates of meetings established. A certificate to be prepared for Richard Janney, minor, to Fairfax MM.

20/6/1822. A certificate for Elizabeth Shoemaker, late Lukens, wife of Geo. Shoemaker, from Gwynedd MM. Pa., dated 31st of 1st mo. last. William Yeates, Jr., John Litle and Samuel Hutchinson appointed to attend burials and to take care of the burial ground belonging to the Washington Preparative Meeting.

18/7/1822. Committee reports about Samuel Wilson. George Drinker, at his request, should be released as overseer, and John Janney appointed in his place. A certificate for Daniel Embree, his wife Sarah and their four children: Rachel, Wm , Margaretta and Hannah Mary, from Bradford MM, dated 3rd ints. Priscilla Hunt, a minister from Indiana, and her companion Rachel Johnson, attended the meeting. A certificate for Rebecca Neill to Hopewell MM; also one for her dau. Lydia Neill to the same meeting. John Rawlings, Jr., has requested our certificate to Wythan MM, Chatensford, Essex Co., England.

22/8/1822. Certificate produced for John Rawlings, Jr. to Wythan MM, Essex, Great Britain. A certificate was requested for William Heston to Gun Powder MM. A certificate was requested for Jos. Heston to Baltimore MM for Western District. A certificate for Amelia Hough from Fairfax MM, dated 27th of 3rd mo. last. The clerk is charged with keeping a suitable book of current record of members, at [at] each Preparative Meeting directed to furnish a correct list of the births and burials which shall have occurred within their respective limits to this meeting in the 12th mo. of each year.

19/9/1822. The clerk being absent, William Stabler was appointed to serve for this time. A request to Wayne Oak MM to deal with Hannah Smyth who has accomplished marriage contrary to discipline.

24/10/1822. A certificate for Jos. Heston to Baltimore MM for Western District. Richard H. Litle has requested a certificate to Philadelphia MM for Northern District to enable him to marry Ruth James a member of that meeting. A certificate for Susannah Ball and her three minor children: Elizabeth H., Jos. P. and William James

Alexandria Monthly Meeting

Ball, to Hopewell MM. Thomas Rutter has removed beyond the limits of this meeting [a certificate was sent to 12th Street MM, Philadelphia].

21/11/1822. A certificate for William Gillingham, his wife Jane and their four minor children: Isaac, Jehu, Elizabeth and Catharine, from Baltimore MM, dated 11th of last mo. A certificate was requested for Thomas S. Stabler to Indian Spring MM.

19/12/1822. Certificate requested for Thomas S. Stabler produced. Records of births and deaths were examined. Alice Spencer has promulgated evil and slanderous reports about another member; she insists on her assertions without being able to substantiate them.

[handwriting of the record becomes less legible]

23/1/1823. Susan Marsh requests to be received into membership. The overseers have removed the following members from the limits of this meeting: David Wilson, wife and children; Peter Saunders, wife and children; Wm. Patterson, wife and children; Abram Howland; John McPherson, Jr.; Noah Swayne.

20/2/1823. A certificate for Wm. Patterson with his wife and son [Ellwood], minor, to Uchland MM, Pa.; one for Abraham Howland to New Bedford MM, Mass.; one for David Wilson, wife and their two minor children: John Warder and Thomas Irwin, to Hopewell MM; one for Peter Saunders and wife with their six minor children: Sarah, John M. McPherson, Joseph, Thomas H. and Samuel C., to Gravelly Run MM, Va.; and one for Jno. McPherson, Jr., to Gravelly Run MM, Va. Reported that Phebe Horner requests to be reinstated. A certificate for Hannah Janney to Indian Spring MM. A certificate for Ruth Litle (nee James, wife of Richard H. Litle) from Philadelphia MM for Northern District, dated 1st mo. 28th 1823.

20/3/1823. A certificate for Thomas Wetherald, a minister, with his wife Ann and their three minor children: Mary, Esther and Joseph E. Wetherald, from Chesterfield MM, N.J., dated 4th. A certificate for Sarah Ann and Harper Soulby, children of Henry Soulby, together with Joseph Harter a youth resident from the monthly meeting of Spalding and Wainfleet in the county of Lincoln, Old England. Caleb Stabler who stood appointed as recorder is about to remove from the limits of this meeting. A certificate was requested for Robert H. Miller to Fairfax MM to enable him to marry Anna Janney.

24/4/1823. John Rawlings, Jr., not having gone to Great Britain, his certificate was returned.

22/5/1823. Robert H. Miller is appointed to office of recorded for term of two years. A certificate was requested for John Rawlings, Jr. to Wythan MM, Essex, Great Britain. A certificate for Phebe Ann Janney, minor, from Fairfax MM, dated 4th mo. 16th 1823. Certificate for Thomas Rutter returned from 12th Street MM, Philadelphia, dated 4th mo. 30th 1823, stating he resided in the limits of the Philadelphia MM for Northern District.

19/6/1823. Certificate for Peter Saunders, wife and children, and that for John McPherson, Jr. to Gravelly Run MM, were returned on account of the unsettled state of their affairs. Ann Elgar and her daus., Eliza and Margaret Elgar, have departed from the consistency of members in dress and address in attending stage plays, balls and places of diversion [disowned]. At the subject of appointing new trustees, they feel that a new deed ought to be obtained from the surviving trustees (only one of whom now resides in Alexandria and he not a member of the Society), for the lot of ground on which the meeting house stands at the southwest corner of St. Asaph and Wolfe streets, and recommend the following named persons, viz. Edward Stabler, Jonathan Butcher, Phineas Janney, George S. Hough and Jonathan Janney, as trustees; deed for burying ground and the lot on which the old meeting house stands is complete, having been renewed on the 24th day of the 4th month 1817 and conveyed to six trustees, five of whim are yet living and all members of this meeting.

24/7/1823. John Janney, an elder and member of Alexandria Preparative meeting departed this life on the 10th of the 5th month in the 58th year of his age. Testimony against Samuel Peach. He is disowned, having accomplished marriage with a woman not in membership. Certificate granted in 4th mo. to Thomas Wetherald to attend meetings in N.J. is returned.

21/8/1823. Testimony against Ann Elgar. A certificate was requested for James Moore, Jr. to Baltimore MM for Western District to accomplish marriage with Esther Sinclair of that meeting. Informed that William Patterson and family for whom a certificate was sent to Uwchland MM, Pa., have removed from within the limits of that meeting.

18/9/1823. Reported that Thomas H. Howland has failed in his business; a considerable period has elapsed wherein he has not paid his creditors [disowned]. A considerable time has past since Thomas V. Huck failed in business; he has not made any arrangement with his creditors.

25/10/1823. Thomas V. Huck has claims due in N.Y. and Va. to the amount of $23,885.63, leaving a balance of $5,148.34 due him. A certificate for Letitia M. Heston to Baltimore MM for Northern District.

20/11/1823. A certificate for Anna Miller from Fairfax MM, dated 9th mo. 10th 1823, and one for Mary M. Scott from the same meeting, dated 8th mo. 13th. Discussion of the Fair Hill Boarding School. A certificate was requested for Joseph Steer, his wife Sarah and their five children: Mary McPherson, James Moore, Isaac Hollingsworth, Lydia Ann and Phebe Moore Steer.

18/12/1823. A certificate from Indian Spring MM for Jacob Janney, his wife Elizabeth and their five minor children: Philip, Lewis, Mary, Henry and Eleanor Janney, dated 21st of 11th mo. 1823. Testimony in the case of Sarah Ann Soulby and Harper Soulby. Sarah Ann and Harper Soulby, children of Henry Soulby, who had a right in the Society which was transmitted to this meeting by a certificate from Spalding and Wainfleet MM in Old England; however their parents manifested an unwillingness that their children remain members; the children are released from membership. Testimony in the case of Joseph Barber. Joseph Barber, having a right in the Society which was transmitted to this meeting by a certificate from Spalding and Wainfleet MM in Old England; however he expresses an unwillingness to remain a member; released. Committee appointed to examine subscriptions to Fair Hill School.

Alexandria Monthly Meeting 29

22/1/1824. A certificate for Mary M. Steer to Fairfax MM. Alexandria Preparative meeting furnished a list of births and deaths within its limits during the year 1823. A certificate was requested for Caleb Stabler to Indian Spring MM.

19/2/1824. A certificate for David Wilson, his wife Hannah and their two minor children: John Warder and Thos. Irwin Wilson, from Hopewell MM, dated 5th inst. A certificate for Jane Janney and one for Pleasant Janney from Goose Creek MM, dated 12th inst.

18/3/1824. A certificate for Esther Moore (late Sinclair), wife of James Moore, Jr., from Baltimore MM, dated 2nd mo. 6th. Also one from the same monthly meeting, for Joel Wright, minor. Informed that Susanna Walker requests to be received into the Society.

22/4/1824. A certificate for Rebecca [illegible], Hannah James Churchman, Elizabeth Stabler and Anna Stabler, to Indian Spring MM. Testimony against Thomas H. Howland.

20/5/1824. A certificate for Oliver Janney, minor, from Fairfax MM, dated 10th of 3rd mo. Samuel Hutchinson expreses concern to accompany his friend Stephen Gullatt. A certificate for Margaret Farr to Plainfield MM, Clark Co., Ohio.

24/6/1824. Mahlon Scholfield request certificate for himself, his wife Ann and their six minor children: Lewis, Elizabeth, Rachel, Ann, Joseph and William, to Hopewell MM.

22/7/1824. Testimony against William Patterson, that during a short residence in Trenton, N.J., he contracted certain debts which he left unpaid; being visited by a committee of Clear Creek MM, Ohio, at our request, he would not admit the charge [disowned]. Committee report on case of Thomas V. Huck. A certificate for Hannah Ross to Hopewell MM.

18/8/1824. David Smedley has for a long time neglected attendance of our meetings and has been in the practice of visiting a house of ill fame; [disowned]. Complaint of Gideon Davis for noncompliance with engagements. A certificate was requested for Ann Lupton and four minor children: Rachel, John, Jane and Mary, to Hopewell MM.

29/9/1824. Certificates for James M. Janney, Israel H. Janney and Sarah Jane Janney, minors, from Fairfax MM, dated 4th mo. 14th. A certificate for Eliza Sands from Indian Spring MM, dated 9 mo. 8th. A certificate for Eliza Mary and Jonathan Barber from Grace Church Street MM, London, dated 5th mo. 5th 1824.

21/10/1824. Letter from Gideon Davis regarding his insolvency and handling his creditors. Informed that Eliza Mary and Jonathan Barber do not reside within the limits of this meeting. Mary Ann Wahl has requested to be received into membership [admitted]. Testimony against David Smedley. A certificate was requested for Beulah Patterson and her children: Samuel Nixon Patterson and Elwood Patterson to Cincinnati MM, Ohio.

18/11/1824. A certificate for James M. Hozier and his wife Hannah, a minister, and their dau. Maria, from Salem MM, Mass., dated 14th of 10th mo. A certificate for Rachel and Ann Ellicott from Baltimore MM for Western District, dated 10th of 9th mo.

23/12/1824. Thomas Spencer, leaving the District, placed his papers and effects in the hands of an agent but has not left property sufficient to discharge his debts [disowned]. Mahlon S. Scott having been imprisoned for debts and obtained the liberty of the goal [jail] bounds by giving security and left the goal limits; has engaged in personal contests and fighting and has at different times given way to intoxication and neglected meetings. Informed that Julianna Bender has accomplished her marriage contrary to discipline. A certificate for Sarah [Corbett] and her dau. Martha, minor, to Hardshaw East MM, England. A certificate was requested for Thomas M. Bond to Fairfax MM.

20/1/1825. Julianna Wilson, late Bender, has accomplished her marriage contrary to discipline [disowned]. A certificate for Margaret Hallowell from Indian Spring MM. A certificate was requested for Benjamin W. Powell to Hopewell MM. A certificate was requested for Asa M. Janney to Hopewell MM.

24/2/1825. A certificate for Benjamin Hallowell from Goshen MM, Chester Co., Pa., dated 2nd inst. Report of Thomas Spencer's case.

24/3/1825. A certificate for Charles Farquhar from Concord MM, Pa., dated the 3rd inst. Some time during the last summer James Irwin joined in a public military muster [disowned]. A certificate for John R. Pierpoint from Hopewell MM, dated 1st mo. 6th. A certificate was requested for James Moore, Jr., his wife Esther and their minor son Thomas, to Baltimore MM for Western District. John Rawlings has been dealing in the article of ardent spirits for some time past.

19/5/1825. Samuel Myers to fill the station of Elder. Mary Cheney late Corbett has expressed that she was sensible of her deviation in the manner of her marriage; the clerk is directed to forward a recommendation that she be disowned to Hardshaw East MM. Elisha C. Dick has for a considerable time past, absented himself from our meetings.

23/6/1825. A certificate for Samuel Canby, his wife Elizabeth and their seven minor children: Thomas, Samuel, Beulah, Joseph, Yardley, Elizabeth and William, and one for Mary Canby, from Baltimore MM for Western District, dated 10th inst. Report of the committee in relation to the property belonging to Washington Preparative Meeting; whether necessary to appoint new trustees; that the deed for the burial ground has been examined by F.S. Key who gave it as his opinion that so far as the Society was interested, it was a good and sufficient deed; that there were some defects in not providing for a succession of trustees. It is believed that the ground on which the meeting house stands is similarly circumstanced with the Burial ground. Of the trustees for the former, only William Morgan is living of the latter there are three living.

21/7/1825. Richard H. Litle, an Elder and member of Alexandria Monthly and particular meetings, departed this life on the 25th of the 2nd month last in the 37th year of his age. Richard R. Lupton, son of Joseph and Esther Lupton and Anna Janney, dau. of Abijah and Jane Janney to marry with consent of her father. He, not being a member of this meeting, produced the consent of his parents in writing. Short Creek MM, OH, reports that a certificate for Mahlon S. Scott had been endorsed by them to Redstone MM. A certificate was requested for William Foulke to Indian Spring MM.

18/8/1825. Certificate received from Hopewell MM dated 4th inst. stating there was no objection to Richard R. Lupton's accomplishing his marriage with Anna Janney.

22/9/1825. A certificate for Lot Holmes, minor, from Fairfax MM, dated 13th of the 7th mo. last; also one for Thomas M. Scholfield from Concord MM, Pa., dated 28th of the same mo. Marriage of Richard R. Lupton and Anna Janney accomplished. Testimony against Thomas Spencer. The mercantile house of which John Morgan was a partner has failed; he has been in practice of using intoxicating drink to excess and frequenting a house where it is sold [disowned 21/9/1826]. Thomas Wilson has accomplished his marriage contrary to discipline [disowned]. John Cowman, Jr. desires to be received into membership [earlier disowned by Indian Spring MM, which meeting consents and he is received].

20/10/1825. A certificate for Margaret Judge, minister, from Indian Spring MM. Lewis Cole [from Fairfax MM], son of Samuel and Lydia Cole, and Amelia Hough, dau. of Mahlon Hough, to marry. Report of case of William Morgan. A complaint against Phebe Horner for determining to hold in bondage until they shall refund the money which was paid for them, two slaves left her by her dec'd. husband [disowned]. A certificate for Deborah Morgan to Hopewell MM.

24/11/1825. Lewis Cole produced certificate from Fairfax MM stating his clearness from other marriage engagements, and consent of his parents in writing; the consent in writing of parents of Amelia Hough was also produced. Testimony received from Elgnad against Mary Cheney, late Corbett. Testimony against Phebe Horner, having come into possession of two slaves which she still continues to hold in bondage. Testimony against Thomas Wilson, having so far transgressed the rules by marrying in a manner contrary thereto. William Stabler is clerk. Testimony against James Irwin, who deviated by joining the military.

22/12/1825. Marriage of Lewis Cole and Amelia Hough accomplished. William Morgan has failed in business; although his insolvency was known to him he drew an order for one year's rent in advance, of a warehouse after he had made a transfer of his right of property [disowned].

19/1/1826. Samuel M. Janney, son of Abijah and Jane Janney, and Elizabeth Janney, dau. of John and Elizabeth Janney, to marry; Abijah Janney expressed his consent.

23/2/1826. At Alexandria MM on 21/12/1820 a certificate for Mahlon S. Scott was received from Short Creek MM, Ohio, and it then appearing that he was not a resident within our limits, the certificate was returned; it further appears that he subsequently became a resident in our limits and on 23/12/1824 at Alexandria MM he was charged with failing to comply with engagements, occasionally giving way to intoxication and entering into personal combat and fighting; and he again removed without our limits [disowned].

23/3/1826. Certificates for Elizabeth and Anna Stabler from Indian Spring MM, dated 4th of the 1st mo. 1826; and one for Thomas S. Stabler from the same meeting, dated 8th of 3rd mo. 1826. Marriage of Samuel and Elizabeth Janney accomplished. Samuel M. Janney, Elisha Talbott, Thomas Levering and John Barcroft appointed to work with clerk in revising the minutes. Request of James M. Hozier to become a member is granted.

24/4/1826. Friend Thomas Wetherald, an approved minister, opened meetings with a concern to attend the ensuing yearly meeting in N.Y. Marriage certificate for Samuel M. and Elizabeth Janney has been recorded. Confirmed Margaret Judge an approved minister. A certificate for John L. Talbott, minor, from Baltimore MM. A certificate for Sarah Eleanor Wetherall [probably Wetherald] from Fairfax MM, dated 14th of 12mo. 1825.

18/5/1826. Mary Cooper late Rawlings has accomplished her marriage contrary to discipline with a person not a member [disowned]. A certificate for Mary S. Hallowell from Concord MM, Pa. A certificate for Susannah Marsh to Rahway & Plainfield MM, East Jersey.

22/6/1826. A certificate was requested for Daniel Embree's son, William L. Embree, minor, to Kennett MM, Chester Co., Pa. A certificate for Anna Lupton, formerly Janney, wife of Richard R. Lupton, to Hopewell MM.

20/7/1826. Ann Butcher, an elder and member of Alexandria Preparative and MM, departed this life on the 2d of the 4th month in the 77th year of her age. Edward Stabler returned the certificate granted to him in the 4th mo. to visit in gospel for friends and others on the eastern shore of Maryland. A certificate was requested for Joshua Riley to Indian Spring MM to enable him to marry Elizabeth Lukens of that meeting. Testimony against Mary Cooper, late Rawlings.

24/8/1826. A certificate was requested for Thomas V. Huck, his wife Mary and their two minor children, Richard and Rebecca, to Hopewell MM. John S. Miller has accomplished his marriage contrary to discipline with a woman not in membership [disowned].

21/9/1826. Testimony against John Morgan, in the excessive use of intoxicating liquors and spending much of his time in taverns, is disowned and no longer a member of the Society.

19/10/1826. Friend Jared Patterson, a minister, attended this meeting and produced a certificate of unity with his prospect as therein expressed from Stillwater MM, Ohio.

23/11/1826. A certificate for Mary M. Scott to Fairfax MM produced.

21/12/1826. A certificate for James A. Hewes [to Philadelphia MM]. Report in case of John McPherson, Jr. In 1824, John McPherson, Jr., then resident in Petersburg, failed in business and availing himself of the insolvency laws, left there without paying his debts; that event was not attributable to extravagance and manifested a disposition

Alexandria Monthly Meeting 33

to do his creditors justice if it had been in his power.

25/1/1827. A calamitous and destructive conflagration having anxiously occupied our attention on the day when this meeting should have been held in course, it was concluded by general consent to meet at this time. William Stabler proposed and appointed as clerk.

22/2/1827. A certificate for Charles Litle and his wife Lydia and their two children: Charles William and Isaac P. Litle, from Hopewell MM, dated 10th mo. 5th 1826. Testimony against John S. Miller.

22/3/1827. Jonathan Scholfield requests to be reunited to our Society [granted]. A certificate for Amelia Coale to Fairfax MM.

19/4/1827. A certificate for Basil B. Hopkins and Richard S. Hopkins, a minor, from Indian Spring MM, dated 3rd mo. 7th, received.

24/5/1827. Propose Abijah Janney for the station of elder. A certificate was requested for William Gillingham, through a friend, his wife and their four minor children: Isaac, Elizabeth, Catharine and Esther, to Baltimore MM for Western District.

23/8/1827. A certificate for Matthew Mitchell, his wife Elizabeth, and their two minor children: Pleasant and Hannah. A certificate for Mary S. Hallowell to Rensaellaerville MM, N.Y. Written communication from Nicholas Brown and Margaret Judge expressing their intention of marriage.

20/9/1827. Nicholas Brown produced a certificate from Yonge Street MM, Upper Canada. Ann Harper, formerly Ellicott, has accomplished her marriage contrary to our discipline. Jonathan Scholfield is reinstated to the Society.

18/10/1827. Marriage of Nicholas Brown and Margaret Judge accomplished. Isaac Holmes and Hannah S. Boone presented proposals of marriage with each other, the former not being a member of our monthly meeting of Goose Creek MM.

22/11/1827. A certificate for Anthony Foulke, his wife Eleanor and their three minor children: Sarah P., Phebe and William, from Indian Spring MM, dated 5th of 9th mo. last. Testimony against Ann Harper, late Ann Ellicott. A certificate was requested for Abner Pope, his wife Maria and their four minor children: Edward, Mary Ann, Abner James and Joseph P., to Baltimore MM for Western District. A certificate for Ann S. Janney and Abigail Shoemaker to Philadelphia MM for Northern District.

20/12/1827. Marriage of Isaac Holmes and Hannah S. Boone accomplished. A certificate for Margaret Brown, late Margaret Judge, wife of Nicholas Brown, to Yonge Street MM, Upper Canada.

End of this book of "Record of the
"Minutes of Alexandria Monthly
"Meeting" to 12th month 1827
Robert H. Miller
Recorder

28/1/1828. A certificate for Samuel E. Smith from Buckingham MM, Pa., dated 5th of the 11th mo. 1827.

21/2/1828. Report in case of Joshua Riley. Joshua Riley has accomplished his marriage contrary to discipline. A certificate was requested for Joseph Drinker to Wayne Oak MM, Va.

20/3/1828. Certificates for Mary Canby and Elizabeth Canby from Indian Spring MM. David Howell, son of James and Sarah Howell, the latter dec., and Hannah S. Janney, dau. of Abijah and Jane Janney, the latter also dec., to marry. Pennell Palmer, son of Moses and Hannah Palmer, and Rebecca N. McPherson, dau. of Daniel and Elizabeth McPherson, to marry [with consent of their parents]. Samuel B. [Shreve] has failed in business. Complaint against Samuel B. Shreve, Brooklyn, 12th month 22nd 1827.

24/4/1828. Certificate received from Hopewell MM dated 10th instant stating that no difficulty presented to prevent David Howell from accomplishing his marriage with Hannah M. Janney. Susanna Smith, formerly Drinker, has accomplished her marriage with her first cousin [disowned].

-/5/1828. Marriage of Pennell Palmer and Rebecca McPherson accomplished. Marriage of David Howell and Hannah M. Janney accomplished. A letter was received from Indian Spring MM requesting this meeting to deal with Amos G. Canby for the non-payment of some debts [has also given way to intemperate drinking].

19/6/1828. A certificate for Hannah M. Howell to Hopewell MM.

21/8/1828. Joseph Bond [from Fairfax MM - with parent's consent], son of Joseph and Elizabeth Bond, the former dec., and Elizabeth Stabler, dau. of Edward and Mary Stabler, the latter dec., to marry. A certificate was requested for Robinson Stabler to South River MM near Lynchburg in order to marry Mary A. Davis of that meeting.

23/10/1828. Marriage of Joseph Bond and Elizabeth Stabler accomplished.

20/11/1828. Certificate for Richard M. Janney from Fairfax MM, held 15th of the 10th mo. A certificate for Sarah Sinclair from Indian Spring MM, held 3d of the 9th mo. Several members have withdrawn from membership.

18/12/1828. A certificate for Jacob Lindly Sinclair, minor, from Indian Spring MM. A certificate was requested for Anthony Foulke, his wife Eleanor and their three minor children [Sarah P., Philip and William W.], to Plainfield MM, Ohio. Informed that Elizabeth Kinsey, formerly Drinker, has gone out in her marriage [disowned].

19/2/1829. A certificate for Caleb [Shreve] Hallowell, minor, from Abington MM, Pa., dated 26th day of the 1st month 1829. A certificate was requested for [Lot] Holmes, to Goose Creek MM.

19/3/1829. Richard M. Janney has requested a certificate to Indian Spring MM in order to accomplish marriage with Sarah J. Hopkins of that meeting. A certificate for Sarah Myers, minor, to Middletown MM, Bucks Co., Pa. A certificate was requested for Thomas Wetherald to York MM, Pa. for himself, wife Ann and their four minor children: Esther, Joseph E., Samuel B. and Thomas.

23/4/1829. A certificate for Richard M. Janney, to Indian Spring MM, to enable him to marry Sarah J. Hopkins of that meeting. A certificate for Hannah S. Hopkins, late Boone, to Goose Creek MM. Andrew Scholfield has for a considerable time absented himself from our meetings and has just joined in the establishment of another meeting name of Friends. A certificate was requested for Ruth Litle to Philadelphia MM at Cherry Street for herself and a minor son John.

21/5/1829. A certificate for Samuel B. Sands from Indian Spring MM. Informed that Daniel Kurtz has applied to become a member of our Society. Reported that Hannah Hozier and Maria Hozier have withdrawn from our meeting.

18/6/1829. A certificate was requested for Pennell and Rebecca N. Palmer (late McPherson) to Concord MM, Pa.

23/7/1829. Joseph P. Ball has accomplished his marriage contrary to discipline [disowned]. Reported that Betsy Scholfield has for a considerable time past absented herself from our meetings and joined in the maintenance of another meeting under the name of Friends.

20/8/1829. A certificate for John Hopkins from Fairfax MM.

24/9/1829. A certificate was requested for William R. Foulke to Pipe Creek MM.

19/11/1829. A certificate for Isaac Vore from Baltimore MM for Western District.

18/2/1830. A certificate for Asa M. Janney, his wife Lydia and their minor dau. Eliza. A certificate was requested for John McPherson, Jr. to Fairfax MM. It appears that Pheby Butcher and Catharina Wilson are no longer members of our Society. Phebe Butcher has for a long time declined attendance of our meetings and she is presently united to another meeting in the name of Friends within the limits of this meeting. Catharine Wilson has for a long time declined the attendance of our meeting and is presently united to another meeting under the name of Friends, within the limits of our meeting.

18/3/1830. Certificate for Elizabeth S. Bond, formerly Stabler, to Fairfax MM.

22/4/1830. A certificate was requested for Jacob Sinclair, minor, to Indian Spring MM.

24/6/1830. Enoch Wilson has for a considerable time past absented himself from our meetings; has attended horse races; now considers himself a member of another meeting within the limits of our meeting [disowned]. Pleasant Bashaw, late Mitchell, has accomplished her marriage contrary to discipline.

22/7/1830. Received from Uwchlan MM, Pa., that Miller Downing who has for several years resided within the limits of this meeting has frequently used intoxicating drink to excess and has been generally absent from meetings. John Barcroft of this meeting has been dealing in spirituous liquors [offers his resignation from the Society].

19/8/1830. A certificate for William Cole from Little Falls MM.

23/9/1830. A certificate for Eli Elliott from Pipe Creek MM, and his wife Margaret and their four minor children: Upton, Ann, Mary and William. Also certificates from the same meeting for Reuben Elliott, Sarah Elliott and Elizabeth Elliott. [They removed to Alum Creek MM at Owl Creek, Ohio in 1833.]

[Minutes continue through 5 mo. 8th 1873].

Alexandria Monthly Meeting 37

Account Book For Friends
Women's Branch Preparative Meeting
1800-1830

The following names are shown in an account book of the friends of Alexandria Preparative Meeting, beginning in the year 1800. Given here are names of subscribers in the sequence as they appear in the record. The monetary amount for individual subscriptions is not provided in the transcription below.

Susannah Hartshorne
Sarah [Matthews]
Ann Butcher (c.1800 to 1825)
Mary Hewes (c.1800 to 1814)
Catherine Pugh (1823-1825)
Mary Janney (c.1800 to 1808)
Ruth Janney (c.1802 to 1805)
Rebeckah Miller (c.1800 to 1810)
Mary Stabler (c.1800 to 1823)
[Mary] Davis
Sarah Gover (1830)
Susan [Russell] (1816 to 1825)
Sarah Pancoast
Mary Wanton (c.1800 to 1830)
Elizabeth Janney (c.1800 to 1807)
Margaret [Hallowell] (1825 to 1830)
Elizabeth [Irwin] (c.1806 to 1830)
Susannah Hartshorne, Jr. (c.1800 to 1820)
Rachel Hewes (c.1803 to 1828)
Ruth Drinker (c.1804 to 1821)
Phebe Butcher (1808 to 1828)
Rebecca Kenworthy (c.1812 to 1815)
Mary [Woodrow]
Elizabeth Ellicott (c.1803 to 1814)
Ruth Janney, Jr.
Margaret Judge (1825-1827)
Judith Lawrence (c.1804 to 1815)
Sarah Vasse (1805-1816)
Ann Shreve (1805-1812)
Elizabeth [Yeates] (1807)
Lydia Horner (1808, 1813, 1817)
Mary Neill (1816)
Sarah [Talbott] (c.1809-1830)
Rebecca Jolliffe (1809-1813)
Ann Scholfield (1809-1813, 1815-1823)
[Rebecca] Lloyd (1809, 1812, 1814, 1816, 1818)
[Mary] Ross (1809, 1812, 1814, 1815, 1817-1819)
[Rebecca] Patton [Paton] (1809, 1812-1814)
Judith [Janney] (1809)
[Ellen] [Scholfield] (1808, 1810-1818)
Elizabeth [Scholfield] (1809-1813, 1815-1828)
Hannah Saunders (1810, 1812, 1814, 1816)
Elizabeth [Litle] (1811, 1812, 1816-1818)
Elizabeth McPherson (1810, 1812, 1814-1816, 1818)
Martha Brown (1811-1813, 1817, 1819, 1820)
Ann [Lupton] (1812)
Grace Shreve (1811-1820)
Sarah Janney (c.1812-1823)
Mary Peach (1813-1830)
--- [Wilson] (1813-1819)
M. Plummer (1813, 1814, 1817, 1818)
Cosmelia Janney (1814, 1816, 1818-1822, 1825-1826, 1828)
Susan Hugh (1814, 1815, 1818-1821)
Mary Grubb (1822, 1823, 1826, 1828)
E. Janney (1814, 1816)
Susan [Hewes] (1822-1830)
Sarah [Yeates] (1815-1822)
Rebecca Niell (1816, 1818, 1821)
Rachel Shreve (1815-1818, 1820-1830)
Mary McPherson (1815, 1816)
Beulah Haines (1817)
Rachel Painter (1817, 1819-1825)
Hannah Wilson (1817)
Sarah Swayne (1817)
Elizabeth Janney (1817, 1819-1830)
Sarah Gover (1818-1827)
Mary Janney (1818-1820, 1822-1829)
Ann Eaches (1818, 1819, 1821, 1823,

1824)
Mary Huck (1819-1821, 1824)
Deborah Stabler (1819-1830)
Ann Janney (1817-1826)
Eliza Morgan (1817, 1819, 1821-1824)
Elizabeth W. Janney (1819-1821)
Amy Ann Miller (1821-1829)
Catharine Wilson (1823)
Abigail Shoemaker (1823, 1824)
Ann Ellicott (1825, 1826)
Susan [Russell] (1827, 1829, 1830)
Sarah Yeates (1823-1830)
Hannah Yeates (1827-1830)
Jane Gillingham (1923)
Amelia Hough (1825)
Ruth [Litle] (1823, 1824, 1827)
Mary Hough (1823)
Deborah Hopkins (1827-1830)
Phebe Horner (1823-1825)
Mary Stabler (1824, 1825, 1827-1830)
Elizabeth Janney (1824-1829)
Mary Peach (1824-1830)
Sarah J. Janney (1824-1830)
Anna Miller (1824, 1826-1830)
Jane Janney (1824-1830)
Pleasant Janney (1824-1828)
Rachel Painter (1826-1829)

Alexandria Monthly Meeting held at Woodlawn

During the Civil War the meeting house was used as a picket post. The soldiers met with the Friends at their meetings for worship.

- - - - - - - - - -

Records of Marriage Certificates

For the record of marriages given below, the names of subscribers are not listed though they do appear in the original record.

William Hartshorne, of the town and county of Alexandria, merchant, and Susannah Shreve of the afsd. town and county, 30/6/1803, Alexandria Meeting House.

Elisha Talbott, of Alexandria, D.C., son of Joseph and Anna Talbott (dec.) of Loudoun Co., Va., and Sarah Saunders, dau. of John and Mary Saunders, the former dec., of the town and District afsd. 2/10/1806.

Edward Stabler, of the town of Alexandria and District of Columbia, son of Edward and Mary Stabler, dec., of the town of Petersburg, Va., and Mary Hartshorne, dau. of William and [Susannah] Hartshorne, the latter dec., of Fairfax Co., Va., having parents' consent, on 28/7/1808.

Certificates of Removal
from
Alexandria Monthly Meeting

Names of Meetings are now indexed in this section, as they are in the minutes previously given.

To Baltimore MM. Isaac McPherson having removed - for his wife Tacy, wife of Isaac McPherson and their children: Jane, Elizabeth, Esther, Mary Ann and William. Note in record that Jane and Elizabeth are daughters of Isaac by a former wife. 23/6/1803.
To Baltimore MM. Ann Coates. 23/6/1803
To Fairfax MM. Dawson Fisher, an orphan, bound to Benjamin Steer, a member of your meeting. 25/8/1803.
To New Garden MM. Isaac Jackson, Jr. 20/9/1804.
To Indian Spring MM. Issachar Scholfield, wife Edith, and their child Thomas. 25/10/1804.
To New Garden MM. Catharine Pugh and her two children: Isaac and Sarah. 25/10/1804.
To New Garden MM. Hannah Jackson. 25/10/1804.
To Nantucket MM for the Northern District. James Coffin Lawrence and his wife Jedidah after a "short stay here," and their minor children: Benjamin, Sally and Lydia. 21/2/1805.
To Fairfax MM. Amos Gibson. 25/4/1805.
To MM in Philadelphia for the Middle District. Thomas and Sarah Matthews and two minor children: Charles and Caleb Bentley. 23/1/1806.
To MM in Philadelphia for the Middle District. William Matthews who has removed with his parents. 23/1/1806.
To Dunnings Creek MM, Pa. William and [Rebecca] Kenworthy. 23/1/1806.
To White Oak Swamp MM, Va. Aaron Hewes, Jr, a minor, who has with the consent of his parents removed and settled within the limits of your meeting; "the employment which he has followed for several years past having from it nature kept him generally away from home." 20/3/1806.
To White Oak Swamp MM, Va. Lydia Green, having removed with her husband. 20/3/1806.
To New York MM. Robert Hartshorne. 26/6/1806.
To Hopewell MM. Ruth Janney and her children: Hannah, Daniel, Rebecca, William, Aquila, Israel and Mary Ann, all minors. 24/7/1806.
To Indian Spring MM. Wm. [Yeates], Jr. 25/12/1806.
To Philadelphia MM. Thomas Matthews, Jr., minor. 25/12/1806.
To Baltimore MM. Elizabeth Janney who "settled with her father's family within the verge of your meeting." 25/12/1806.
To Baltimore MM. Levis Janney and his wife Mary and their son, a minor, Benjamin. 25/12/1806.
To Baltimore MM. John Shreve. 26/2/1807.
To Indian Spring MM. Deborah Stabler, "having returned to the verge of your meeting," and two minor children: Caleb and Henry. 24/9/1807.
To Baltimore MM for the Western District. Samuel Heston. 26/11/1807.
To Nantucket MM for the Southern District. Charles Spencer Lawrence, minor,

"whom we are informed has removed within the verge of your Meeting to live with his Uncle James C. Lawrence." 26/11/1807.
To Philadelphia MM for the Northern District. John Wilson, minor. 25/2/1808.
To Baltimore MM for the Western District. Samuel B. Bedgood. 23/11/1809.
To New York MM. Pattison Hartshorne, Jr. 21/12/1809.
To Fairfax MM. Elisha Janney and his wife Mary, "tho' Elisha's outward affairs (in consequence of his failing in trade) are not satisfactorily settled, as it regards some of his creditors, yet we hope should he ever be able to make these satisfaction, he will be disposed to do it." With 8 minor children: Ruth, Albinah, John, Mary, Anna, James, Aquila and Cornelia. 26/4/1810.
To Baltimore MM for the Western District. Jesse Talbott, his wife Hannah and their son John Litle Talbott. 20/12/1810.
To Philadelphia MM. Mary Shotwell. 21/3/1811.
To Fairfax MM. Moses Janney and Judith his wife and their two minor children: Isaac and Oliver. 21/3/1811. This certificate was returned.
To Fairfax MM. Robert Gover. 26/9/1811.
To Fairfax MM. John Morgan. 23/1/1812.
To Indian Spring MM. William [Yeates], Jr. 23/1/1812.
To Philadelphia MM in the Northern District. William Thomas. 21/5/1812.
To Cedar Creek MM, Hanover Co. Fleming Bates, his wife Unity Bates and their five minor children: Benjamin, Spence, Deborah, Lemuel, Unity and Hannah. 24/9/1812.
To Philadelphia MM. Warwick Price Miller, minor. 22/10/1812.
To Baltimore MM for the Western District. William R. Wanton. 24/12/1812.
To Hopewell MM, Frederick Co., Va. Mary Buchannan. 25/2/1813.
To Baltimore MM for the Western District. David Saunders. 25/6/1814.
To Croswicks MM, N.J. Sarah Ann Hewes. 8/9/1814.
To Croswicks MM, N.J. Deborah Hewes. 8/9/1814.
To Fairfax MM. Sarah Janney, "having settled with her parents within the verge of your meeting." 26/1/1815.
To Plainfield MM, Ohio. Thomas F. Horner, minor. 20/4/1815.
To Philadelphia MM for the Western District. Aaron Hewes and his wife Mary. 25/5/1815.
To Philadelphia MM for the Western District. Sarah Powers Hewes. 25/5/1815.
To Philadelphia MM for the Western District. Mary Ann Copeland Hewes. 25/5/1815.
To Hopewell MM. William Jolliffe, his wife Rebecca and their five minor children: Mary, John, Elizabeth, William and Joseph. 25/10/1815.
To Baltimore MM for the Western District. Charles Litle, a minor, 21/9/1815.
To Goose Creek MM, Loudoun Co., Va. William Kenworthy and his wife Rebecca. 23/11/1815.
To Indian Spring MM, Md. Isaiah Hopkins. 21/12/1815.
To Baltimore MM for the Western District. William R. Wanton, a minor. 25/1/1816.
To Fairfax MM. Rebecca [Leslie]. 22/8/1816.
To Indian Spring MM. John Hughes, a minor. 21/11/1816.
To Baltimore MM for the Western District. Nathaniel Ellicott, his wife Elizabeth, their four minor children: Nathaniel, Mary, Jonathan and Andrew. 26/12/1816.
To Baltimore MM for the Western District. Edward Stabler. 23/1/1817.
To Baltimore MM for the Western District. John A. Ellicott. 20/2/1817.
To Baltimore MM for the Western District. Hannah Ellicott. 20/2/1817.

Alexandria Monthly Meeting 41

To Fairfax MM. Samuel McPherson and his wife Mary. 20/3/1817.
To Indian Spring MM, Md. Mecajah Welding. 22/5/1817.
To Short Creek MM, Ohio. Mary Grubb on behalf of Alexandria MM (District of Columbia). 25/12/1817.
To Indian Spring MM. Jacob Janney, his wife Hannah and their five children: Philip, Lewis, Mary, Ann and Henry. 22/1/1818.
To Baltimore MM for the Western District. Maria Pope, formerly Parkins, having removed to reside with her husband. 23/7/1818.
To Buckingham MM. Elizabeth Shaw. 22/4/1819.
To Baltimore MM for the Western District. Susanna H. Hurdle. 22/7/1819.
To Goose Creek MM. Hannah Wilson, having removed with her husband. 22/7/1819.
To Hopewell MM. Margaret Wood, having removed with her husband. 22/7/1819.
To Sadsbury MM, Pa. William Temple. 23/9/1819.
To Philadelphia MM at Green Street. William Morgan, minor. 23/9/1819.
To Plainfield MM, Ohio. Martha B. Horner, minor, dau. of John and Lydia Horner. 23/12/1819.
To Fairfax MM. Isaac Beale. 23/3/1820.
To Chesterfield MM, Great Britain Mary Sutton. 25/5/1820.
To Baltimore MM for the Western District. Ann H. Carey, formerly Irwin, having removed with her husband, John C. Carey 22/6/1820.
To Miami MM. Mary [Neill], having removed with her husband. 21/9/1820.
To Indian Spring MM, Md. John McPherson and his wife Hannah. 23/11/1820.
To Indian Spring MM, Md. Rebecca McPherson. 23/11/1820.
To Fairfax MM, Va. Rebecca Swayne. 21/12/1820.
To Plainfield MM, Belmont Co., Ohio. Lydia Horner. 21/12/1820.
To Fairfax MM. Thomas Swayne. 21/12/1820.
To Fairfax MM. Joshua Swayne. 21/12/1820.
To Indian Spring MM, Md. Sarah Canby. 25/1/1821.
To Hopewell MM, Va. Daniel Haines, who has left a number of unsettled debts which he is at present unable to pay; no complaint has been ever been made against him and we hope he is disposed to pay them whenever he may become possessed of the means. 22/2/1821.
To Goose Creek MM, Loudoun Co., Va. Jesse S. Wilson. 22/3/1821.
To Hopewell MM. William H. Brown. 24/5/1821.
To Indian Spring MM. Joseph Canby. 21/6/1821.
To Indian Spring MM. Amos Gilbert, minor. 21/6/1821.
To Indian Spring MM. Thomas Canby. 26/7/1821.
To Chesterfield MM, N.J. Thomas Shreve, a minister in esteem, having with his minor children, Elizabeth, Margaret, Grace, Thomas and Mary, removed to reside within the limits of your meeting. 23/8/1821.
To Chesterfield MM, N.J. Grace Shreve. 23/8/1821.
To Baltimore MM for the Western District. Jane Heston. 23/8/1821.
To Baltimore MM for the Western District. Charles Heston and Joel Wright, minors. 24/1/1822.
To Philadelphia MM for the Northern District. Israel Janney, Jr., and his wife Elizabeth and two minor children: Caroline W. and Charles W. 24/1/1822.
To Baltimore MM for the Western District. Thomas Morgan, minor. 24/1/1822.
To Indian Spring MM. Ruth Hannah Janney, having moved with her parents. 24/1/1722.
To Indian Spring MM, Md. George Janney and his wife [Susannah], and their six

minor children: Jacob, Esther, Isaiah, Susan, George and Sarah. 24/1/1822.
To Indian Spring MM, Md. Susanna H. Hurdle. 21/3/1822.
To Fairfax MM. Richard Janney, minor. 20/6/1822.
To Hopewell MM. Rebecca [Neill]. 18/7/1822.
To Hopewell MM. Lydia Neill, with her mother [Rebecca Neille]. 18/7/1822.
To Gunpowder MM, Md. William Heston. 19/9/1822.
To Hopewell MM. Susanna Ball and three minor children: Eliza H., Joseph P. and Wm. James Ball. 24/10/1822.
To Baltimore MM for the Western District. Jos. Heston. 24/10/1822.
To Twelfth Street MM, Philadelphia, Pa. Thomas Rutter. 21/11/1822, returned.
To Whitham MM at Chelmsford, Essex, England. John Rawlings, Jr. 22/8/1822, returned.
To Indian Spring MM, Md. Hannah Janney. 20/2/1823.
To Hopewell MM. David Wilson and his wife Hannah and their children: John Warder and Thomas Irwin. 20/2/1823.
To Gravelly Run MM, Va. John McPherson, Jr. 20/2/1823.
To Uchland MM, Pa. William Patterson, although he has left unpaid debts. 20/2/1823.
To Gravelly Run MM, Va. Peter Saunders. 20/2/1823.
To Bedford MM, Mass. Abraham Howland. 20/2/1823.
To Witham MM, Essex, Great Britain. John Rawlings, Jr. 19/6/1823.
To Baltimore MM for the Western District. Letitia M. Heston. 23/10/1823.
To Indian Spring MM. Caleb Stabler. 18/2/1824.
To Indian Spring MM. Elizabeth Stabler. 22/4/1824.
To Indian Spring MM. Anna Stabler. 22/4/1824.
To Indian Spring MM, Md. Rebecca [Russell]. 22/4/1824.
To Indian Spring MM. Hannah J. Churchman. 22/4/1824.
To Plainfield MM, Clark Co., Ohio. Margaret [Farr]. 20/5/1824.
To Hopewell MM, Va. Hannah Ross. 22/7/1824.
To Hopewell MM, Va. Mahlon Scholfield and his wife Ann and their 6 minor children: Lewis, Elizabeth, Rachel, Ann, Joseph and William. 22/7/1824.
To Hopewell MM. Ann Lupton and her four minor children: Rachel, John, Jane and Mary. 23/9/1824.
To Cincinnati MM, Ohio. Beulah Patterson, having removed with her husband, and her two minor children: Samuel W. and Ellwood. 18/11/1824.
To Hardshaw East MM, England. Sarah Corbett and her dau. Martha Corbett, a minor. 23/12/1824.
To Fairfax MM, Va. Thomas M. Bond. 20/1/1825.
To Hopewell MM, Va. Benjamin W. Powell. 24/2/1825.
To Hopewell MM, Va. Asa M. Janney. 24/2/1825.
To Fairfax MM, Va. Mary [Moore] Steer. 22/1/1824.
To Fairfax MM, Va. Joseph Steer, his wife Sarah and their four minor children: James Moore, Isaac Hollingsworth, Lydia Ann and Phebe Moore. 22/1/1824.
To Baltimore MM for the Western District. James Moore, Jr., and his wife Esther and their minor son, Thomas. 19/5/1825.
To Hopewell MM, Va. Deborah Morgan. 20/10/1825.
To Hopewell MM, Va. Anna Lupton. 22/6/1824.
To Kennett MM, Chester Co., Pa. William L. Embree, minor, son of David Embree. 20/7/1826.
To Hopewell MM. Thomas V. Huck with his wife Mary and their two minor children:

Richard and Rebecca Neil. 21/9/1826.
To Fairfax MM. Mary M. Scott. 23/11/1826.
To Philadelphia MM, Pa. James A. Hewes. 25/1/1827.
To Fairfax MM, Va. Amelia Cole [Coale], having removed with her husband. 22/3/1827.
To Baltimore MM for the Western District. William and Jane Gillingham and their four minor children: Isaac, Eliza, Catharine and Esther. 21/6/1827.
To Rensellair Ville MM, N.Y. Mary S. Hallowell. 8/3/1827.
To Philadelphia MM for the Northern District. Ann S. Janney. 22/11/1827.
To Philadelphia MM for the Northern District. Abigail Shoemaker. 22/11/1827.
To Yonge Street MM, Upper Canada. Margaret Brown [wife of Nicholas Brown] late Margaret Judge. 20/12/1827
To Baltimore MM for the Western District. Abner Pope, Maria his wife and their four minor children: Edward, Mary Ann, Abner James and Joseph P. 20/12/1828.
To Main Oak MM, Va. Joseph Drinker. 20/3/1828.
To Hopewell MM, Va. Hannah M. Howell, late Janney, having removed with her husband. 19/6/1828.
To Plainfield MM, Ohio. Anthony Foulkes and his wife Eleaner and their three minor children: Sarah P., Phebe, William W. 22/1/1829.
To Goose Creek MM, Loudoun Co., Va. Lot Holmes. 19/3/1829.
To Middletown MM, Bucks Co., Pa. Sarah Myers, minor, 19/3/1829.
To Goose Creek MM. Hannah J. Holmes [wife of Isaac Holmes, nee Boone]. 23/4/1829.
To Philadelphia MM at Cherry Street. Ruth Litle and her minor son John James Litle. 21/5/1829.
To Concord MM, Pa. Pennell Palmer and his wife Rebecca N. [nee McPherson]. On behalf of the Alexandria MM in the District of Columbia. 23/7/1829.
To Pipe Creek MM, Md. William R. Foulke. 22/10/1829.
To Green Street MM, Philadelphia. Margaret Bender. 24/12/1829.
To Fairfax MM, Va. John McPherson, Jr. 18/3/1830.
To Fairfax MM. Elizabeth S. Bond [nee Stabler, wife of Joseph Bond]. 18/3/1830.
To Indian Spring MM. Jacob Sinclair, a minor. 24/6/1830.
To Goose Creek MM. Eliza Canby. 21/10/1830.

[Record continues to 8th 11 mo. 1877].

Alexandria Monthly Meeting
Membership

The record is inscribed Alexandria Monthly Meeting, Membership, 1823-1881. An index appears at the front of the original record. This is a compilation of families with annotations added by William Wade Hinshaw at a later date. Entries are sometimes difficult to decipher in the original record. Information is presented here in alphabetical order by surname for ease of use.

Abbreviations used by this compiler:

b.	- born	c.	- circa
d.	- died	dis.	- disowned
MM	- Monthly Meeting	m.	- married
m(1)	- married first	m(2)	- married second
mo.	- month	rem.	- removed
ret.	- returned	yrs.	- years

BAKER. Joshua Baker d. 19/1/1843 in his 77th year.
BALL. Children of Susan Ball: Eliza; Joseph Parkins; William James Parkins. Note: Susannah (Brown) Parkins widow of Joseph Parkins of Hopewell, m. John Ball. Joseph and William rem. to Hopewell MM, 1822.
BARBER. Eliza Barber, rem. from Grace Church Street MM, London 1824, rem. to Hanover, Pa.
    Jonathan Barber, rem. from Grace Church Street, MM, London 1824, rem. to Hanover, Pa.
    Joseph Barber, rem. from MM, of Spalding and Wainfleet MM, county of Lincoln, Old England, 3rd mo. 1823 - dis. 12th mo. 1823.
    Mary Barber, rem. from Grace Church Street, MM, London 1824, rem. to Hanover, Pa.
BARCLOSS. John Barcloss, dis. 1830.
BENDER. Josiah Bender
    Margaret Bender (rem. to Green Street MM, Philadelphia 1829) and her dau. Juliana (dis. 1825).
BOND. Thomas M. Bond rem. to Fairfax MM, 1825.
BROOKE. Samuel Brooke d. 24/8/1828 in his 77th year.
BUTCHER. Ann Butcher d. 2/4/1826, age 77 years nearly.
    Jonathan Butcher (d. 21/9/1841) and his wife Phebe (withdrawn 1830), had the following children: Catharine Ann, withdrawn 1836; John, dis. 1838; Jonathan, d. 18/10/1838; Robert Hume, dis. 1842.
CANBY. Children of Samuel Canby (d. 13/9/1826 at Occoquan) and his wife Elizabeth (d. 1825): Thomas Y., rem. to Makefield MM, Pa. 1835; Samuel, Jr., rem. to Baltimore MM, for Western District 1841; Beulah, d. 1825; Joseph, rem. to Cherry Street MM, Philadelphia 1837; Yardley, rem. to Athens, Ill. more than 20 years ago and has never applied for certificate (1859); Elizabeth, rem. to Makefield MM, Pa. 1835; William, rem. to Waynesville MM, 1835; Ann, b. and d. 1825. The family rem. from Baltimore MM, for Western District 1825.
    Eliza Canby, rem. from Indian Spring MM, 1828, rem. to Goose Creek MM,

1830.
Mary Canby (dau. of Samuel and Elizabeth), rem. from Baltimore MM, for Western District 1825, rem. to Makefield MM, Pa., 1835.
Mary Canby, rem. from Indian Spring MM, 1828, rem. to Goose Creek MM, 1839.
CHURCHMAN. Hannah Churchman rem. to Indian Spring 1824.
COLE. William Cole, rem. from Little Falls MM, Md., 1830, rem. to Cherry Street MM, Philadelphia 1836.
CORBETT. Martha [Corbett], dau. of [Sarah], rem. to Hardshaw East MM, England 1824.
Sarah [Corbett] rem. to Hardshaw East MM, England 1824.
COWMAN. John Cowman, Jr. came in by request in 1826, d. 25/9/1843 in his 50th year.
DAVIS. Gideon Davis m(1) ca. 1805, Nancy Hughes (d. 7/4/1833, aged 52 years). Their children: Herephila, rem. to New Garden MM, Ohio, 1839; Rodney, b. 6/4/1808, d. 18/6/1891, m. Elizabeth Boone, rem. to Hopewell MM, 1833; Morgan; Levi; Patty, d. 6/8/1835; Catharine, b. 20/9/1823; John C., b. 18/12/1825; Arnold Boone, b. 19/5/1828, d. 23/7/1830.
DICK. Elisha C. Dick relinquishes his right 21/7/1825.
DRINKER. George Drinker, son of Joseph and Hannah Drinker, Philadelphia, Pa., b. 5/12/1766, d. 1/2/1846, m. Ruth Miller (d. 8/7/1857). Their children: William; Hannah, dis. 1823; Susannah, dis. 1828; Joseph, rem. to [Weyanoke, Charles City Co.] MM, Va. 1828; Elizabeth, dis. 1829; Samuel; Rebecca, dis. 1841.
EACHES. Ann Eaches d. 4/7/1850 in her 53rd year.
ELGAR. Ann Elgar and her children: Elizabeth; Margaret. Disowned 1823 for inconsistency in dress and address.
ELLICOTT. Ann Ellicott, rem. from Baltimore MM, for Western District 1824, dis. 1827.
Rachel Ellicott, rem. from Baltimore MM, for Western District 1824, d. 1825.
ELLIOTT. Jesse H. Elliott, rem. from Pipe Creek MM, 1831.
Elizabeth Elliott, rem. from Pipe Creek MM, 1830, rem. to Alum Creek MM, held at Owl Creek, Ohio, 1833.
Reuben Elliott, rem. from Pipe Creek MM, 1830, rem. to Alum Creek MM, OH, 1834.
Sarah Elliott, rem. from Pipe Creek MM, 1830, rem. to Alum Creek MM, held at Owl Creek, Ohio, 1833.
ELLISON. William C. Ellison rem. to Cherry Street MM Philadelphia 1839, certificate returned.
EMBREE. Children of Daniel Embree and his wife Sarah: Rachel; William L.; Margaretta; Hannah M. The family rem. from Bradford MM, [Pa.] and rem. to Cincinnati MM, 1831. [William L. rem. to Kennet MM, Pa., Chester Co., 1821; however his name was on the certificate to Cincinnati in 1831.]
FARQUHAR. Charles Farquhar, rem. from Concord MM, Pa., 1825 [see below].
FARR. Margaret Farr rem. to Plainfield MM, Clark Co., Ohio, 1824.
FOULKE. Children of Anthony Foulke and his wife Eleanor: Sarah P.; Phebe; William W. The family rem. from Indian Spring in 1827 and rem. to Plainfield MM, Ohio, 1829.
William Foulke, rem. from Indian Spring, Md., 1818, rem. to Pipe Creek MM, 1829.
GARDNER. Merab Gardner, rem. from Nantucket North District MM, 1828, rem.

to Nantucket MM, 1839.
GILLINGHAM. Children of William Gillingham and his wife Jane: Isaac; Jehu, d. 16/10/1823; Elizabeth; Catharine; Esther, b. 1825. The family rem. from Baltimore MM, for Western District in 1822; they rem. back to Baltimore MM, for Western District in 1827.
GOVER. Anthony P. Gover, m. at Fairfax MM, 1815, to Sarah Janney (d. 2/7/1840), dau. of Elisha and his 1st wife Albinah (Gregg) Janney. Their children: Mary Albina; Jane; Cornelia and Caroline, twins, b. 21/4/1823 (Caroline, d. 21/7/1823).
GUY. Miranda Guy late Morgan.
HALLOWELL. Benjamin Hallowell, rem. from Goshen MM, Chester Co., Pa., 1825 and to Indian Spring MM, 1843, m. 13/12/1824 Margaret Farquhar at Sandy Spring, Md. She rem. from Indian Spring MM, in 1825 and rem. to Indian Spring MM in 1843. Their children: James, b. 9/1/1825, d. 9/7/1831; Charles, b. 2/5/1827, d. 17/7/1831; Henry C. and Mary J., twins, b. 16/6/1829 (Henry C. rem. to Indian Spring MM in 1843, m. Sarah Miller 16/7/1859 and Mary J. d. 5/7/1835); Caroline, b. 20/8/1831, rem. to Indian Spring MM 1843, m. [Francis] Miller 9th mo. 1852; Benjamin, Jr., b. 17/12/1834, d. 7/5/1835; John E., b. 8/2/1836, rem. to Indian Spring MM, 1843; Benjamin, Jr., 16/1/1838, rem. to Green Street MM Philadelphia 1856; Mary S.
  Caleb Shreve Hallowell, rem. from Abington MM, Pa., 1829 [see below].
  Mary S. Hallowell, rem. from Concord MM, Pa., 1826, rem. to Rensallaerville MM, NY, 1827.
HARTSHORNE. William Hartshorne (b. in N.J. 1742, d. 13/12/1816 in his 75th year), son of Hugh and Hannah ([Patterson]) Hartshorne, m(1) 1767 Susannah Saunders (dau. of Joseph; she d. in Fairfax Co., Va., 26/10/1801) at Philadelphia Meeting; m(2) 30/6/1803 at Alexandria Meeting, Susannah (Wood) [Shreve], widow of Benjamin [Shreve]. (Susannah was rec'd. at Fairfax 26/8/1786, on a certificate from Upper Springfield MM, N.J., dated 2/6/1786, and became a charter member of Alexandria MM. William Hartshorne came to Fairfax MM in 1773 with certificate from Philadelphia MM. Sarah S., dau. of William and his 1st wife Susannah, m. Phineas Janney [see above].
HESTON. Joseph Heston rem. to Baltimore MM Western District 1822.
  Letitia M. Heston rem. from Baltimore MM, Western District 1823.
  William Heston rem. to Gunpowder MM 1822.
HEWES. Children of Rachel and Abram Hewes: Eliza, d. 23/1/1844; James A., rem. to Philadelphia MM, 1827; Mary M., dis. 1835.
HOLMES. Lot Holmes, rem. from Fairfax MM, 1825, rem. to Goose Creek MM, 1829.
HOPKINS. Basil B. Hopkins, rem. from Indian Spring MM, 1827, rem. to Baltimore MM, for Western District 1839.
  Deborah Hopkins, received from Indian Spring MM, 1817, rem. to Baltimore MM for Western District 1836.
  John Hopkins, rem. from Fairfax MM, 1829, relinquished his right.
  Richard S. Hopkins, rem. from Indian Spring MM, 1827, d. Baltimore 1859.
HORNER. Phebe Horner, came in by request 1823, dis. 1825.
HOUGH. Amelia Hough, rem. from Fairfax MM 1822, rem. to Fairfax MM, 1827.
  George S. Hough, d. 17/1/1847, m. 2/1/1812 Susan B. Carr, dau. of David and Ann Hamilton. Their children: Edward S., d. 1881; Harrison, dis. 1841;

Catharine, relinquished her right 1843; Sophia, dis. 1843; George S., Jr., d. 1823.
Mahlon Hough and Mary (rem. to Fairfax MM, 1839). Their dau. Amelia m. Lewis Coale of Fairfax MM, 1/12/1825.
Robinson Hough died 8/12/1826.
HOWLAND. Abram Howland rem. to New Bedford MM, Mass. 1823.
Thomas H. Howland dis. 1824.
HOZIER. Child of James M. Hozier (relinquished his right in 1826) and his wife Hannah (withdrawn 1829): Maria, withdrawn. The family rem. from Salem MM, Mass. in 1824.
HUCK. Thomas V. Huck, m. 3/12/1818 Mary Neill. Their children: Richard S., m. Sarah Stabler; Joseph Neill, dead; Rebecca Neill, b. 1824. The family rem. to Hopewell MM, in 1826.
HUGHES. Isaiah B. Hughes d. 10/3/1822.
HURDLE. Susannah H. Hurdle rem. to Indian Spring MM.
HUTCHINSON. Children of Samuel Hutchinson (d. 12/9/1824, age 58 years), taken in by request: Thomas and John ("believed to be long since dead.")
JANNEY. Abijah Janney, d. 14/1/1842 in his 67th year, m(1) Jane McPherson. Their children: Samuel M., m. 9/3/1826 Elizabeth Janney dau. of John and Elizabeth Janney; Asa Moore, m. Lydia, rem. to Hopewell MM, 24/2/1825; Anna, rem. to Hopewell MM, 1826; Richard M., rem. to Fairfax MM, and ret. 1828, rem. to Baltimore MM, for Western District 1831; Hannah M., m. 1/5/1828 David Howell, rem. to Hopewell MM, 6th mo. 1828; Thamsin, d. 10/10/1836; Abijah Janney m(2) Mary (nee [Mitchell]) widow of John Ellicott (Mary d. Philadelphia, 25/5/1843 in her 60th year). Their children: Edward Abijah b. 20/6/1818, d. 18/9/1838 in Ohio; Tacey M., rem. to Deer Creek MM, Md. 22/5/1837; Jane m. Richard H. Stabler; Henry, b. 21/8/1827, d. 19/8/1828; Rachel b. 10/8/1825, rem. to Goose Creek MM, 22/5/1851; Rebecca, b. 29/1/1829, dis. 1852; Francis Hague b. 28/6/1831, d. 22/6/1883, dis. 1858.
Asa M. Janney and Lydia (rem. from fairfax MM, 1830). They rem. to Goose Creek MM, in 1861. Their children: Mary Jane, b. 15/8/1827, d. 11/9/1829; Eliza, m. 18/5/1851, Wm. Henry Pleasants; Ellen Haines, b. 13/8/1831, rem. to Goose Creek MM, 1861; Abijah Jr., b. 17/3/1834, d. 14/11/1843; Cosmelia, b. 13/1/1836, rem. to Goose Creek MM, 1861; Tamsin, b. 16/6/1838, rem. to Goose Creek 1861; Hugh S., b. 24/11/1841, d. 4/1/1843; Lydia N. 14/8/1844, rem. to Goose Creek MM, 1861.
Cosmelia Janney, received 1819, d. 6/4/1834 in her 74th year.
Jacob Janney and his wife Eleanor; Caroline, b. 5/1/1824; Edward H., b. 3/11/1825; Isaiah B.H., d. 28/2/1828 in his first year; James Fenton, b. 28/6/1829, rem. to New Garden MM, Ohio, 1834; Ellen E.
Jacob Janney and his wife Hannah; children: Philip H., d. 7/9/1825, age 18; Lewis, relinquished his right in 1831; Mary, dis. 1834; Henry, rem. to New Garden MM, Ohio, 1834. Jacob and his wife Hannah and family rem. from Indian Spring MM, 1823.
Hannah Janney, Sr. rem. to Indian Spring MM 1823.
Israel H. Janney, rem. from Fairfax MM 1824, discontinued 1851.
James M. Janney, rem. from Fairfax MM 1824, discontinued 1851.
Jane Janney, rem. from Goose Creek MM, 1824, d. 12/3/1847.
John Janney, d. 10/5/1823, aged 58 yrs., m(1) Elizabeth Hopkins. Their

children: Joseph b. 17/11/1800; Elizabeth b. 17/10/1802, d. 24/12/1873, m. Samuel McPherson 1826; Samuel Hopkins b. 15/6/1804, d. 21/2/1887, dis. 1831 for marrying Elizabeth [Mark], non-member; John Hopkins b. 1806, d. c.1870, dis. 1831 for marrying Margaret Tyson, his 1st cousin. John Janney m(2) 1817 Ann Shoemaker (d. 10/5/1823, age 58).

Jonathan Janney, b. 20/3/1785, d. 21/12/1838 near 8:00 p.m., m. 9/1/1790 Elizabeth McPherson (d. 27/3/1843) dau. of Isaac and Elizabeth. Their children: Anna, b. 22/2/1811, d. 2/12/1886 unmarried, dis. 1848; Isaac McPherson, b. 4/12/1812, d. unmarried, dis. 1837; Richard Tunis, d. 4/4/1814, drowned at sea 1846; Jane Elizabeth, b. 10/10/1818, d. 1825; Margaret, b. 1825, dis. 1848; Jonathan, Jr., b. 25/2/1829, relinquished by removal beyond the reach of Friends; Emma, b. 7/2/1820, dis. 1848; John Thomas, b. 4/1/1836, m. 18/7/1863 Frances Martin Long.

Joseph Janney m(2) Hannah Hopkins, both dis. for marrying, she being his dead wife's sister. Their child: Hannah Ann, dis. 1833.

Oliver Janney, rem. from Fairfax MM, 1824, rem. to Cherry Street MM, Philadelphia 1834.

Phebe Ann Janney, rem. from Fairfax MM, 1823, m. 28/6/1832 Joseph H. Miller. [see below]

Phineas Janney, d. 18/10/1852 in his 75th year, m(1) 13/11/1779 Ruth Lupton at Upper Ridge Meeting House under Hopewell MM; m(2) 28/11/1811 Sarah S. Hartshorne (d. 1/5/1853 in her 68th year), dau. of Wm. Hartshorne and his 1st wife Susanna Saunders. No issue by either marriage.

Pleasant Janney, rem. from Goose Creek MM, 1824, rem. to Goose Creek MM, 1848.

Richard M. Janney, rem. from Fairfax MM, 1828 and to Baltimore MM, for Western District in 1831.

Samuel M. Janney m. 9/3/1826 Elizabeth Janney, dau. of John and Elizabeth Janney. Their children: John Jr., b. 17/1/1827; Ellen, b. 27/11/1828, d. 22/11/1830; Jane Eliza, d. 26/3/1832; Cornelia, b. 3/1/1833, d. 19/3/1922 unmarried; Anthony Benezet, b. 11/4/1834, d. 1837; Mary Ann, b. 1837; Edward Abijah, b. 24/6/1839, d. 18/7/1842; Phineas, b. 24/3/184-, d. 31/12/1914, m. 1868 Clara Connelly. The family rem. to Goose Creek MM, in 1839.

Sarah Jane Janney, rem. from Fairfax MM 1824, m. Gerard H. Reese, rem. to Lombard Street MM, Baltimore 1846.

JAWIN. Children of Thomas (d. 28/1/1827 in his 68th year) and Elizabeth (d. 1847) Jawin: Thomas, Jr., dis. 1817; Ann, m. 20/3/1820 to John E. Carey, rem. to Baltimore 1820; Mary, dis. 1833; James, dis. 1825; William H., dis. 1832; Hannah, m. David Wilson.

JUDGE. Margaret Judge, rem. from Indian Spring MM. 1825, rem. to Yonge Street MM, Upper Canada, 1827.

KINSEY. Ezra Kinsey, d. at Hillsborough 12/6/1826.

KURTZ. Daniel Kurtz, received by request 1829; d. 9/8/1846, age 60 years.

LEVERING. Children of Thomas (withdrawn - see minute 3rd mo. 1829) and Rachel A. Levering ("left Friends"): Griffith ("left Friends"); Joseph, d. 9/2/1823; Thomas, b. 27/7/1823, d. 22/11/1825; Mary, b. 21/9/1826, d. 17/5/1830; Samuel, b. 22/9/1828, "left Friends."

LITLE. Charles Litle, d. 2nd mo. 1839, m. 24/4/1822 Lydia Parkins. Their children:

Charles William; Isaac P.; Nathan Parkins, b. 7/12/1827; Sidney; John Henry Easton. The family rem. from Hopewell MM, 1827. The family rem. to Hopewell MM, in 1840 except for Isaac who rem. to Concord MM, Ohio, in 1840 and John Henry Eaton who rem. to Baltimore MM, for Western District in 1840.

John and Sarah Litle and their children: Robert S.; Samuel B.; William; Richard, b. 16/6/1824; Sarah Ann, 19/7/1826; John, b. 9/9/1829. The family removed to Indiana "more than twenty years ago say about 1836 and have never applied for certificate: relinquished their right."

Richard H. Litle, d. 25/2/1825 in his 37th year, m(1) 26/12/1810 to Elizabeth Talbott (dau. of Joseph and Ann). Their children: Hannah, rem. to Baltimore MM, for Western District 5th mo., 1839, dis. 6th mo. 1839; Rebecca d. 1824; Richard H. Litle m(2) Ruth James. She rem. from Philadelphia MM, Northern District 20/2/1823; rem. Cherry Street MM, of Philadelphia 1829. Their children: John James, rem. to Cherry Street MM, of Philadelphia 1829; Richard b. and d. 1825.

LUKENS. Rachel Lukens, rem. from Gwynedd MM, [Pa.] 1831 [see below].

LUPTON. Children of David and Ann Lupton (McPherson): John; Rachel; Jane; Mary. Ann and her children rem. to Hopewell MM in 1824.

MARSH. Susan Marsh, came in by request 1823, rem. to Rahway & Plainfield MM, E. Jersey 1826.

McPHERSON. Children of Elizabeth (d. 7/11/1843 in her 63rd year) and Daniel McPherson: Rebecca N., m. 30/4/1828 Pannell Palmer, rem. to Concord MM, Pa. 1829; Mary Ann, dis. 1833; Samuel; Elizabeth, Jr., d. 26/1/1845, age 31; Joseph G., d. 22/3/1843 in his 28th year; John D.; Emily; Jane, d. 10/4/1843 in her 23rd year; Charles, rem. to Little Falls MM, Md.

John McPherson, Jr. rem. to Fairfax MM, 1830.

MILLER. Mordecai Miller (d. 2/4/1832) and Rebecca; children: William H., m. 12th mo. 1820 at Fairfax MM, Amy Ann Philips; Robert H., m. Anna Janney, dau. of Elisha and Mary Janney; John S., dis. 1827; Samuel; Joseph H., m. Phebe Ann Janney, dau. of David and Elizabeth Janney.

Robert Hartshorne Miller m. Anna Janney, dau. of Elisha and Mary Janney, rem. from Fairfax MM, 1823, d. 24/2/1885. Their children: Warwick Price, b. 26/9/1824, rem. to Sandy Spring MM, 1838; Charles, b. 26/2/1826, m. Ellen Morgan; Elisha, b. 6/10/1827, resigned his right; Francis, b. 31/7/1829, m. 23/9/1852 Caroline Hallowell, dau. of Benjamin and Margaret Hallowell; Cornelia Janney, b. 17/10/1831, rem. to Baltimore MM, for Western District 1850; John Saunders Janney, b. 7/12/1833; Sarah, b. 24/2/1836, m. H.C. Hallowell; Mary Anna, b. 4/3/1838, m. H. Reese, rem. to Baltimore MM, 1858; Benjamin Hallowell, b. 20/5/1840, rem. to Sandy Spring 1863; Caroline S., b. 2/8/1842, m. Roger Farquhar, Sandy Spring; Eliza Hewes, b. 20/2/1844, resigned.

William H. Miller m. 12th mo. 1820 at Fairfax, Amy Ann Philips. Their children: Rebecca, relinquished her right 1843; Mary Hewes, rem. to Fairfax MM, 1850; Caroline, b. 1825, d. 26/8/1826 at Waterford, Va.; Thomas P., b. 20/2/1827, d. 11/9/1828; Mordecai, Jr., b. 5/10/1828, d. in New Orleans; Edgar, b. 26/6/1830; Thomas Phillips, b. 2/2/1833, d. 28/8/1834; Sarah P., b. 15/10/1834, d. 19/3/1835; Susan, b. 5/9/1836; Arthur, b. 4/7/1838; Llewellyn, b. 14/1/1840; Thomas P., b. 31/8/1841;

Samuel. The family rem. to Fairfax MM, in 1850.
MITCHELL. Children of Matthew [Mitchell] (d. 9th mo. 1832) and his wife Elizabeth: Pleasant, dis. 1830; Hannah. The family rem. from Fairfax MM, in 1827.
MOORE. Children of James Moore, Jr. and his wife Esther (Sinclair): Thomas, b. 19/9/1824. Esther rem. from Baltimore MM, for Western District 6/2/1824. The family rem. to Baltimore MM for Western District in 1825.
MORGAN. Children of John (dis. 1826) and Eliza Morgan: Joseph, d. 11/1/1836; Mary Ann, dis. 1836; Hannah, d. 16/11/1844 in her 25th year; Thomas P., left Friends (see minutes 3rd mo. 1851); Elizabeth, b. 25/11/1823, relinquished her right 1843; Ellen M., b. 29/11/1825, m. 23/12/1850 Charles Miller.
Deborah Morgan, rem. from Fairfax MM, 1816, rem. to Hopewell MM, 1825.
William Morgan, dis. 1825, m. 1791 at Gunpowder MM, Md. to Sarah Price (d. 15/9/1845 age 76 years). Their children: William, Jr.; Jane, d. 16/6/1837 in her 29th year; Thomas, d. in New Orleans in 1832.
MYERS. Samuel Myers and his wife Paulina and their children: Sarah H.; Mary; Hannah; Joseph, d. 11/9/1826 in his 6th year; Rachel, b. 2/7/1823; William M., b. 26/11/1825; Julia Ann, b. 29/9/1828; Jane. Sarah rem. to Middletown MM, Bucks Co., Pa., 1829. The remainder of the family rem. to New Garden MM, Columbiana Co., Ohio, 1833.
Sarah H. Myers, rem. from Middletown MM, PA, 1832, rem. to New Garden MM, Columbiana Co., Ohio, 1833.
NEILL. Children of Joseph and Rebecca Neill (rem. to Hopewell MM): Lydia, rem. to Hopewell MM; Mary, m. 3/12/1818 Thomas V. Huck; Lewis.
PAINTER. Rachel Painter dis. 1834
PALMER. Pennell Palmer, m. 30/4/1828 Rebecca McPherson, rem. to Concord MM, Pa. 1829.
PATTERSON. Children of William (dis. 7th mo. 1824) and Beulah Patterson: Samuel Nixon; Ellwood. The family rem. to Cincinnati MM, Ohio, 11th mo. 1824.
PEACH. Samuel Peach dis. 1823.
Samuel son of Samuel and Mary (d. 1/7/1844 in her 81st year) Peach, dis. 1823.
PIERPOINT. John R. Pierpoint, rem. from Hopewell MM, 1825 [see below].
PLUMMER. Gerard Plummer and his wife Mary (d. 1824) had the following children: Rebecca; Richard Hopkins; Mary Ann; Thomas; Gerard, Jr., b. and d. 1824. Gerard and his children, Rebecca and Mary Ann rem. to Baltimore MM, for Western District 1846; Richard rem. there in 1831 and Thomas in 1839.
POPE. Abner Pope m. 30/4/1818 to Maria Parkins. Their children: Edward; Mary Ann; Abner, Jr., b. 7/4/1824; Joseph D.
POWELL. Benjamin W. Powell rem. to Hopewell MM 1825.
RAWLINGS. Children of John Rawlings (dis. 1831) and his wife Mary: John, Jr., rem. to Wytham MM, Essex, Great Britain, 1823; Samuel, d. 12/9/1825, age 27 years; Mary, dis. 1826; Robert, dis. 1831; James, dis. 1831.
RILEY. Joshua Riley, "deceased."
RINKER. Joseph Rinker d. 23/10/1832.
ROBERTSON. Mary Robertson, "deceased."
ROSS. Children of Mary Ross, formerly Janney of Fairfax MM, and David Ross, son

Alexandria Monthly Meeting   51

of David and Katherine (Thomas) Ross: Charles, dis. 1838; James, dis. 1851; Samuel, removed to Yonge Street MM, Upper Canada 1834; John C., rem. to Plainfield MM, Ill. 1851; Mary S, d. 25/5/1834. Hannah Ross, rem. from Hopewell MM, 1818, rem. to Hopewell MM, 1824.
RUSSELL. Children of James [Russell] (rem. from Fairfax MM, 1815) and Susannah: John Thomas, rem. to Yonge Street MM, Upper Canada 1834; Joseph J., rem. to Yonge Street MM, Upper Canada 1833; Hannah Ann; Rebecca; Susannah; James; Charles. James and Susannah and the remainder of the family (Hannah Ann, Rebecca, Susannah, James and Charles) rem. to Honey Creek MM, Ind. 1840.
Rebecca Russell rem. to Indian Spring MM 1824.
RUTTER. Thomas Rutter, rem. from Philadelphia MM Southern District 1818, rem. to 12th Street MM Philadelphia 1822, MM for Northern District Philadelphia 1823.
SANDS. Eliza Sands, rem. from Indian Spring MM 1824.
Samuel B. Sands, rem. from Indian Spring MM, 1829, rem. to Green Plain MM, Ohio, 1836.
SAUNDERS. Peter Saunders (d. 26/2/1825) m. Hannah McPherson. Their children: Sarah Pancoast, m. 1834 Silas Dunbar; John M.; McPherson; Joseph; Thomas H.; Samuel C.; Mary, b. 1824. The family rem. to Gravelly Run MM, 1823 (certificate not received) and to Cherry Street MM Philadelphia in 1834.
SCHOLFIELD. Andrew Scholfield and his wife Elizabeth, withdrawn 1829.
Jonathan (readmitted 1827, dis. 1835) and Eleanor* Scholfield; children: Samuel W.; Sarah Ann, m. 18/10/1832 Charles W. Swain, rem. to Newtown MM, Pa. 1833; Phebe Ellen*; Mary Eliza*; William A.*; David B.*, b. 30/9/1819; Margaret A.*, b. 26/11/1821; Joseph*, b. 7/6/1828; Maria Pope*, 15/5/1823; Susanna*, 23/7/1825. *(rem. to Milford MM, Milton, Ind., 3rd mo. 1835)
Joseph L. (d. 19/9/1848, age 89) and Mary (d. 1860) Scholfield; children: Joseph; Hannah R., m. Henry Janney, rem. to New Garden MM, Ohio, 1838; Sarah, rem. to Green Street MM, Philadelphia 1854.
Mahlon Scholfield and his wife Ann had the following children: Ann; Lewis; Elizabeth; Rachel; Joseph; William. The family rem. to Hopewell MM in 1824.
Thomas M. Scholfield, rem. from Concord MM, Pa., 1825, rem. to Still Water MM, Ohio, 1832.
SCOTT. George Scott d. 12/10/1845, age 45 years.
Mahlon S. Scott, came in 1824, dis. 1826.
Mary M. Scott, rem. from Fairfax MM, 1823, rem. to Fairfax MM, 1826.
William A. Scott (d. 30/7/1846, age 73) and his wife Ann (d. 18/9/1846, age 89).
SHOEMAKER. Abigail Shoemaker d. 18/12/1826, age c.82 years; Abigail Shoemaker, Jr., rem. to Philadelphia MM, for the Northern District 1827.
Arnold and his wife Hannah; children: Hannah Shoemaker, m. Isaac Holmes 5/12/1827, rem. to Goose Creek MM, 1829; Elizabeth, m. Rodney Davis, "belongs to the Orthodox Friends"; Mary Spencer; Isaiah; Anna; Susan; Ellen; Samuel Spencer, b. 6/2/1823. Arnold and Hannah and their children, Isaiah, Anna, Susan, Ellen, Samuel Spencer, rem. to Springborough MM, Ohio, in 1837.
George Shoemaker, d. 20/7/1865, m. 1821 at Gwynedd MM, Pa. to Elizabeth Lukens (d. 25/2/1881). Their children: Willm. Lukens, b. 19/6/1822;

Edward, b. 23/10/1825, m. 12/7/1860 Fanny B. Walton; David L., b. 21/10/1827, dis. 1853; Elizabeth Lukens ("now Buckey") and Rebecca Albertson (d. 5/10/1830) (twins b. 2/12/1829); Mary A., b. 25/4/1832, now Walton, rem. to Spruce Street MM, Philadelphia; Francis Dodge, 3/3/1834; Charles, b. 3/3/1834, d. 1845; George, b. 25/7/1836.

Tacey Shoemaker rem. to Horsham MM, Montgomery Co., Pa. 1848.

SHREVE. Samuel B. Shreve, son of Benj. and Hannah, m. 2/12/1813 to Rachel Smedley (dau. of David and Rachel). Samuel rem. to Burlington MM, 1851.

SINCLAIR. Jacob Lindley Sinclair, rem. from Indian Spring MM, 1828, rem. to Ind. Spring MM, 1830.

Sarah Sinclair, rem. from Indian Spring MM, 1828 [see below].

SMEDLEY. David Smedley, dis. 1824.

SMITH. Samuel E. Smith, rem. from Buckingham MM, Pa., 1828, left Friends [see below].

SOULBY. Harper Soulby, rem. from MM, of Spalding and Wainfleet, county of Lincoln, Old England, 3rd mo. 1823 - dis. 12th mo. 1823.

Sarah Ann Soulby, rem. from MM, of Spalding and Wainfleet, county of Lincoln, Old England, 3rd mo. 1823 - dis. 12th mo. 1823.

SPENCER. Children of Thomas Spencer and his wife Alice (both dis. 1823): Mary Ann; Rebecca.

STABLER. Caleb Stabler rem. to Indian Spring MM, 1824.

Edward Stabler, b. at Petersburg 28/9/1769, d. 18/1/1831, son of Edward and Mary Stabler, m(1) Mary Pleasants [see Fairfax MM, d. 29/4/1853 in her 70th year]. Their children: William, d. 24/9/1852 in his 57th year, m. 1818 at Chesterfield MM to Deborah Hewes (d. 27/5/1876); Elizabeth rem. to Indian Spring MM 1824, ret. 1826, m. 1828 Joseph Bond, rem. to Fairfax MM 1830; Anna rem. to Indian Spring MM, 1824, ret. 1826, rem. again 1846; Robinson m. Mary Annie Davis from South River MM, Va. (see below); Thomas S., rem. to Indian Spring MM 1822, ret. 1826. Edward Stabler m(2) Mary Hartshorne. Their children: Mary P.; Susan; Edward H.; Rebecca; Henry (see below); Richard H. (see below); Sarah, m. Richard S. Huck 26/1/1847, rem. to Baltimore MM, for West District 1848; Francis, b. 1825, m. Cornelia Janney Miller d/o Robert and Anna Miller (see above); Caroline H., b. 15/2/1828, d. 3/2/1831; Harriet, b. 30/4/1830, d. 25/7/1847.

Robinson Stabler m. Mary Annie Davis (d. 5/8/1838) from South River MM, Va. Their children: Sarah Zalinda, b. 21/10/1829, d. 3/11/1834; Anna E., now Harthorne, dis. 19/10/1854; William Davis; Thomas.

William Stabler, d. 24/9/1852 in his 57th year, m. 1818 at Chesterfield MM, Deborah Hewes (d. 27/5/1876).

STEER. Joseph Steer and his wife Sarah and their children: Mary M.; Phineas J.; James M.; Isaac H.; Lydia Ann; Phebe M. All the family except Phineas rem. to Fairfax MM, in 1824; he rem. there in 1833.

SUTTON. James Sutton dis. 1834.

SWAYNE. Children of Sarah Swayne (d. c.1851) and her husband John: Mary Ann, d. c.1835; John Thomas, rem. "beyond the reach of Friends."

Noah Swayne dis. 1839.

TALBOTT. Elisha [Talbott], d. 11/8/1832, m. Sarah Saunders. Their children: Mary Ann, d. 28/7/1831; Rebecca, d. 12/2/1832; Jno. Saunders, dis. 1851; Joseph C., rem. to Baltimore MM, for Western District 1833; Elisha, Jr.;

William W., left Friends (see minutes, 3rd mo. 1851); Richard Litle, b. 19/9/1827, left Friends (see minutes, 3rd mo. 1851).
John L. Talbott, rem. from Baltimore MM, for Western District 1826, d. at Detroit.
UNDERHILL. Levi Underhill m. -/7/1818 to Elizabeth Mattingly. Their children: Sarah; Daniel; Levi Athan, b. 12/5/1823, d. 14/7/1829; Willm. Francis, b. 17/10/1827; Elizabeth. The family rem. to New York MM, 1835.
VASSE. Sarah Vasse, rem. from Philadelphia MM, 1802, d. 24/8/1829.
VORE. Isaac Vore, rem. from Baltimore MM, for Western District 1829.
WALKER. Rosanna Walker, came in by request 1824, d. 20/8/1838.
WALL. Mary Ann Wall, came in by request 1824, rem. to Goose Creek MM, 1831.
WANTON. Mary (Saunders) Wanton d. 26/11/1846, age 84.
Philip Wanton, dis. for drinking 1806, m. 1792 at Fairfax MM, Mary Saunders (widow of John Saunders and dau. of David and Sarah Pancoast). Their children: Hannah, d. 13/10/1860, age 67; William R., rem. to Baltimore 1816; Mary H., m. 26/9/1833 to John R. Pierpoint.
WETHERALD. Children of Thomas Wetherald and his wife Ann: Mary; Esther; Joseph E.; Samuel B., b. 12/7/1825; Thomas, Jr., b. 22/6/1827. The family rem. from Chesterfield MM, N.J. in 1823. They rem. to York MM, Pa., in 1829.
WETHERALL. Sarah Eleanor Wetherall, rem. from Fairfax MM, 1826.
WILSON. Catharine Wilson, withdrawn (see minutes 2nd mo. 1830).
David Wilson, d. 1824, m. 4/3/1813 to Hannah Irwin (dis. 1833). Their children: John Warder, "residing in New Orleans"; Thomas Irwin, d. 24/5/1840 at 5 a.m. The family rem. from Hopewell MM, in 1824.
Enoch Wilson, dis. 1830.
Samuel Wilson, dis. 1822.
Thomas Wilson, dis. 1825.
WRIGHT. Joel Wright, rem. from Baltimore MM, Western District 1824, "believed to be deceased."
YEATES. Children of William Yeates, Jr. (d. 22/7/1849) and Hannah (d. 23/12/1834): Elizabeth, d. 6/12/1848; Henry, rem. to Cherry Street MM, Philadelphia 1835, d. 26/4/1845 in his 29th year; Ann; Sarah, b. 29/3/1823, d. 18/2/1843; Rachel, b. 15/10/1824, d. 12/10/1836.
William Yeates, d. 6/9/1826 at Brooklyn, N.Y., m(1) Elizabeth. Their child William, Jr. (see above). William, Sr. m(2) Sarah who d. 19/8/1826.

For later information see William Wade Hinshaw, Encyclopedia of American Quaker Genealogy, Vol. VI - Virginia.

CHRIST (EPISCOPAL) CHURCH, FAIRFAX PARISH
Extracts from the Vestry Book
Genealogical Data

Vestry book begins August 26, 1765, and ends November 1, 1842. First portion abstracted.

26 Aug 1765. At a Vestry Meeting of the Parish of Fairfax. Present: John West, William Payne, William Adams, John Dalton, Thomas Wren, Edward Duling, Richard Sandford, Thomas Shaw, Townshend Dade.

I, A.B. do declare that I will be conformable to the doctrine of the Church of England as by law Established -- John West, William Payne, Jr., William Adams, John Dalton, Thomas Wren, Edward Duling, Richard Sandford, Daniel French, Thomas Shaw, Townshend Dade. John Minor is appointed Clerk of the Vestry.

Ordered that John West, William Payne, John Dalton and Daniel French or any three of them apply to the clerk of the vestry of Truro Parish for a copy of all such records relative to the cost of the Glebe lands, buildings, church plate, and fifty thousand pounds of tobacco which has been levyd. upon the inhabitants of the said Parish of Truro and Fairfax; take care of the poor until the laying of the parish levy; William Adams, Thomas Wren and Edward Duling agree with workmen for repairing the church.

Ordered that Samuel Hamon be appointed Reader at the Falls church. Ordered that John Dalton buy and provide a church Bible and two prayer books for the use of the lower church and a Book proper for the records of the Parish and bring his charges of the same.

30 Nov 1765. Payments were made to the following persons: Sybil West; William Crawford; [Margaret] McFall; Peter Perry; John Muir; Margaret [Evans]; Edward [Trammell], sexton; John Rhodes; Elizabeth Palmer; Matthew Bradley; William Ramsay; John Muir; Robert Wilson; Margaret McFall for the care of Eliza Barker; John Dalton for a coffin for Eliza Barker; Henry Biddle; John Tomlin; Messrs. [John] Carlyle and [John] Dalton; Doctor William Rumney; Revd. Mr. Scott; John Parker; James Goodin; John Bowling; Joseph Smith; Peter Perry; Gerrard Trammel for [lining] and collering the surplice[1]; Benjamin Sebastian; Bartholomew Bolton, a poor man; Thomas Wren, Reader at the Falls Church; to building churches; Peter Wagener for copying Truro list of tithables.

Ordered that the Church Wardens receive of every tithable in the Parish 47 pounds of tobacco or levy the same by distress. William Payne and John West are appointed church wardens for the year 1766.

---

[1] "Surplice" is a loose-fitting broad-sleeved white vestment, properly of linen, worn over the cassock by clergymen and choristers.

Indentures made: Between William Payne and John West binding John Longden to William Carlin; binding Uriah Colton to William Carlin; binding John Darby to Betty Ramsay.

Agreeable to an order of the last vestry that John West, John Dalton and Daniel French to inspect into the records of Truro Parish to see the cost of the Glebe lands, buildings and church plate.

30 Dec 1765. Gerrard Trammel agrees to do the usual duties at the Falls Church for 400 lbs. tobacco as sexton. The Rev. Townshend Dade produced his credentials as a minister of the Church of England and offered his services as incumbent for this Parish and as such is received. Thomas Wren is appointed clerk for the Falls Church. Church wardens advertise the want of a Glebe for this parish. Ordered that the church wardens advertise the want of a vestry house to be built, sixteen feet square, clap board work and inside chimney to be covered with 3 feet shingles, plank floored.

17 Mar 1766. The dimensions of the vestry house are as follows: It shall be built sixteen feet square, with an outside chimney, planked above and below to be covered with three feet oak shingles, the joysts to be beaded, the upper floor to be planed below. The doors rabbitted and beaded, a glass window with eight lights, the floor to be laid with pine planks, the room sides and gable ends to be tarred. The pitch to be nine feet, a back and hearth to be made of clay. The whole to be framed and finished in a workmanship manner by the first day of the Nov next for Two Thousand Five Hundred Pounds of transfer tobacco.

Henry Darne, undertaker. Ordered that William Payne, Edward Duling, William Adams and John Dalton attend the persons that offer their land for sale and view the same and report to the vestry on Saturday before May Court at "Cameron," their opinion of the land in proportion to the value demanded.

17 May 1766. Present: John West, William Payne, William Adams, John Dalton, Thomas Wren, Charles Broadwater, Daniel French, Edwd. Duling, Thomas Shaw, Edwd. Blackburn, Richard Sandford. Ordered that the church wardens prosecute the appeal made against Richard Griffis, and pay to Barnaby Noland such a sum of tobacco as they shall think necessary for his support, and pay to Mary Murry forty shillings for the maintaineance of a bastard child.

16 Oct 1766. Present: John West, William Payne, John Dalton, Charles Broadwater, Townshend Dade, William Adams, Richard Sandford, Edward Duling, Thomas Shaw, Thomas Wren, Daniel French.

Fairfax Parish. Payments were made to the following persons: Rev. Mr. Townshend Dade for 11 months, and also for the "deficiency of a Glebe;" Thomas Wren at the Falls Church; Gerrard Trammel, sexton at the Falls Church; John Rhodes, sexton at Alexandria; Matthew Bradley for keeping his son, a disabled child; Nicholas Garret for maintenance of a base born child; John Asberry per account; Messrs. [John] Carlyle and [John] Dalton for church books & a bolt and lock on account; Daniel French for the support of [Catherine] Carter; Colo. John West for elements for the church; John Minor for serving as clerk.

Ordered that the church wardens take care of Andrew Robertson, a poor man. An indenture between John West and William Payne, church wardens, and Andrew Nelson. The church wardens to advertise the building of a church at the Falls old church, twenty two hundred square from outside to outside, for the walls to be raised to admit of galleries. William Adams and John Dalton are appointed in this parish as church wardens. Ordered that the church wardens advertise the want of a Glebe to be bought and those inclined to sell land let them meet at the Falls Church the first Monday in March ensuing, or send in [their] proposals. John West resigns his place as a vestry man and requests the vestry to make choice of some other person.

15 Nov 1766. Fairfax Parish. Payment made to: Archibald McDonald for digging the grave and burial of Elizabeth Young; George West per account; Henry Riddle per account; Peter Perry for the maintenance of Thomas Richards; James Connel per account; Carlyle and Dalton per account; Alexr. Williams "2 levys being wrong charges." An order of the vestry of Truro Parish was produced to this parish desiring a view of the work done to the Falls Church by Charles Broadwater, they appointed Thomas Price to view the work, and also James Wren. Edward Blackburn resigned his place as vestryman, replaced by James Wren.

27 Nov 1766. Fairfax Parish. Payments made to: Maj. [Peter] Wagener per account; James Russell for 2 mos. services as clerk; William Carlin for his services as clerk 9 mos.; Mary Bryan for keeping Zephaniah Bryan, an object of charity; Margaret McDonald for keeping James Battle, a poor man; Dr. William Rumney per account; Colo. John Carlyle for mending benches; Francis [Summers]; William Trossel for making a coffin for Geo. Palmer; Elizabeth Palmer for boarding a child 4 mos., and burial; Henry Darne per account.

Ordered that the church wardens receive of every [tithable] in this parish 65 lbs. tobacco or levy the same by distress. It is ordered that the church wardens advertise the building of two churches 2400 sq. feet each to be built of brick from outside to outside and the walls to be raised to admit of galleries. [One at Alexandria and the other "where the old Falls Church now stands."]

1 Jan 1767. Present: William Adams, John Dalton, John West, William Payne, Edward Duling, Thomas Shaw, Richard Sandford, Daniel French, Thomas Wren and James Wren. Church wardens advertise in the Maryland and Virginia Gazettes the letting out two churches to the lowest bidder. James Wren produced a plan, 60 feet by 40 feet, to build a church at Falls for £599.15. James Parsons agrees to build a church at Alexandria for £600, agreeable to a plan by James Wren for which plan Wren is to receive 40 shillings, and bill of scantling.

The Church at the Falls and Alexandria to be twenty eight feet from the foundation, that is three bricks and a half to the sleepers, three bricks to the water table, and two and a half from thence. The quoins and arches to be of pubd. brick, the pediment to the doors of rubd. work in the Tuscan order. The outside of the wall to be done with place bricks, the mortar to be two thirds lime and one sand. The inside half lime and half sand. The isles to be laid with tile or flags, the lower windows to contain eighteen lights each of nine by eleven, the upper windows, twelve lights each. Besides the compass head. The sashes of the lower windows to hang with weights and pulleys, and to be clear of sap, to have a medallion cornish under the eaves. The roof to have three pair of pine-apple rafters or as the workmen call it a princeable roof to be framed in the best manner and to be covered with ince pine or poplar plank laid close to the shingle, on the singles to be of the bst juniper cypress, three quarters of an inch thick, eighteen inches long and to show six inches. The floor to be laid with inch and quarter pine plank and to be raised four inches above the isles. The pews to be three feet six inches high besides the coping, with doors to all, to be neatly wainscoted with quarter round on both sides and raised panrel on one, and to be neatly coped with some handsome moulding, the seats to be twelve or thirteen inches broad, the outdoors to be folding and in width [blank] feet, hung with proper hinges locks and barrs, to be raised pannel on both sides, locust sills to the frames and archetraves on the outside. The altar piece pulpit and canopy to be compleated in the Ionic order. The walls and ceiling to be well plastered with three coats, with cove cornish. The whole to be neatly painted and finished in the best manner. The isles to be six feet.

14 May 1767. Present: John West, William Payne, Edward Duling, Thomas Shaw, Charles Broadwater, William Adams, Richard Sandford, Daniel French, Townshend Dade, Thomas Wren, James Wren and John Dalton. An indenture between William Adams and John Dalton, church wardens, binding Cloe Stephens, an orphan, aged 13 to Nomy Ramsay to instruct her in needlework and mantua making and to learn her to read and write English. Upon a petition to the vestry of sundry inhabitants praying an addition to the church of ten feet in width that is to be built at Alexandria, it is agreed to that they make such addition agreeable to [their] contract with James Parsons, the present undertaker, who has agreed to build the said Church and lay off pews, by a plan produced and numbered 4, 5, 15, 18, 29, 14, 19, 28, 13 and 20, which said pews are to be sold by the said James Parsons, for his benefit, but with this exception, that no one is permitted to be a purchaser but inhabitants in this parish, or those that pay taxes in the same.

18 Aug 1767. Ordered that Thomas Triplett, Humphrey Peake and Abednego Adams or any two of them attend as processioners to see the lines of the land renewed in that part of the parish whose beginnings are between Little Hunting Creek on Potomac River, Great Hunting Creek up the Broad Lick Run and to the parish line, and that they do the same between the last day of Sept next.

Ordered that Robert Alexander, Moses Ball and William Hardin or any two of them attend as processioners to see the lines of land renewed in that part of the parish whose beginning are between Great Hunting Creek up the main road to Avery's road, thence down the road to Rock Creek Ferry then down Potomac River to the mouth of Great Hunting Creek thence up the creek to the aforesaid road.

Ordered that John Hunter, Henry Darne and George Thrift or any two of them attend as processioners to see the lines of the lands renewed in that part of the parish who beginning are from Avery's road to the Old Court House, thence down the main road.

Ordered that John Anderson, Charles Thrift and James Jenkins or any two of them attend as processioners to see the lines of the lands renewed in that part of the parish who beginning are from the Old Court House to Difficult Bridge, thence down the run to Potomac thence down the river to the Falls warehouse and thence up the main road to the beginning.

Ordered that Joseph Cockerille, John Summers Jr. and John Hurst or any two of them attend as processioners to see the lines of the lands renewed in that part of the parish who beginning at the Difficult Bridge up the run to the parish line and along the said line where it crosses the Backlick road thence up the said road to the Falls Church thence up the county road to Difficult Bridge.

Ordered that William Summers, Francis Summers and John Ratcliff or any two of them attend as processioners to see the lines of the lands renewed in that part of the parish who beginning are from the Falls Church down Cameron road to Great Hunting Creek thence up Backlick run to the parish line, thence along the line to where it crosses the back road, thence up the said road to the Falls church.

14 Oct 1767. An indenture between William Adams and John Dalton, church wardens: binding John Perkins, an orphan, age nine years an apprentice to Thomas Lister who is to learn him the trade of a shoemaker and to read and write English. Binding Samuel Williams, an orphan, age four years an apprentice to John Williams who is to learn him the trade of a cordwainer and to read and write English. Binding Daniel Diskins, an orphan, age five years as an apprentice to John Summers who is to learn him the trade of a shoemaker and to read and write English. Binding Ann Spurling, a bastard child, age eight years to George Williams who is to learn her to read and write English. Mr. Henry Gunnell was elected a vestry man in the [room] of Thomas Wren, deceased.

23 Nov 1767. Fairfax Parish. Payments made to: Rev. Mr. Dade, salary; Clerk of the vestry; Clerk of the Church of Alexandria, William Carlin; Clerk of the Falls Church, Thomas Wren; Benjamin West as Clerk from the death of Mr. Wren; Gerrd. Trammell, sexton at the Falls Church; John Rhodes, sexton at Alexandria; Mr. Townshend Dade for a levy overpaid for the last year; William Horsman for three levys overpaid for the last year; John Summers for a levy overpaid for the last year; Francis Summers for a levy overcharged in 1765 as per account; Joseph Smith per account; Edward Blackburn for maintaining a bastard child; Maj. Peter Wagener; John Rhodes for his attendance on John Kilmaster; Robt. Jones for his trouble in tending and burying Edwd. Holt; Mr. William Adams; Mr. John Dalton; Mr. Sampson Darrell; Michael Reagan; Mr. Wm. Grayson; Mr. William Rumney; Robert Jones for boarding an old woman; Mr. John Muir; Mr. Henry Riddle; Isaac Ross for keeping Hannah Clements, a molatto child; Richd. Hollinsbury for [maintenance] of Sepr. Rolings; Matthew Bradley for the [maintenance] of his son John Bradley; Mary Bryan for maintenance of her son, Zephaniah; George Magness for nursing Thomas Flemings' servant woman's child; Thomas Shaw for six benches; Messrs. Carlyle and Dalton; Stephen Pusey for nursing a child for three weeks; Nicholas Garrett for one levy over paid; Nicholas Garrett for keeping and maintaining a base born child; Sandford Remy for maintaining base born child three months; John Moxley for keeping Henry Summersett who is to be kept twelve months from this date for £5.0.00 which sum now levied is to be deducted at the laying of the next parish levy; Rev. Mr. Dade for deficiency of a Glebe and for deficiency for the last year's salary for the want of a Glebe.

21 Dec 1767. Payments made to: John Win for boarding Eliza Winn; Gerrard Trammil for attending six vestrys. Ordered that the church wardens receive from every tithable 57 lbs. tobacco or levy the same by distress. Edward Duling and

Charles Broadwater are appointed church wardens. Ordered that the collectors pay to James Wren four thousand lbs. of tobacco.

Parish of Fairfax. Payments received from: Andrew Robertson; Mr. Henry Riddle; Mr. William Payne; Sylvester Adams; John Lister; Robert Jones; Peter Wise; Craycraft and Barne's note; Keziah Jenkins.

8 Feb 1768. Charles Broadwater refusing as one of the church wardens to collect the parish levy, it is ordered that Edward Duling is appointed collector for the present year; ordered that James Wren fix the church as near the north of the old church so that it fronts directly south.

19 Apr 1768. Work to be inspected of the upper church to be built by James Wren, undertaker.

30 Jul 1768. An indenture between Charles Broadwater and Edward Duling, church wardens, binding Henny Carter, a mulatto girl, aged eleven years to Michael Ragan who is to learn her to read and write English. Inquiry into the late behavior of the Rev. Townshend Dade in Mr. John Hunter's family.

28 Nov 1768. Payments made to: Rev. Mr. Dade's salary; Clerk of the vestry; William Carlin, Clerk of Alexandria church; Benj. West, clerk of the Falls Church; Gerrard [Trammell], sexton of the Falls Church; John Rhodes, sexton at Alexandria; William Boswell for two levys over paid last year; Robert Jones for a levy overpaid for the last year; John Summers, Sr. for one levy overpaid; William [Deebie], Edward Duling, John Williams, Henry Riddell and Henry Ansley - all per account; John Moxley for support of Henry Summerset to this date; John Moxley per account; Gerrard Bowling as per account; Benjamin Sebastian for maintenance of bastard child to date; Robert Jones for maintaining Thomas Richards [for] twelve mos.; Matthew Bradley for support of his son; Mary Bryan for support of her son; John Stone for the maintenance of a poor child of Jeremiah Cohagan; Shadrack Hill for maintaining Elizabeth Stichborne for keeping her in sickness and burying her; James Connell for making two coffins; Mary Hooper for maintaining her son for nine mos.; Sandford Remy for keeping a bastard child to date; Maj. [Peter] Wagener as per account; Thomas Parsons for a levy overpaid for the last year; Rev. Mr. Dade for deficiency of a Glebe; Elizabeth Palmer for the clothing her; James Wren as per account for moving and building the chimney and fittings in the vestry house with brick; Sampson Darrell per account; Dr. [William] Rumney per account; Gerrard Trammell for attending the vestrys

Ordered that the collectors receive from each tithable person sixty pounds of tobacco or levy the same by distress. Daniel French and Thomas Shaw are appointed church wardens for the ensuing year.

An indenture between Charles Broadwater and Edward Duling binding Gilbert Bains, an orphan, aged eight years to William Carlin who is to learn him the trade of a taylor and to read and write English.

Thomas Shaw declining to collect and Daniel French not being present, William Adams is appointed to collect the parish levy.

Ordered that John West apply to Mr. John Alexander of Stafford [Co.] for deeds for one acre of land near Alexandria which the church is erected upon.

24 Jul 1769. An indenture between Daniel French and Thomas Shaw binding Robert Mills, an orphan, aged twelve years to Edward Rigdon who is to learn him the trade of a joiner and to read and write English. Mr. William Payne exhibited an account [payments] to this vestry as follows: Henry Darne; John Dalton; Henry Riddle; Mary Murry for keeping a bastard child for three months, and to William Reedy for keeping the same child 3 mos.

Fairfax Parish. Payment by William Elliott. It is agreed by the vestry to buy the land on which Mr. Townshend Dade lives containing four hundred acres; the plantation making a complete Glebe.

28 Nov 1769. An indenture between Thomas Shaw and Daniel French, church wardens, binding William Grimes, an orphan, aged fourteen years in February last to Thomas Doudill to learn the trade of a tile cooper and to read and write English. A bond from Rodger Chew, Thomas Brownly and Peter Wise, indemnifying the parish from any charge that may arise from a bastard child born of Elinor Robertson, of which the said Rodger Chew is the reputed father.

Fairfax Parish. Payments made to the following persons: Rev. Mr. Townshend Dade for his salary; the clerk of the vestry; William Carlin clerk of Alexandria; Benjamin West, clerk at the Falls church; Gerrard Trammell, sexton; John Rhodes, sexton; Capt. [Sampson] Darrell for keeping a bastard child 14 mos.; Gerard Bowling for keeping Richard Hunt 12 mos.; John Williams Lock for 1 levy overpaid; Capt. John Dalton for James Boid; Matthew Bradley for the support of his son; Owen Williams for keeping a sick woman 6 mos.; Kizzia Williams for nursing a sick woman; Michael [Gretter] as per account; John Lomax for Thomas Richards; Richard Morris as per account; John Muir for Richards; John Muir for Elizabeth Broady; Thomas Shaw as per account; Daniel French as per account; John Stone for keeping an orphan child 12 mos.; Mary Hooper for keeping Thomas Hooper a lame youth, her son; Mary Bryan for keeping Zephaniah Bryan her son; Maj. Wagener as per account; Pierce Baly as per account; Benjamin Sebastian as per account; John Lomax for the support of Mary Rigdon; John Urton for his support; John Summers, Sr. for the support of Francis Ballinger; Edward Blackburn to be paid to Mr. Muir; the Rev. Mr. Dade for the deficiency of a Glebe; John Williams, Red Oak; George Murphey for the support of Elizabeth Palmer; Mr. James Wren for stone steps for the church and extraordinary work to the windows; Gerrard Trammel for attending the vestry. Ordered that the collector receive from every [tithable] person in this parish fifty lbs. of tobacco or levy the same by distress. Townshend Dade and James Wren are appointed church wardens for the ensuing year.

20th Dec 1769. Mr. James Wren has completed the work of the Falls Church agreeable to his contract.

Church wardens to allot the seats for the parishioners according to dignity. It is ordered that the old church be sold immediately and to be removed by the last of February a distance sufficient from the new building.

An indenture between church wardens binding James Mitchel an orphan aged about 4 years in Oct last to Samuel Johnston to learn the trade of a shoemaker and to read and write English.

At a vestry held for the parish of Fairfax the 12th day of May 1770, an offer being made by Daniel Jennings of his tract of land for a Glebe.

An application of James Hooper, a lame parishioner, and at present a charge upon the parish, being desirous of being bound as an apprentice to Jacob Dane, a taylor, has agreed with the said Dane to take him as an apprentice four years and has further agreed to pay him at two payments £7.4 each payment. The said Jacob to prepare indentures conformable. Ordered that John Summers bring his account of his charge expended for Frances Ballinger to the next vestry.

An indenture between Townshend Dade and James Wren, church wardens, binding: Isaac Halbert, an orphan, aged fourteen years to learn the trade of sadler; Sarah Blinstone aged three years and Thomas Blinstone aged 15 months to Sampson Darrell; Mr. James Wren produced an account for writing the commandments at £8 and ordered that he be paid the same.

27 May 1770. Application being made to the vestry by William Adams, gentleman, for payment of a secretary's note in a suit carrying on against the Rev. Mr. Dade by several persons some of which are not of the vestry. They gave for an answer, they will not pay the said note, as the said suit is not carried on by the vestry. John Dalton, one of the prosecutors, said the vestry had nothing to do with it and that he would pay the said note. Ordered that the collector pay Mr. French £3 which was levied for Owen Williams; also pay Mr. Wagener £2.18.4; also pay Pierce Bayly 9 shillings, 4 pence. It is agreed with Daniel [Jennings] to take the land whereon he lives containing as is supposed to be about 400 and more acres. The said Daniel Jennings agrees that Mr. George West, the surveyor, is to lay [off] the several [partitions] at his expense adjoining to find out the real quantity now in his possession. For which the church wardens and vestry agree to pay him at the rate of 15 shillings per acre. Daniel Jennings is to deliver up all the premises on the land on the 15 of Dec. next, except his dwelling house and kitchen which he reserves for his use till the 1 day of May next ensuing. Mr. James Wren produced an account of glass he has left unused which is seventy-eight panes which amount to £2.14.1 now deposited for the use of the parish.

12 May 1770. Ordered that John Summers, Sr. bring in his account of his expense of Frances Ballinger to the next vestry. On application of James Hooper, a lame parishioner and at present charged upon the parish being desirous of being bound an apprentice to Jacob Dane, a taylor, has agreed with the said Dane to take him as an apprentice four years, and has further agreed to pay him at two payments seven pounds, four shillings each payment.

17 Sep 1770. Conformable to an agreement entered into by the vestry for the purchase of the land for a Glebe from Daniel Jennings, a survey being made by Mr. John West, Jr. whereby it appears that there is 516 acres. Ordered that deeds be made and church wardens rent out the land for one year.

26 Nov 1770. Payments made to: The Rev. Townshend Dade for his salary and cash; John Minor, clerk of vestry; William Carlin, clerk at Alexandria; Benjamin West, clerk at Falls Church; Gerrard Trammel, sexton at the Falls Church and taking care of the surplice; Matthew Bradley for taking care of his son, John; Mary Bryan for the support of her son, Zephaniah; Rev. Mr. Dade for deficiencies of a Glebe; the sexton at Alexandria; Gerrard Bowling for boarding Richard Hunt; Sylvester Adams per account; Robert Lindsay per account; Doctor Townshend per account; William Housman for keeping Mary Ashberry; Moses Ball, Jr. for a child's coffin; John Williams for keeping Eliza Broadbent; Shadrack Hill for keeping Mary Gammel; Maj. Peter Wagener per account; William Balmain per account; John Summers; John Stone for keeping a child of Tony Cohagan; Thomas Shaw per account; William Middleton per account; William Adams by William Middleton; Gerrard Trammel per account; John Hurst per account; John Dalton per account; Tony Thrift per account; Margaret Piper per account; James Connelly per account; Edward Blackburn to be paid to John Muir; George Murphey for keeping Elizabeth Palmer; Gerrard Trammel for finding fire wood for the vestry; James Boid for Henry Summerset to be paid Mr. Carlyle; John West, Sr., assignee for James Boid; Daniel Mills for maintenance of a bastard child; Townshend Dade for [setting?] a poor man over the ferry; Mackenzie Porter for his maintenance; James Wren per account; Richard Morris per account to be repaid to James Muir; Rev. Mr. Dade for deficiency of a Glebe. John West, Sr. and Henry Gunnel, Sr. are appointed church wardens for the ensuing year. John Gunnel is appointed collector for this parish. It is further ordered that he receive from every tithable person fifty pounds of tobacco or levy the same by distress.

Thomas Shaw and Daniel French exhibited an account to this vestry and ordered to be recorded an is as follows: The Parish of Fairfax; James Wren his payment for building a church at the Falls; James Parsons his payment for building a church at Alexandria.

The Parish of Fairfax. Payments were made by the following persons: Michael Gretter; John Mason; Hector Ross; James Moon; James Parsons; and William Adams. By fines received William Gunnell, James Muir, Robert Adam, Agnes Brooks, Isaac Ross. By fines received - Ann Langham and John Mason.

William Adams and James Wren exhibited an account to this vestry and ordered to be recorded as follows: Daniel French per order of Owen Williams; Maj. Peter Wagener; Daniel Jennings; John Rhodes one levy over charged; Michael [Gretter]; Daniel Jennings; James Wren; Pierce Bayly.

Fairfax Parish. Payments were made by: a fine from Mr. Hughes; by order from late church wardens on Sanford and Rhodes; Hector Ross.

An indenture between church wardens binding George Francis who was ordered to be bound in August court, an orphan, aged 15 years to Thomas Monroe who is to learn him the trade of a cooper. Ordered that John West is appointed Treasurer for the parish.

5 Aug 1771. Entry of vestry for 25 Sep 1766 found to be missing.

Christ (Episcopal) Church, Fairfax Parish, Alexandria, Virginia   63

25 Sep 1766. Agreeable to an order made the 17 day of March for building a vestry house which was undertaken by Henry Darne the said house has been deeded and recorded. Pay Darne 2,500 lbs. of transfer tobo. for building said house, he presented his account for planking and securing fourteen windows and making a horse block.

Elizabeth Young, the property of Blanch Flower Dunkin, made application to this vestry for support, it appearing to them by the conviction and an assignment from Robert Adam, Gent. that she is not clear from her said service till the 12 of May, 1767. It is ordered that the church wardens make application to a magistrate for a warrant to move her out of the parish to her said master. William Payne, church warden.

25 Nov 1771. Payments made to: William Carlin, clerk of Alexandria; Benjamin West, clerk of Falls Church; John Rhodes, sexton for Alexandria; Rev. Mr. Dade for a deficiency of a Glebe; John Ramsay for the support of Paul Emmitt and Eve, his wife; William Horsman for keeping Mary Ashberry; John Williams for keeping Richard Hunt 5 mos.; Matthew Bradley for keeping his son, John to account for burying him; Margaret Long for burying Henry Cathers and her trouble in his sickness; John Summers, Sr. for keeping Thomas Sutton 10 mos.; Edwd. Rigdon for Henry Cathers; Robert Harrison for drawing a set of deeds; John Summers for keeping Henry Ballinger from May to date; Wineford Vinara for keeping and burying Mary Gabel; James Buckly for keeping [Catherine] Parsons 4 mos.; John Bowling for keeping Sarah Thompson 6 mos.; Abraham Wright for keeping Sarah Thompson 2½ mos.; Richard Leake for keeping Sarah Thompson 2½ mos.; Margaret West for keeping Sarah Thompson 2½ mos.; John Stone for keeping a child of Janey Cohagan; Joseph Smith for keeping Mary Oakly 4 mos.; Sarah Marvel for keeping Mary Oakly 2 mos.; John Dalton for necessary for Mary Oakly; Rodger Chew for necessary for Mary Oakly; Michael Coyle for necessary for Mary Oakly; Peter Perry for Mary Oakly; James Stewart per account; Mary Bryan for keeping her lame son; George Murphey for Elizabeth Palmer and his wife; Gerrard Trammel for keeping Elizabeth Broadb[ent] 12 mos.; John Branner per account; Dr. [William] Rumney per account; John Muir per account; Robert Adams per account; William Balmain per account; Michael Greter [Gretter] for burying of Cope; William Gunnell, for a judgment obtained grand jury on account; John Mason, Jr. for a judgment obtained grand jury on account; Gerrard Trammel, sexton at Falls Church; Gerrard Trammel for making fires, attending to vestry and cleaning the church yard; Colo. John West for finding elements; Doctor Alexander for attending Mary Gamon; John Minor for extraordinary expenses.

An indenture between the church wardens binding: Henry Allen, a base born child; Jane Ashberry, as an apprentice, to Robert Lindsay; John Parker, who is seven years old, as an apprentice to Andrew Waits who is to learn him the trade of a brewer; James Longworth aged 14 as an apprentice to Cyrus Copper who is to learn him to read and write.

Fairfax Parish. Payments made to: Mr. Henry Piper assignee of John Muir who is as the Doctor the assignee of Daniel Jennings, a bond passed by Townshend Dade and James Wren; Mr. Harry Piper assignee of John Muir who was the assignee of Daniel Jennings, a bond passed by church wardens, on account; James Parsons for work at Alexandria church; William Gunnel for pricing of 29 hhds of tobacco; John West, Jr.

To Fairfax Parish. By 29 hhds tobacco recd. of Mr. John Gunnell and sold to Mr. Harry Piper.

Ordered that David Talbert, Presly Cox, Humphrey Peake and Abednego Adams or any two of them attend as processioners to see the lines of the land renewed in that part of the parish, whose beginning are between Little Hunting Creek on Potomack river. Great Hunting Creek up the backlick run and to the parish line.

Ordered that Robert Alexander, James Green, Gerrard Alexander and William Hardin or any two of them attend as processioners to see the lines of the land renewed in that part of the parish whose beginning is between Great Hunting Creek up the main land to [Avery's] road, thence down the road to Rock Creek Ferry, thence down the river to the mouth of Hunting Creek and from then up the said creek to the crossing at Cameron.

Ordered that Henry Darne, George Thrift and James Robertson or any two of them attend as processioners to see the lines of the land renewed in that part of the parish whose beginning are from Avery's road to the old court house thence down the road to the Falls warehouse, then down the river to Avery's road from thence to the beginning.

Ordered that John Anderson, Charles Thrift and John Jackson or any two of them attend as processioners to see the lines of the lands renewed in that part of the parish whose beginning are from the Old Court house to Difficult Bridge thence down the run to Potomack thence down the river to the Falls warehouse and thence up to the main road to the beginning.

Ordered that Benjamin Moody, John Summers and John Hurst or any two of them attend as processioners to see the lines of the lands renewed in that part of the parish whose beginning are at Difficult Bridge up the run to the parish line and along the said line to where it crosses the backlick road thence up the said road to the Falls church thence up the county road to the beginning.

Ordered that William Summers, Francis Summers, Daniel Summers and David Price, or any two of them attend as processioners to see that lines of the land reviewed in that part of the parish whose beginnings are from the Falls Church down Cameron road to Great Hunting Creek, thence up the backlick run to the parish line thence along the line to where it crosses the back road thence up the said road to the Falls Church. Ordered that John West receive the rents due from the Glebe land and to tenant them as he shall see necessary.

William Payne and William Adams are appointed church wardens for the ensuing year.

Ordered that William Payne collect from every tithable in the parish 50 pounds of tobacco on levy the same by distress.

Ordered that the sexton at Alexandria examine into and fix the mode of corpses burying in the said church yard, that they be buried at least six feet deep, and in case said sexton can't conveniently execute the said order, it is then ordered Peter Perry perform the same. John West and Henry Gunnell, church wardens.

8 Jun 1772. Finishing of the church at this place was to be put up to the lowest bidder; John Carlyle, Gent., being the lowest bidder undertakes to finish.

23 Nov 1772. Indentures made by church wardens: binding John Carroll to David Gordon, as an apprentice aged 16 years who is to learn him the trade of a cooper and to learn him to read and write English; binding William Floyd, aged 9 years an apprentice to William Carlin who is to learn him the trade of a taylor and to learn him to read and write English; binding Mary and Sarah Hawkins, the one 8 years and the other 5 years, as apprentices, to William Richards who is to learn them and to read and write English; binding Milly Ballinger, aged 10 years as an apprentice to Francis Summers who is to learn her and to read and write English; binding Alice Ashberry, aged 10 years, as an apprentice to Thomas Wren who is to learn her and to read and write English; binding Elizabeth Banks Watts, aged 6 years, as an apprentice to David Gordon who is to learn her and to read and write English; binding Mary Watts, aged 6 years, to Archibald Cunningham who is to learn her and to read and write English.

The Parish of Fairfax. Payments made to: Rev. Mr. Dade; John Minor; William Carlin; Benjamin West; Gerrard Trammel, sexton; John Rhodes, sexton; Thomas Beach for burying Mary Hughes; Dr. Alexander; Dr. [Williams] Rumney; Roger Chew for making two coffins; John Muir; John and George Forster; John Dalton; Mr. Peter Wagener; Christian Murphey; Elizabeth Palmer; Mary Bryan for the support of her son; Margaret Piper for the support of her son; Edward Ruksby[1]; John West for finding elements to the church four times; Thomas Shaw; John Summers, Sr.; John Rhodes; Peter Perry.

Ordered that John Dalton and Edward Duling are appointed church wardens for the ensuing year. Ordered that the church wardens collect from every tithable person in this parish 45 pounds of tobacco or levy the same by distress.

27 Feb 1773. The vestry having received the church at Alexandria do receive the same from the undertaker, Colo. John Carlyle and is satisfied that the said church is finished in a workmanlike manner. Ordered that William [Copens] and Joseph Gourd do view the stone steps at Alexandria Church doors, and report to the next vestry.

The vestry then proceeded to sell the pews, as agreed 14 May 1767, and the following conditions are published. The conditions are: anyone purchasing a pew that is not a subscriber, pay down £15 of the purchase money and for the remainder must give their bond with security to the church wardens for the use of the parish payable in six months. Whatever the amount of sales are if it falls short of what the parish are in advance in finding the church, the ten pews are chargeable with the fifth part of the said sum deficient, no one is permitted to be a purchaser but inhabitants of this parish or those who pay taxes in the same, and the purchaser of each pew is obliged in case

---

[1] This surname is found spelled many ways, and it may be that we have confused it entirely. On several occasions it appears like "Bushby," while on a number of other cases we find "Rooksby," "Ruksby" or similar spelling. For the sake of consistency, we have inserted [Ruksby], as this surname is recognized in the area. Fairfax records are sprinkled with entries for an Edward Ruxby, 1751-1752, and an Edward Ruxsberry, 1815-1816.

of repairing being made for the said church to pay when demanded one tenth part of the one fifth of the said repairs, as there [their] fixed quota and agreeable to the original contract, otherwise the said pew becomes a forfeiture for the use of the parish.

Pew No. 28 sold to John Muir for £36.5.0
Pew No. 29 sold to John West, Jr. for £33.0.0.
Pew No. 18 sold to Thomas Fleming for £21.5.0.
Pew No. 19 sold to John Carlyle for £30.0.0.
Pew No. 20 sold to William Ramsay for £33.0.0.
Pew No. 15 sold to John Dalton for £20.0.0.
Pew No. 14 sold to Robert Alexander for £30.10.0.
Pew No. 13 sold to Robert Adam for £30.0.0.
Pew No. 4 sold to Townshend Dade for £28.0.0.
Pew No. 5 sold to George Washington for £36.10.0.

15 Mar 1773. Ordered that the church wardens advertise the letting of a Glebe house forty two by twenty eight in the clear to be built of brick the walls to be 19 feet from the bottom of the cellar, to be two brick thick to the water table and a brick and a half to the top of the wall. The outside to be laid with two thirds lime and one sand, the inside to be half and half. To be plastered, painted, and finished in a workmanlike manner. The plan will be produced at letting the aforesaid building, which will be on Monday, 26th day of April at the Rev. Dade's. At the same time will be let out to be built a kitchen, [meat] house, dairy, a barn, stable, and some other outhouses and paling in a garden.

24 May 1773. Lenghthy descriptions of structures to be built on Glebe land, including: dwelling house, rooms and dimensions, construction materials; dairy; meat house; barn; stable; corn house; and a garden.
   a.   Dwelling House (portion). Of brick and 28 feet in the clear. The walls from the foundation to be two bricks thick to the water table, and one and a half from that to the top; the cellar to be four feet under ground and to include the dancing room and passage, in it and from the bottom of the cellar to the upper parts of the first floor to be seven feet and from the upper part of the first floor to the upper part of the second floor to be eleven feet, two [partition] walls in the cellars under the girders of brick nine inches each, with proper doors in the cellars and through the [partition] with good and sufficient locks and hinges to them, and the cellars cleared out. The chimney to be seven feet above the ridge. The frame of the lower floor to be sawed out of white oak, clear of sap. The upper framing to be sawed out of white oak or poplar to be got very substantial and well framed the bricks to be laid in mortar two thirds lime and one third sand for the outside, the inside half and half. The floors to be laid with inch and a quarter pine plank. The upper floor to be grooved and tongued, the stairs to run up in the passage with hand rail and banisters, and a door underneath to go down into the cellar with a broad step ladder; all the doors on the lower floor to have six panels each and frames to have double [architraves]... Windows below with eighteen lights in each, ten by eight with inside shutters to them, four end windows eight lights each, ten by eight, six dorment windows twelve lights each, ten by eight, with good and sufficient frames with locust sills to all... Two portals the one in the hall, the other in the

Christ (Episcopal) Church, Fairfax Parish, Alexandria, Virginia 67

dining room to have the upper door glass...
b. Kitchen (complete). On the Glebe land, twenty feet by sixteen feet in the clear, a pair of stoves to run up on the outside and a closet on the other. The frame to be sawed out of white oak, the sides and ends to be weather boarded, with clapboards clear of sap, the roof to be covered with fetherage shingles to be got out of red oak and well seasoned. The inside filled in with brick and the floor laid with brick or soil and under pinned and the loft laid with plank one plain plank door and one window, eight lights and one window in the loft with a shutter, proper shelves and dressers put up, the eaves boxed and barged and common boards to be painted, the sides ends and roof to be tarred, the whole to be well framed and everything done to make the said kitchen in compleat in a plain workmanlike manner.
c. Dairy (complete). Twelve feet square, eight feet pitch, the frame to be sawed out of white oak, to be weather boarded with pine plank to have a pidgeon roof and covered with the best juniper cypress shingles, to be got, eighteen inches and to shew six, and to have a handsome lattice round the eaves to project eighteen inches and cornished. The inside to be lathed and plastered, one battined door with a sufficient lock and hinges, and proper shelves put up. The floor to be laid with brick or soil and underpinned with brick, the whole to be painted, and everything to be done to make the said dairy compleated in a neat plain and workmanlike manner.
d. Meet [Meat] House (complete). Twelve feet square eight feet pitch, the frame to be sawed out of white oak to be weather boarded with pine plank, a plain cornish and in the eaves. The roof to be covered with the best juniper cypress singles got eighteen inches and to shew six, to be well framed with a pidgeon roof, one battened door, with sufficient lock and hinges, the whole to be painted and under pinned with brick and everything done to make the said meet house compleat in a plain neat and workmanlike manner.
e. Barn (complete). Thirty-two by twenty feet, ten feet pitch, the frame to be sawed out of white oak, the sides and ends to be weather boarded with clapboards free of sap, the roof to be covered with fetherage shingles, got out of red oak timber and clear of sap. Twelve feet in the middle of the floor to be laid with two inch white oak plank and exited down the rest to be laid with inch and nailed with 20 penny nails, the whole to be well framed with proper doors lock and hinges, and to be well tarred, and evrything done to make the said barn compleat in a workmanlike manner.
f. Stable (complete). Twenty-four feet by sixteen feet, the body to be of sawed logs four inches thick to be doweled and dovetailed, eight feet pitch, the rafters sawed and the gable ends to be weather boarded, with clapboards clear of sap. The roof to be covered with fetherage shingles to be got out of red oak timber and clear of sap, the loft planked, proper door with sufficient lock and hinges, the ends and roof well tarred and everything done with salls, racks, and maingers to make the said stable compleat in a workmanlike manner.
g. Corn House (complete). Sixteen feet by ten feet, sawed logs for the body and floor, six feet pitch, and dovetailed, the roof and gable ends to be covered with clapboards got out of red oak timber clear of sap, a good and sufficient lock to the door and the ends and roof tarred, and everything done to make the said cornhouse compleat in a workmanlike manner.
h. House of Office (complete). Eight feet by six feet weather boarded with pine plan, and covered with cypress shingles, one battened door with three lights of

glass over it, proper seats put in the whole painted and compleated in a workmanlike manner.

i. Garden (complete). One hundred feet square the poles five feet high and neatly headed, the panels not to exceed ten feet in length, the rails and poles to be sawed out of white oak, locust posts, the rails and posts mortised and tenanted and put three feet in the ground and everything done in a compleat and workmanlike manner.

24 Nov 1773. The Parish for Fairfax. Payments made to: Rev. Mr. Dade; John Minor; John Rhodes, sexton at Alexandria; John Ball, clerk at Falls Church; John Ball for attending the church at Alexandria; Elizabeth [Gretter]; Robert H. Harrison; Witherson Grigsby; Dr. William Rumney; John Muir; John Duke for Glasford & Henderson; John Read; Richard Morris; Rodger Chew; Mary Bryan for keeping her son; Christian Murphey for her support; Elizabeth Palmer for her support; Edward [Ruksby] for support; Mary Howard for her support; John Summers, Sr. for one levy; Francis Summers; Thomas Shaw; to Peter Wagener for four copies of the last tithes; James Muir provided the grand jury which he was fined on should appear to be overset; William Donaldson for serving as clerk at Alexandria for 9 mos.; Paul Emmit for his support; William Buckley; Margaret Piper for the support of her son; Gerrd. Bowling the balance of his account for keeping Rd. Hunt, 1771; James Parsons, Wm. West and John Minor for the stone steps at Alexandria, which same is to be proportioned by Col. John West and John Dalton reserving James Parson's proportion for the use of the parish agreeable to William Copens and Joseph Gourd's report; Edward Duling; John Dalton; Gerrard Trammel for making fires and serving as sexton; James Wren for his plan of the Glebe house; William Parkerson for his plan of the Glebe house.

By 1385 [tithables] @ 5 lbs. tobacco per pole.

An indenture between church wardens: binding Joshua Rhodes, an orphan, aged ten years to Thomas Moxley who is to learn him the trade of a ship carpenter and to read and write English; binding Matthew Patterson, an orphan, aged four years to Daniel Mills who is to learn him the trade of a cooper and to read and write English; binding Pierce Baily West, an orphan, to William Patton who is to learn him the trade of a taylor and to read and write English; binding John Hughes, an orphan, to Thomas Moxley who is to learn him the trade of a ship's carpenter and to read and write English.

A bond from Elias Porter and Peter Wise to indemnify the parish from any expense attending a base born child of Susanna West. The church wardens returned John Ratcliff's bond for the parish collection.

Payments made to: Elizabeth Ramsay for making shifts and aprons; to bind Betty and Eave [Emmit][1]; Paul [Emmit] by agreement with him for distance; Mrs. Rind for the same; cash paid Hammond, & per account for church chest; Mary Hame; William [Copens] for coming to view the steps at church; Robt. Condran for fixing the pins in the windows; Mr. Herbert for a Bible and two prayer books for the Falls Church;

---

[1] Surname appears as "Ermat," "Esmit," or "Ermett."

Christ (Episcopal) Church, Fairfax Parish, Alexandria, Virginia   69

Messrs. Ray, Owen Williams, Rev. Morris, Colo. [John] Carlyle balance of account per agreement in finishing the church; Mr. Ramsay.

Payments received from: Colo. Washington; Mr. Robt. Adam; Robert Adam & Co. per note; Maj. Broadwater.

1773 Fairfax Parish. Payments received from:
Jan 18, Mr. Henry Gunnell for fines in killing deer.
May 10, Michael Ashford for his daughter, Ann.
Jun 22, Mr. Henderson on account of Truro Parish.
Oct 20, Robert Lindsay and John Brauner.
By pews sold in Alexandria Church, viz.

No. 28	John Muir	£21.5.0		
No. 29	John West, Jr.	18.0.0		
No. 18	Thomas Fleming	6.5.0		
No. 19	John Carlyle	15.0.0		
No. 20	William Ramsay	18.0.0		
No. 15	John Dalton	5.0.0		
No. 14	Robert Alexander	15.10.0		
No. 13	Robert Adam	30.0.0	£15.0.0	
No. 4	Townshend Dade	23.0.0	13.0.0	
No. 5	George Washington	36.10.10	21.10.0	148.10.0
By hds. received from John Ratcliff.			162.10.-	
by 3 p'cent hhd.			29.96	
			192.06	115.4.8

To cash from John Luke in part of a bond due; from Glasford & Henderson by Henry Riddle; by interest received from Glasford and Henderson as settled; by cash received from Robert Lindsay, interest.

Ordered that the church wardens settle with Mr. William Grayson for his fees on parish fines. Messrs. Charles Broadwater and Henry Gunnell are appointed church wardens for the ensuing year. Henry Gunnell, Sr. is appointed collector for the ensuing year. It is further ordered that he collect from every tithable person in this parish fifty four pounds of tobacco or levy the same by distress.

26 Nov 1774. The Parish of Fairfax. Payments made to: Rev. Mr. Dade; John Minor; John Rhodes; John Ball, clerk at the Falls Church; John Longden, clerk, at Alexandria; Gerrard [Trammell], sexton at the Falls Church; Dr. Smith; Dr. Rumney; John Muir; Shadrach Hill; Rodger Chew; Timothy Kennedy; Peter Perry; Thomas [McClosses?]; Thomas Davis; Richard Morris; Edward [Ruksby] for his support; Margaret Piper for keeping a sick woman and burying a child; Henry Gunnell, Sr. for elements for the church; John Dalton; Paul [Emmit] for his support; Francis Summers; Christian Murphey for her & her daughter's support; Mary Bryan for keeping her son; Mary Howard for her support; John Graham for keeping a sick man after accounting for his clothes and keeping Joseph Keeth, including his bed clothes; Peter Wagener for four lists of [tithables]; Gerrard Trammell for making fires.

By 1524 Tithables at 40 [lbs.] of Tobacco per pole.

Ordered that Townshend Dade and Henry Gunnell are appointed church wardens for the ensuing year. Church wardens to employ a person to build a hen house on the Glebe land, sixteen feet by ten feet, to be built of hewed logs covered with shingles, and two [battened] doors with a partition through the middle.

Ordered that the church wardens sell the effects of Mary Bryan now in the hands of Capt. [John] Dalton for the benefit of the parish.

Fairfax Parish. Payments were made to the following persons: John West, treasurer; John Hurst for removing a poor woman; Gerrard [Trammell] for order of vestry; Owen Williams.

Fairfax Parish. By cash received of Wm. Adams for the several fines for killing deer out of season delivered him by Mr. Bryan Fairfax.

Ordered that Henry Gunnell pay to Benjamin Ray one hundred and three pounds agreeable to contract. It is further ordered that he pay Mary Broadwater 3 shillings and 9 pence. Ordered that the church wardens demand of John Ratcliff the balance due upon his bond and upon refusal to bring suit immediately. Ordered that Mr. James Wren do such things as he shall see necessary to the spring at Falls Church. Henry Gunnell and Charles Broadwater, church wardens.

28 Nov 1775. Fairfax Parish. Payments made to: Rev. Mr. Dade; John Minor; John Rhodes, sexton at Alexandria; Elisha Powell, clerk at Alexandria Church; Gerrard Trammell, sexton at Falls Church; Edward [Ruksby] for his support; Paul [Emmit] for his support; Christian Murphey for her and her daughters support; Mary Bryan for the support of her son; Elizabeth Payne for keeping Thomas Howard a child, 10 mos.; John Muir; Cumberland [Ferguson]; Townshend Dade; Rodger Chew; Peter Perry; Elizabeth Ramsay; William Wilson; Dr. William Rumney; Robert Lindsay; John Dalton; Francis Summers; Capt. Henry Gunnell; Gerrard Trammell for making fires.

Ordered that a bond from Edward Ramsay to save the parish harmless for a bastard child be recorded. Henry Gunnell and Townshend Dade, church wardens.

16 Apr 1776. Ordered that a bond of Joseph Cockrill and Jeremiah Williams to save harmless the parish for a bastard child be recorded. Ordered that the church wardens pay Mr. John Dalton 37 shillings 6 pence money advanced by him for the support of a poor man. Ordered that the collector pay Colo. John West £40 of tobacco for a levy overcharged last year.

25 Nov 1776. Fairfax Parish. Payments made to: Rev. Mr. Dade; John Minor; Elisha Powell, clerk at Alexandria Church; John Ball, clerk at the Falls Church; Gerrard Trammell, sexton Falls Church; Edward [Ruksby] for his support; Elizabeth Payne for keeping Thomas Howard, an orphan for 12 mos.; Susan Edwards, sexton, Alexandria from Feby.; Christian Murphey for her and her daughters support; Mary Bryan for keeping her son; Gerrard Trammell for keeping fires at Falls Church; Peter Wagener for recording a deed to this parish; Peter Wagener for list of [tithables] for 75 and 76; John Dalton for finding elements for the church; James Hurst for filling up eleven graves; William Bolling for burying William Castello and finding him eleven days; John Rhodes his proportion as sexton; Francis Summers for keeping the poor;

Margaret Payne for making salves for the hospital; Rodger Chew, a coffin for Charles Whitmore; Peter Perry for his care and burying Michael Lyon, a poor man, a traveler, and Whitmore's grave; Dr. Smith his account from Novr. 1774 till May 1775.

Elisha Powell is appointed clerk to the Falls and Alexandria churches and to be allowed at the rate of fifteen hundred pounds of transfer tobacco. Ordered that the church wardens apply to John Williams for his account against the estate of William Clifton as well as the estate of Robert Boggess and on their receiving proper vouchers for them to make application to the Executors or Administrators of said estate.

To cash paid Benjamin Ray; to Capt. James Wren; to Rodger Chew; to Dulick Willis for 2 shirts; to William Wilson; to three persons double listed viz. Jacob [Hubbut?] 3, Thomas Bates 1, Thos. Fletcher 1; to six persons that listed themselves in this parish that lived in Truro: Simon Bowling 2, James Ferrell 2, Thomas Gough 1, John [Peesch] 1, Joshua [Peesch] 1, Nathaniel Wickliff 3, at 40 lbs. [of tobacco] per pole.

Fairfax Parish. Payments made to: James Wren, church warden; goods bought from Mr. James Buckhanan for the poor; Francis Summers to pay Taylor for making Frost a jacket; Rev. Mr. Dade for building his house on the Glebe; Francis Summers to buy goods for the poor; Capt. Dalton.

Fairfax Parish. Payments received from: Capt. Gunnell late church warden; Rodger Chew; Mr. William Wilson; Capt. Gunnell his [claim]; Francis Summers. Capt. [Henry] Gunnell late church warden by the hands of William Gunnell. William Payne and John Dalton are appointed church wardens for the ensuing year. Thomas Triplett, Chichester and Henry Darne are appointed vestrymen in this parish in the room of Col. John West, dec., and William Adams and Edward Duling who have resigned. John Hunter appointed clerk of vestry.

Ordered that the church wardens endeavor to procure a Master for Benjamin Watson in the Taylor's business.

24 Mar 1777. Ordered that the church wardens pay James Webb seven mos. board for Alexander Frazier at the rate of ten shillings per month from the 25 of Apr 1776 until the 25th of Oct; to the Rev. Townshend Dade for his deficiencies from the 16 Oct 1776 until the 1 Jan 1777; to Elisha Powell for his deficiencies as clerk for both churches from 25 Nov 1776 to 1 Jan 1777; to Gerrard Trammell, sexton at Falls Church from 25 Nov 1776 until 1 Jan 1777; to Susannah Edwards, sexton at Alexandria church from 25 Nov 1776 to 1 Jan 1777. John Seale appointed clerk of vestry in room of Mr. John Hunter who is chosen as vestryman. Ordered that John Minor, the late clerk, deliver to John Seale the present clerk, the books and papers now in his possession belonging to this parish.

31 Mar 1777. Mr. John Muir is appointed a vestry man in the room of Mr. Townshend Dade, deceased. William Payne, gentlemen is appointed collector for this parish. Ordered that he receive thirty nine pounds of tobacco from each [tithable] person in this parish.

21 Aug 1777. Ordered that the church wardens pay Joseph Marle £24 as an apprentice for Benjamin Watson. Ordered that Francis Summers employ the

parishioners under his care in anything that he may think they are capable of doing and render an account thereof to this vestry at the laying of the next levy and in case they disobey, Mr. Summers has full power to deal with them as the law directs.

Mr. Charles Alexander is appointed a vestry man in the room of Mr. John Muir who refuses to serve. Mr. Presley Cox is appointed a vestry man in the room of Mr. Thomas Shaw, deceased. Mr. Josias Watson is appointed a vestry man in the room of Mr. John Dalton, deceased. Ordered that Colo. Broadwater, Capt. William Payne, Capt. Henry Gunnell and Mr. Richard Sanford wait upon Rev. Mr. Townshend Dade to know his reasons why he rejects his Duty as a minister in the churches of this parish. William Payne, church warden.

24 Nov 1777. Payments made to: Edward [Ruksby] for his support; Elizabeth Payne for keeping Thos. Howard; Christian Murphey for her support; Mary Bryan for keeping her son; Gerrard Trammell for attending the vestry; Colo. Peter Wagener; Francis Summers as for keeping the poor; Dr. Robert Lindsey as for attending parishioners; Priscilla Thomas for the support of her son; Wm. Adams for the support of Sarah Mason eleven mos. and 24 days from 1 Apr 1777; Dr. Walter Smith; F. Summers; Dr. Robt. Lindsay; Wm. Adams.

George Chapman is appointed a vestryman in the room of Josias Watson who refuses to serve. Ordered that William Payne, Henry Gunnell, James Wren, John Hunter, Presley Cox, Charles Alexander and Henry Darne wait upon the Rev. Townshend Dade on Tuesday the 25th of this instant for to know whether he will resign the Glebe, as he fails to do his Duty as a mininster.

8 Dec 1777. Ordered that church wardens pay Elisha Powell for his services as a clerk last year out of the money in hand. Capt. William Payne and Capt. Richard Conway [are] appointed church wardens for the ensuing year. Ordered Capt. William Payne to collect from each tithable person in the parish 25 pounds of transfer tobacco and in case of failure he levy the same by distress.

Capt. William Payne is appointed collector for the Fairfax Parish of the ensuing year. Rev. Dade entered into bonds for his appearance and faithful performance and Duty as a minister.

23 Feb 1778. Rev. Dade refuses to acknowledge bond, is summoned before two justices of the peace in the town of Alexandria on third Monday in March next, at the house of Adam Lynn.

27 Jun 1778. Ordered that Rev. Townshend Dade's resignation of the Rectory and Parsonage, be received and recorded. *In the name of God Amen. I Townshend Dade, Rector and Incumbent of the parish Church at Fairfax in the County of Fairfax and commonwealth of Virginia, Voluntarily and for good causes and considerations hereunto especially moving to be exonerated from the care and [burden] of the said Rectory, Do by [these] presents expressly and absolutely renounce & resign into the hands of the present vestry of the said parish my said Rectory and Parsonage aforesaid. Together with all and singular its Rights, Members and appurtenances, and all my Right and Title to, and Possession thereof, and do leave the same vacant to all intents and purposes whatsoever. In witness whereof I have hereunto set my hand and seal this 25th Day of June Anno*

Domini 1778. [signed] Townshd. Dade (seal).

Ordered that William Payne, Charles Broadwater, Charles Alexander immediately take possession of the glebe of this parish for the use of this parish and contract with the tenants thereon for the rents that shall become due at the expiration of this year. Ordered that the church wardens of this parish do advertise in Virginia and Maryland Gazettes the vacancy of the parish in order to procure a minister.

11 Jul 1778. The Rev. Mr. Spence Grayson having made application to be received as the minister of this parish, it is ordered that his letter upon that head, be answered. William Payne, Richard Conway, church wardens.

28 Sep 1778. The question being put for the choice of a mininster, the Rev. William West is chosen by the vestry of this parish.

An indenture from William Payne and Richard Conway, church wardens, to: Joseph Marle binding Joseph Young, thirteen years old, as an apprentice, December Court 1776; to John Shortbridge binding John Gray as an apprentice, nine years old, the 15th day of May last October Court, 1776; to Alexander Smith binding David [McDormanto?], twelve years the thirteenth of Jun 1776, and William Gray, five years old last March, May Court, 1778; to Joseph Caverly binding George Broccus, six years old, as an apprentice, June Court 1778.

26 Oct 1778 Fairfax Parish. Payments made to the following persons: Francis Summers for keeping the poor; Dr. Robert Lindsey for attendance of the poor; Patty Moxley for keeping Ann Olister five months; Margaret Payne for services done the poor; Elizabeth McFarlane for keeping Alexr. Frazier; Edward [Ruksby] for his support; Christian Murphey for her support; Capt. Richard Conway; Gerard Trammell for attending the vestry; John Seale, clerk of the vestry; William Adam for keeping Zephaniah Bryan; Colo. Peter Wagener for five lists of tithables; Dr. Robert Lindsey undertakes to make a cure of William Graham at 100 pr ct on his medicines each portion at £4 and if not cured his board to be paid for as other parishioners. Gerard Trammell for mending the graves.

William Payne, Esq. and Mr. Charles Alexander [are] appointed church wardens for the ensuing year. William Payne, Esq. is appointed collector for the ensuing year and ordered that he collect ten pounds of tobacco from each tithable person in this parish.

William West accepts offer of parish, promising to be here by the last of November next to do his duty as a minister.

17 Feb 1779. Upon the resignation of the Rev. William West, the Rev. Mr. David Griffith having made application to be received as the mininster of this parish and being unanimously chosen, it is ordered that the church wardens put him in possession of the Glebe of the said parish. William Payne, Charles Alexander, church wardens.

10 Nov 1779. Payments made to: Francis Summers; 5 yds. linnen for Ben. Watson; pr shoes for John Williams; 7 1/2 yds linnen per Frazier; 3 1/2 yds linnen for John Williams; James Webb; Capt. [John] Dalton; William Bowling; James Hurst; Maragaret Payne; Doctor Smith; Joseph Marle as an apprentice fee for B. Watson;

linnen paid Francis Summers; 7 hhds. tobacco sold Capt. Conway; James Parsons and levy John Payne for both churches; Winefred Vinnard; Mrs. Slaughter for 1775 2 levies and for 2 leavies in 1776; John Bolton; John Fisher, Jr.; James Mattox; John Smith; George Williams; Joseph Woodward; John Hahn; William Johnson; Charles Jenkins; Michael Lindsay; John Read; S. Perkins; Eli Perkins; John Skelton; William Taylor; M. McDermot; Mr. Watson; Elija Payne; John Frizby; C. Doyle; Peter Perry; Roger Chew; William Taylor.

Payments received from: Maj. Wren; Mr. Adams for 7,763 lbs. tobacco sold him; Capt. Conway for 6,383 lbs. tobacco sold him; Mr. Watson for 2,893 lbs. tobacco sold him; John Frizzell, two levies; Phil. Mason; Grace Lyons; Baptist Tuttle; Charles Craig; John Cross; James Watts; Wm. Ward; William Reedy; Phil. Adams; Peter Pierce; Jas. Rollins; J. Wren; Charles Alexander; Mrs. Slaughter; Michael Thorn; O. Talbert; Jeremiah Thrift; John Frisby; Conrad Doyle.

1778 Fairfax Parish. Payments made to: Wm. Adams; Robert Lindsey; Priscilla Thomas; Elisha Powell 1500 lbs. tobacco in cash; Francis Summers; for 3 yds. of cloth of Mary Atchison; for a pair shoes and stockings, and 5 yds. of country cloth for for B. Watson; Margaret Newton, a poor woman; Colo. Mason 11 levies twice charged last year; Elizabeth Payne; 3½ yds. linnen for Frazier; 8½ yds. linnen for the poor Frazier and Watson; Edward Rooksby [Ruksby] 1 levy repaid for last year; 17 hhds. tobacco sold Mr. Watson; Capt. Seale for 200 nails.

Payments were made by: Lawrence Monroe for gaming; Thomas Lewis for hunting on the sabbath; John Lewis for hunting on the sabbath; Eley Monroe fine; 15,408 lbs. tobo. sold Mr. Watson for cash; Charles Jenkins last year returned.

29 Nov 1779. Fairfax Parish. Payments made to: Francis Summers for keeping the poor; Edward [Ruksby] for his support; Margaret Payne; Christian Murphy for her support; Gerard Trammel, Sr.; John Seale; Colo. Peter Wagener; Elisha Powell, clerk Falls Church; Susannah Edwards of Alexandria Church; Dr. Rumney; Gerard Trammell, clerk, Alexandria church; Doctor Robert Lindsey as per acccount; John Rollins for keeping Edward Frazier 8 mos.; Elinor Daily for keeping Zephaniah Bryan; Osburn Talbert; Opie Lindsey; Elizabeth McFarling for the board of Alexander Frazier 4 mos.; Gerrard [Trammell], Sr. for horse racks; William Payne, Esq. to be paid out of the above tobacco; Charles Alexander as for finding elements for the church at Alexandria. Church wardens furnish Margaret Chambers with such clothing as they shall think necessary.

1779 Fairfax Parish. Payments made to: Francis Summers; Doctor Lindsey; Patty Moxley; Margaret Payne; Edward [Ruksby]; Elizabeth McFarling; William Adams; William Adams for Christian Murphey; Capt. Richard Conway; Gerard Trammell; John Seale; Peter Wagener; Gerard Trammell; Elisha Powell & Conn; Susannah Edwards; 4 yds. cloth for B. Watson; 3 yds. Bays for Watson; 7½ yds. linnen for B. Watson; 7½ yds. linnen for Newton; one pair shoes for Newton; one pair shoes for B. Watson; 7 yds. linnen for Frazier; pair shoes for Frazier; Ann Williams for nursing Baily and Robinson; 6 yds. linnen for Jane [Russell]; paid Joseph Marle; 5¼ yds. linen for Frazier; 6 yds. serge for Jane [Russell]; 3 yds. linnen for B. Watson; 3 yds. linen for Mary Hutchison; John Bowling for a coffin for Baley and for a coffin for Robinson; 1½ yds. broadcloth and 2 yds. planes for Zephaniah Bryan; 1 3/4 yds. planes and 1½ linnen for Mary Hutchinson; Peter Wagener, clerk's fees; Pierce Baley jury [against] Barnes; William Adams.

Payments made by Thomas Wright 2 levies and William Payne.

An indenture from the church wardens: to George Shortbridge binding Elizabeth Long, nine years old, and Richard Falkner, six years old, next March Court 1779; to Joseph Robinson binding Samuel Mason, the term of 2 years and 9 mos., also Adam Bence, sixteen years old last March, September Court 1779; to Richard Taylor binding Elizabeth Darby, thirteen years old the 4th day of Jan last, July Court, 1779; to William Hartshorn to bind Amelia Williams, ten years old next Christmas, November Court 1777; to Gerrard [Trammell] Conn binding Samuel Hill, sixteen years old, March Court 1779; to Thomas Reed binding Mary Hutchinson, ten years old the 15th of July last, August Court 1779; to Robert Allison binding Conrod Bannenger, eighteen years old, March Court 1779; to Washer Blunt binding Robert Headrick, seventeen years old, April Court 1778; to Peter Wise binding George Robinson, fourteen years old, March Court 1779; to Enoch Spinks binding Joel Cooper for the term of five years, March Court 1779; to Isaac Gooslen binding Thomas Brocchus, five years old, also Benjamin Clark, twelve years old, Sep Court 1779; to Thomas Wilkinson binding Thomas Lane, fifteen years old, the 13th day of March last, August Court 1779; to John Vernon binding William Reynolds, seventeen years old, 23rd day of May last, August Court 1779; to Joseph Birch binding John Hartlove, eight years old, September Court 1779.

Nelson Reid agrees to take John Young at the rate of 1,200 lbs. of Tobacco pr annum, the parish finding him with bed and clothing sufficient. William Payne, Richard Conway, gentlemen are appointed church wardens for the ensuing year. William Payne, Charles Alexander, church wardens.

12 Apr 1780. Reconcile accounts. Francis Adams, who was appointed a collector of [Fairfax] parish for the year 1776 has never settled any account with the vestry. William Payne is appointed collector for this present year & ordered to collect from each tithable person in this parish thirteen pounds of Tobo. Mr. Richard Sandford resigns his seat as vestryman in this parish. John Parke Custis is appointed a vestryman in the room of Mr. Richard Sandford.

23 Oct 1780. The vestry has estimated the price of Mr. Griffith's tobacco at 40 pounds per hundred. Mr. William Herbert is appointed a vestry man in the room of Mr. Thomas Triplett, deceased. William Payne, Richard Conway, church wardens.

27 Nov 1780. Mr. George Chapman resigns his seat as a vestryman.

Payments made to [partial list]: Edward [Ruksby] for his support; Gerrard Trammell; 10 yds. linen for Jean Honest and Hutcherson; 5 yds. linen to Nelson Reed for John Young; 4 yds. linen for Benj. Watson; 9 yds. linen for Margaret Newton; 1 pr shoes and stockings and 4 3/4 yds. corse cloth for Frazier; Dr. William Rumney; 13 yds. linen for Rachel Lucas and Jean Russell; 10 yds. for Macalister and Bryant; Nelson Reed for John Young.

Colo. Robert Townshend Hooe is appointed a vestry man in the room of Mr. George Chapman who has resigned. William Payne and William Herbert are appointed church wardens for the ensuing year. Mr. George Minor is appointed clerk of the vestry in the room of John Seale who has resigned, and ordered that the said Seale deliver the Parish records and papers to the said George Minor.

An indenture from the church wardens: to John Williams binding Sarah Halbert, ten years old next May; to James Jenkins binding John Hessee, eight years old last August; to John Smith Prather binding Peyton Bates, twelve years old; to Drummond Wheeler binding Daniel Wilson, two years the 10th of April; to Thomas Jenkins binding Cherity Cook, 14 mos. old; to Thomas Wright binding William Rhoades, fourteen years old 22 Jul next; to William Richards binding Hannah Riston, four years old last March; to John Gosbel binding William Morris, ten years old; to James Lawrence binding Rebecca Nicholson, ten years old last May; to Andrew Judge binding John Rutledge, four years old the third day last October; to Edward Ramsay binding William Winslow, seventeen years old the 28 next April; to Edwd. Ramsay binding Thomas Ramsay, sixteen years old the 18th of last February; to George Duncan binding Samuel Skidmore, sixteen years old the 11th of October last; to William Allison binding Mary Halbert, fourteen years old next November. William Payne, Richard Conway, church wardens.

30 Nov 1781. Payments made to: Edward [Ruksy] for his support; George Minor, clerk of vestry; Thomas Daly for keeping Zeph. Bryan 7 mos.; Nelson Reed for keeping John Young; William Adams for keeping Sarah Mason; Ignatius McFarlin for keeping Mary McFarlin; Rev. David Griffith; Nelson Reed; Shadrack Hill for keeping Margaret Chambers; John Rollins for keeping Alexander Frazier 11 mos.; Francis Summers; Robert Lindsay for keeping William Graham; Dr. William Rumney; James Richards for keeping Esabella Patterson; Gerard Trammell for attending the vestry; Ellender Dayley's heirs for support of Zeph. Bryan 5 mos.; the Rev. David Griffith; James Reed for his support.

Fairfax Parish 1781. Payments made to: 6 yds. linen for Margaret Chambers; Feb 2 to 8 yds. linen for John Young and Nelson Reed; paid John Rollings 13 mos. board of Alexander Frazier; Francis Summers; Robert Lindsey; [Shadrack] Hill; Timothy Melance for moving John Witton to Summers; 2 hhds. tobacco sold Charles Acquart; 3 hhds. sold Capt. Taylor; Nelson Reed to 9 yds. linen for Margaret Chambers; 8 yds. linnen for Zeph. Bryan; 8 yds. for Jean Russell; 3 yds. linnen for Ann Hutcherson; Mr. William Herbert (omitted); Francis Summers; Thos. Dayly.

William Payne and William Herbert are appointed church wardens for the ensuing year.

29 Nov 1782. An indenture from the church wardens: to Charles Little binding John Blinston, nine years old in April 1780; to Sarah Triplett binding Jane, a mulatto girl, three years old June 1780; to [Allen] Gunnell binding John Honest, a mulatto boy, thirteen years old August 1780; and to William Summers binding Thomas Holbert, five years old September 1780.

Payments made to: Edward [Ruksby] for his support 12 mos.; George Minor, clerk of vestry; Thomas Dayly for keeping Zeph. Bryan 12 mos.; Nelson Reed for keeping

Christ (Episcopal) Church, Fairfax Parish, Alexandria, Virginia   77

John Young 12 mos.; Ann Bowling for keeping Sarah Mason 12 mos.; Ignatius McFarling for keeping Mary McFarling 12 mos.; Gerard Trammell for attending the vestry; James Reed for his support 12 mos.; John Adams for the support of Susannah Lister 12 mos.; William Horseman for his support 12 mos.; Joseph Burgess for his support and wife's 12 mos.; Sampson [Cockrill]; Francis Summers; Nelson Reed; James Robertson; James Richards; Robert Lindsey; the Rev. David Griffith; William Bowling for keeping John Nash; Gerrard Trammell for repairs of steps at the vestry house; Eliza Edwards for her support 12 mos.; Martha Broadwater for her support 12 mos.

William Brown is appointed vestry man in the room of John [Parke] Custis, deceased. George Gilpin is appointed a vestry man in the room of [Presley] Cox, deceased. William Payne is appointed a vestry man in the room of his father, William Payne, deceased.

Charles Alexander and John Hunter are appointed church wardens for the ensuing year. John Ratcliff is appointed collector for this parish.

27 Nov 1783. Fairfax Parish. Payments made to: Mrs. Rucksby [Ruksby]; Thomas Dayly for keeping Zeph. Bryan for 12 mos.; Nelson Reed for keeping John Young 12 mos.; Sarah Mason; Ignatius McFarlin for keeping Mary [McFarlin]; Gerrard [Trammell] for attending the vestry; George Minor, clerk for vestry; John Adams for Susannah Lister; William Horsman for his support; Joseph Burgess for his support; Robert Lindsey for keeping William Graham; Elizabeth Edwards for her support; Francis Summers as per account; Martha Broadwater for her support to be furnished by the church wardens; Nelson Reed; Mary Malone for her support to be furnished by the church wardens; Mary Earp; Eliza Payne; Ann Waters for her support to be furnished by the church wardens; Mary Ellison; Thomas Dayly for keeping William Rogers 13 days; Moses Ball for burying a poor child; William Bowling for keeping a poor child; William Anderson for keeping a poor child and burying her; and John Hanley for his support to be furnished by the church wardens.

Payments made to: Benjamin Leonard for keeping a poor woman; Thomas Hart for burying a poor woman; Capt. Henry Lyle for 2 weeks board of Mary Middleton; William [Shakespeare] for keeping a poor child 8 1/2 and furnishing some things; Mr. Charles Alexander produced his account for the year 1783 and settled the balance due the parish - is 1,196 lbs. crop tobacco and £8.19.3; William Herbert produced his account for the year 1782 and settled the balance due the parish is 154 lbs crop tobacco; Mr. John [Ratcliff] produced his account as collector for the year 1783 and there is a balance on neither side; Mr. John [Ratcliff] produced his account for the year 1773 there appeared to be a balance of £7.8.11 which he paid to the vestry; and James Wren and William Brown are appointed church wardens for the ensuing year.

Ordered that the present church wardens settle with Mr. John Hunter, one of the late church wardens and receive the balance of his account, if any. Also an inquiry be made respecting two blankets that were furnished the poor put in the hands of Francis Summers. John [Ratcliff] is appointed collector of the parish for the ensuing year.

On the motion of the Rev. David Griffith, William Brown, William Herbert, George Gilpin, Charles Alexander and Robert T. Hooe for leave to erect galleries in the church of Fairfax Parish at Alexandria for the purpose of building pews.

22 Nov 1784. Payments made to: Thomas Dayly for keeping Zeph. Bryan; Thomas Dayly for keeping William Rogers 12 days; Nelson Reed for keeping John Young; Sarah Mason for her support; [Gerrard] Trammell for attending the vestry; George Minor, clerk of vestry; John Adams for keeping Susannah Lister; Joseph Burgess for his support; Robert Lindsay, dec.; Francis Summers; Elizabeth Edwards; Joseph Birch; Elizabeth Payne; Ann Watters to be furnished by the church wardens; James Thrift; Henry Biggs and wife; William [Shakespeare] for keeping a poor child and other per account; Elizabeth Downey for keeping her father; [Margaret] Mcguire for support of her child; Ann Thrift for keeping a poor woman in flux 5 weeks; Margaret Hardy.

Present William Payne. Richard [Ratcliff] is appointed collector of the parish for the ensuing year. Mr. Richard [Ratcliff] produced his account in behalf of his father for the year 1784 and settled it. The vestry has estimated the price of Mr. Griffith's subscription of tobacco at 24/per c. James Wren and William Brown.

27 Nov 1784. Fairfax Parish. Payments made to: William Wools; Jean McPherson; Jessie [McPherson]; Robert Rankin for keeping Joseph Haggin. Charles Alexander settled up his account and paid the balance to Dr. William Brown. Doctor William Brown produced his account for the year 1784 and settled the same. Mr. John Hunter produced his account. Robert T. Hooe and William Payne are appointed church wardens for the ensuing year.

An indenture between James Wren and Dr. Brown, church wardens binding: Amelia Gorbell to John Elton according to law; Sally Ambrose to Henry Gunnell according to law; Francis Adams to Michael Clark according to law; Thomas Preston to John Elton according to law.

17 Mar 1785. Fairfax Parish. Payments made to: Thomas Dayly for keeping Zeph. Bryan 4 mos.; Nelson Reed for keeping John Young 4 mos.; Sarah Mason for keeping John Young 4 mos.; Gerrard Trammell for attending vestry 4 mos.; George Minor, clerk for vestry; John Adams for keeping Susannah Lister 4 mos.; Joseph Burgess for his support; Susannah Lindsay for the poor 4 mos.; Francis Summers for keeping a poor woman 4 mos.; Eliza Edwards; Elizabeth Payne; Henry Biggs and wife; William Shakespeare for keeping a poor child; Margaret Hardy; Anenias Payne for keeping John Henly and wife, 4 mos.; William Frazier for keeping the poor for 4 mos.; Mary Hagan for support of Rebecca Giddings for 4 mos.; William Hunt for keeping a poor woman and child, 4 mos.; Jeremiah Thrift for keeping Mary Watson; William Lyles & Co. for relief of a poor woman; William Herbert for a coffin; William Miller for keeping Stephen Snell 6½ weeks at 12/ as per agreement with the church wardens; Dr. William Brown for his services visiting the poor; Hugh Middleton for keeping and burying a poor woman.

An indenture between the church wardens of Fairfax Parish: to William Duvall binding Zacheriah Corbett, 15 years old, 27 Sept 1784; to John Wise binding Pretius Talbot, 12 years of age, Jun 1781; to Collin McIver binding William Bartleman, 14 years old, November Court 1784; to [Valentine Uhler] binding William Young, aged 16 Jan 1782. Robert T. Hooe and William Payne, church wardens.

An indenture between the church wardens of Fairfax Parish: to Aaron Hewes binding Sarah Nash, 11 years old, Dec 1783; to John Crew binding George Reynolds, 15 years old, Jul 2, 1783; to John Sutton binding Elizabeth Evey, 14 years old, April Court 1784; to Washer Blunt binding Mary Sullivan, 10 yrs. old last May the 8th day, agreeable to order of court, June 1784; to Washer Blunt binding Thomas Young, 14 years old, June Court 1784, and John Donaldson, 14 years old August 23, 1784; to Peter Dow binding John Moxley, 11 years old, November Court 1784; to Robert McDougal Taylor binding Samuel Muir, 17 years old March 1785, November Court 1785; to Washer Blunt binding Harrison Polly Runnalds, 15 years old, September 30, 1784, November Court 1784; to William Frazier, blacksmith, binding John Taylor, 8 years old, Apr 20, 1785; to Edward Ramsay binding Mary Campbell, 5 years old July 1785, August Court 1785; to Michael Stieber binding James Miles 15 years old, January 10, 1787, February Court 1787; to Samuel Smith binding Nancy Cassgrove, 8 years old last December, June Court, 1787.

18 Apr 1785. Fairfax Parish. In account with William Payne; 1785 to cash paid William Frazier; cash paid Thomas Dove to buy corn; Henry Valient 1 bushel meal and some bacon; 1786 to cash paid Colo. Hooe; May 29, by cash of William Hartshorne. To build a gallery in and steeple to the church at Alexandria. Conditioned on pews or parts of pews shall be for use of subscribers, or their paying annually to vestry for use of the Protestant Episcopal Church in Fairfax Parish or if the parish should be divided to the minister and vestry of the Episcopal Church, Alexandria. Not less than 24 pews to be erected in gallery, besides a convenient space for an organ. Ballot for pews.

10 Aug 1786. Petition presented to next General Assembly, praying that the act incorporating the Protestant Episcopal Church may be repealed. We, the subscribers do hereby agree that the pews we now hold in the Episcopal Church at Alexandria shall be forever charged with an annual rent of £5 Virginia money ... this 25th day of April in the year of our Lord 1785.

David Griffith at signing and sealing for G. Washington. W. Bird	G. Washington [seal] W. Bird [seal]
T. Herbert & P. Alexander	Thomas Herbert [seal]
Giles Cook for T. West	Thomas West [seal]
Burr Powell for W. Herbert	W. Herbert [seal]
Geo. Chapman for R. Adams	Philip Alexander [seal]
Robert Macgill for M. Madden	Robert Adam [seal]
	M. Madden [seal]

We, the subscribers, do give our votes for James Keith, William Herbert, William Brown and Richard Arell or any three of them as managers, to contract for and see completed the gallery and steeple to be built in and to the Episcopal Church of Alexandria. (signed) Charles Simms, John Hawkins, R.T. Hooe, Samuel [Montgomery] Brown, George Gilpin, John Potts, Jr., Charles Alexander, Oliver Price, Cyr. Copper, Wm. Ward, Thomas Moxley, Lawrence Hooff, Jos. Caverly, James Keith, Richard Conway and Wm. Lyles. Ordinance for regulating the appointment of vestries.

22 Aug 1787. Oliver Price is appointed clerk of the vestry and clerk of the church at Alexandria; resolved as soon as bier & pall can be procured they be deposited in the care of the clerk who is to charge every person applying six shillings for the use of them both. Resolved that Ephraim Weiley be appointed sexton to the Church at Alexandria, and that he shall have the exclusive privilege of digging all the graves in the Protestant Episcopal burying grounds and that he shall not demand more than five shillings for each grave large or small, and shall also have the use of a house for his residence so soon as one can be built on a part of the said burying ground. Provided that if any member of the church incapable of paying for the digging of a grave, shall apply to the church wardens in Alexandria, or in his absence to any member of the vestry, leave may be granted by said church wardens or vestry man to such person to dig or have dug a grave for his or her deceased friend. The depth of each grave shall not be less than five feet and be filled by the sexton at the time of interment and be left by him in decent order. Resolved that a subscription be opened for enclosing the burying ground in the town of Alexandria, for making the necessary repairs to the church. Thirteen unappropriated pews on the lower floor at Alexandria to be let out. Sum of six shillings be paid for every grave hereafter to be dug in the Protestant Episcopal burying ground in Alexandria, provided that any poor person may with the leave of one of the church wardens or in their obsence a member of the vestry, a member of the vestry in writing under their hand, bury their dead gratis.

15 Mar 1790. The Rev. Bryan Fairfax is inducted as Minister of the parish by a unanimous vote. The minister only shall occupy Glebe lands or rent them to one tenant only whom he may choose.

18 Apr 1791. Resolved that Roger West is appointed church warden in the room of Doctor William Brown whose ill state of health prevents him from serving in that capacity. Resolved that Robert T. Hooe be appointed a lay deputy to attend on the part of this parish at the next convention of the Protestant Episcopal Church to be held at Richmond.

1 Mar 1792. William Herbert produced an account proven for collections and interments. Resolved that George Gilpin and Thomas Fairfax are chosen vestry men in the room of William Brown, deceased, and Lewis Hipkins who does not attend to his appointment. Resolved with the approbation of the present minister, that the Rev. Bernard Page is received by this vestry as an assistant minister in the parish of Fairfax.

6 Jul 1792. In consequence of a letter from Rev. Bryan Fairfax, communicating to the vestry his resignation as minister of Fairfax Parish, resolved that the church wardens wait upon that gentleman and express their concern that the reasons contained in his letter are found to operate to the discontinuance of so meritous a character as this minister. Joseph Thomas is hereby appointed collector of all monies that may be now due and pay the same unto the hands of William Herbert, Esq., treasurer of said parish and that Mr. Thomas be allowed 5 per cent commission on all monies so collected and paid by him. Resolved that Andrew Munroe be and is hereby appointed collector of all monies that may be due or shall become due the Episcopal Church of Fairfax Parish at or near the Falls church. That so fast as he collects any money, he pay the same into the hands of William Herbert, Esq., Treasurer of Fairfax parish. And that the Mr. Munroe be allowed 5 per cent commission on all monies so collected and by him paid. W. Payne and Roger West, church wardens.

16 Aug 1792. Vestry rejects placing Mr. Bernard Page as permanent minister, and writes to Rev. Thomas Davis with an offer. Nicholas Fitzhugh is appointed a vestryman in the room of Mr. James Wren who has resigned.

5 Oct 1792. Rev. Thomas Davis is inducted as minister of Fairfax Parish, and Bernard Page will preach at the two churches in the parish that are not occupied by the minister himself.

Pews in the Gallery
Names of Subscribers

Pew Number	1 October 1804	
32	John Muncaster	Pews in the Gallery
33	James Keith	
34	James Craik	
34	Messrs. Scott and Swann	
36	Charles Simms, Sr.	
37	Lawrence Hooff	
38	Philip Marsteller	
39	Christopher Gird	
40	~~Jonah Thompson~~	
41	Capt. Roberts	
42	R.T. Hooe	
43	Ch. & Edmd. Lee	
44	Richard Conway	
45	Jonah Thompson	
46	George Gilpin	
47	Benjamin [Dulany]	
1	Guy Atkinson	Pews below Stair
2	J. Gillis & Mr. Davis ½, McLean ½	
3	R.B. Jamesson	
4	Messrs. Dade's ½, Ch. Alexander ½	
5	Wm. Reiley, Edmd. Denny, C. Powell	
6	John Lewis & Bryan Hampson	
7	John N. Lyles, H. Rose & John McKeay	
8	Capt. Roberts	

Payments:
10 April 1804, Mr. Guy Atkinson, No. 1.
11 May, John Richeter, Duke St.
18 May, Matthias Snider
24 June, Thomas Potts
18 July, Samuel Keitch
20 July, Forrest Richardson
1 April, Jos. Thornton
11 Aug, Ben Cocke
Andrew Bartlett
Freiderick [Koones]
1 Oct, John Bonsal

Christ (Episcopal) Church, Fairfax Parish, Alexandria, Virginia   83

6 Apr 1804
Pews below counted

Pew No.	Names of Subscribers
9	For blacks
10	Poor whites
11	[vacant]
12	Nicholls & Hall
13	William Wilson ½, J. Potts ½
14	Wm. Hodgeson for W. Oxley
15	Thomas Williams ¼, James Patten ¼, Nicholas Fitzhugh ½
16	John Watts ¼, Benj. Cocke ¼, John Bonsal ¼
17	George Taylor & Gurden Chapin
18	Thos. Tucker and Doctor Douglass
19	J. Lawrason
20	Dade & Slacum

Pews below

Pew No.	Subscribers Name
21	Jonathan Mandeville for himself ½
22	G. Deneale, Jno. Roberts and Wm. Newton
23	John Gadsby
24	Jacob Resler and Fredk. May
25	Blacks
26	Poor whites
27	Strangers
28	John Winterberry & M. Butts
29	Lewis Deblois
30	Wm. Herbert
31	P.R. Fendall and W. Fitzhugh

18 November 1803. At a meeting of the subscribers of the Protestant Episcopal Church in Alexandria, resolved that George Deneale and George Taylor do cause a footway to be paved or gravelled from Washington Street to the church. Resolved that Hezekiah Smoot be appointed Treasurer and John Tucker and Hezekiah Smoot are appointed to collect the quarters salary due the first of October last. G. Deneale, Secy. Church wardens only to grant permits for interments.

18 May 1804. Resolved that the Rev. Mr. Davis do return thanks of the vestry to George Washington Parke Custis, Esq. for the Church Bible, presented by him to the Alexandria Episcopal Church. Resolved that Mr. Davis do pay to John Buchanan, treasurer of the Episcopal convention, ten dollars on account of the cups which were presented to those gentlemen of the [Bar] who volunteered their services in favor of the church property.

14 Jun 1805. Daniel McLean and William Herbert be appointed a committee to examine into the situation of the Glebe, state the quantity of land in cultivation, in meadow, and in wood. Plan to raise money to purchase a burial ground.

1 Apr 1806. Messrs. [McLeod] and Lumsden exhibited an account against the church for painting.

1 Jul 1806. Proposals received from the following persons who offer to sell situations for a burying ground and were referred to the committee appointed on that business:
a. Samuel Craig offers a square adjoining Spring Garden belonging to the estate of W. Mitchell, deceased, at seven hundred dollars.
b. P.G. Marsteller offers a square near thereto for five hundred dollars.
c. Colin Auld and Wm. Wilson offer a square of two acres bounded by the Run and Capt. Conway's lot for six hundred and twenty dollars an acre.

It appears that the land belonging to the parish formerly of Fairfax County in the state of Virginia, but now of the County of Alexandria in the District of Columbia was sold and conveyed by one Daniel Jennings and Anne, his wife, in the year of our Lord 1770, unto Townshend Dade, Sr. and James Wren, then church wardens of the said parish and to their successors in office for the use of the parish. By the terms of this conveyance, the vestry had no other power over the land than that of holding it for the use of the church, they therefore cannot by virtue of the conveyance itself, sell the land.

Christ (Episcopal) Church, Fairfax Parish, Alexandria, Virginia 85

Plat of Christ Church Burial Ground (East)

1st Street West of West Street

The following state of the burial lots of the Methodist burial ground on the west side of West Street (100 ft.) comprising one hundred & thirty six burial lots of the following description. Body lot 26 by 8 ft., 24 do. 24 by 8 ft., 32 12 by 8 ft. = 136. Laid off on March 1809 by a scale of 25 feet in an inch.

(21) There is a ten foot avenue between C Church and the Methodist burial grounds on the west. Spot given to each.

Copy retraced by W. Pippenger

Christ Church Burial Ground (Wilkes Street)
Names of Burial Plot Owners, 1812

1. James Keith, Sr.
2. Daniel Minor
3. The Rector
4. Edmund F. Lee
5. J. & N. Carson
6. Jos. T. Lawrason
7. Seth Cartright
8. George Taylor
9. John Zimmerman
10. Wm. Hodgeson
11. Henry Washington
12. Gurden Chapin
13. Thomas Swann
14. John Roberts
15. Mrs. Benj. Davis
16. Mrs. Benj. Davis
17. Peter Foster
18. Peter Foster
19. Charles Page
20. John Korn
21. Augustine Newton
22. George Deneale
23. Joseph Myers
24. Joseph Myers
25. Henry B. Dagen
26. James Keyling
27. C.F. Lee
28. Cuthbert Powell
29. Mark Butts
30. Daniel McClean
31. Russel Stephens
32. Drucilla Evans
33. Horace Field
34. Horace Field
35. Thomas Jacob
36. George Slacum
37. Joseph Thomas
38. Richard Weightman
39. Bat$^{\text{st.}}$ Daingerfield
40. David Mankin
41. Hugh Morrison
42. Joseph Thornton
43. Nat. Fitzhugh
44. J. Tucker & B. Bell
45. J. Thompson & sons
46. A. Chase & J.L. McKenna
47. John Dixon, baker
48. George Dixon
49. Joseph Ingle
50. Joseph Ingle
51. Wm. O'Conner
52. Thomas K. Bealle
53. John D. Simms
54. Thomas Towers
55. Thomas Broechus
56. Alexander Moore
57. James P. Bowie
58. Eliza O. Cracroft
59. Thomas Watkins
60. John Wise
61. Wm. Morgan
62. Wm. Herbert
63. John Sellers
64. Henry Piercy and James Mandeville
65. Eliza Potts
66. Charles J. Catlett
67. Cam$^{\text{s.}}$ Griffith
68. John Muncaster
69. Tholemias Berry
70. Wm. Herbert
71. Lilly Linton
72. Jonathan Mandeville
73. Alexander Gordon
74. Charles Davis, Owen Magrath and Berryman
75. Guy Atkinson
76. George Gilpin
77. Thos. Braddick
78. Strangers, Mrs. McCue, Jemima Jenkins
79. Thomas Murray
80. Richard Rock
81. John W. Smith
82. Edward Davis
83. Alexander Moore
84. Wm. Mazingo
85. Nat. Wattles
86. Doctor Wm. Washington
87. Mary Dulany
88. Ann Howard
89. [Thomson] F. Mason

90 Isaac George
91 James Atkinson
92 John Hughes
93 John Lloyd
94 William Cranch
95 Wm. G. Adams
96 Samuel S. Fearson
97-101 Vacant

102 Wm. C. Shilman
103 Edward Latham
104 B. Coves
105 Clagett
106 Massie
107-129 [vacant]

- - - - - - - - - - -

Rectors of Fairfax Parish
1765-1861

Rev. Townshend Dade, 1765-1778
Rev. William West, 1778-1779
Rev. David Griffith, 1779-1789
Rev. Bryan Fairfax, 1790-1792
Rev. Thomas Davis, 1792-1806
Rev. Wm. L. Gibson, 1807-1809
Rev. Robert Barclay, 1810-1811

Rev. Wm. Meade, 1811-1813
Rev. Oliver Norris, 1813-1825
Rev. Reuel Keith, 1825-1827/8
Rev. George Griswold, 1828-1829
Rev. John P. McGuire, 1829-1830
Rev. Charles Mann, 1830-1834
Rev. Charles B. Dana, 1834-1861

Vestrymen of Christ Church
Fairfax Parish, Alexandria, 1765-1843

Name	Year	Name	Year	Name	Year
Adams, William	1765	Frobell, J.	1829	Masters, Solomon	1837
Adams, Francis	1815	Fletcher, George	1840	Minor, Daniel	1836
Alexander, Charles	1777	Gunnell, Henry	1767	Mason, Dr. Richard C.	1838
Alexander, Charles, Jr.	1810	Gilpin, George	1792	Mason, Gen. John	1842
Alexander, Dr. Wm. F.	1833	Grubb, John	1841	Nicholls, James B.	1795
Atkinson, Guy	1827	Herbert, Noblet	1820	Powell, Robert	1785
Atkinson, James	1831	Herbert, William, Jr.	1825	Payne, William	1765
Broadwater, Charles	1765	Hunter, Dr. John Chapman	1796	Payne, William, Jr.	1782
Blackburn, Edward	1765	Hunter, John	1776	Powell, Cuthbert	1804
Brown, Dr. William	1782	Herbert, William	1780	Page, Washington C.	1832
Chapman, George	1777	Hooe, Robert Townshend	1781	Roberts, John	1804
Conway, Richard	1777	Hooe, James H.	1818	Sanford, Richard	1765
Cox, Presley	1777	Hooe, Bernard	1825	Shaw, Thomas	1765
Crease, Anthony	1814	Harris, Benjamin	1790	Smoot, Hezekiah	1804
Crease, John H.	1831	Hipkins, Lewis	1790	Simms, Charles	1804
Clagett, Horatio	1820	Hodgeson, William	1813	Swann, Thomas	1807
Clagett, Richard H.	1833	Irwin, James	1839	Smith, Dr. Augustine J.	1810
Custis, John Parke	1780	Jackson, John	1790	Scott, Richard M.	1813
Courts, Dr. John	1785	Keith, James	1804	Semmes, Dr. Thomas	1818
Dalton, John	1765	Keith, James, Jr.	1818	Stuart, Dr. David	1787
Dalton, Tristram	1809	Keene, Newton	1821	Taylor, George	1804
Deneale, George	1804	Lyles, William	1789	Terrett, William H.	1795
Duling, Edward	1765	Little, Charles	1790	Tucker, John	1804
Dade, Townshend	1765	Lee, Ludwell	1795	Thompson, Craven Peyton	1818
Dade, Baldwin	1793	Lee, Edmund J.	1804	Thompson, Israel P.	1828
Darne, Henry	1774	Lee, Cassius F.	1837	Triplett, Thomas	1778
French, Daniel	1765	Lloyd, John	1829	West, John	1765
Fairfax, Bryan	1785	Latham, Edward	1839	West, Roger	1791
Fairfax, Thomas	1792	McLean, Daniel	1804	West, Thomas	1785
Fitzhugh, Nicholas	1793	Moore, Wm. S.	1815	Wren, Thomas	1765
Fitzhugh, William F.	1798	Muncaster, John	1807	Wren, James	1767
Fendall, Philip R.	1792	Morgan, William	1837		

Record of Burial Permits, Christ Church Churchyard

The following information is found in Mary G. Powell's transcript of the vestry book.

The record of burial permits begins after the establishment of the Protestant Episcopal Church in 1785. At a vestry meeting held August in 1787, it was resolved to procure a bier and pall, and to change each person applying six shillings for use of both, or three for either. Ephraim Weiley was appointed sexton to the church at Alexandria, and had exclusive right to dig graves, and not allowed more than five shillings for each. A small house was built in the grounds for him, and any member of the church not able to pay for his or her deceased friends buried or for a grave could procure a permit gratis from the church warden, or in his absence, from any member of the vestry. The depth of each grave was required to be not less than five feet, and to be filled in by the sexton at the time of interment. A subscription was opened in 1787, for enclosing the burial ground.

In April 1804, the permits for interments, the rent of bier and pall, and other fees arising were used for discharging contingent expenses. Right of burial was restricted to church members and their families in 1804. Right restricted to members who paid 20 shillings for each interment in 1807. The right of burial ceased after May 1, 1809, except in the case of Peter Wise who had leave granted in 1815 to be buried near his deceased wife. In 1841, the citizens of Alexandria were given space to erect a monument in the churchyard and remove there the remains of Mr. Charles Bennet.

In the 1870s, the remains of a number of Confederate soldiers who had died in the hospitals of Alexandria during the Civil War were brought to the churchyard and interred under a mound, and a suitable stone placed there with the names of these men, so far as could be obtained, inscribed thereon. At this date, 1913, many of the old stones are in good condition, not a few are much in need of repair and many have been entirely lost from their old positions. The parish hall built 1855 covers many graves, a few of the stones removed at that time are placed against the east wall of the church.

The only record of burials we have commences after the enclosure of the grounds and probably when mention is made of "the removal of the corpses of Mr. Robert Muir inside the churchyard," it has reference to one who was originally buried north of the church in ground afterward given up to the town and heirs of Mr. Catlett where many graves have been discovered by house builders (N.W. corner of Cameron St.).

The church was built in the middle of the land given by John Alexander of Stafford [Co.], which contained one acre; this embraced 237 feet 6 inches of the lot north of Cameron Street occupied by Charles S. Catlett, and which he claimed, and which after some controversy, the vestry gave up to him. It was disputed by the vestry but finally allowed.

Between November 5, 1787 and December 8, 1796, 452 burial permits were given. Of these, 138 were for men, 122 for women, and 192 for children. Many burials before and after these dates were made around the Church. Those graves north were either unmarked or else despoiled of their stones. It is thought probable that the negroes and poor whites were buried north of the Church.

1787
Nov 5 - Dr. Mr. Hogarthy of the Tobacco Warehouse, to operating a grave
Nov 12 - Mrs. McMahon
Nov 12 - James Boyd, gratis
Nov 18 - Henry Boswell
Nov 19 - Mr. Matchum
Dec 24 - Jesse Taylor, Esq.
Dec 25 - William Dunn, gratis
Dec 28 - Mr. Adam Tatespaugh for body of Hindman
Dec 28 - Susannah Edwards for the body of her daughter, Sarah Edwards

1788
Jan 8 - Mr. Redmon for the body of a man who died at his house
Jan 9 - For one of Mr. Fendall's negroes, gratis
Jan 9 - Estate of Mr. Colin McIver, dec.
Mar 6 - Estate of Jacob Hess
Mar 8 - George Hill for his wife's grave
Mar 19 - Thomas White Burr for his sister
Mar 15 - Capt. Joseph Greenway for Capt. James Woodward
Mar 29 - Thomas Sangster for Mary Sangster
Mar 29 - Mr. Wilson for a negro woman
Apr 3 - Black Bob for an infant
Apr 16 - James Irvine for Mrs. Wall
Apr 19 - Ninian Anderson for Mrs. Black
Apr 23 - Mr. Lawrence Hooff for his child
Apr 23 - Priscilla Vilner for an infant she has lost
May 1 - Mrs. Anderson for her husband
May 2 - Capt. Jesse Taylor for a negro
May 7 - Estate of Richard Westley, gauger, and which his family are to pay if able
May 16 - Estate of Richard Westley, gauger, for a child near its father
Jul 1 - Mr. Peter Carville for his wife, Mrs. Carville
Jul 25 - Hannah Chamberlain's child, a poor woman
Jul 30 - A poor woman's child
Aug 10 - Mr. John Korn's, child
Aug 23 - Mr. John Page for Mr. Arthur Maxwell
Aug 26 - Mr. Edward Beacher for a child
Aug 28 - A poor child by application of Mrs. Copper
Aug 28 - Col. John Fitzgerald for a negro child
Aug 31 - Mrs. Hayley Cooper for a child
Sep 1 - Benjamin Lageton's child
Oct 26 - Andrew Hayes for a child
Nov 4 - Mr. John Kean for a child
Aug 17 - James Irvine for the burial of Wall, a poor man, gratis

Sep 8 - John Jolly for his wife
Oct 8 - Richard Barnet for his child
Oct 14 - James Lawrason for his child
Oct 22 - The overseer of the poor, for a poor man, gratis
Oct 25 - Mr. John Helm for his child
Dec 3 - The estate of Alexander Keith at the request of his widow

1789
Jan 7 - Adam Tatsepaugh for his child
Jan 12 - Michael Flinn
Jan 21 - John Bright's child on its grandfather's grave, gratis
Jan 24 - Charles Bouchire for his child
Feb 2 - John Yost for Mr. Bashaw's wife, paid
Feb 21 - John Bright for his wife, paid
Feb 10 - George Murray, a poor man, gratis
Feb 16 - --- Ducket paid Dr. Brown by Geo. Coryell
Mar 7 - William Allison to bury his wife
Mar 28 - Colo. Samuel Hanson for a child
Mar 18 - Wm. Spence for a child without expense
Mar 14 - Mrs. Patton, gratis
Apr 12 - John Comb's child, paid
Jun 9 - Mrs. Hayley's child
Apr 9 - Patrick Sollar, gratis
Jun 21 - Andrew Wales for Benjamin Black
Jul 4 - Mr. George Richards
Jul 28 - Mr. Wooten for Zane
Aug 2 - Mr. Barclay for his child
Aug 4 - William Herbert, Esq. for burial of a child
Aug 27 - For the burial of a child
Aug 15 - Mr. Carville for James Hayley
Aug 13 - Joseph Frazier for a child
Aug 12 - Jeremiah Couder alias Chevalier, gratis
Aug 19 - Mrs. Mar's child
Aug 20 - John Murtland's child
Sep 4 - Mrs. Couder alias Chevalier to bury her child, gratis
Sep 11 - A free negro's child, gratis
Sep 12 - A poor woman, gratis
Sep 12 - A child of Wm. Noel, paid
Oct 29 - A child of James Duff
Oct 30 - Jacob Cook, a poor man, gratis
Oct 30 - Ann Mason's child, gratis
Nov 16 - Mr. Rector's child
Nov 27 - John Horner's child
Dec 24 - Mr. Sangster's child

1790
Jan 7 - Mrs. Carville's child, he having paid six shillings to the churchyard

Christ (Episcopal) Church, Fairfax Parish, Alexandria, Virginia

Jan 16 - Erasmus Welsh, gratis
Feb 23 - John Evans, gratis
Mar 8 - Mrs. Jacobs, gratis
Mar 13 - Mrs. Cookson, gratis
Mar 17 - Mr. Patton by his son
Apr 2 - Michael Gohegan, gratis
Apr 30 - Mrs. Evans, wife of Ephraim Evans
May 3 - Adam Frasier for his child
Jun 4 - Washer Blunt for Thomas Wilkerson
Jun 11 - Lawrence Hooff for his child
Jun 15 - William Hodges for William Alexander
Jun 28 - T. Baily for Mrs. Zanes's child
Jul 15 - Mrs. Parthenia Dade, gratis
Jul 16 - Thomas Copper for his child
Jul 20 - Mr. Joseph Maria Perrin for the body of a French emigrant
Jul 22 - Andrew [Nose?] for his child in the churchyard
Jul 30 - Mr. Page for his father
Jul 30 - One of the family of Mr. Randolph
Aug 1 - Thomas Hedrick's child
Aug 9 - A child of Betty Talbuts
Aug 6 - Patrick Burns for his child
Aug 16 - Mr. Hedrick's child
Sep 9 - Mr. Kean's child
Sep 27 - Adam Shurn's child
Oct 4 - John Helm's child
Oct 4 - William Hodgeson
Oct 5 - Josiah Emmet's child
Oct 6 - For Mr. Patrick Burns for Mr. Harris
Oct 13 - Adam Shurn for his wife
Oct 24 - Mary Keaton for Ann Taylor
Dec 10 - Betsey Lott's child, gratis
Dec 11 - Primus Coburn's child
Dec 13 - Thomas Redman for his father
Dec 19 - Henry Boyer's child

1791
Jan 20 - Adam Butt's wife
Jan or Feb - Mr. Mann's child
Jan 28 - Mr. Hawke's wife
Feb 1 - Mrs. Burnes for her husband, John Burnes
Feb 7 - Mr. Love's child
Feb 26 - Mrs. Chapin
Mar 4 - Mr. Spangenburg
Mar 28 - Mr. John Muir and the removal of the corpse of Mr. Robert Muir inside the churchyard
May 21 - Mrs. Cook
Jun 20 - Priscilla Jennison
Jul 1 - George Boswell
Jul 11 - Mr. Murtland's child
Jul 15 - John Smith
Jul 16 - Nelly McDonald's child
Jul 22 - Patrick Hagerty
Jul 30 - Negro Anthony's child

Jul 4 - John Longden's child
Aug 11 - Child
Aug 13 - Col. Marsteller's child
Aug 14 - Mr. Kean's child
Aug 18 - William Ayres
Aug 20 - Mr. Waitman's child
Aug 20 - The body of a child
Aug 20 - Mr. Butler's child
Aug 22 - Mr. Horner's child
Aug 24 - Thomas Ryan
Aug 23 - Jacob Shuck's child
Aug 24 - Mr. Pile's child
Aug 31 - Joseph Kimber's wife
Dec 31 - Mr. Evans' child

1792
Jan 14 - John Harper's child
Jan 3 - Mr. Howard's child
Jan 10 - Mrs. Sanford's child
Jan 11 - Mr. McDonald
Jan 25 - McCue's child
Feb 1 - Jermey Fergurson
Feb 9 - Mrs. Butts
Feb 10 - Mrs. Little
Jan 30 - Adam Feizer's child
Feb 28 - Mr. Fairfield
Mar 16 - Mr. Adam Bloss
Mar 19 - Mr. Roger Chew
Mar 19 - Robert Sanford
Mar 23 - Mr. McMaken's child
May 7 - Christian Brenar
May 12 - Mrs. Ann Hedrick
May 23 - Mr. Good
May 27 - Mr. Randall's child
Jun 21 - Mr. Boyer's child
Jul 13 - Mr. Weston's child
Jul 28 - Mrs. Tarleton's child
Nov 4 - Sarah Kennedy
Nov 30 - Jean Sangster
Dec 4 - Mr. Limerick's child
Dec 9 - Thos. Reider
Dec 11 - Mrs. [Lowndes]
Dec 16 - Mrs. Hassel
Jan 31 - Mr. Griffith's child

1793
Feb 20 - Mr. John Levan's child
Mar 18 - James Shaw
Mar 28 - Mary Powell
Apr 14 - Mr. Good's child
May 19 - Polly White
May 25 - Mr. Hill's child
Jun 2 - Bodies of Mrs. McDaniel and Mrs. Rick's children
Apr 2 - Mrs. Crawford's child
Jun 5 - Mrs. Evans' child
Jun 5 - Mrs. Montgomery to be paid by Oliver Price

Jun 7 - Mrs. Matchen's child
Jun 11 - The body of a stranger
Jun 26 - William Green
Jun 26 - Mrs. Jacob's child
Jun 28 - Mrs. [Hannah] Bryce
Jun 28 - Mrs. Kimber
Jul 5 - Mrs. [Catharine] Spickett
Jul 3 - Mr. Crowe's and Mr. White's children
Jul 17 - Katherine Kelly to be paid by Oliver Price
Jul 16 - Miss Hanson
Jul 18 - John Makin's child
Jul 19 - Sarah Fletcher
Jul 20 - Mrs. Simmons' child
Jul 21 - Mrs. Pickering's child
Jul 21 - Mrs. Lightfoot
Jul 30 - Mrs. Lowther
Jul 31 - Mrs. Young's child
Aug 3 - Mr. Francis Peyton's child
Aug 8 - Mrs. Reardon's child
Aug 8 - Michael Pepper
Aug 19 - Capt. Rice
Aug 12 - Mr. Evans' child
Aug 20 - Mrs. Bright
Aug 28 - Mr. Morrow's child
Aug 31 - Mr. Gill and Bier
Sep 1 - Mr. Boswell's child
Sep 3 - Mr. Wherry's child
Sep 9 - Mrs. Anderson
Sep 10 - Robert Harle's child
Sep 16 - Mr. Renolds' child
Sep 17 - Mr. Dubis
Sep 19 - Mr. Dunlap's child
Oct 5 - Mr. Good's child
Oct 7 - James Connor
Sep 23 - Permit the body of Mrs. Byrill to be buried in the churchyard
Oct 9 - Capt. Morris's child
Oct 10 - Eleanor Bailey
Oct 11 - Mr. Ostand's child
Oct 19 - Alexander Weiley
Nov 11 - Miss Thompson
Nov 12 - Mr. Joseph Emmet
Nov 13 - Mr. Pindall
Nov 14 - Mr. Meeks
Nov 16 - Mr. Summers' child
Nov 17 - Mr. Thomas' child
Nov 25 - Joseph Larkin
Dec 18 - Mr. Burns' child
Nov 2 - Prisey
Nov 3 - Mr. Hains
Oct 25 - Mr. Boswell's child
Oct 20 - Mr. Wm. Simmons
Oct 19 - Henry Redman
Oct 30 - Alexander Weiley
Dec 12 - P. Montgomery
Dec 27 - Capt. Brookes

1794
Jan 4 - Mr. Talbert's child
Jan 8 - Mrs. Bentz
Jan 8 - Mrs. Butts
Jan 12 - Mrs. Collier
Jan 15 - Mrs. Shuck's child
Jan 23 - Derrington's child
Jan 25 - Thomas Crawford
Feb 14 - Mrs. Mooney
Feb 15 - Mr. Reed
Feb 18 - Mr. Leip's child directed to pay Mr. Price a dollar for permit of Mr. Hooe
Mar 23 - Mr. Newman's child
Mar 26 - Mr. Wass
Mar 27 - Wm. Boswell's child
Mar 4 - William Sebastian
Apr 18 - Wm. Bowie's child, paid Oliver Price a dollar
Apr 15 - Andrews Hayes' child, paid Oliver Price a dollar
Jun 5 - Mr. Reintzel's child
Jun 6 - Mr. Craik
Jun 25 - Mrs. Crowe, Mrs. Galahan, Mrs. Fulton and Mrs. Butts
Jul 2 - Mr. Horner's child
Jul 5 - Mr. Patton's child
Jul 15 - Mr. Mark's child
Aug 1 - Mr. Seymour's child
Aug 4 - Mrs. Patterson
Aug 5 - Mr. Smith
Aug 12 - Mr. Zimmerman's child
Aug 22 - Mr. Jackson
Aug 25 - Mr. May's child
Sep 3 - Mr. Mayhall
Sep 5 - Mr. Williams' child
Sep 8 - Mr. Shiese
Sep 9 - Mr. Clifford's child
Sep 10 - Mr. Wright's child
Sep 19 - Mr. Cox

1795
May 3 - John Grymes
May 6 - Mrs. Rantor
May 6 - Mr. Custis
May 28 - Mrs. Butts
Jun 4 - Mr. Tatsebaugh
Jun 5 - Mr. Samuel Goode's child
Oct 26 - Miss Pursley
Feb 26 - Mrs. Shaw
Feb 7 - Mrs. Glassell
Feb 27 - The body of a stranger
Mar 4 - Mrs. McMasters
Mar 9 - Martin McDermott
Mar 29 - Lewin Weston
Mar 27 - William Connell
Mar 27 - Mr. Lumpkin's child

1794
No date - Mr. Well's body
Sep 6 - Mr. Love's child
Sep 30 - Mr. Foard's child
Sep 25 - Mr. Glover's child
Oct 1 - Mr. Kean Bowman
Oct 3 - Doctor Gillies's child
Oct 4 - Mr. Andrews
Oct 6 - Mr. Jobbin's child
Oct 10 - Mr. George Goodes
Oct 16 - Mr. Sailer(?)'s and Mr. Pease's child
Dec 9 - Mr. Hewes and Mr. Hayes
Dec 14 - Miss Mandeville
Oct 23 - Mrs. Hill's boy
Oct 25 - Mrs. Chavelier's child
Oct 25 - Mrs. Sloane
Oct 8 - Mr. Hogarty and Mr. Tucker
Oct 27 - B. Downes and Mr. Semple's boy
Nov 15 - Mr. Duffey's child
Nov 24 - Mrs. Creagor's child

1795
Jan 27 - Mrs. Patterson
Jan 31 - Mr. Boyer's child
Feb 17 - Mr. John Jordan
Apr 8 - Mrs. Lyles
Apr 12 - Mrs. Brickets
Apr 12 - Miss Moore
May 5 - The body of a stranger
May 16 - Mr. Emmet's child
May 16 - Mr. Edmunston
May 17 - Mr. Shepherd
May 19 - Mr. Ramsay's child
May 20 - Mr. Livingston's child
May 30 - Mr. Brookbank
Jun 4 - Mr. Patton's child
Jun 5 - Mr. Haycock's child
Jun 6 - Mr. Farmer's child
Jun 18 - Mr. James Murray
Jun 24 - Mr. Murtland's child
Jun 30 - The body of a stranger
Jul 24 - Mr. Galvin's child
Jul 25 - Mr. Earle's child
Jul 25 - Mr. Heartely's child
Jul 28 - Mr. Hall
Jul 31 - Mr. Armistead's child
Sep 10 - Mr. Weightman's child
Sep 1 - Mr. Smith
Sep 6 - Mr. Moody
Sep 7 - Mr. Butts
Sep 10 - Mr. Clementson's child
Aug 1 - Doctor [William] Ramsay
Aug 10 - Mr. Thornton's child
Aug 17 - Mr. Dixon
Sep 13 - Mr. Foushee's child
Sep 14 - A stranger
Sep 19 - A negro child
Sep 19 - Mr. Wagener's child
Oct 1 - Mr. [Valentine] Uhler
Oct 4 - Mr. Rounter
Oct 5 - Mary Harrison, daughter of Richard Harrison, Esq.
Oct 4 - A stranger
Oct 12 - Mr. Chunn's child
Oct 13 - Mr. Allison's apprentice
Oct 18 - Mr. Shurn
Oct 17 - Mrs. Bonner
Oct 14 - Negro Peter
Oct 19 - Mrs. Hewett
Oct 20 - Mr. Sponnigil's child
Oct 25 - Rebecca Pan
Oct 27 - Mr. Powers
Oct 29 - Catherine Dutler
Nov 3 - Miss Boucher
Nov 3 - Mrs. Hale
Nov 4 - Mr. Kidd
Nov 2 - Mr. & Mrs. Dead and Miss Dead
Nov 3 - Mr. Goodes
Nov 12 - Mrs. Doyle
Nov 2 - Mrs. Clifford's child
Nov 18 - Negro Stephen
Nov 1 - A. Williams
Dec 14 - Mr. Davis
Dec 21 - Mrs. Wilk's child
Dec 28 - Mr. Reid

1796
Jan 5 - Mr. Lutz
Jan 16 - Mr. West's child
Feb 7 - Mr. J. Lynn
Feb 8 - Mr. Sluse
Mar 15 - Mr. Reynolds' child
Mar 26 - George Mason
Jun 9 - Mrs. Jones
Aug 2 - Ann Doyle
Aug 10 - Hannah Casey
Aug 11 - Limerick's child
Aug 11 - Mr. Thornton's child
Aug 15 - William Wheeler
Aug 15 - P.G. Marsteller
Aug 17 - The body of a child
Aug 17 - Mr. Evans' child
Aug 23 - S. Harris
Sep 4 - Mr. Gird
Sep 8 - Mrs. Howard
Sep 10 - Mrs. [Biggs]
Sep 15 - Mrs. Brown & Mr. [Slade]

Extracts From Tombstone Inscriptions
in Christ Church Churchyard
October 1818

The following inscriptions were made by Mary Gregory Powell, historian, in 1914.

Confederate Monument

How Sleep the brave who sink to rest.
By all their country's wishes blest.

Beneath this mound lie the remains of
34 Confederate Soldiers
Which were disinterred from the Alexandria Soldier's Cemetery (Federal) and reinterred in this ground on the 27th day of December 1879, under the auspices of the Southern Memorial Association of Alexandria, Va.

William Bamburg, 42 Miss.; William T. White, Sergeant 25th S.C.; Daniel V. Frazier, Corporal, 7 S.C.; H.L.B. Fleming, 25 S.C.; G.S. Herron, 7 S.C.; Henry G. Proctor, 25 S.C.; Erastus W. Hays, 25 S.C.; Wm. W. Taylor, 25 S.C.; Henry A. Strom, 14 S.C.; David Rogers, 1 S.C.; Charles Firtich, 25 S.C.; Thomas W. Montgomery, 25 S.C.; Jacob Redmon, 25 S.C.; Abner M. Buzhardt, 1 S.C.; Gambriel Cox, 1 N.C.; Westley W. Skipper, 30 N.C.; Anderton Brown, 3 N.C.; Lemuel Cheeney, 44 N.C.; Ashbury Tarpley, 12 Miss.; John Carter, 10 Fla.; James E. Elder, 25 Tenn.; Robert J. Morris, 16 Miss.; R. Pittman, 60 Ga.; James M. Stuart, Corporal 48 Va.; Alexander Lyles, Richardson's Battery, Va.; Gustavus W. Portlock, 61 Va.; James Augustine, James Cox and Thomas Royal, a Lieut. and one private unknown.

These men were prisoners of war who died in the Federal Hospitals in this city.

Resurgemus.

Roger Chew died Mar 18, 1811 age --- yrs.

--- Hughes died Oct 8, 1794 aged 3 yrs.

Mary Moore the wife of John Moore, who died Apr 24, 1795 aged [45] yrs.

John Boyar died 19 Nov 1802 in the 46th year of his age.

Eleanor Wren, the wife of Mr. Daniel Wren, died Apr 1, 1798 aged 33 yrs. This stone was placed over her by order of her disconsolate husband who was left with two children to lament her loss. John William Renwick, her son being only three yrs. old when his mother departed this life and Dinah Eleanor Wren their daughter only 7 days.

Sarah, the wife of John Wren, died Aug 13, 1792 aged 28 yrs.

Christ (Episcopal) Church, Fairfax Parish, Alexandria, Virginia   95

Robert Muir, son of Hugh Muir of Dumfries, Scotland, died Dec 21, 1786 aged about 38 yrs.

John Muir, Late merchant of Alexandria, eldest son of Hugh Muir, merchant of Dumfries, in Scotland who died Mar 29, 1791 in the 60th year of his age.

John Hutchings, only son of John and Ann Hutchings, borough of Norfolk. Born November 13, 1774, died September 27, 1800 aged 25 yrs.

Sacred to the memory of Col. Charles Simms, an officer in the Army of Independence and for many yrs. an honored citizen of Alexandria, Mayor of that city in 1814. He died in the year 1819. He was one of the founders of the Society of the Cincinnati and a personal friend of General Washington.

Mary Wilson, died May 20, 1807, aged 34 yrs.

Cyrus Toffler, died 17 Aug 1803, aged 20 months.

Jonathan Toffler, died July 24, 1797, aged 18 months.

Alexander Latimer of Alexandria, died Dec 22, 1806 aged 42 yrs.

Hannah Limerick, wife of John Limerick, b. Apr 1762, died Jun 17, 1802 aged 40 yrs.

[Mary] Crowe, wife of Lanty Crowe of Alexandria, died Jun 24, 1794 aged 32 yrs.

Edward Lewis, died Jan 6, 1800 aged 53 yrs.

John Myers of Jarmney, died 17 Mar 1802 age of 42 yrs.

David Herlihy died Jul 23, 1795 aged 1 year and six months.

George Mason of Alexandria died 24 Mar 1796 aged 47 yrs.

Charles Bennet, born in Charles County, Md., Apr 24, died age 70 yrs. A public benefactor.

William Slade, son of Charles and Mary Slade died Jul 1800.

Henry Boyar died March 7, 1799 aged 43 yrs. and 14 days.

James B. Roberts, son of Robert and Bridget Roberts, died Jan 12 January 1803 aged 4 yrs. and 6 months.

James McHenry of Alexandria died Dec 29, 1796 aged 31 yrs.

Michael McMahan of Alexandria died Mar 24, 1786 aged 28 yrs.

Fanny Herbert, wife of Thomas Herbert who departed this life, the 4th day of March 1803 in the 45th year of her age.

Hetty Meeks, wife of Edward Meeks, merchant of Alexandria and late of New York, died Feb 23, age 29 yrs.

Henry Zimmerman died Nov 16, 1806 in the 52nd year of his age.

Rebecca, consort of John Young, died Jul 15th aged 33 yrs.

Henry Brent died Jul 29, 1800 aged 23 yrs. and 15 days.

Bethanath McLean, son of Daniel and Lucretia McLean, b. Nov 25, 1795; Aug 15, 1798.

William Daingerfield Ross, son of Edward and Isabella Ross died November 25, aged 27 yrs.

Jacob Resler died Oct 10, 1803 aged 17 yrs. and 11 months.

Leah Campbell, wife of Jas. Campbell died Oct 11, 1803 aged 59 yrs.

William Dunn of Alexandria died Dec 25, 1787 aged 39 yrs.

Mary Ann Thornton, wife of William Thornton.

George Sexsmith, son of Matthew Sexsmith, died Jun 30, 1797 aged 1 year and 8 months.

Caleb Smith, Jr. died Jul 14, 1803 aged 38 yrs.

William Thomas, son of Richard and Mary Thomas of Cecil County, Md. [part of inscription below soil]

Fanny McCue [dau.] of Henry and Rebecca McCue who died on the 24 March 1782 aged 8 yrs.

Thomas Croucher of Dumfries, died May 22, 1792 in the 25th year of his age.

J.G.R. - 1798 [footstone]

Dorothy Harper, uxor of John W. Harper, died Sep 3, 1800, aged 42 yrs. 8 months.

Mr. Isaac Pierce, born in Boston, son of Isaac Pierce, distiller, died March 26, 1721, aged 24 yrs.

T.W. Webb who departed this life, Jul 28, 1799 aged 54 yrs.

William Swann
Jane Selden
Ann Swann and Wilson Swann

David C. Hough died Aug 31, 1800 aged 15 months and 4 days.

Capt. Mumford late of New London, in the Colony of Connecticut died at Georgetown, July 7, 1773 in the 28th year of his age.

Thomas Leap, son of Jacob and Ann Leap, died Feb 18, 1794.

Margaret Lyles, wife of Zachariah Lyles, died Apr 7, 1793 aged 32.

Elizabeth Stoops, wife of William Stoops died March 8, 1800, aged 23 yrs.

George Isler of Alexandria, died Oct 17[92].

Jacob Hess b. 17 May 1740, died March [6, 1788] aged 47 yrs. and 20 days.

Mrs. Elizabeth Davis, the late consort of Rev. Thomas Davis, Rector of Fairfax [parish]. She was related to some of the most respectable families of Virginia and Maryland. Lived, deservedly, esteemed by all the worthy of her acquaintance and died justly lamented on the 9th of May 1803. Anno Etatis 59.

Mrs. Anne Warren, daughter of John Brunton of England and wife of William Warren, Esq. of England. One of the managers of the Philadelphia and Baltimore Theatres. By her loss, the American stage has been deprived of one of its brightest ornaments. The unequaled excellence of her theatrical talents was only surpassed by the many virtues and accomplishments which adorned her private life. In her were combined the affectionate wife, the tender mother, and the sincere friend. Died in Alexandria 28th day of June 1808.

TRURO PARISH
Extracts From the Vestry Book

Vestrymen

Adams, Gabriel	1732-1733
Ashford, Michael	1733-1734
Awbrey, Francis	1733-1734
Barnes, Abraham	1750-1765
Barry, Edward	1732-1744
Baxter, James	1734-1736
Baxter, John	1743-1744
Boggess, Robert	1744-1765
Broadwater, Charles	1732-1733, 1745-1765
Bronaugh, Capt. Jeremiah	1733-1744, 1747-1750 (died)
Cockburn, Martin	1770-1779
Coffer, (Capt.) Francis	1776-1785. Notice was to be given to Francis Coffer desiring him to let the vestry know whether he will continue to serve the parish as vestryman or not, 23 Feb 1784.
Coffer, Thomas Withers	1765-1784 (died)
Colvill, John	1737, 1739-1741, 1743. On 23 Sep 1734 it was noted that John Colvill, Gent. one of the members of the Vestry, is bound for Great Britain; he has promised to use his interest to procure a discreet and Godly Minister of the Church of England to come over and settle in our said parish...
Colvill, Colo. John	1745-1748
Deneale, Wm.	1781-1785
Ellzey, Thomazin	1765-1785
Ellzey, Capt. Lewis	1744-1748, 1765
Emmons (Emonds), Edward	1732-1748
Fairfax, Hon. William, Esqr.	1754-1757 (died)
Fairfax, George William	1757-1776. Appointed vestryman in room of his father the Hon. Col. William Fairfax, deceased, 28 Nov 1757
Ferguson, John	1733-1737, 1739-1744
Fleet, Capt. Lewis	1745
Ford, Edward	1776
Ford, John	1765
Ford, Thomas	1765-1776 (died)
French, Daniel	1744-1746
Gardiner, William	1765-1776
Gardner, Wm.	1765-1769
Gibson, John	1784-1785
Godfrey, William	1733-1734, 1736-1744
Green, Rev. Charles	1737-1764
Gunnell, Henry	1756-1765
Hamilton, James	1749-1756

Henderson, Alexander	1765-1785
Heryford, John	1732-1743
Hutchinson, Andrew	1744-1748
Lewis, John	1732-1733
Lewis, Thomas	1734-1744
Linton, William	1765-1770 (died)
Mason, Col. George	1749-1785
Massey, Rev. Lee	1767-1777
McCarty, Capt. Daniel	1749-1784 (resigned)
McCarty, Dennis	1732-1741
Minor, Capt. John	1744-1748
Moore, Cleon	1781-1785
Osborne, Capt. Richard	1732-1748
Payne, William, Jr.	1756-1765
Payne, William, Sr.	1750-1765
Payne, Edward	1765-1774
Peake, William	1733-1744, 1744-1762 (died). George Washington, Esqr. was appointed one of the vestrymen in the room of William Peake, Gent., dec., 25 Oct 1762
Pollard, Capt. Thomas	1774-1784 (removed)
Posey, Capt. John	1765-1770 (removed)
Sturman, John	1733-1746 (resigned)
Tillett, Giles	1733-1734
Triplett, William	1776-1785
Turley, John	1749-1756
Wagener, Peter, Sr.	1765, 1772-1774 (died)
Wagener, Colo. Peter	1778
Washington, Capt. Augustine	1735-1737
Washington, George, Esqr.	1762-1765, 1765-1784. Appointed one of the vestrymen in the room of William Peake, Gent., dec., 25 Oct 1762. John Gibson, Gent., elected vestryman to fill the room of his Excellency General Washington "who has signified his resignation in a letter to Danl. McCarty, Gent.," 23 Feb 1784
Washington, Edward, Jr.	1779-1785. Appointed vestryman in the room of Edward Ford who refused to serve, 9 Dec 1779
Washington, Lund	1784-1785
Waugh, James	1784-1785
West, Hugh	1744-1754 (died). On 1 June 1754, William Fairfax, Esqr. was appointed a vestryman in the room of Mr. Hugh West, dec.
West, Capt. John	1744-1748, 1750-1765
Wren, Thomas	1749-1764

Sextons

Awbrey, John. Sexton above Goose Creek, 1740, 1742 (6 months). In the 1741 proceedings he was paid as the sexton "at the chappell."

Bennett (Bennit), Mary. Sexton at New Church, 1743-1744. Later she was shown as sexton at the Upper Church, 1745-1754. In the 1755 proceedings she was listed as deceased, replaced by John Palmer.

Bennett, Thomas. Sexton at New Church, 1735, 1737-1742, replaced by Mary Bennett (Bennit).

Carroll, Nicholas. Sexton at Pohick, 1739-1742

Christmass, Charles. Sexton at Pohick Church, 1733-1738. On 8 Oct 1739 reference is made to the widow of John Christmass, late sexton at Pohick.

Connell, Simon. Late sexton at Pohick, 10 Oct 1743

Connell, John, 11 Oct 1736

Davis, Elizabeth. Sexton at Pohick, 1765-1766.

Gladin, William. Sexton at Alexandria, 1756-1760.

Grove, William. Appointed sexton at the new church, 29 June 1747 and remained until 1748.

Howell, Philip. Sexton at Pohick Church, 1745-1752.

Jennings, Alexander. Sexton at Goose Creek, 1748.

Leatherland, Ann. Sexton at Pohick, 1743. She was listed as "late sexton at Pohick," on 1 Oct 1744.

Lewis, Richard. Sexton at Pohick Church, 1753-1756.

Lewis, Jane. Sexton at Pohick, 28 Nov 1757

Littlejohn, Samuel. Sexton at Littlejohn's for his services, 1766-1767.

McDowell, Mary. Sexton "above Goose Creek," six months, as of 14 8ber 1742, "at the Chappell," 1743-1744, "at Goose Creek," 12 Oct 1747. Although not named she was probably sexton at Goose Creek in 1745-46 also.

Moore, James. Sexton at the new church from 9 Sep 1768 to 26 Nov 1770; sexton at the "upper church," 1771-1776.

Moxley/Thrift. Jos. Moxley or George Thrift to be sexton at the upper Church if either of them will accept it. [Apparently neither did.] 27 Nov 1758

Palmer, John. Replaced Mary Bennit, deceased as sexton at Upper Church, 1755., "at Falls Church," 1757-1758.

Palmer, James. Sexton at the Upper Church, 1756 and at the Falls Church, 1757-1758.

Pierce (Pearce), Elizabeth. Sexton at Pohick, 1758-1764. [Although in 1761-2 the sexton at Pohick was not specifically named in the salaries, she probably held the position at that time.]

Platt, George. Sexton at Pohick, 1744; replaced by Philip Howel in 1745.

Rhodes, John. Sexton at Alexandria, 1763-1765.

Roe, Oliver. Sexton at Pohick Church, 1735

Trammell, Gerrard. Sexton at Falls Church or Upper Church, 1759-1760-1765.

Wright, Charles. Sexton at Pohick, 20 Nov 1767, 1769-1776

Clerks

Adams, Francis. Clerk of the Vestry, 1777-1779 (resigned).
Allen, John. Paid for attendance as clerk, 7 Oct 1745.
Allen, Robert. Clerk at Goose Creek Church, 1746.
Atkins, Daniel. Clerk at the Upper Church, 1773-1775, 1778. Clerk of both churches, 1776.
Barry, Edward, Clerk of the Vestry, 1732-1744. Clerk of Pohick, 1736. Edward Barry resigned the office of Clerk of Pohick Church on 8 Oct 1739.
Barry, John. Clerk of Pohick Church, 1743-1760, 1766-1775. Listed as "clerk," 1761-1765. Clerk of the Vestry, 1765-1772, 1774-1775. Clerk of Littlejohn's 2 months in 1766. While clerk at Pohick he was also clerk at the "new Church in 1744, clerk at Alexandria in 1759 and clerk at Belhaven in 1760. On 3 Nov 1775 he was listed as deceased.
Bowie, John. Clerk of Pohick Church, 1740-1741.
Champneys, William. Appointed clerk at the new church, Oct 1746; served in that position until 1748.
Dainty, John Wybird. Clerk of the Upper Church, 1745-1756 [continuous except for about 5 months in 1751 in which James Feagan apparently acted.]. On 28 Nov 1757 authorization was recorded to purchase clothes for John Wybird Dainty, to be laid out - per church wardens.
Donaldson, William. Clerk at Upper Church, 22 Nov 1754-1756.
English, Walter. Clerk of the New Church, 1743
Evans, Thomas. Clerk at Goose Creek, 1748.
Feagan, James. Clerk at Upper Church, 1751.
Graham, John. Mentioned as clerk of the Court, 1748, 1751.
Hull, Samuel. Clerk of the chappell above Goose Creek, 1735, 1736, 1739, 1740.
Johnson, Joseph. Clerk of the new church, 1735-1736, 1739-1742.
Lane, Henry Smith. Clerk of the Vestry, 1779.
Lewis, Thomas. Clerk at Falls Church, 1759-1760
Lumley, John. Clerk at Falls Church and Alexandria, 1757; deceased as of 27 Nov 1758.
Massey, Rev. Lee. Clerk of the Vestry, 1775-1777 (resigned).
Mosley, Joseph. Clerk at Goose Creek, 1747.
Richardson, John. Clerk at chappel above Goose Creek, 1741-1745.
Terrett, William Henry. Clerk of the Vestry, 1744-1756.
Wagener, Peter. Mentioned as clerk of the court, 1759, 1760, 1763, 1767, 1771, 1774-1777. Clerk of the Vestry, 1781.
West, John, Jr. Clerk of the Vestry, 1756-1764.
West, Benjamin H. Clerk at the New Church, or Upper Church, 1770-1772.
Williams, Elijah. Clerk at Littlejohn's, 1767-1768. Clerk at the New Church, 1769-1769.

Readers

The following readers were mentioned in the minutes:

Johnson, Joseph, reader at the new church and the chappel above Goose Creek, 1733;
Joseph Johnson, reader at the new Church, 1737-1738
Hull, Samuel, reader at the chappel, 1737 and 1738
Williams, Elijah, 1765-1766 (reader at Samuel Littlejohn's), 1769-1771

Birth Records
Recorded 12 Oct. 1734 to October 1737

George Heryford, son of John and Jane Heryford, b. 19 Feb 1733; bapt. 21 March following.

Anne Barry, daughter of Edward and Mary Barry, b. Saturday, 8 Aug 1730; bapt. 27 Sep following.

Mary Barry, daughter of Edward and Mary Barry, b. 18 Jan 1732; bapt. 23 March following.

Humphrey Peake, son of William and Sarah Peake, b. 31 Jan 1732; bapt. 23 March following.

Sarah Peake, daughter of William and Sarah Peake, b. 10 Nov 1734; bapt. 19 Dec following.

Elizabeth Barry, daughter of Edward and Mary Barry, b. 28 Sep 1735; bapt. by Rev. Mr. James Keith, 2 Feb following. John Baxter, Godfather; Mary Payne and Anne Ashford, Godmothers.

Frances Heryford, daughter of John Heryford and Jane his wife, b. 21 May 1737; bapt. by Rev. Mr. Joseph Blumfield, 29th of the same month.

Stacey Ellzey, daughter of Lewis Ellzey and Mary his wife, b. 3 May 1734; bapt. 7 June following.

Sarah Ellzey, daughter of Lewis and Mary Ellzey, b. 24 April 1736; bapt. 12 May following.

Patience Ellzey, daughter of Lewis Ellzey and Mary his wife, b. 16 Sep 1737; bapt. 19 April following.

Orphans/Apprenticeship Indentures

In obedience to an order of the Court of Prince William County, dated 23 Oct 1737, Jeremiah Bronaugh and Thomas Lewis, Church Wardens, bind William Gowen, an orphan child, aged 10 yrs., as a servant and apprentice to John Straughan, until age 21 - to learn the trade of tanning.

Indenture made on 28 March 1738 between Thomas Lewis and Edward Barry, Church Wardens of Truro Parish in Prince William County, and Michael Reagan, bind Joseph Housley, an orphan child, as an apprentice to said Michael Reagan, to learn the trade of carpenter, until he reaches the age of 21.

On 28 March 1738 the same church wardens bind William Collins, an orphan child, as a servant and apprentice to Michael Reagan, to learn the trade of shoemaker, until he reaches the age of 21.

On 15 Aug 1737 the same Church Wardens bind to Rodham Neale, Anne Dickson, a bastard child, aged 1 yr. 1 mo. (dau. of Mary Dickson), as a servant to said Rodham Neale, until she reaches the age of 18.

By order of the County Court dated 25 April 1737 the church wardens bind John Piper, an orphan son of Margaret Piper, as apprentice to Gerrard Trammell, to learn the trade of shoemaker, until he reaches the age of 21; he is forbidden to commit fornication or contract matrimony.

By order of the County Court dated 25 April 1737 the church wardens bind Sarah Piper, an orphan daughter of Margaret Piper, as apprentice to Gerrard Trammell, until age 21 under same restrictions as John Piper.

Indenture made 25 June 1738 by the church wardens with John Turley, in obedience to a court order dated 20 May 1736 bind Alexander McKenney, an orphan, son of John McKenney, lately deceased, as a servant and apprentice to said John Turley, until age 21, to learn the trade of cooper.

Indenture made 25 June 1738, by church wardens and John Turley, binding Anne McKenney, orphan daughter of John McKenney, as a servant and apprentice to said John Turley, to age 18.

Indenture made 28 Feb 1738 between the church wardens and Jacob Laswell, binding William Chandler, an orphan child of William Chandler, lately deceased, as an apprentice to said Jacob Laswell, to age 21, to learn the trade of carpenter.

Indenture made 28 Feb 1738 between the church wardens and Jacob Laswell, binding Benjamin Chandler, an orphan child of William Chandler, lately deceased, as an apprentice to said Jacob Laswell, to age 21, to learn the trade of carpenter.

Indenture made 27 April 1740 between church wardens and Richard Kirkland, binding Betty Shorten as an apprentice or servant to said Richard Kirkland until she arrives at the full age of 18.

At a Fairfax Co. Court May 20, 1746, Alexander Roe was bound to Richard Nelson to learn the shoemakers trade.

At a Fairfax Co. court on 18 Oct 1748 ordered that the church wardens of Truro parish bind Anthony Avery a mulatto the son of Ann Yoen to John Gladwin and Frances his wife.

Ordered that the church wardens be appointed to look out for proper persons to whom may be bound the children of James Glocester, Margaret Moore, Winefred Jones and the grandchildren of James Grimsley, 23 Feb 1784.

Burials

The following were shown as payments for burials. Dates shown are dates of payment. Named in capitals are the deceased.

Richd. Stephens for keeping and burying Eliz. ALLEN, 12 Nov 1759.
Thomas Lewis for burying Joseph BARNES, 20 June 1733.
John Sweet for burying George BARNETT, 11 Oct 1734.
William Brookshire for burying William BEALE, 20 June 1733.
William Peake for burying Thomas BUCHANAN, 6 Oct 1740.
John Barry for burying Mary BURK, 9 Oct 1764.
James Deneal for attending John CASTLE in his sickness and burying him, 26 Nov 1770.
John Barrett for burying Dorothy CHESHER, 28 Nov 1768.
Hannah Conner for the support of Patrick CONNER 9 months, burying him, etc., 23

Feb 1784.
John Gladin for keeping and burying John CURRY, 7 Oct 1745.
George Ross for taking care of & burying Mary DULANY, 12 Nov 1759.
Henry Baylie for burying Ann FOOTE and finding coffin, 27 Nov 1777.
Thomas Evans for burying Ralph FRANKLAND, 10 Oct 1748.
Hugh West for burying Thomas GAHAGAN, 20 June 1733.
Timothy Lyons for attending and burying Nicholas GALE, 5 Oct 1761.
William Reardon for burying George GIBBENS, 1749.
Thomas West for tending Mary GRAY in her sickness and burying her, 7 Oct 1745.
Mr. Willm. Ramsay, Gent. for burying Jos. HOLDSWORTH, 27 Nov 1758.
Elizabeth Ward for burying Sarah HOLMES, 20 June 1733.
Thomas West for burying Henry HUSSEY, 20 June 1733.
Mary Wagener for burying Michl. KENNON, 12 Nov 1759.
Samuel Conner for burying Samuel KENT, 6 Oct 1740.
John Sweet for keeping Noble LAWRENCE two months and burying him, 11 Oct 1736.
Thomas Saunders for burying Cath. McCARTY, 25 Oct 1762.
Thomas Sanders for the support of Catharine McCARTY 4 months and burying her, 29 Nov 1760.
John Patterson for a coffin for Martha MILLER, 5 Oct 1761
Mary [Coffer] for burying James NEWSON, 20 June 1733.
Miss Valinda Wade for taking care of Priscilla PIPSECOE in sickness and burying her, 28 Nov 1768.
Thomas Ford for burying Phillis REILEY, 11 Oct 1734.
Shadrack Green for burying Mary RHODES, etc., 27 Nov 1781.
Sarah Mills for attendance and burying Thomas ROBINSON, 22 Nov 1773.
William Brummett for a coffin for Thomas ROBINSON, 22 Nov 1773
Silvester Gardner for maintaining Samuel RUSSELL 13 months, burying and finding a coffin, etc., 23 Feb 1784.
Benj. Sad for burying Terence RYLEY, 1756.
Zephh. Wade for burying Peter and Ann SHINBANK, 6 Oct 1740.
William Cullison for burying John SOLOMON, 3 Nov 1775.
Henry Treu for keeping & burying Hannah STEVENSON, 12 Oct 1747.
Thomas Moss for boarding Mary STRAUGHAN 3 months and 5 days and burying her, 12 Nov 1759.
Richard Carpenter for a balance for burying Benjamin WHITEHEAD, 10 Oct 1748.
Robt. Douglass for burying Joseph WILSON, 9 Oct 1764.
William Hall for burying Alexander YOUNG, 2 Oct 1738.
John Price for keeping and burying a child assigned to Robert Boggess, 1749.
John Hollis for burying a poor man, 8 Oct 1750.
William Kidwel for burying a poor man, 8 Oct 1750.

Needy Persons

Payments were made to the following persons for the keeping or maintenance of parishioners as indicated. Dates given are the dates of the minutes in which payment was authorized by the Vestry.

The following persons were compensated for support:

Joseph Boling for keeping a poor child, 8 Oct 1750
John Dalton per account for goods for a poor woman, 10 Oct 1748
William Gossom for keeping a child, 1754-1756
Dr. John Hunter for ballance of his account for sundry services to the poor, 1749
Dr. John Hunter for sundry service and medicines to the poor Geo. Johnston for paying for the removal of a poor man to Doctor Hunter for a pair of shoes for one of the poor patients, 27 Nov 1758; Maryland, 5 Oct 1761
John Keen for maintaining a poor child, 1745-1752
Eliza. Palmer for keeping an idiot, 5 Oct 1761
Thomas Simmons for maintaining a poor child, 10 Oct 1748
John Summers for nursing a child, 10 Oct 1748

Persons in Capital Letters are those supported:

John ALVERSON, 27 Jan 1785
Edward Emons for Ann ANDERSON, 7 Oct 1745
Samuel ATHEY for one months board, 28 Nov 1774
Sarah Martin for maintaining Sarah BAILY the ensuing year, 22 Nov 1773
Isaac Gates for boarding Christian BAIN while sick, 25 Oct 1762
Charles Griffin for boarding Margt. BEARD, 10 Oct 1748
Doctor Robinson for medicines and attendance to John BENNIT, 7 Oct 1745
Zephaniah Wade for boarding John BENNIT 4 months, 7 Oct 1745
Philip BEVAN for his support, 1770
Mrs. Eliza. Broadwater for maintaining Mary [BIGGS], 2 Oct 1752
William Trammell for keeping Mary BIVINS, 6 months, 10 Oct 1743
William Trammell for maintaining Mary BIVINS, 6 Oct 1740
---- King for accommodating Jas. BOILSTON, 6 Oct 1740
William Gladdin for keeping John BOILSTON, 12 Oct 1741
Thomas BOSLEY to be laid out by the church wardens, 1 Dec 1769
Thomas BOSWELL and wife, 23 Feb 1784
Benedicter BOSWELL, 27 Jan 1785
Matthew BRADLEY for supporting his son John who is unable to gain his livelihood being bed rid and lost the use of his limbs, 1762-1764
Jane Kent for boarding Philip BRIANT, etc. the year past, 22 Nov 1776
Barton Martin for boarding Philip BRIANT the year past, 27 Nov 1777
Sarah Athey for boarding Margt. BRONAUGH one year, 3 Nov 1774 - March 8 last 1776
William Trammell for maintaining Mary BROWN, 12 Oct 1741 and 14 8ber 1742
Grafton Kirk for maintaining Philip BRYAN to be paid to Alexr. Henderson per order, 1771, 1772
Benonie Kent for maintaining Philip BRYAN, 22 Nov 1773
Jean Kent for maintaining Philip BRYAN, 28 Nov 1774

Philip BRYAN for his support, 1777-1781, 1784
George Simpson for cloathing William BURGESS for 12 months form this date, 28 Nov 1768
Nicholas CARROLL, one of the poor of the parish, 1744, 1745
John Hollis for the board of Dorothy CHESHER from 25 May to this date, 20 Nov 1767
James GLOCESTER and wife, 23 Feb 1784
Mary COMPTON for support of her sick husband, 7 Oct 1745
Alexander Henderson assee of Isaac Halbert for the maintenance and clothing Richard CONDREN from 17 Feb 1780 to 1 Dec 1781, 27 Nov 1781
James Moore, sexton for board and cloathing for Richard [CONNER] per account, 27 Nov 1777
Hannah CONNER for the support of her father to this day, 27 Nov 1781
Charles CORNISH for his relief, 14 Oct 1751
Relief of John CRINLIN, to be lodged in the hands of the church wardens, 10 Oct 1748
John Gladding for accommodating John CURREY, a year, 1 Oct 1744
Mary DAVIS for the support of her father till his death and her mother to this day, 9 Dec 1779
Mary DAVIS for the support of her mother for 1781-1784
Robert DAVIS for clothing for the year ensuing, 21 Nov 1778
Colo. Daniel McCarty for the support of Robert DAVIS for the year 1779, 9 Dec 1779
John Alverson for board for Sarah SHELTON and Robt. DAVIS for time past, 21 Nov 1778
William Simpson for boarding Robert DAVIS 6 months, 27 Nov 1777
Doctor James Lawrie for medicines, etc. to Jane EVANS, 3 Oct 1763
David FITHEY for himself and wife, 1773-1774
John Swallow for maintaining George FLETCHER one of the poor of this parish, 5 Oct 1761
John Summers for his trouble with Hannah FORBES, 12 Oct 1747
Towards the relief of Hannah FORBES to be in the Churchwardens hands, Oct 1746
Isaac GATES and wife, 23 Feb 1784, 27 Jan 1785
The wife of James GLOCESTER, 27 Jan 1785
William GOSSAM ensuing year, 28 Nov 1774
Thomas West for boarding Mary GRAY 5 1/2 months, 1 Oct 1744
John Moore for maintaining James [GRIGSBY] 11 months to this day, 27 Jan 1785
James Doyle for maintaining Charles GRIFFIN, 9 Oct 1764
Sarah Mills for supporting an orphan of [James] GRIGSBY, 23 Feb 1784
John Moore for supporting James GRIGSBY four months, 23 Feb 1784
Ann [GRIGSBY], an orphan, 27 Jan 1785
John GRYMES, 27 Jan 1785
Elijah Williams for boarding Elizabeth HAIRBOTTLE and attending one day as clerk omitted, 28 Nov 1768
Stephen King for boarding and nursing Ann HAMILTON, 3 Nov 1775
John Hurley for taking care of Arrabella HAMILTON, Oct 1746
Richard Stephens for keeping Eliza. HANSON four months, 1749
Mary HASKINGS for her support, 28 Nov 1774
Thomas Craford for boarding Margt. HASLIP, 22 Nov 1754
John HOLLIS, to support son John, a disabled person, 1745-1747

Truro Parish, Fairfax County, Virginia 107

John HOLLIS, Junr., for two yrs. support, 1749
John HOLLIS for his support, 1766, 1767
Richard HOPKINS, 23 Feb 1784
Edward Shelvin for boarding Philip HOWEL, 22 Oct 1753
John Manley for keeping Rebecca HUTTON, 10 Oct 1743
Support of Sarah JACKSON and Philip BRYAN and provide cloathing for Sarah WEST who have been heretofore supported by the Parish, 22 Nov 1773.
Ordered that church wardens furnish Sarah JACKSON and Arthur TOUGH with such necessary cloaths as they want and being in their account, 1 Dec 1769
Ordered that church wardens furnish Sarah JACKSON and Arthur TOUGH with such necessary cloaths as they want and being in their account, 1 Dec 1769
Support of Sarah JACKSON and Philip BRYAN and provide cloathing for Sarah West who have been heretofore supported by the Parish, 22 Nov 1773.
Grafton Kirk for maintaining Sarah JACKSON, 1762, 1764-1775 1776, 1778, 1779 [Paid to Alexr. Henderson]
Ordered that church wardens furnish Sarah JACKSON and Arthur TOUGH with such necessary cloaths as they want and being in their account, 1 Dec 1769
Henry Harman for board, etc. for Sarah JACKSON for time past, 21 Nov 1778
Joseph JACOBS for his wife, 1772-1774, 1784
Massey JOHNSON, 27 Jan 1785
William Gladding for accommodating Samuel KELLY, a year, 1 Oct 1744 and two months as of Oct 1746
Benjamin King for the support of Prise KENT for the year past and ensuing year, 28 Nov 1774
John KERR for his relief, 1748 and 1749
Absolom Kent for keeping John KERR two yrs., 14 Oct 1751
Henry Worthen for supporting Sampson KING one month to this day, 27 Jan 1785
Edward Ford for the benefit of Sarah Reed's children for maintaining Sampson and Stephen KING, 2 months, 27 Jan 1785
John Sweet for keeping Noble LAWRENCE, 11 Oct 1736
Isaac Gates for boarding Martha LAWSON for 10 months, 29 Nov 1760
Rich. LIGHTFOOT to be laid out for him by the Church wardens if needful, 28 Nov 1768
Richd. LIGHTFOOT to be laid out by the church wardens, 29 Nov 1771
Eliza. Young for boarding Charlotte LINDSAY 2 months, 3 Oct 1763
Judith LONGDON for taking care of a dead woman, 29 Nov 1760
Mary [LLOYD], 27 Jan 1785
Robert [LLOYD] for his support, 20 Nov 1767
Martha LUDWELL for her support, received payments on: 22 Nov 1773, 28 Nov 1774, 27 Nov 1777, 21 Nov 1778
Francis Coffer for Martha LUDWELL for shoes, 21 Nov 1778
Catherine McCARTY for her support for 16 months past to be paid to Thos. Sanders her son-in-law, 12 Nov 1759
William Saunders for keeping Mary McKABOY, 1752-1754
Samuel Wilson for maintaining Isaac MILLS, 11 Oct 1734
Robert MILLS who is aged and decrepit and a part of his support, 25 Oct 1762
Robert MILLS towards his support, 3 Oct 1763
Sarah MILLS for maintaining crippled son until he is bound apprentice which should be speedy as possible, 9 Oct 1764
Mary MOBBS, to be laid by the church wardens, 1 Dec 1769

Margaret MOORE and her children, 23 Feb 1784
Richard Stephens for keeping Mary MURPHY and child 4 months, 22 Nov 1754
Walter Taylor for keeping John MURRAH 3 months and 20 days, 8 Oct 1750
Robert Church for maintaining Michael NEWMAN 3 months and 10 days, 27 Nov 1781
Shadrack Green for maintaining Michl. NEWMAN to first day of next month, 27 Nov 1781
Samuel Alexander for maintaining Michael NEWMAN 10 months last past, 27 Nov 1781
Mary NOBBS for ensuing year, 21 Nov 1778
Mary NOBLE, a poor woman, 1 Oct 1744
Elizabeth PALMER for support of her lame idiot son to be laid out for her use by the church wardens, 1759, 1760, 1762 and 1763
Elizabeth PALMER, a poor woman, 9 Oct 1764
John Martin, Junr., for boarding Sarah RAILEY from 6 Oct 1776 to 6 Sep 1777, 27 Nov 1777
Joseph RANSOM for his child to be applied by C.W., 28 Nov 1774
Rich. RANSOM towards his support for 1768 and 1769
Absalom REID for his support, 21 Nov 1766
Widow RICHARDSON for her support, 12 Oct 1747
Widow [RICHARDSON] for her support, 10 Oct 1748
Thomas Douglas for taking care of base born child of Mary ROBINSON who died in child bed, 25 Oct 1762 (date of minutes)
Wife of Andrew ROBINSON, a poor woman, 9 Oct 1764
Thomas [Simpson] for maintaining Oliver ROE 20 June 1733
Ordered that Charles [Russell] have 500 lbs. of tob. yearly for keeping Samuel [RUSSELL] and the vestry agree to indemnifie him for carrying him out of this parish into the upper parish, 22 Oct 1753
Samuel [RUSSELL] for his support, 1764, 1770-1781
Samuel Conner for keeping Samuel RUSSELL, 14 8ber 1742
Saml. Connor for keeping and clothing Saml. RUSSELL, 1758-1760, 1763
Charles Russel for keeping Saml. RUSSELL 2 yrs., 1755
William Reardon for keeping Saml. RUSSELL, etc., 1756-1757
John Raly for maintaining Saml. RUSSELL, 1764 and 1765
Saml. RUSSELL for his support being allowed to remove to Cameron Parish this claim to continue to be paid to Mr. Alexr. Henderson per order of Saml. RUSSELL, 1767-1769
John Sertar for cloathing Saml. RUSSELL, 9 Oct 1764
Lewis Sanders for the support of Eleaner SANDERS, 29 Nov 1771
Michael SCANDLAND for his relief, 1748, 1751, 1752
Robt. Lindsay for Sarah SHELTON per account, 21 Nov 1778
Ordered that Sarah SHELTON, a poor child, be sent to Doctor James in St. Mary's Co., Maryland and employ him to cure her of her present disorders, 2 Oct 1777
John Alverson for board for Sarah SHELTON and Robt. DAVIS for time past, 21 Nov 1778
Simon SIMMONS, 27 Jan 1785
Doctor James Nesbett for taping and medicines to John SOLOMON's wife, 21 Nov 1766
Arthur Garrett for taking care of John SOLOMON, 28 Nov 1768
Doctor James Lawrie for [Mr.] SPARROW, 3 Oct 1763

Truro Parish, Fairfax County, Virginia   109

Mary STRAUGHAN for her support, 22 Oct 1753
Mrs. Masterson for keeping Mary STRAUGHAN 2 months, 22 Nov 1754
Nichs. Martin for boarding Mary STRAUGHAN, 27 Nov 1758
Doctor James Lawrie for Eleanor SWALLOW, 3 Oct 1763
George TASKER, 27 Jan 1785
Arthur TOUGH for his support, 1769, 1771, 1773-1775, 1781
Edward Washington for the support of Arthur TOUGH and his wife for the yrs. 1782-Feb 1784
Elinor Barnsby for boarding Ann VANDIVER, 22 Nov 1754
Mary WATERS, a poor woman, 1 Oct 1744
William Trammell for keeping Eliza. WELSH, 10 Oct 1743
James Taylor for keeping Thomas WEST, 22 Nov 1754
Edward Violet for keeping Thomas WEST, 22 Oct 1753
Thomas Ford for maintaining Sarah WEST for the ensuing year, 1773 and 1774
Drummond WHEELER for his relief, 8 Oct 1750
Charles Griffin for keeping Thomas WILKISON to be paid to Mr. Hugh West, 12 Oct 1747
Thomas WILKINSON to be laid out for him by the church wardens, 1768 and 1769
John Peters for boarding Margaret WILKS, 10 Oct 1748
Alexander Henderson for Catherine WILLIAMS, 28 Nov 1774
Joseph Williams for Catherine WILLIAMS, 28 Nov 1774
David WILLIAMS and wife for their support, 1 Dec 1769
Thomas Williams, for Jean WILLIAMS, 28 Nov 1774
Doctor Robinson for physick and attendance to Susa. WILLIAMS, 7 Oct 1745
Doctor to Susanna WILLIAMS and agree with some person to board her and take care of her until she is under the Doctor's hands. 15 April 1745.
Mary Bennit for taking care of and nursing [Susanna] WILLIAMS, Oct 1746
William Davis for taken care of Susanna WILLIAMS, Oct 1746
Wm. Kitchen for taking care of Susanna WILLIAMS, 12 Oct 1747
Benoni Halley for keeping [Susanna] WILLIAMS 8 months, 10 Oct 1748
Sarah Brookshire for keeping Susanna WILLIAMS 4 months, 10 Oct 1748, 8 Oct 1750
Joseph WILSON towards his support to be laid out by the Church Wardens for his use, 29 Nov 1760
Joseph WILSON, one of the poor of this parish for the support of himself and wife - to be paid to Wm. Payne, Sr. for their use, 25 Oct 1762
Joseph WILSON towards support of himself and wife, 3 Oct 1763
Charles WRIGHT and child, 27 Jan 1785

Other Accounts

ANDREWS. Rev. Mr. John Andrews for 2 sermons, 2 Feb 1765
ASHFORD. Michl. Ashford, Jr. or his assigns, 2 Feb 1765
AYRES. John Ayres to be paid for his plan and estimate [for the new church], 2 Feb 1765
BAYLY. Peirce Bayly for the balance due to him per account, 1 Dec 1769; Peirce Bayly for crying the pews, 22 Nov 1773; Peirce Bayly assignee of James Leach, 23 Feb 1784; Henry Bayly per account, 27 Jan 1785
BAYNE. Mr. Edward Bayne per account, 26 Nov 1770
BENNIT. Mary Bennit for washing the surplices, 1746, 1748

BERKELEY. William Berkeley agreed to build a mansion house on the Glebe
BLACKBURN. Richard Blackburn agreed to build a church at the crossroads near Michael Reagan's .. 1733
BOGGESS. Robert Boggess, 1745-1749, 20 Nov 1772, 28 Nov 1774
BOSLEY. Thomas Bosley for work done on Pohick Church, 14 Oct 1751
BRADLEY. Matthew Bradley, 2 Feb 1765
BROADWATER. Charles Broadwater for an addition to the Upper Church, 8 Oct 1750 and for making a door to the desk and hinges, 8 Oct 1750; "for Walker's account," 2 Oct 1752; Capt. Broadwater for Eliz. Collum's attendance at the church wardens suit vs. Cole, 28. Nov 1757
BRONAUGH. Capt. Bronaugh for a balance of his account, 10 Oct 1748
BROWN. James Brown, 22 Oct 1753
BUSHBY. William Bushby per account, 28 Nov 1774
BUTSFIELD. Dr. William Butsfield per account, 5 Oct 1761
BUTTERS. Mary Butters per account, 25 Oct 1762
CARLYLE & DALTON. Messrs. Carlyle & Dalton per Mary Straughan, 1756; Messrs. Carlyle & Dalton for Crittendon Monday's claim, 28 Nov 1757; Messrs. Carlyle & Dalton per account, 1757, 1758, 1760, 1761, 1764, 1765
CASTELLO/COSTELLO. Bridget Castello per account, 29 Nov 1760; Bridget Costello per account, 12 Nov 1759
CHARLTON. Jane Charlton, 1756
COCKBURN. Martin Cockburn, C.W. per account, 22 Nov 1773; James Cockburn per account, 9 Oct 1764
COCKE. Catesby Cocke per account, Oct 1746; Maj. Cocke as per account, 7 Oct 1745
COFFER. Francis Coffer for a horse block and benches at the upper church, 28 Nov 1774; per account, 28 Nov 1774; Thomas W. Coffer per account, 1 Dec 1769
CONNELL. James Connell for a coffin, 12 Nov 1759; per account, 29 Nov 1760
CONNER. Edward Conner as per account, 5 Oct 1761
CRANFORD. William Cranford, 2 Feb 1765
CRAWFORD. Messrs. Crawford and Dunmoor per account, 9 Oct 1764
CULLISON. William Cullison per account, 20 Nov 1767
DALTON. Capt. John Dalton per account, 22 Nov 1754
DARNES. Henry Darnes, 1756
DENEALE. William Deneale per account, 27 Jan 1785
DICK. Doctr. Dick per account, 23 Feb 1784
ELLZEY. Mr. Thomazin Ellzey for running the line from Johnson's Ferry, 2 Feb 1765; per account, 20 Nov 1767
EMBERSON. Richard Emberson per account, 27 Jan 1785
EVANS. Margt. Evans per account, 2 Feb 1765
FLAX. Francis Flax per account, 5 Oct 1761, 25 Oct 1762
FORD. Mr. Thomas Ford per account, 26 Nov 1770, 28 Nov 1774
FRENCH. Daniel French for 3 acres and 260 perches of land laid off for the use of the parish as per plat 424, 1 Dec 1769 and for repairs done to Pohick Church and Vestry house, 4 June 1753; Daniel French and others, 26 Nov 1770
GARDNER. William Gardner ballance per account as church warden, 20 Nov 1767
GATES. William Gates, 29 Nov 1760, 1 Dec 1769
GIBSON. John Gibson per account, 28 Nov 1774; John Gibson assee. of James Nisbett, deceased, estate of James Nesbett, 23 Feb 1784
GOAD. Joseph Goad per account, 28 Nov 1757, 27 Nov 1758, 29 Nov 1760

GRAHAM. John Graham per account, 12 Oct 1747, 8 Oct 1750
GRANT. Mary Grant per account, 1755
GRAYSON. William Grayson per account, 20 Nov 1767, 28 Nov 1768; William Grayson appointed attorney in fact for the Parish, 1 Dec 1769
GREEN. Charles Green for paying Thomas Chambers for work done to the church doors, 14 Oct 1751
GREY. Martha Grey per account, 1755
GRIFFIN. Charles Griffin per account, 14 Oct 1751
GUNSTON. Mary Gunston, 1756
HALE. Michael Hale per account, 3 Nov 1775
HALLEY. Benoni Halley per account, 28 Nov 1768
HAMILTON. Robert Hamilton per account, 5 Oct 1761
HARGIS/REARDON. Abraham Hargis and William [Reardon] per accounts, 1755
HARLE. William Harle for work done to the church, 7 Oct 1745; for horse blocks and window shutters, Oct 1746; for repairs to Upper Church, 10 Oct 1748
HART. Doctor Daniel Hart per account, Oct 1746
HENDERSON. Alexander Henderson per account, 3 Nov 1775; assignee of Robert Church assee of Henry Bayly, 23 Feb 1784
HERYFORD. John Heryford on 4 June 1734, agreed to sell 300 acres near the plantation of David Jones for a glebe
HIGGINSON. John Higginson per account, 14 Oct 1751
HOLLISS. John Holliss per account, 27 Nov 1758
HOWELL. Philip Howell for washing the surplices, etc., 1745, 1748
HUNTER. Doctor John Hunter per account, 1747, 1750-1760, 1762
HURST. John Hurst per account, 1759
HUTCHINSON. Ordered that the clerk of the vestry prepare deeds for Mr. Andrew Hutchinson's conveying of 2 a. to this parish for the use Hugh Thomas, undertaker to build the aforesaid church. 21 May 1745
JOHNSON. William Johnson per account, 1760
JOHNSTON. George Johnston appointed to act as attorney for this Parish and that he return a list of all the judgments obtained by him to the Church Wardens by 1 Nov annually, 2 Feb 1765
JONES. David Jones, tarring the church, 20 June 1733
JOURDAN. Angel Jacobus Jourdan per acount, 3 Nov 1775
KIRK. Grafton Kirk per account, 3 Oct 1763
LANGTON. Judie Langton per account, 12 Nov 1759
LAWRIE. Dr. James Lawrie per account, 1756, 1762, 1764
LEWIS. Jane Lewis, 1756
LINDSAY. Robert Lindsay per account, 1772
LINTON. Mary Linton per account, 1775, 1776
LITTLE. Webster Little per account, 1776
LITTLEJOHN. Samuel Littlejohn for 5 months rent, 2 Feb 1765
LYON. Timothy Lyon per account, 1758, 1759
MARTIN. John Martin per account, 1776
MASON. George Mason, Esqr. for finding elements twice, 20 Nov 1767
MCCARTY. Mr. Daniel McCarty for advertising the letting the church, 1 Dec 1769; for the ballance of his account in 1769, 29 Nov 1771
MCFALL. Margt. McFall per account, 2 Feb 1765
MIDDLETON. Luther Middleton per account, 27 Jan 1785
MIDDLETON. Honor Middleton per account, 5 Oct 1761

MILLS. William Mills, a chain carrier, 2 Feb 1765
MOORE. James Moore for digging a grave, 1 Dec 1769
MUIR. John Muir per account, 3 Oct 1763, 2 Feb 1765
NESBETT. Doct. James Nesbett per account, 1767, 1770, 1773-1776
OSBORN. Richard Osborn, Gent., for repairs, etc. to Pohick Church, 10 Oct 1748
PALMER. Elizabeth Palmer, 2 Feb 1765
PAYNE. Edward Payne in part of his charge for painting the church and interest of money, 28 Nov 1768
PERRY. Peter Perry, 2 Feb 1765
POSEY. Capt. John Posey for balance of his account, 28 Nov 1768
PRICE. Ordered that Thomas Price view the work done to the Falls Church, 2 Feb 1765.
RAMSAY. Wm. Ramsay per account, 1755, 2 Feb 1765
REARDON. William Reardon per account, 22 Oct 1753
REMY. Jacob Remy for pailing in the new church making horse blocks and tarring the church and pails our proportionable part, 1749
RHODES. John Rhodes as per account, 5 Oct 1761
RICHARDS. John Richards, seats at Upper Church, 27 Nov 1758
RIGBE. George Rigbe, 1756
ROBERTSON. Dr. Jno. Robertson per account, 1747, 1748, 1750, 1751; John Robertson, Jr. per agreement, 2 Feb 1765
RUMNEY. Dr. Wm. Rumney per account, 1764, 1765
ROSS. Mr. Hector Ross for Leod. Harper, 2 Feb 1765; for Zepha. Swallow(?), 2 Feb 1765; for Saml. Gates, 2 Feb 1765; assd. by Jonathan Stone, 2 Feb 1765; per account, 1769, 1771, 1773
SANDERS. James Sanders, per account, 1756, 1757
SANDERS. William Sanders, 1756
SCOTT. Rev. Mr. James Scott per account, 1765, 1766; for 6 sermons, 20 Nov 1767; one sermon omitted, 28 Nov 1768
SEBASTIAN. Mr. Sebastian for fee v. [Messrs.] Rose & Mead & Tomlin, 1756; Benjamin Sebastian per account, 1755, 1757, 1760
SIMPSON. William Simpson, son of Joseph, per account, 1776; William Simpson per account, 27 Jan 1785
SMITH. Joseph Smith, per account, 9 Oct 1764
SMITH. Doctor Richard Smith per account, 10 Oct 1748
SUMMERS. John Summers per account, 10 Oct 1748, 22 Nov 1754; John Summers, William Harle and Thomas Darne are appointed and ordered to view the new church and to report on oath to the vestry on the condition of the work. Oct 1746
TAYLOR. Walter Taylor per account, 14 Oct 1751
TERRETT. Wm. Henry Terrett for drawing deeds from Hutchinson to the parish, 7 Oct 1745; recording proofs & reports & extraordinary service, 7 Oct 1745; per account, 1747, 1752
THOMAS. Hugh Thomas, 7 Oct 1745
TRAMMELL. John [Trammell] to be paid 50 shillings for 2 acres at the Upper Church, Oct 1746; for the church land and book bought for the church, 12 Oct 1747
VIOLET. Edwd. Violet and wife attendance as evidences, 1758
WAGENER. Maj. Peter Wagener per account, 1753-1758, 1761, 1764, 1766, 1768, 1769; copying 6 lists of tithables in 1765 ..[and other copying], 2 Feb 1765; Peter Wagener, Jr. per account, 20 Nov 1772; the copying 3 lists of tithables, 22 Nov

1773; Colo. Peter Wagener for 3 lists of tith[able]s for the year 1778; also to him 4 lists for the year 1779

WAITE. Thomas Waite undertook to build the dwelling house and other houses on the Glebe, 2 Oct 1752. Mr. Waite to be replaced in his work at the Glebe buildings as he did not complete his work according to his agreement, 27 Nov 1758

WASHINGTON. George Washington, Esqr. per account, 20 Nov 1767; Edward Washington per account, 1771-1777

WEST. George West, 2 Feb 1765; Capt. John West, 7 Oct 1745; payments made by Capt. John West and Hugh West, 12 Oct 1747; Capt. John West for part of building the desk at Alexandria, 1754; John West, Jr., for elements and sheriff's account, 1762; John West, per account, and for providing elements, 1763, 1764; John West, Jr., per account, 2 Feb 1765; Hugh West for a record book, Oct 1746 and for bringing said book from Williamsburg, Oct 1746; Hugh West per account, 1751-1753, 1756, 1757; Hugh West, 4 lawyers fees, 27 Nov 1758; Hugh West, attorney, 1759-1761; Hugh West, Depy. Attorney per account (to be settled), 25 Oct 1762, 3 Oct 1763, 2 Feb 1765; Hugh West's widow for Elemts. for the church on account, 22 Nov 1754; Mrs. Sibyl West, her account for elements for churches, 1755-1757, 1760; per account, 1758-1762, 1765

WHEELER. Drummond Wheeler for attendance at the church wardens' suit vs. Cole, 28 Nov 1757

WILLIAMS. Elijah Williams, 13 days extra service, 21 Nov 1766 Elijah Williams per account, 1 Dec 1769; Owen Williams, 1756; Thomas Williams, per account, 22 Nov 1776

WILSON. James Wilson as per account, 27 Nov 1758; Robert Wilson per account, 25 Oct 1762, 2 Feb 1765

WITHERINGTON. Mary Witherington per account, 1756

WREN. James Wren as per account, 25 Oct 1762; James Wren and Owen Williams to value the work to be done by Mr. [Charles] Broadwater on the new addition, 28 March 1763.

WRIGHT. Charles Wright for making a back and hearth, 20 Nov 1767

YOUNG. John Young per account, 25 Oct 1762; Elizabeth Young, 2 Feb 1765

Processioners

Processioners (persons ordered to verify the boundaries of the land owned by freeholders) for the yrs. 1751, 1755, 1759, 1767, 1771:

Adams, Abednego
Adams, William
Ashford, William
Barnes, Abraham
Boggess, Robert
Broadwater, Guy
Cash, Joseph, Sr.
Cox, Presley
Dalton, John
Darrell, Sampson
Demovill, Sampson
Donaldson, James
Dozier, James Iugo
Ellzey, Capt. Lewis
Ford, Thomas
French, Daniel
Glading, William
Halley, James, Sr.,
Hampton, John
Harrison, Thomas
Hawley, James
Hereford, John
Hunter, John
Keen, William
Littlejohn, Marielles
Masterson, Edward
Peake, John
Pearce, Simon
Piper, David
Posey, John

Ratcliff, John
Reardon, William
Rhodes, John
Robertson, James
Sebastian, Benjamin
Shaw, Thomas
Simpson, George
Simpson, Moses
Simpson, Richard
Smith, Thomas
Smith, Nathaniel
Stephens, Joseph
Triplett, William
Violet, Edward

Adjustments in Levies

In 1735, each tithable person in the parish was required to pay a levy of seven pounds of tobacco. By 1767, the rate had increased to 41 pounds per year. On occasion, these assessments were found to be made incorrectly and were adjusted.

Robert Douglass for a levy wrong charged, 29 Nov 1771.
Neamiah Davis for a levy wrong charged, 29 Nov 1771.
William Donaldson for 8 levies overcharged at 23, 27 Jan 1785.
Michael Scanlin, a poor inhabitant of this parish requests and is granted to be levy free, 12 April 1737.
Upon his petition, John Shubbord is set levy free, 2 Oct 1738.
Upon the petition of John Currey he is set levy free, 8 Oct 1739.
Upon the petition of Thomas Bennett he is set levy free, 8 Oct 1739.
On the petition of Nicholas Carroll he is set levy free, 6 Oct 1740.
On the petition of John Richardson he is set levy free, 6 Oct 1740.
Joseph Wilson is exempt from parish levy for the future, 28 Nov 1757.
John Gray for 1 levy overcharged, 7 Oct 1745.
Lewis Saunders was exempted from paying parish levy, 7 Oct 1745.
Gabriel Adams was exempted from parish levy, 7 Oct 1745.
Valentine Peyton, gent. for 1 levy overcharged, Oct 1746.
Matthew Bradley for one levy overcharged, 12 Oct 1747.
John Graham for 6 levies overcharged, 10 Oct 1748.
Valinda Wade for 4 levies overcharged, 10 Oct 1748.
Baldwin Dade for 1 levy overcharged, 10 Oct 1748.
John Carlyle for 3 levies overcharged, 10 Oct 1748.
William Moore for 1 levy overcharged, 10 Oct 1748.
Thomas Moxley for 1 levy overcharged, 10 Oct 1748.
Maj. Lawrence Washington for 27 levies overcharged last year, 8 Oct 1750.
Colo. William Fairfax for 6 levies overcharged, 8 Oct 1750.
George Taylor for 3 levies overcharged, 8 Oct 1750.
James Hamilton for 1 levy overcharged, 8 Oct 1750.
William Ramsay for 5 levies overcharged, 14 Oct 1751.
Colo. Fairfax for 6 levies overcharged, 14 Oct 1751.
Thomas Wren for 1 levy overcharged, 14 Oct 1751.
John Higginson for 1 levy overcharged, 14 Oct 1751.
William Clifton for 1 levy overcharged, 14 Oct 1751.
John Hollis for 1 levy overcharged, 2 Oct 1752.
Samuel Canterbury for ditto, 2 Oct 1752.
Rev. Mr. Charles Green for ditto, 2 Oct 1752.
Mrs. Lewis for 1 levy overcharged, 22 Oct 1753.
John King for 3 levies overcharged, 22 Oct 1753.
William Glading for 1 levy overcharged, 22 Oct 1753.
John Summers Jr. for 1 levy overcharged, 22 Oct 1753.
John Baptist Anderson for 1 levy overcharged, 22 Oct 1753.
Joseph Cash for 1 levy overcharged, 22 Oct 1753.
James Tillet for two levies overcharged, 22 Nov 1754.
William Peake for 2 levies overcharged, 22 Nov 1754.
James Donaldson, a levy overcharged, 1755.
Richard Nelson, 2 levies overcharged, 1755.

George Flynn, 4 levies overcharged, 1755.
Pat Grace, 1 levy overcharged, 1755.
Benja. Elkins, 1 levy overcharged, 1756.
William Donaldson for 1 levy overcharged, 28 Nov 1757.
Gerrard Trammell, charged a levy tho' a patroller, 27 Nov 1758.
Peter Shoemaker, 3 levies in 1757 wrongly charged, 27 Nov 1758.
John Gore and Geo. Norman for 1 levy each, 27 Nov 1758.
William Massey, Thos. Wyat, Saml. Boutcher & George Wyn, 1 levy each, 27 Nov 1758.
Ben. Wickliffe, a levy overcharged in 1755, 27 Nov 1758.
James Crawley to be for the future levy free, 27 Nov 1758.
Thomas Linas for 2 levies overcharged, 22 Nov 1754.
Daniel Summers for a levy overcharged, 9 Oct 1764.
Thomas Bosley exempted from paying Parish levy for the future, 20 Nov 1767.
John Posey for 11 parish levies overcharged last year, 3 Oct 1763.
Edward Bates for his levies the 2 last yrs. tho' a patroller, 3 Oct 1763.
Wm. Turner for 5 levies wrong listed, 9 Oct 1764.
George Simpson for 2 levies wrong listed, 2 Feb 1765.
Wm. Courts, for 2 levies overcharged in 1767, 1 Dec 1769.
Thomas Wren paid fine of Ann Sebastian, 5 Oct 1761.

First Presbyterian Church, Alexandria, Virginia   117

FIRST PRESBYTERIAN CHURCH

Register of Baptisms, Marriage, and Funerals
during the Ministry of the Rev. Dr. James Muir
in the Presbyterian Church
of
Alexandria, D.C.

Rev. Dr. James Muir (1756-1820), served the First Presbyterian Church from May 1789 until his death in 1820. He kept the subject record, presumably in his own hand. It is noted that the marriages and funerals are those at which Rev. Muir officiated, and did not necessarily take place at the First Presbyterian Church, now known as the Old Meeting House. Rev. Muir left a paper trail of his interests in the history of the church, as can be found in the Presbyterian Historical Society, Philadelphia. In this collection can be found one of the earliest accounts of the founding of this congregation. Due to failing health, the minister in 1817 visited Bermuda. He died at "Colross," the home of one of his parishioners, Jonathan Swift, near Alexandria on August 8, 1820. His wife Elizabeth Wellman, died in March 1830.

Abbreviations Used:

b. born
dau. daughter
d. died
mos. months
yrs. years

Page numbers referenced below are those written in at the bottom of the page, and not those at the top of the page in the original record.

pg. 1 Baptisms
5 Apr 1802 Austin, Henrietta dau. of John Austin and Mary Ann, b. 22 Jun 1800
5 Apr 1802 Austin, Emily dau. of John Austin and Mary Ann, b. 24 Mar 1802
23 May 1804 Alexander, Mary Ann Frances dau. of Charles Alexander, Jr. and Mary B., 3 mos.
10 May 1807 Adams, Robert
10 May 1807 Adams, Margaret, above 2 children of ------ Adams and his wife
24 May 1813 Alexander, Alfred son of Charles Alexander and Mary B. his wife, b. 20 May 1813

pg. 2 Marriages
20 Dec 1791 Richard Archdeacon and Margaret Lennox
12 Oct 1797 Amos. Alexander and Ann Ricketts
17 Oct 1797 Nathaniel Atkins and Sarah Hoskins
15 Mar 1798 William Allison and Sarah Green
22 Nov 1798 John Austin and Mary Ann Perry
6 Dec 1798 Nathaniel Allen and Mary Weston
9 Apr 1801 Bryan Allison and Anne Barr
27 Aug 1801 Bernard Andol and Eleanor Stone

25 Feb 1802 James Adams and Catharine Bruner
5 Mar 1802 Leonard Adams and Nancy Davis
23 Jun 1802 Parnell Antrim and Sarah Manley
2 Sep 1802 James Anderson and Nelly Weyley
17 Feb 1803 Elias Allison and Nancy Kent
30 Mar 1803 Amos. Allison and Anne Geiger
7 Apr 1803 Guy Atkinson and Albina Birch
10 Jan 1805 Amos. Alexander and Elisabeth Wroe
25 Dec 1806 George Ashford and Susanna Compton
28 Jul 1807 John Armstrong and Susan Caywood
20 Dec 1814 Francis Adams and Mary R. Newton
22 Feb 1816 John Adam and Mary Dunlap
Dec 1795 Benjamin Andrew and Eliza Davies
7 Apr 1810 Jacob Andrew and Polly Baxter

Funerals
13 Jul 1796 Andrews, -----, 1 year, died of flux
28 Jul 1796 Arell, H., 77 yrs., consumption
4 Jun 1797 Adams, Anne, 44 yrs.
10 Mar 1798 Andrews, ------, 10 mos.
14 Jun 1801 Allison, Robert, 6 yrs., consumption
Mar 1804 Alexander, Mrs., 34 yrs., consumption
29 Apr 1804 Austin, -----, stillborn
7 Nov 1811 Anderson, James, 40 yrs., rupture
9 Nov 1811 Adams, Mrs., 39 yrs.
6 Sep 1814 Allison, Robert, killed in battle
9 Sep 1815 Austin, an infant

pg. 3 Baptisms
6 May 1796 Bowie, Forrest son of William Bowie and Mary Goldsmith, b. 5 Apr
2 Oct 1797 Bent, Eliza Lewis dau. of Samuel Bent and Elisabeth, his wife, b. 18 Aug
9 Oct 1797 Bogue, John son of John Bogue and Judith his wife, b. 5 Oct
1 Dec 1797 Bowie, William son of William Bowie and Mary his wife
10 May 1799 Black, David son of Capt. Black and Eliza his wife, b. 25 Apr 1799
16 Aug 1801 Bartleman, Margaret Douglass, dau. of Wm. Bartleman and Margaret his wife, b. 12 Apr 1801
11 Jul 1803 Black, Esther Ann dau. of Capt. David Black and Eliza his wife, b. 1803
5 Sep 1803 Bartleman, Isabella dau. of William Bartleman and Margaret his wife, b. 21 Aug 1803
26 Oct 1806 Black, James son of David Black and Eliza his wife, b. 4 Oct 1806
20 Apr 1807 Bell, Ross son of --- Bell and --- his wife, age 6 mos.
27 Jun 1808 Butts, Mark son of Capt. Butts and --- his wife, age 1 yr.
3 Jan 1811 Black, Margaret dau. of Capt. David Black and Eliza his wife, age 9 mos.
13 Mar 1812 Brocchus, Matilda dau. of --- Brocchus and --- his wife, age 8 mos.
12 Jul 1812 Bailey, Robert son of --- and --- his wife, age 5 mos.
9 Sep 1812 Black, Helen Anne dau. of David Black and Eliza his wife, b. Apr 1812
11 Oct 1812 Bonsall, John, in consequence of a profession of his faith and obedience before the Church assembled in the morning for public worship

First Presbyterian Church, Alexandria, Virginia 119

9 May 1813 Bartleman, Rebecca Lane b. 20 Sep 1807
9 May 1813 Bartleman, Anne Edwards b. 1 May 1810
9 May 1813 Bartleman, William b. 10 Mar 1813, above three children of William Bartleman and Margaret his wife
23 Aug 1813 Boyd, Ann dau. of --- Boyd and ---his wife
23 Nov 1814 Black, Charles William son of David Black and Eliza his wife, b. 20 Jan 1811
16 Jun 1814 Blacklock, Jean Allen Taylor dau. of Nicholas F. Blacklock and Eliza I. his wife, 8 mos.

pg 4. Marriages
10 Aug 1790 William Brook and Margaret Trout
19 Nov 1790 Samuel Bruffield and Sarah Farrell
7 Dec 1790 Thomas Beech and Margaret Riley
22 Dec 1790 Thomas Blackburn and Mary Jenkins
17 Feb 1791 Robert Benson and Elisabeth Moon
Jul 1792 Samuel Bass and Sarah Rhoe
Nov 1792 John Boyd and Elisabeth Macmannin
Sep 1793 James Burke and Ann Power
Dec 1793 Isaac Brammell and Ann Henniken
Mar 1794 Andrew Ballinger and Elisabeth Morgan
May 1794 Francis Bontempt and Catharine Paterson
Jul 1794 William Bagnet and Nancy Robinson
Nov 1794 Richard Bray and Rosanna Neil
Jan 1795 G.W. Bailey and Sarah Sisson
Feb 1795 Archd. Browne and Eleanor Beall
Jul 1795 Thomas Bellmire and Sarah Bruffield
Oct 1795 Vincent Branson and Lydia Cole
Nov 1795 William Buckland and Ann Lynn
Nov 1795 John Bright and Sybil Williams
7 Jan 1796 Peter Billey and Mary Simpson
3 Apr 1796 James Brown and Catharine Steuart
14 May 1796 Joseph Bolling and Nancy Moxley
17 May 1796 William Bayliss and Susanna Johnston
30 Jun 1796 James Baker and Mary Valient
11 Nov 1796 Hanson Bryan and Eleanor Fludd
8 Dec 1796 William Beech and Sally Harrison
19 Feb 1797 George Brookes and Sarah Boswell
22 May 1797 George Brickles and Elisabeth Greene
2 Nov 1797 Peter Behier and Elisabeth Lavazon
1 May 1798 Mark Butts and Elisabeth Winterberry
11 Sep 1798 David Brown and Mary Moxley
5 Jan 1799 James Birch and Priscy Green
10 Nov 1799 James Browning and Sarah Ann Brook
3 Dec 1799 William Burgess and Nelly Thomson
3 Dec 1799 Jacob Bedinger and Eliza Pepper
24 Dec 1799 Ignatius Brooke and Martha Rollins
29 Dec 1799 Geo. Blagden and Ann Davies
12 Apr 1800 William Bartleman and Margaret Douglass
6 Jan 1801 John Beech and Mary Glasgow

12 Feb 1801 Robert Bayliss and Peggy Power
 5 Mar 1801 Joseph Brumley and Mary Smith
14 Mar 1801 Geo. Bowling and Sarah Staples
 5 Nov 1801 Thomas Brocchus and Rachel Ashton
23 Dec 1801 James Biggs and Rebecca Talbutt
31 Dec 1801 Allan Ball and Anne Wiley
15 Aug 1802 William Braithwait and Elisabeth Corry
 9 Jan 1803 Jesse Barnes and Susanna Green
20 May 1803 William Barry and Mary Cook
 3 Jul 1803 James Brittingham and Polly Brown
 4 Aug 1803 Isaac Barrett and Lucy Burgess
16 Aug 1803 Elias Boyer and Ann Bruce
23 Feb 1804 John A. Burford and Hannah Dyson
29 Mar 1804 Charles Baggott and Elisabeth Bagget
30 Aug 1804 John Bennett and Anne Perry
24 Feb 1805 George Bowling and Elisabeth Veitch
27 Mar 1806 John Blue and Catharine Evans
20 Apr 1806 Peter Behier and Ann King
14 Dec 1806 John Ballinger and Sarah Freeman
19 Apr 1807 Carr Bailey Jr. and Catharine A. Hunter
 3 Oct 1807 William Bond and Nancy Taylor
26 Jun 1808 Severon Ballard and Liven Ballard
14 Jul 1808 Robert Baggett and Sarah Dyer
 5 Sep 1809 Thomas Brooke and Sarah Coffin
15 Mar 1810 Geo. Barnett and Mary Ann Cranston
28 Jun 1810 Rev. Francis Barclay and Helen B.C. Brown
11 Mar 1811 James Berry and Ann Davies
22 Oct 1811 [John Douglas] Brown and Mary [Goulding] Gretter

pg. 5 Marriages
 2 Aug 1812 John Brown and Margaret Coates
 1 Oct 1812 Thomas Beech and Cordelia Smith
24 Mar 1814 Samuel Bartle and Susan Rhodes
27 Mar 1815 Henry Blackford and Sarah Parsons
30 May 1815 Henry Brawner and Kitty McCrea
24 May 1815 John Beale and Mary McKeivor
30 May 1815 Samuel Baker and Susan Gladden
 2 Sep 1815 Aaron Bruce and Nancy Smith
 8 Sep 1815 Isaac Birch and Elisabeth Walker
18 Nov 1815 Walter B. Brockett and Elisabeth Byrne
21 Nov 1815 Thomas [Bavers] and Delilah Davis
14 Dec 1815 Robert Brockett, Jr. and Elisabeth Longden

pg 4. Funerals
 7 Apr 1796 Bertram, an infant
13 Jun 1796 Bent, Nancy, 21 mos. consumption
16 Dec 1796 Baden, ---, 37 yrs., consumption
27 Mar 1797 Barber, ---, drowned
15 Jan 1799 Barber, child
 3 Sep 1799 Bogue, Mrs. Judith, 40 yrs., dropsy

9 Dec 1800   Balfour, Mrs., 60 yrs., dropsy
6 Dec 1802   Brochus, ---, 3 mos., bowel complaint
13 Dec 1803 Balfour, James, 65 yrs., decay
28 Jun 1803 Black, Robert, Doctr., 27 yrs., bilious fever
16 Jul 1803 Brown, ---, 10 mos., bowel complaint
19 Aug 1804 Baillie, Robert, 60 yrs., putrid ch.
23 Jun 1806 Bartleman, George, 8 mos., bowel complaint
11 Aug 1806 Baldwin, stillborn
31 Nov 1806 [Blunt], Washer, 68 yrs., decay
18 Jan 1807 Bayley, Carr, 25 yrs., sudden
30 Mar 1809 Ball, ---, 20 mos., hooping c.
5 Aug 1811   [Blunt], Polly, 20 yrs., decay
23 Oct 1811 Black, Esther Ann, 10 yrs., water in the head
5 Jul 1813   Bartleman, William, 3 mos., 24 days, complaint dubious
6 Sep 1814   Bowen, ---, killed in battle
30 Sep 1815 Black, Charles W., 1 yr., 8 mos., croup
17 Nov 1815 Boyd, ---, 3 mos.

pg. 6 Baptisms
13 Jul 1796 Cooke, Julia Esten dau. of Stephen Cooke and Catharine Esten, b. 6 Jul 1796
8 Oct 1797   Cooke, Catharine Esten dau. of Dr. Stephen Cooke and Catharine his wife, b. 10 Sep 1797
19 Jun 1798 Crawford, Martha dau. of John Crawford and Martha his wife, b. 29 Dec 1797
23 Jul 1799 Crawford, William son of John Crawford and Martha his wife
23 Apr 1800 Cruse, James son of Thomas Cruse and Anne his wife, b. 2 Apr 1800
4 Jan 1801   Cazenove, Paul son of A.C. Cazenove and --- his wife, 2 mos. old, since dead
10 Jun 1801 Crooke, Priscilla dau. of --- Crooke and --- his wife, b. Nov. 1800
17 Apr 1802 Collard, Eliza Simms dau. of Samuel Collard and Rachel his wife
30 May 1802 Collard, James Irvin son of Samuel Collard and Rachel his wife
19 Nov 1803 Collins, --- son of --- Collins and his wife, 7 mos. old
22 Oct 1805 Cazenove, Charles b. 16 Aug 1801
22 Oct 1805 Cazenove, Ann Maria b. 5 Aug 1803, above 2 children of Anthony Charles Cazenove and Anne his wife
11 Jan 1807 Colston, --- dau. of --- Colston and --- his wife, 3 weeks
27 Oct 1809 Collard, Ellen dau. of --- Collard and --- his wife, 7 weeks
8 Jun 1810   Cazenove, Paulina b. 13 Apr 1806
8 Jun 1810   Cazenove, Lewis Albert b. 30 Nov 1807, above 2 children of Anthony C. Cazenove and Anne his wife
27 Mar 1811 Conway, Richard son of Robert Conway and Peggy his wife, b. Dec 1810
5 Sep 1811   Cole, Elisabeth dau. of Thomas and Trephesa his wife, 4 yrs.
5 Sep 1811   Cole, Mary dau. of Thomas and Trephesa his wife, 9 mos.
6 Jul 1813   Conway, --- of Robert Conway and Margaret his wife
7 Jun 1815   Cazenove, Octavius Anthony, b. 27 Dec 1813
7 Jun 1815   Cazenove, Charlotte Busten b. 14 Jan 1812, above 2 children of A.C. Cazenove and Anne his wife

15 Oct 1815 Conway, Robert son of Robert Conway and Margaret his wife, b. Oct 1813
15 Oct 1815 Conway, Joseph son of Robert Conway and Margaret his wife, b. 6 Jul 1815

pg. 7 Marriages
11 May 1789 Daniel Carlisle and Martha Douglass
2 Aug 1789   John Cranston and Nancy Cooper
17 Mar 1799 John Cowan and Sarah Downs
23 Jun 1799 Peter Carvel and Catherine Lowe
11 Aug 1799 James Callahan and Rebecca Wallhouse
21 Sep 1799 Richard Croak and Elisabeth Blackburn
27 Nov 1799 Hezekiah Clark and Margaret Clark
7 Feb 1791   Thomas Conn and Cassina Lake
Jun 1792   Samuel Clinton and Susanna Lindsay
Jul 1792   Thomas Cooke and Susanna King
Sep 1792   Seth Cartwright and Mary Levering
Oct 1792   Dennis Conney and Susanna Cockrill
Oct 1792   Samuel Clements and Eleanor Garrett
Jan 1793   Gurden Chapin and Margaret Reeder
Oct 1793   Patrick Carey and Jane Reed
Sep 1795   Joseph Curtis and Elisabeth Chisholm
Sep 1795   Charles Chick and Eleanor Gooding
14 Nov 1795 Robert Clark and Nancy Montgomery
17 Jun 1796 Benjamin Carey and Catherine Lutz
15 Oct 1796 John Crispin and Kitty Potter
3 Nov 1796   Duncan Charles and Margaret Stone
1 Dec 1796   George Cook and Polly Spickett
15 Dec 1796 Nathaniel Cannon and Elizabeth Hall
15 Dec 1796 John Crawford and Martha Delawhan
19 Dec 1796 Francis Conner and Elisa. Appleby
9 Feb 1797   Premier Coburn and Jane Moody
1 Jun 1797   Samuel Caither and Mary Mearsheimer
1 Aug 1797   Nehemiah Clifford and Jenny Fergusson
12 Sep 1797 Thomas Copper and Sarah Trotter
14 Apr 1798 Daniel Courts and Margaret Pearson
22 Oct 1798 Peter Cornetady and Kitty Wedgworth
9 Mar 1799   Jesse Cox and Nancy Harris
24 Mar 1799 William Cross and Sarah Johnston
2 Apr 1799   Thomas Copper and Nancy Cockrill
2 May 1799   John Joseph Casso and Margaret Heath
9 Jul 1799   John Cozeen and Ann Avery
18 Jul 1799 Samuel Collard and Rachel Darrell
20 Oct 1799 John Cohagan and Anne Wright
30 Dec 1799 John Clark and Cloughley Luckett
18 Jul 1799 John Card and Mary J. Allen
14 Aug 1800 Thomas Colbert and Jane Earp
5 Jan 1801   John Chishom and Mary Ann Grigsby
30 Apr 1801 William Cohen and Catharine Carey
4 Oct 1801   Lewis Chasson and Ann Truman

17 Dec 1801 Daniel Coffin and Sarah Findlay
21 Jan 1802 Thomas Crandle and Sarah Strait
7 May 1802 Henry Church and Margaret McCallister
9 May 1802 Sinclair Carroll and Agnes Johnston
2 Jun 1802 William Clements and Sarah Booth
5 Jun 1802 John Newton Cannon and Ann Wattles
5 Jun 1802 John Coffin and Eliza. Bennett
13 Jun 1802 William A. Collins and Sarah Statford
25 Nov 1804 John Christman and Elizabeth Barr
1 May 1806 Charles I. Catlett and Anne Fairfax
6 Nov 1806 Thomas Cole and Tryphesia Hand
25 Nov 1806 Samuel Carson and Jane Hamilton
30 Nov 1806 Joseph Crandell and Jane Talbott
12 Mar 1807 Gilbert Church and Sarah Hayes
23 Aug 1807 John Covert and Elizabeth Dorcey
17 Aug 1808 Joseph Carne and Rebecca Davis
29 Nov 1808 John Christie and Jane Jackson
17 May 1809 Lewis Crosby and Sarah Ann Russell
21 May 1809 John Carson and Elisabeth Jerome
22 May 1809 Robert Conway and Margaret Sweet
15 Apr 1811 Christian Christopher and Harriet Cox
1 Jan 1812 Samuel Cramm and Mary Hickman
24 May 1812 John Cohagen and Elizabeth Bowie
20 Oct 1813 John Hipperly Crease and Jane Newton
12 Nov 1814 Benjamin Cawood and Anna Ferguson
10 Oct 1815 Isaac Clark and Mary Smith

Funerals
13 Mar 1796 Creek, William, 33 yrs., dropsy
16 Jul 1796 Cooke, Julia Essen, 9 days, flux
27 Aug 1796 Charles, Mary, 33 yrs., consumption
9 Sep 1796 Cushan, Capt., 30 yrs., fever
10 Jul 1797 Craig, Mary, 1 yr., consumption
19 Aug 1797 Crank, a child
18 Aug 1797 Crandell, Mrs., 28 yrs., consumption
4 Sep 1797 Compton, William, 45 yrs., flux
11 Sep 1799 Carey, Miss Mildred, 38 yrs., consumption
19 Jan 1800 Crandell, Mrs., 46 yrs., consumption
4 Jan 1801 Cazenove, a child, not known
24 Sep 1801 Crandell, Samuel, 19 yrs., yellow fever
20 Nov 1801 Creighton, Dr. Robert, 67 yrs., consumption
21 Jul 1803 Crandell, child, bowel hives
5 Oct 1803 Crandell, John, 25 yrs., fever
22 Nov 1804 Cranston, ---, 30 yrs., fever
22 Jan 1805 Church, an infant
21 Feb 1805 Clifford, Mrs., belonging to another denomination
1 Jul 1806 Cranston, ---, 8 yrs., drowned
11 Oct 1806 Craig, Jeanna, 50 yrs., fever
24 Jan 1808 Craig, Samuel, 45 yrs.
8 Oct 1808 Crandell, ---, 40 yrs., consumption

17 Feb 1811 Chandler, Mrs., of Rhode Island, 21 yrs., consumption
4 Apr 1811   Cooper, Samuel, 26 yrs.
6 Mar 1813   Church, ---, 36 yrs.
27 Sep 1813 Crandell, Joseph, 25 yrs., consumption
12 Sep 1814 Craffts, Anne, 25 yrs., consumption

pg. 8 Baptisms
28 Aug 1796 Dykes, Andrew son of Mungo Dykes and Ann Wade, b. 11 Jul
1 Sep 1797   Davidson, William son of James Davidson and Margaret his wife, b. 18 Aug
5 Mar 1798   Dundas, Thomas son of John Dundas and Nancy his wife, b. 19 Jun 1797
6 May 1798   Dykes, Nancy Longden dau. of Mungo Dykes and Ann his wife, b. 11 Mar 1798
12 Dec 1798 Douglass, Archibald Orme son of Daniel Douglass and Charlotte his wife, b. 26 Sep 1797
18 Mar 1799 Davidson, James son of Col. James Davidson and Margaret his wife, b. 17 Feb 1799
17 Feb 1800 Dick, Margaret dau. of David Dick and Elisabeth his wife, b. 3 Jan 1799
2 Mar 1801   Davidson, Eliza dau. of Col. James Davidson and Margaret his wife, b. 7 Jan 1801
30 Jan 1803 Dundas, Henry Thompson son of John Dundas and Nancy his wife, b. Oct 1802
9 Feb 1806   Dundas, Edward Burnes son of John Dundas and Nancy his wife, b. 12 Sep 1805
4 Jan 1807   Dixon, Mary Ann dau. of John Dixon and Mary his wife, b. Nov 1806
19 Jun 1808 Dye, Reuben son of Reuben Dye and Elisabeth his wife, b. 1 year
8 Oct 1808   Dunlap, Mary in consequence of a public profession of her faith, age 18 yrs.
25 Jan 1809 Deakins, Margaret dau. of William Deakins and Jane his wife, b. in May 1808
24 Oct 1809 Daingerfield, John son of Col. B. Daingerfield and --- his wife, aged -- mos.
25 Oct 1809 Dyer, Julia Ann, b. 17 Dec 1799
25 Oct 1809 Dyer, Caroline, b. 23 Sep 1804
25 Oct 1809 Dyer, Mary, b. 30 Oct 1806
25 Oct 1809 Dyer, Harriet, b. 18 Jan 1809, above 4 children of Anthony Dyer and --- his wife
13 Nov 1809 Dunlap, James son of William Dunlap and --- his wife, 3 yrs. old
19 Mar 1811 Dunlap, Esther Ann dau. of William Dunlap and --- his wife, 3 weeks old
22 Apr 1812 Dean, William
22 Apr 1812 Dean, John, above 2 children of Joseph Dean and Hannah his wife
15 Jun 1814 Douglass, Louisa dau. of James Douglass and Eliza his wife, age 4 mos.

pg. 9 Marriages
25 Jul 1789 David David and Mary Keith
31 Dec 1789 James Daniel and Sarah Wright
3 Apr 1789   Swann Dolphin and Rebecca Carne
1 Jun 1790   Walter Dulany and Anne Farrell

First Presbyterian Church, Alexandria, Virginia   125

3 Apr 1791   John Wallace Douglas and Mary Moxley
22 Dec 1791   Mungo Dykes and Anne Wade
Jan 1792   Jonathan Devann and Becca Iams
Oct 1792   Miles Dorsey and Sina Molan
Jan 1793   James Doring and Jane Vaughan
Jan 1793   James Dougherty and Nelly St. George
Nov 1793   Gideon Dyer and Mary Barwell
Aug 1794   Samuel Devaughn and Anna Glasgow
Sep 1794   John Lame [Douglass] and Anne Camerson
28 Aug 1795   Daniel Douglass and Charlotte Orme
7 Jul 1795   John Dove and Nancy Grant
14 Nov 1795   John Dunlap and Elisabeth Hanna
5 Feb 1796   John Duffey and Mary Deeble
3 Jul 1796   George Deneale and Mary Patten
7 Jul 1796   Jesse Dunbar and Elisabeth Griffin
24 Nov 1796   Ganet Doyle and Martha Denick
9 Mar 1797   George Darling and Mary Isler
3 May 1797   Philip Dymem and Fanny Walker
3 Aug 1797   Jesse Dunbar and Sarah Stricklen
9 Sep 1797   Andrew Duncan and Anne Bellona
23 Mar 1798   William Dulany and Ann Simms
7 Nov 1799   Joseph Green Daffen and Eliza Cook
11 Feb 1800   Edward Drake and Juliana Cazenove
27 Apr 1800   Elijah Davis and Elisabeth Brittingham
11 Jun 1801   Daniel Dalton and Margaret Emmett
29 Jun 1801   Arthur Dougherty and Rebecca Smith
17 Dec 1801   Robert Duncan and Hannah Bennett
14 May 1802   Daniel Davis and Frances Grimes
1 Apr 1804   Michael Detterly and Mary Coones
23 Apr 1804   Colin Dowdall and Margaret Stokely
17 Jul 1804   Reuben Dye and Elisabeth Turner
9 Dec 1804   Charles Drew and Polly Huble
14 Apr 1805   John Dixon and Mary Jura
21 Aug 1806   Davey Davey and Betsey Bowling
9 Jul 1807   Basil H. Davidson and Eliza Hunter
10 Feb 1808   Thomas Drinnan and Mary Taylor
14 Sep 1808   John Duffey and Mary Kinsell
23 May 1809   Charles Stuart Dade and Jane Adam
16 Aug 1810   John Darnell and Rhodey Taylor
18 Sep 1810   David Dick and Sarah Ann Posey
21 Oct 1810   James Dunn and Penelope Cayton
12 Dec 1811   Francis Dade and Harriet Shephard
25 Apr 1812   Richard DeButts and Louisa Dulany
13 Feb 1812   F.C. DeKrafft and Harriet Scott
17 Nov 1812   James Douglass and Eliza Kincaid
18 Mar 1813   Francis Dyer and Margaret Hunter
11 Jul 1814   Aaron Dewitt and Eliza Mark
18 May 1815   Horatio Day and Martha Dunnington

Funerals

28 Apr 1797	Dyson, a child, age 1 year
19 Sep 1798	Dykes, Elisabeth, 6 mos., gravel.
3 Sep 1801	Davidson, Eliza, 6 mos., lingering illness
25 Oct 1801	Duffey, ---, 1 yr., consumption
14 Feb 1803	Delia of Mr. Patten, 40 yrs., consumption
7 Sep 1803	Douglass, Daniel, 35 yrs., bilious fever
3 May 1804	Duffey, ---, stillborn
19 Jun 1805	Duffey, ---, 10 days
26 Sep 1806	Dundas, Edward, 1 yr. 11 days, croup
27 Sep 1806	Douglass, Mary, 81 yrs., old age
28 Oct 1806	Dunbar, Silas, 17 yrs., fever
2 Nov 1806	Dunlap, John, 50 yrs., lingering illness
8 Jan 1807	Deakins, child, 2 hours
18 Jan 1807	Davey, Davey, 50 yrs., fever
3 Sep 1807	Dixon, ---, 9 mos., bowel complaint
11 Oct 1807	Douglass, Sarah, 40 yrs., consumption
1 Mar 1808	Duffey, ---, stillborn
7 Mar 1808	Duffey, Mrs., 40 yrs., childbirth
15 Oct 1809	Dunlap, an infant, 4 mos.
13 Mar 1811	Dunlap, Mrs. of William, 36 yrs.
31 Mar 1811	Dennett, John L., 26 yrs., short illness
11 Sep 1812	Dunlap, Elisabeth, 54 yrs., long illness
1 Sep 1813	Dundas, John, 54 yrs. 6 mos., dropsy
19 Oct 1813	Darling, George, 75 yrs., worn out

pg. 10 Baptisms

21 Feb 1796	Fleming, Peterson of Andrew Fleming and Catherine Steele, b. 25 Nov 1795
20 Mar 1798	Fleming, Robert son of Andrew Fleming and Catherine Steele, b. 6 Mar 1798
2 Jun 1799	Fleming, Andrew son of Andrew Fleming and Catherine Steele, b. 1 Apr 1799
14 Oct 1800	Farrell, Mary dau. of Thomas Farrell and Mary his wife, b. Mar 1800
23 Aug 1801	Fleming, Margaret dau. of Andrew Fleming and Catherine his wife, b. 26 Apr 1801
23 Oct 1803	Fleming, Mary dau. of Andrew Fleming and Catherine his wife, b. 7 Jun 1803
17 May 1807	Fleming, Anna dau. of Andrew Fleming and Catherine his wife, b. 26 Oct 1806
14 Aug 1808	Fleming, Elisabeth dau. of Andrew Fleming and Catherine his wife, b. Jul 1808
20 Oct 1809	Floyd, Mary in consequence of a public profession of her faith and obedience
3 Nov 1810	Fleming, Andrew Jamison son of Andrew Fleming and Catherine his wife, b. 23 Aug 1810
2 Mar 1814	Fleming, John son of Andrew Fleming and Catherine his wife, b. Dec 1813
8 Feb 1816	Fleming, Catherine Sabel dau. of Andrew Fleming and Catherine his wife, b. 3 Jan 1816

First Presbyterian Church, Alexandria, Virginia   127

pg. 11 Marriages
25 Nov 1789 William Fieldon and Catherine Derea
27 Jul 1790 Dennis Foley and Elisabeth Dunn
6 Sep 1790   Henry Frederick and Sarah Macmannin
23 Oct 1790 Joseph Feagans and Mary Lester
2 Mar 1791   Thomas Flatford and Sarah Wiley
20 Nov 1791 Reuben Fairfield and Ann Beall
Jan 1792   John Forster and Ann Gilpin
May 1792   Joseph Fulford and Polly Spicott
Jun 1792   Bennett Freeman and Peggy Guzman
25 Apr 1793 Andrew Fleming and Catharine [Steele]
Jan 1794   Thomas Farrell and Ann Weston
Jun 1794   Robert Farrell and Peggy Insley
Nov 1794   Zaccheus Ferguson and Susanna Wallace
Mar 1795   Thomas Fitzpatrick and Ann Wilkinson
28 Oct 1795 Samuel Freeman and Nelly McDonald
4 Mar 1796   Henry Finlay and Polly Carroll
21 Apr 1796 William Fletcher and Catherine Wright
5 Sep 1796   Andrew Ford and Jane Muley
17 Jun 1797 Leonard Fry and Marry Allan
5 Nov 1797   Thomas Francis and Margaret Smith
27 Jul 1798 Samuel Flower and Mary Lowden
28 Jun 1799 William Foxton and Hannah Ricks
9 Sep 1799   John Fawcett and Janet Mitchell
10 Jun 1804 Matthew Francis and Ann Durrington
4 Nov 1804   Horatio Field and Elisabeth Boyer
30 May 1805 John Fairbrothers and Elisabeth Ends
20 Apr 1806 Abraham Faw and Sarah Moody
10 May 1807 John G. Francis and Jane Mays
2 Jul 1809   John Fulmore and Mary Ann Gallie
25 Jul 1811 Daniel Foxwood and Sarah Hill

Funerals
28 Sep 1801 Fleming, Peter, 6 yrs. 10 mos. 2 days, dropsy in the head
20 Jan 1805 Faw, Mrs. 35 yrs., herself
2 Oct 1805   Fleming, Andrew, 6 yrs. 5 mos., fever
18 Jul 1807 Fleming, Ann, 5 mos., bowel complaint

pg. 12 Baptisms
18 Aug 1807 Gilman, Laura Ann dau. of Ephraim Gilman and his wife Ann, b. 30 Oct 1806
13 Dec 1807 Gilman, Laura Ann dau. of Ephraim Gilman and his wife Ann, 6 weeks old
28 Apr 1808 Gray, Emma dau. of Robert Gray and his wife, b. Jan 1808
16 Apr 1809 Gilman, Julia Augusta dau. of Ephraim Gilman and Ann his wife, 3 mos.
3 Feb 1811   Gilman, Lucy dau. of Ephraim Gilman and Ann his wife, 7 yrs.
9 Dec 1812   Gilman, Eugenia dau. of Ephraim Gilman and Ann his wife, 8 mos.
16 Nov 1814 Gilman, Cornelia dau. of Ephraim Gilman and Ann his wife

pg. 13 Marriages
20 Dec 1789	Thomas R. Glover and Elisabeth Steward
29 Feb 1790	Joshua Guest and Catherine Reintzell
16 Mar 1790	John Garrow and Susanna Davis
8 May 1790	John Grimes and Hannah Bedinger
17 Feb 1791	John Gill and Esther Lowrey
Oct 1792	Anthony Glandes and Tabitha Armstrong
Jun 1793	Elias Thomas Gretter and Mary Gretter
Nov 1793	John Greenwood and Elisabeth Beltz
Jan 1794	Samuel Gates and Martha Wiley
Feb 1794	John Giborie and Jeanie Garat
20 Apr 1795	Edward Gray and Mary Darly
Dec 1795	John Grimes and Jane Hannah
28 Jun 1796	Thomas Graffort and Mary Fulford
30 Oct 1796	Caleb Green and Hannah Robinson
4 Mar 1797	James Gullatt and Elisabeth Cooper
2 Jun 1797	Thomas Garner and Elisabeth Green
26 Dec 1797	William Gates and Jemima Thomas
7 Sep 1798	John Gunnell and Letty Hall
20 Sep 1798	Jeremiah Galloway and Polly Stewart
30 Dec 1798	Isaac Gibson and Susanna G. Foushee
3 Feb 1799	Obediah Gunn and Ann White
13 May 1799	James Gill and Elisabeth Small
9 Sep 1800	John Gooding and Margaret Angely
9 Oct 1800	Robert Gray and Polly K. Nelson
18 Dec 1800	William Gullatt and Elisa. Taylor
26 Feb 1801	Grigsby Grady and Mary Baggett
12 Sep 1801	James Gray and Priscilla Weeds
8 Mar 1802	Geo. Green and Catherine Patterson
17 Jul 1803	Joseph Gowan and Mary Sherron
24 Nov 1803	Robert Grimes and Priscilla Gray
3 Apr 1804	William Grymes and Letty Lanham
5 Jun 1804	Andrew Goss and Sarah Pearson
8 Sep 1804	Thomas Green and Susan Lanham
7 Oct 1804	Frederick Gesh [Gasch] and Molly Catherby
12 May 1807	Martin George and Catherine Kline
12 Sep 1809	William Garner and Margaret Simms
7 Feb 1811	Francis Gonsalves and Mary Byrne
5 Feb 1812	Frederick Green and Catherine Cheverill
22 Feb 1814	Levy Gray and Ann Osburn
29 Mar 1815	John Glanders and Fanny Myers
16 Oct 1815	James Green and Esther H. [Hudson]

Funerals
10 Mar 1797	Greenaway, Rebecca, 38 yrs., fever
8 Oct 1803	Graham, David, 45 yrs., fever
18 Aug 1807	Gilman, Laura Ann, 10 mos.
25 Aug 1807	Gillies, Doctor James, 49 yrs., decline
26 Jul 1812	Gullatt, Mrs. Betsey, 30 yrs.
5 Sep 1813	Gird, son of J. Gird, 1 yr. 6 mos.

Jul 1815   Gilman, 9 mos.

pg. 14 Baptisms
24 Jan 1796	Holmes, Margaret dau. of Isaac Holmes and Christian McGregor, b. 2 Dec 1795
18 Jul 1798	Hall, Mary Grace Craig dau. of William Hall and Grace his wife, b. 5 Feb 1798
2 Nov 1801	Harper, Joshua Riddle son of John Harper and Mary his wife, b. Mar 1796
25 Dec 1803	Hall, John Shephard son of William Hall and Elisabeth his wife, b. 8 Apr 1803
5 Jan 1804	Hartshorne, Saunders William son of William Hartshorne, Jr. and Mary his wife, b. 18 Dec 1803
24 Mar 1805	Hall, James son of William J. Hall and Elisabeth his wife, b. 10 Jan 1805
10 Aug 1807	Hampson, Leonora dau. of Bryan Hampson and --- his wife, b. 15 Jan 1807
19 Feb 1809	Hunter, William Forest son of --- Hunter and --- his wife, 4 mos.
19 Feb 1809	Hunter, Samuel Earle son of William Hunter and --- his wife, 11 yrs.
25 Mar 1809	Hunter, Hatty Hatton dau. of Colin Hunter and Hatty Hatton his wife, 3 mos.
18 Jul 1809	Hampson, Paul son of Bryan Hampson and --- his wife, b.
11 Mar 1809	
25 Jul 1809	Harper, Mrs. wife of William, in consequence of her profession of her faith and obedience
26 Jul 1809	Harper, Joel, age 15 yrs.
26 Jul 1809	Harper, Charles, age 13 yrs.
26 Jul 1809	Harper, Joseph, age 9 yrs.
26 Jul 1809	Harper, Washington Terrett, age 7 yrs., above 4 sons of William Harper and Mary his wife
16 Jun 1810	Harper, John, captain
16 Jun 1810	Harper, Sarah, his wife, both in consequence of a profession of their faith and obedience
20 Jun 1810	Harper, Mary Anne
20 Jun 1810	Harper, William, above 2 children of Capt. John Harper and Sarah his wife
8 Aug 1810	Hoy, Charlotte, dau. of --- Hoy and Nancy his wife, b. 12 Jul 1810
31 Oct 1810	Harper, Mary, wife of Capt. Robert Harper in consequence of a profession of her faith and obedience
7 Nov 1810	Hunter, --- dau. of Wm. Hunter and--- his wife, 6 weeks old
3 Apr 1811	Hunter, Janet dau. of Colin Hunter and Hatty Hatton his wife, 3 mos. old
10 Apr 1811	Harper, Julia dau. of Capt. John Harper and Sarah his wife, 3 mos.
27 Nov 1811	Hill, Silvam dau. of Lawrence Hill and Jane his wife, 2 mos.
13 Mar 1812	Hoye, --- dau. of --- Hoy and--- his wife, 3 mos.
7 Aug 1812	Harper, William, Jr., in consequence of a profession of his faith and obedience
7 Aug 1812	Harper, Mary dau. of Wm. Harper, Jr. and --- his wife, 7 mos.
30 Dec 1812	Hill, Lawrence son of Lawrence Hill and Jane his wife, 2 mos.
30 Jun 1813	Hunter, John son of Colin Hunter and Henrietta his wife, b. 2 Jun

27 Sep 1813 Harper, Martha Ann dau. of William Harper, Jr. and his wife, 3 weeks
17 Nov 1813 Harper, William Wells, son of Robert Harper and Mary his wife
12 Apr 1815 Hunter, Henrietta Hatton dau. of Colin Hunter and Henrietta his wife, b. Feb 1815

pg. 15 Marriages
9 Aug 1789   Peter Hoatz and Becky Shultz
19 Mar 1790 John Hill and Mary Perry
1 Aug 1790   Thomas Hardyman and Mary Carter
26 Feb 1791 Barton Hill and Tracey Ashford
16 Aug 1791 Daniel Hurley and Nancy Bedinger
24 Oct 1791 Richard Harrison and Ann Craik
22 Dec 1791 Morris Hurley and Jane Chattham
Jul 1792   John Hookes and Mary Burnes
Jan 1793   Charles Hogue and Sarah Magness
Feb 1794   Martin Hogner and Christiana Rich
Mar 1794   Pollard Hardgrove and July McCrety
29 Oct 1794 Robert Hamilton and Hester Gray
29 Oct 1794 Charles Hardy and Patience Garlick
29 Oct 1794 Wm. Haycock and Sarah Mason
Nov 1794   James Hammond and Rosanna Bowen
Oct 1795   James Harper and Anna Rice
Dec 1795   David House and Lucretia Tenison
15 Feb 1796 John Horner and Phebe Clevenger
13 Apr 1797 Robert C. Hall and Eleanor Nottingham
28 May 1797 John Hodgkins and Rachel Dalton
16 Sep 1798 Henry Hollinduff and Margaret Felsh
26 Dec 1799 Fielder Hayes and Elenor Vermillion
4 Oct 1800   James Hall and Rebecca Fisher
6 Oct 1800   John Hardy and Elisa. Robertson
30 Oct 1800 Robert Hooper and Mercy Courtney
28 Jan 1801 Benjamin Hawkins and Nancy Willis
1 Mar 1801   William Hengarty and Rachel Kitely
11 Sep 1801 David Hamilton and Ann Gray
22 Sep 1801 Charles Horwell and Ann Phenix
17 Dec 1801 Joseph Harris and Winifred Dorsey
24 Dec 1801 Charles Heath and Melinda Kent
15 May 1802 Thomas Hughes and Amelia Egling
13 Jun 1802 George Huntley and Sarah Pepper
17 Apr 1803 Garret Haden and Eleanor Wood
8 Oct 1803   Martin Hoverman and Elisabeth Waper
26 Feb 1804 Enoch Harley and Debby Dennison
5 Jun 1805   John Harper and Sarah Davis
6 Jul 1806   Benjamin Hood and Ann Limerick
25 Dec 1806 Wm. Huntington and Elisa. Smitherman
26 Nov 1807 John Bennett Hill and Mary Underwood
10 Jul 1808 Stephen Haden and Elisabeth Harden
18 May 1809 Robert Harper and Mary Ann Davis
29 Mar 1810 Lawrence Hall and Jane Perry
19 Aug 1810 Reuben Hoit and Cleary Flanagan

First Presbyterian Church, Alexandria, Virginia   131

19 Dec 1811   Philip Hunt and Rebecca Yost
25 Oct 1812   Charles Hallwood and Rosley Russell
4 Nov 1813   James Harris and Lucy Longden
30 Dec 1813   William H. Hannon and Mary Hodgkin
13 Oct 1814   George Harrison and Polly Snyder
24 Oct 1815   Hynam Harrower and Eliza. McDonald

Funerals
8 Jun 1796   Hannah, John, 1 yr., fever
22 Aug 1797   Harper, Edward, 7 1/2 yrs., drowned
18 Oct 1797   Harper, John, 9 mos., pleurisy
15 Feb 1798   Hunter, George, 56 yrs., intemp.
10 Mar 1798   Hall, Mrs. Grace, 18 yrs., childbirth
27 Jun 1798   Hunter, Alexander, 52 yrs., decline
24 Jul 1799   Harper, John, 11 mos.
24 Mar 1803   Harper, Rosa, 36 yrs., consumption
1 Jun 1803   Hunter, ---, 22 yrs., inflammation
21 Jul 1803   Harper, ---, 8 mos.
18 Oct 1803   Hunter, William, 54 yrs., fever
18 Oct 1803   Hunter, Robert son of William above, 17 yrs., fever
22 Nov 1803   Hannah, Alexander, 74 yrs., old age
4 Dec 1803   Harper, Edward, 40 yrs., consumption
9 Mar 1804   Hubbold, John, 40 yrs., pleurisy
12 Mar 1804   Harper, Robert, 20 yrs., consumption
7 May 1804   Harper, Capt. John Sr., 76 yrs., old age
5 Dec 1804   Hall, John Shepard, 1 yr. 9 mos.
4 Apr 1806   Harper, ---, 18 mos., fever
12 Jan 1807   Harper, Sophia, 14 yrs., consumption
31 Mar 1807   Harris, ---, 8 mos., hives
22 Oct 1807   Hamilton, Susanna, 60 yrs., fever
22 Sep 1808   Hodgson, Charles Henry, 5 yrs. 6 mos., decline
20 Nov 1809   Hunter, Mrs., 52 yrs., palsey
1 Dec 1809   Harper, Joseph, 58 yrs., palsey
16 Apr 1810   Hall, William J., 38 yrs., intemperance
4 Mar 1812   Harding, Mrs. Mary, 82 yrs., old age
1 Dec 1813   Harper, of Capt. Jn. Harper, 2 mos.
8 Jun 1814   Hepburn, Agnes, 87 yrs., old age
20 Jul 1815   Hunter, of Wm., 15 mos., hives
22 Sep 1815   Hunter, Mrs. Cordelia M., 59 yrs.

pg. 16 Marriages
28 Oct 1795   Jasper Isralean and Eliza. Taylor
   Dec 1795   Joseph Ingle and Mary Simmon
25 Nov 1802   Rev. James Inglis and Jane Swan Johnston

Funerals
20 Dec 1814   Irwin, Thomas, 40 yrs.

pg. 17 Baptisms
15 May 1796   Jamieson, George son of Andrew Jamieson and Mary Little, b. 29 Apr
15 May 1796   Jamieson, Robert son of Andrew Jamieson and Mary Little
14 May 1797   Johnston, James son of John Johnston and ---- his wife, b. 4 Nov 1796
21 Jan 1798   Johnston, Sarah Carter dau. of Capt. Johnston and his wife Jean [or Jane], b. Dec 1797
12 Dec 1798   Johnston, John son of John Johnston and Mary his wife, b. 12 Nov 1798
29 Jul 1799   Johnston, Jane dau. of Capt. Johnston and Jane his wife, b. Jun 1799
17 Mar 1800   Jamieson, Mary dau. of Andrew Jamieson and Mary his wife, b. Nov 1799
24 Feb 1801   Johnston, John Dunlap son of Capt. Johnston and Jane his wife
15 Feb 1802   Johnston, William son of John Johnston and Mary his wife, b. Jan 1802
5 Jan 1804   Johnston, James Haynes son of --- Johnston, Norfolk, and his wife, 3 yrs.
10 Dec 1804   Johnston, Mary Magdalene dau. of John Johnston and Mary his wife, b. 6 Apr 1804
28 Sep 1806   Johnston, Charles Anthony son of John Johnston and Mary his wife, b. 4 Feb 1806
5 Sep 1808   Johnston, Margaret M. dau. of John Johnston and Mary his wife, b. 15 Dec 1807
15 Dec 1808   Johnston, Charles son of Capt. Johnston and Jane his wife
15 Dec 1808   Johnston, Alex. MacKenzie son of Capt. Johnston and Jane his wife, 8 mos.

pg. 18 Marriages
5 Jan 1790   William James and Mary Smith
22 Dec 1791   John Johnston and Mary LeTrait
Feb 1792   Joshua Jordan and Rebecca Crampton
Feb 1793   Johnston Jenkins and Sarah Lightfoot
Feb 1794   Andrew Jamieson and Mary Sweet
Mar 1795   Thomas Jones and Ann Jones
Mar 1795   Jesse Jordan and Mary Cavender
Jul 1795   Thomas Jones and Amelia Locker
Dec 1795   Charles Jones and Prudence Shuen
1 Dec 1796   William Jackson and Kitty Fleming
25 Dec 1796   George Johns and Mary Ann Richards
21 Jul 1798   William Johnston and Mary Rezin
28 Oct 1800   Peter Johns and Elisabeth Bower
19 Nov 1800   Jonathan Jones and Sarah Jones
13 Jun 1804   Samuel Johnston and Aminta King
4 Nov 1804   Henry James and Susanna Taylor
21 Feb 1805   Mos.es Janney and Judith Lawrence
8 Mar 1807   John Johnston and Mary Hodgkins
17 May 1808   Catesby Jones and Alice Welch
11 Sep 1808   David Jobson and Sarah Keating
22 Jan 1809   Edward H. Jacobs and Ann Boyd
5 Nov 1809   Hezekiah Johnston and Nancy Talbot
22 Nov 1810   Henry C. Joachim and Lettice Harding
9 Jun 1815   William Jackson and Bridgett Roberts

First Presbyterian Church, Alexandria, Virginia   133

Funerals
24 Aug 1796   Jamieson, George, 3 mos., flux
24 Feb 1797   Johnston, Anne, 4 yrs. 4 mos. 9 days, whooping cough
30 Aug 1799   Johnston, Jane, 5 wks
30 Sep 1801   Johnston, John, near 3 yrs., [whooping] cough
2 Nov 1801   Johnston, ---, 9 mos., [whooping] cough
15 Feb 1803   Jamieson, Mary, 3 yrs. 3 mos., consumption
9 Jul 1804   Jamieson, Charles, 59 yrs., jaundice
10 Apr 1810   Janney, Mrs., 49 yrs., bilious cholic
3 Jul 1811   Johnston, Mary Ann, 8 mos.
19 Jul 1811   Johnston, Dennis McCarty, 46 yrs.
2 Dec 1811   Johnston, Jane, 39 yrs., bilious fever
13 Apr 1812   Janney, Abel, 57 yrs.

pg. 19 Baptisms
28 Feb 1796   Kelly, Rebecca dau. of John Kelly and Elena Putney, b. 29 Mar 1795
28 Feb 1796   Kelly, Mary Ann dau. of James Kelly and Rachel Allen, b. 27 Dec 1794
9 Oct 1797   Kidwell, John son of Benjamin Kidwell and Elisabeth his wife, b. 31 Oct 1796
26 Nov 1799   Kennedy, William son of Dr. James Kennedy and Letty his wife, b. 17 Aug 1798
14 Apr 1801   Kincaid, Isabel dau. of John Kincaid and --- his wife, 8 weeks
3 Jun 1801   Kerr, Alexander son of Alex. Kerr and --- his wife
15 Jun 1814   Kincaid, --- dau. of John Kincaid and --- his wife, 10 yrs.

pg. 20 Marriages
12 Dec 1791   John Keith and Elisabeth McMahon
Oct 1792   Samuel Keach and Mary Harman
Apr 1794   William King and Elizabeth Harper
Dec 1795   Benjamin Kidwell and Eliza Hamilton
20 Mar 1796   Damulian Kingsbury and Ann Hardy
31 Mar 1796   James Kingsbury and Rebecca Castile
5 Jun 1796   Mos.es Kenny and Elisabeth Baker
23 May 1797   William Kirby and Susanna Hayne
15 Jun 1797   James King and Ann Pindall
3 Jun 1798   Samuel Kirk and Barbara Britton
30 May 1799   James Keene and Jane Clark
15 Jan 1801   Edward Keating and Martha Dunn
25 Jun 1801   Samuel King and Elizabeth Gates
23 Jan 1802   John Kent and Martha Ballard
22 Jul 1802   James Keith and Esabella McMahon
9 Sep 1802   Alexander Kibby and B. MacFarlane
12 Jun 1806   Benjamin King and Eliza. Dorcey
1 Nov 1810   Mos.es Kenny and Sally Lewis
23 May 1811   Newton Keene and Nancy Moore Dundas
12 Oct 1815   John Knowles and Mary Ann Westcott

Funerals
20 Nov 1802   Kilton, ---, 2 yrs.
1 Jan 1811   Kincaid, John, 60 yrs., apoplexy

8 Jan 1816   Kennedy, James, Dr., 63 yrs.

pg. 21 Baptisms
25 Jun 1797   Locke, Joseph son of Tho. Locke and Catherine his wife, b. 15 May
8 Apr 1798   Lotz, Susanna Hartshorne dau. of J. Lotz and Susanna his wife, b. 6 Nov 1797
10 Jun 1798   Logan, --- dau. of Samuel Logan and Fanny his wife, b. Dec 1797
15 Jul 1798   Lumsden, John son of John Lumsden and Margery his wife, b. Jun 1798
12 Dec 1798   Lemoine, John Estave son of John Lemoine and Susanna his wife, b. 30 Jul 1798
3 Dec 1799   Lotz, Rosanna Elisabeth dau. of J. Lotz and Susanna his wife, b. Oct 1799
25 Oct 1801   Logan, Anna Maria dau. of Randolph Logan and Eliza. his wife, b. 8 Sep 1801
8 Mar 1803   Lotz, John Christian son of J. Lotz and Susanna his wife, b. Feb 1803
12 Jun 1803   Ladd, Samuel son of Wm. Ladd and --- his wife, 6 weeks
11 May 1806   Ladd, Joseph son of Wm. Ladd and --- his wife, 3 mos.
11 Oct 1807   Ladd, Elisabeth Ann dau. of Wm. Ladd and --- his wife, 7 weeks
12 Oct 1807   Long, William Harper son of Seth Long and Sarah his wife, 2 mos.
22 May 1809   Long, Jane Barba. dau. of William Long and Susanna his wife, b. 3 Aug 1808
21 Jul 1809   Long, Mary Donaldson dau. of Seth Long and Sarah his wife, 6 mos.
15 May 1813   Lewis, --- dau. of Laurence Lewis and Eleanor his wife, 6 weeks

pg. 22 Marriages
19 Aug 1790   Henry Lowe and Mary Burnett
12 Sep 1790   John Limerick and Susanna Adams
15 Nov 1790   Richard Lane and Hannah Bayley
26 Feb 1791   John Lehon and Sarah Williams
21 Sep 1791   William Lizurm and Sarah Merick
Oct 1793   John Lowe and [blank] Brammell
Mar 1795   John Levenston and Elisabeth Talbutt
Sep 1795   William Lyles and Nancy Farnester
Sep 1795   William Lightfoot and Patty Brown
Dec 1795   Zachariah Lyle and Polly Edwards
22 Feb 1797   Alexander Latimer and Massie Burkett
2 Apr 1797   Elias Longden and Eliza. Baden
27 May 1797   Samuel Logan and Fanny McGahan
19 Aug 1797   John Lumsden and Margery Oates
7 Sep 1797   Samuel Lewis and Sarah Jenkins
23 Nov 1797   John Lanham and Cassa Thom
24 Dec 1797   William Lightfoot and Eliza. Wallis
8 Feb 1798   Benjamin Lindsay and Amelia Robinson
2 Mar 1799   Alexander Lammond and Charlotte Tull
3 Jun 1799   David Lewis and A. Davis
6 Mar 1800   Barton Linch and Sarah White
25 Jun 1800   John Lindsay and Athy Cooper
29 Jun 1800   James Locker and Susanna King
20 Nov 1800   Randolph Logan and Eliza. Conn
12 Apr 1801   Henry W. Landress and Nancy Davis

First Presbyterian Church, Alexandria, Virginia 135

14 Jun 1801 John M. Lightfoot and E. Sanford
19 Oct 1801 William Ladd and Sophia A. Stidolph
22 Oct 1801 John Lanham and Olpha Longden
 5 Sep 1802 John Lanham and Ann McFaden
 8 Feb 1803 William Laurence and Rebecca Marle
14 Dec 1803 John Lomax and Elisabeth McLea
17 May 1804 William Linter and Letitia Hardy
26 Feb 1805 Andrew Lyon and Mary Massey
31 Oct 1805 Henry Lyles and Mary Davis
22 Jul 1806 Thomas Lowe and Mary Cannon
21 Aug 1806 George Limmerman and Ann Simpson
 9 Oct 1806 Seth Long and Sarah Harper
18 Dec 1806 William Lewis and Salome Way
29 Oct 1807 William Long and Susanna Stewart
 3 Nov 1808 John G. Ludberg and Sarah Crandell
14 Jan 1810 William Lawson and Patsey Fiegate
 3 Feb 1810 John Lanham and Catherine Snell
10 Feb 1810 George Linton and Henrietta McKinney
12 Nov 1812 George Lightfoot and Ann Sanford
 7 Sep 1813 George C. Longden and E.A. Scott
 6 Oct 1813 James Locker and Mimay Simpson
13 Jan 1814 Joseph Laurence and Mockey Grinnel
23 Mar 1814 Benjamin Leslie and Rebecca Kinsey
27 Mar 1815 Rev. James Lawrie and Elisabeth B. Hall
29 May 1815 Thomas Lewis and Nancy Evans
 6 Sep 1815 James Laurence and Betsey Brim
23 Jul 1803 Henry White Landres and Maria Thompson

Funerals
10 Jan 1796 Long, Rebecca, 45 yrs., fever
14 Nov 1799 Lumsden, John, 1 yr. 6 mos., flux
 5 Jul 1800 [Lyle], ---, 9 mos., smallpox
17 Oct 1800 Lumsden, ---, 3 mos.
 5 Dec 1800 Ladd, Capt. Wm., 68 yrs., pleurisy
20 Jul 1802 Ladd, ---, 2 hours
 5 Oct 1803 Low, Mrs., 45 yrs., fever
14 Jul 1804 Ladd, ---, 17 yrs. 2 mos.
25 Nov 1804 [Lyle], ---, 21 yrs., consumption
30 Jun 1806 Long, Samuel, 26 yrs., short illness
 1 Nov 1807 Ladd, Mrs. Sarah, 77 yrs., jaundice
20 Oct 1812 Logan, Mrs., 30 yrs., consumption

pg. 24 Marriages
 2 Aug 1789 William Moony and Nancy Jackson
 9 Sep 1789 James Mills and Eleanor Aubrey
24 Sep 1789 John Mullon and Catherine Dunkin
 2 Oct 1790 James Murray and Nancy Pittman
 9 Mar 1791 James Martin and Sophia Galloway
-- Jan 1792 George W. Murray and Olivia Lowry
   May 1792 Robert [Mease] and Betty Stewart

Sep 1792   Stephen Moore and Mary Skinner
Sep 1792   John Murray and Elizabeth Wilcock
Nov 1792   Thomas Massey and Eliza. Richards
Dec 1792   Thomas Mezarvey and Mary Stone
Dec 1793   James Mayhall and Nelly Cole
Dec 1793   William G. Marks and Peggy Emery
Dec 1793   Thomas Mos.s and Ann Fullerton
Nov 1794   James Murray and Margaret Butt
Dec 1794   Neil Moony and Winny A. Smith
23 Apr 1796   Daniel Mandell and Nancy Newman
18 Sep 1796   John Munro Moore and Elisabeth Clemster
2 Nov 1797   Israel Musgrove and Grace Woodrow
25 Nov 1797   William Middleton and Lucy Ironmonger
1 Mar 1798   John Moyer and Maria Juliana Reisch
8 Mar 1798   Levin Morris and Frances Piles
7 Mar 1799   William Mills and Elisabeth Tolson
3 Apr 1799   Daniel Mandell and Emma Lustre
8 May 1799   William Martin and Nancy Bagnett
13 May 1799   William Morgan and Eleanor Mayhall
12 Sep 1799   Benjamin Moody and Elisabeth Blunt
14 Nov 1799   John Meyers and Margaret Boyer
10 May 1800   Samuel Mocklar and Mary Clark
21 Jun 1800   Charles Mankin and Polly Vowell
26 Dec 1800   John Muir and Polly Long
5 Mar 1801   James Mayhall and Anne Ellis
11 May 1801   Edward Murray and Hepsiba Goodwin
24 Oct 1801   Francis Murray and Lucretia Catterton
5 May 1803   Rev. William Maffitt and Harriet Turberville
23 Jun 1803   Robert Mercy and Susanna Mertland
27 Oct 1803   Thomas Murray and Mary Pindall
28 Nov 1803   Jabez Matthews and Sarah McPherson
1 Sep 1804   Benjamin Mason and Mary Ann Stone
17 Oct 1805   William Martin and Mary Woodrow
26 Feb 1806   William Nelson Mills and Ann Leap
13 Jun 1806   John Mason and Jane Lethue [Lithcoe]
9 Apr 1807   John [Mearechtree?] and Catherine Nelville
7 Apr 1809   Hanson Moreland and Sarah Atkins
14 Mar 1811   John Murphy and Margaret McManing
22 Sep 1812   Lee Morris and Sarah Walker
30 Sep 1813   David Marle and Eliza. Harriet Smith
5 Oct 1815   Robert Miller and Elisabeth Howard

Funerals
20 Mar 1796   Morrison, ---, a few days
7 Jun 1796   Mills, John Melville, 6 mos., smallpox
9 Jun 1796   Milburn, Joseph, 2 yrs., smallpox
25 Jun 1797   Miller, Caroline, 6 mos., consumption
18 Sep 1797   Miller, Mrs., 33 yrs., consumption
26 Mar 1798   [Mease], Mrs. Eliza, 46 yrs., bilious fever
15 Sep 1799   Muir, Elisabeth, 10 mos.

20 Jan 1800 Monroe, Mrs., 28 yrs., childbirth
28 Dec 1802 Mitchell, Capt. Wm., 42 yrs., decline
10 Mar 1803 [Mease], Robert, 57 yrs., decline
29 Jun 1803 Masterson, Sarah, 56 yrs., cancer in the brain
13 Sep 1803 Madden, Nancy, 18 yrs., fever
17 Sep 1803 Matheson, Kenneth, 30 yrs., fever
22 Oct 1803 Moody, Mrs. Elisabeth, 25 yrs., fever
-- Jan 1804 Matheson, ---, 3 mos., decline
11 Mar 1809 Marclay, ---, 4 yrs., burnt to death
11 Sep 1815 Mark, John Lisle, 5 mos., bowel complaint
8 Jan Marsteller, Mrs. P., 41 yrs., consumption

pg. 25 Baptisms
28 Oct 1796 McGarr, Margaret dau. of James McGarr and Mary McLean, b. 13 Sep
14 May 1797 McCleish, Archibald son of Archd. McCleish and Elisa. his wife, 13 Mar
25 May 1797 McLeod, Helen dau. of John McLeod and Helen his wife, b. 4 May 1797
11 Jun 1797 McLeod, John son of Daniel McLeod and Mary Ann his wife, b. 21 May 1797
1 Aug 1797 McCrea, Kitty dau. of James McCrea and Kitty his wife, b. 30 Jun
15 Jul 1798 McFaden, Nancy dau. of James McFaden and Ann his wife, b. 6 May 1798
16 Dec 1798 McLeod, Philip son of Daniel McLeod and Mary Ann his wife, b. Oct 1798
19 Apr 1799 McKenzie, John son of Capt. James McKenzie and Margaret his wife, b. Nov 1798
25 Apr 1799 [McCleish], William son of Archd. McLeish and Elisabeth his wife, b. 26 Jan 1799
7 Oct 1799 McIver, Mary Grace Hall dau. of John McIver and Margaret his wife, b. 30 Apr 1798
7 Oct 1799 McIver, John son of John McIver and Margaret his wife, b. 30 Apr 1798
5 Oct 1800 McKnight, William Henry son of John McKnight and Catherine his wife, b. 24 Aug
20 Sep 1801 McLeod, Mary Ann dau. of Daniel McLeod and Mary Ann his wife, b. Aug 1801
30 Sep 1801 McKenzie, Alexander son of James McKenzie and Margaret his wife, b. 7 Sep 1800
16 Nov 1802 McKnight, Martha Bryan dau. of John McKnight and Catherine his wife, b. 7 May
3 Dec 1802 McKenzie, James son of Capt. James McKenzie and Margaret his wife
12 Aug 1803 McCleish, George son of Archd. McCleish and Elisabeth his wife, 8 mos.
25 Dec 1803 McIver, Evander son of John McIver and Margaret his wife, 8 yrs.
8 Jul 1804 McClellan, Mary dau. of John McClellan and --- his wife
21 Sep 1806 McKnight, Charles Augustus son of Capt. John McKnight and --- his wife, 7 weeks
8 May 1807 McGehanny, Margaret dau. of A. McGehanny and --- his wife, b. 8 Feb 1807
13 Jun 1807 McKinney, Mary Ann, 6 yrs.
13 Jun 1807 McKinney, Helen, 3 mos., above 2 children of John McKinney and his

3 Jan 1808	McKnight, Margaret dau. of Capt. John McKnight and --- his wife, 7 weeks
20 Mar 1808	McNemara, Jo. Henry son of Capt. John McNemara and his wife, 6 weeks
15 May 1808	McCrea, Rebecca dau. of James McCrea and Catherine his wife, 2 yrs.
14 Jul 1808	McDonald, Wm. King son of John McDonald and Ann his wife
17 Aug 1808	McKenzie, George son of James McKenzie and Margaret his wife, b. Apr 1808
22 May 1809	McKnight, Susanna dau. of John McKnight and Catherine his wife
20 Dec 1809	McCrea, Ann Allison, 10 yrs.
20 Dec 1809	McCrea, James [Mease], 7 yrs.
20 Dec 1809	McCrea, William Allison, 5 yrs.
20 Dec 1809	McCrea, Henry, 1 yr. 8 mos., above 4 children of James McCrea and Catherine his wife
29 May 1810	McIntyre, Sarah dau. of Charles McIntyre and Sarah his wife, 2 mos.
27 Mar 1811	McKenzie, Louis son of James McKenzie and Margaret his wife, b. Nov 1810
17 Apr 1811	McKnight, Mary Elisabeth dau. of Capt. John McKnight and Catherine his wife, 5 mos.
16 Mar 1813	McKnight, Christiana Perry dau. of Capt. John McKnight and Kitty his wife, 5 mos.
7 Jul 1813	McKenzie, Andrew Jamieson son of James McKenzie and Peggy his wife, b. 24 Oct 1812
7 Jul 1813	McIntyre, Catherine Ophelia dau. of Charles McIntyre and his wife
26 Mar 1814	McIntyre, Margaret Ann dau. of Charles McIntyre and his wife
23 Nov 1814	McKnight, Catherine Ann dau. of John McKnight and Cathr. his wife, 9 mos.
15 Oct 1815	McKenzie, Harriet Rebecca dau. of James McKenzie and Margaret his wife, b. 6 Apr 1815

pg. 26 Marriages

3 Dec 1789	James [Mease] McCrea and Catherine Wise
7 Nov 1790	John McIver and Margt. Coupar
13 Aug 1791	John McBride and Polly Watts
24 Dec 1796	Hugh McGaughan and Priscilla Rawlins
28 Jan 1797	James McFadden and Ann Keating
23 Jun 1798	Alexander McKenzie and Ann Lymburn
5 Feb 1799	Patrick McCarty and Sarah Weightman
2 Apr 1801	Isaac McLean and Mary Turner
17 Sep 1801	Daniel McDougall and Mary Talbutt
27 Oct 1801	Bernard McCormack and Lucy Murphy
21 Jan 1802	George McFarlane and Kitty Richards
13 May 1802	John McCobb and Sarah Weston
27 Mar 1803	Peter McCrea and Mary Reynolds
24 Apr 1803	James McDimmick and Lydia Talbutt
3 Jul 1803	Thomas McCauglin and Mary Taylor
26 Feb 1807	John McDonald and Anna King
26 Oct 1807	Patrick McCutcheon and Lucy Keaton
26 Mar 1808	Thomas McLean and Ann Shephard

First Presbyterian Church, Alexandria, Virginia   139

27 Dec 1808 Charles McIntyre and Sarah Heineman
 2 Dec 1809 Patrick McNeil and Maria Night
22 Feb 1814 William McIlhenny and Hannah Ingram
 5 Oct 1815 Robert Miller and Eliza. Howard

Funerals
 1 Jun 1796 McLeod, John, 8 yrs., scarlet fever
13 Jun 1796 McKenzie, John, 26 yrs., scarlet fever
 1 Jul 1796 McLeod, John, 7 yrs. 6 mos., flux
11 Jul 1797 McCrea, Nancy, 3 yrs., flux
25 Nov 1797 McLeod, John, 6 mos. 3 days, hives
24 Apr 1799 McFaden, James, 38 yrs., consumption
12 Jul 1799 McFaden, Nancy, 1 yr. 2 mos.
10 Jun 1800 McLeod, ---, a few mos.
 3 Sep 1801 McCrea, --- of James, 18 mos., consumption
 7 May 1802 McDougall, ---
30 May 1804 McCulloch, Mrs., 37 yrs., consumption
 6 Mar 1805 McKay, Elisabeth, 19 yrs., cancer
 3 Aug 1807 McKnight, Ch., 1 yr
17 May 1808 McCrea, Rebecca, 2 yrs., croup
 7 Aug 1808 McCrea, Capt. John, 36 yrs., victim to ---
26 Jul 1812 McKnight, William, 80 yrs., old age
13 Sep 1812 McDonald, John, 26 yrs.
 3 May 1813 McCleish, Jane, 15 yrs., inflammatory fever
 8 Aug 1813 McGehanny, Margaret, 5 yrs. 5 mos., fever
21 Jan 1815 [McCleish], James, 55 yrs., epidemic
 3 Mar 1815 McKinney, Mrs. S., 50 yrs., epidemic
 6 Apr 1815 McKenzie, Mrs. Ann, 43 yrs., epidemic
10 Jul 1815 McKecknie, ---, 67 yrs.

pg. 27 Baptisms
13 Sep 1796 Neill, Jane Christie dau. of John Neill and Rebecca Offutt, b. 21 Aug
25 Jan 1809 Newton, Albert Orlando son of William Newton and Jane B. his wife,
             b. 26 Oct 1805
25 Jan 1809 Newton, Sinah Ann dau. of William Newton and Jane B. his wife, b. 15
             Nov 1807
12 Jun 1811 Newton, Joseph Monroe son of William Newton and Jane B. his wife,
             b. ---
12 Jul 1812 Newton, Augustine W. son of William Newton and Jane B. his wife, b.
             1 Jul 1812
16 Sep 1812 Nash, Jane Ann dau. of --- Nash and his wife Jane, b. 9 May 1809
16 Sep 1812 Nash, Mary Murdoch dau. of --- Nash and his wife Jane, b. 12 May 1811
12 Nov 1815 Nicholson, Mary Ann dau. of Henry Nicholson and Margaret his wife,
             b. 11 Jul 1815

pg. 28 Marriages
19 May 1789 William Norris and Sarah Evans
 7 Aug 1789 George Nash and Ann Ripton
17 Mar 1791 Joseph Nainby and Eleanor Buffiere
    Feb 1792 William Newton and Jane Steuart

Mar 1793 James Nebton and Mary Pettit
Aug 1793 Scudamore Nickolls and Selina Roberdeau
Aug 1794 Henry Nicholson and Precious Talbott
28 Oct 1795 John [Neill] and Rebecca Offutt
27 Oct 1803 Henry Nicholson and Ann Ballard
7 Mar 1808 Augustine Newton and Ann Sophia Gadsby
6 Aug 1808 John Nevitt and Lucy Beakley
8 Sep 1808 John Nowland and Susanna Windsor
14 Jun 1814 Henry Nicholson and Margaret Heineman

Funerals
17 May 1806 Nivin, Duncan, 40 yrs., suddenly
10 Aug 1807 Nicholas, Lewis, Gent., 90 yrs., old age
9 Feb 1812 Nelson, Mrs., 56 yrs., pleurisy
28 Dec 1814 Newton, William, 50 yrs., epidemic
25 Feb 1815 Newton, Mrs. Jane B., 39 yrs., decline

pg. 29 Baptisms
2 Apr 1797 Orr, Eleanor dau. of Dr. Orr and Lucinda his wife, b. Dec 1796

pg. 30 Marriages
Sep 1792 John Outten and Phillis Evans
Mar 1793 Henry O'Neal and Rosetta Howard
28 Sep 1798 John Oakley and Margaret Deakins
16 Mar 1799 Thomas Osburn and Susanna Beedle
16 Feb 1804 Henry Oswald and Martha Kelly
25 Dec 1806 William O'Connor and Sophia G. Williams
31 Jan 1808 John A. Overman and Catherine Durington

pg. 31 Baptisms
24 Jul 1796 Perry, Matilda dau. of William Perry and his wife, b. 24 Jun
14 Nov 1796 Patten, Isaac Roberdeau son of Tho. Patten and Mary Roberdeau, b. 20 Sep
6 May 1798 Patten, Susan dau. of Tho. Patten and Mary Roberdeau, b. 13 Dec 1797
25 Sep 1798 Perry, Charlotte dau. of William Perry and his wife, b. 3 Mar
25 Jul 1799 Pratt, Mary Sullivan Western dau. of Levin Pratt and Elisabeth his wife, b. 26 Dec 1798
5 Sep 1800 Patten, Joseph May son of Tho. Patten and Mary his wife, b. 1799
18 Oct 1800 Page, Washington Craig son of Charles Page and his wife, b. 24 Jul 1800
18 Mar 1802 Patten, Elisabeth Catherine, dau. of Tho. Patten and Mary his wife, b. 19 Nov 1801
11 Sep 1803 Perry, Daniel C. son of Wm. Perry and --- his wife, b. Jul 1802
25 Nov 1803 Porter, Maria Mercer dau. of Tho. Porter and Sarah his wife
25 Nov 1803 Porter, Sarah Ramsay, dau. of Tho. Porter and Sarah his wife
9 Mar 1806 Patten, Selina Blair dau. of Thomas Patten and Mary his wife, b. 13 Sep 1805
21 Sep 1806 Piercy, George Ashbeel Green son of Geo. Piercy and --- his wife, 7 mos.
9 Aug 1807 Patten, Thomas Roberdeau son of Tho. Patten and Mary his wife, b. Jan 1807

First Presbyterian Church, Alexandria, Virginia   141

31 Jul 1808 Piercy, C. McKnight dau. of Geo. Piercy and --- his wife (of Washington), 6 mos.

pg. 32 Marriages
9 Nov 1790   Edmund Poole and Susanna Wiley
15 Oct 1791 William Parkhouse and Elisabeth Lane
Oct 1792   Dennis Poole and Elisabeth Allison
Jan 1793   Richard Pickerill and Susanna Welch
Nov 1793   Thomas Patten and Mary Roberdeau
Apr 1794   Peter Plear and Nancy Stiebby
Jun 1794   Henry Poole and Catherine Stone
Jun 1794   John Peters and Mary North
Jul 1794   Isaac Pickerill and Charity Wheat
Sep 1794   William [Patterson] and Mary Cozzens
Oct 1795   John Parsons and Frances Perry
15 Mar 1797 John Perkins and Priscilla Willing
30 Mar 1797 Thomas [Penny] and Eliza. Lightfoot
8 Apr 1797   John Potts and Margaret Cooke
1 Jul 1797   James Patterson and Ann McHenry
18 Dec 1797 John [Penny] and Elisabeth Hill
7 Jun 1798   Thomas Preston and Jane Jackson
19 Dec 1799 Samuel Pumphrey and Rebecca King
21 Jan 1800 Edward Powell and Mary Sisson
18 Nov 1800 Hezekiah Payne and Ann Gray
29 Nov 1800 William Pomery and Elisabeth Wright
28 Dec 1800 James Parker and Dorcas Golier
12 Feb 1801 Reuben Porter and Franny Chadwell
23 Dec 1802 Enoch Pelton and Sarah M. Patterson
28 Apr 1803 Lewis Piles and Anne Harriss
22 May 1803 Joseph Patterson and Elisabeth Keene
23 May 1803 Francis Perkins and Anne Smith
2 Aug 1803   Joseph Plumb and Elisabeth Marle
6 Sep 1803   Daniel C. Puppo and Elisabeth Stroman
27 Oct 1805 John Parker and Mary Hill
24 Feb 1807 Francis Dade Pomery and Nancy Garrett
16 Sep 1807 William H. Perry and Mary F. Madden
21 Jul 1810 Zacha. Paul and Elisabeth Bowling
26 Feb 1811 Thomas West Peyton and Sophia M. Dundas
27 Aug 1811 Walter Parsons and Sarah Williams
20 May 1812 Henry Posey and Elisabeth King
3 Sep 1812   Thomas Pierce and Elisabeth Mandley
16 Dec 1813 Geo. Parks and Sarah Church

Funerals
2 Apr 1797   Pomery, ---, 2 mos.
5 Sep 1799   Porter, James, 2 yrs., hives
1 May 1800   Porter, Thomas, 44 yrs., fever
17 Mar 1801 Patten, Susan, 3 yrs. 3 mos., fever
13 Jun 1802 Powell, ---, 1 yr., measles
12 Dec 1802 Patten, Elisabeth C., 3 yrs. 22 days, teething

29 Jul 1805 Puppo, ---, 1 yr. 2 mos., croup
7 Mar 1807 Pittman, ---, 3 mos., found dead in bed
21 Aug 1808 Perry, Daniel C., 64 yrs., fell into a kettle of boiling tallow
2 Nov 1808 Patten, Mary, 34 yrs., consumption
8 Sep 1811 Piercy, ---, 9 mos.

pg. 33 Baptisms

22 May 1796 Riddle, James Dall son of Joseph Riddle and Sarah Kearsley, b. 17 Jan
20 Jul 1796 Rogerson, Robert son of Thomas Rogerson and Anstis Olney, b. 17 Apr
21 May 1797 Riddle, John Harper son of Joshua Riddle and Frances his wife, b. 11 Jan 1796
18 Jul 1798 Reeder, John son of Alexr. Reeder and Rebecca his wife, b. 30 Jan 1797
12 Oct 1798 Russell, James Blackburn son of James Russell and Nancy his wife, b. 7 Sep 1798
12 May 1799 Riddle, Eliza Mitchell dau. of Joseph Riddle and Sarah his wife, b. Nov 1798
29 Sep 1799 Richardson, Foster son of Capt. Richardson and --- his wife, b. 15 Sep 1799
25 Dec 1800 Riddle, John Adams son of Joseph Riddle and Sarah his wife, b. 3 Jul
16 Mar 1801 Russell, Mary Ann dau. of James Russell and Nancy his wife, b. 10 Oct 1800
28 Oct 1802 Riddle, Julia Mina dau. of Joseph Riddle and Sarah his wife, b. Jul 1802
18 Apr 1804 Russell, Hannah Throgmorton dau. of James Russell and Nancy his wife, 9 mos.
23 Jul 1804 Reynolds, --- dau. of --- Reynolds and his wife, 3 weeks
1 Aug 1804 Riddle, Joseph son of Joseph Riddle and Sarah his wife, 6 mos.
23 Aug 1804 Riddle, Anna Maria dau. of Joshua Riddle and Frances his wife, 3 yrs. Jan next
23 Aug 1804 Riddle, Bushrod Washington of Joshua Riddle and Frances his wife, 1 yr. Sep next
2 Mar 1806 Riddle, Jane dau. of Joseph Riddle and Sarah his wife, b. 30 Jul 1805
9 Sep 1806 Ramsay, Ann McCarty
9 Sep 1806 Ramsay, Jane Allan Taylor
9 Sep 1806 Ramsay, Robert Johnston
9 Sep 1806 Ramsay, Amelia, above 4 children of Dennis Ramsay and Jane his wife
20 Mar 1807 Riddle, Robert son of Joseph Riddle and Sarah his wife, b. 1 Nov 1806
29 Aug 1808 Riddle, Sarah Ariana dau. of Joseph Riddle and Sarah his wife, b. Jul 1808
25 Jan 1809 Ricketts, John Thomas, b. 10 Oct 1805
25 Jan 1809 Ricketts, Mary Elisabeth, b. 3 Mar 1808, above 2 children of David Ricketts and Elisabeth his wife
19 Feb 1809 Richardson, Daniel son of Capt. Richardson and his wife, 3 yrs.
5 Jun 1811 Riddle, Joseph son of Joseph Riddle and Sarah his wife, b. Apr 1810
15 Nov 1811 Reynolds, Sarah dau. of --- Reynolds and Sarah his wife, 6 weeks
5 May 1812 Ramsay, George Washington Dennis, son of Dennis Ramsay and Jane his wife, 3 yrs.
26 Dec 1814 Riddle, Charlotte Vowell dau. of Joshua Riddle and Frances his wife, 6 mos.

pg. 34 Marriages
24 Oct 1791 John Reed and Catherine Day
   Jan 1792 Michael Reardon and Mary McNamer
   Jul 1792 John Reardon and Rachel Brooks
   Nov 1793 Henry Redman and Mary Kelly
   Feb 1794 James Reed and Charlotte France
   Jun 1794 John Robertson and Elisabeth Snalum
   Feb 1795 Joshua Riddle and Fanny R. Harper
   Mar 1795 Alexander Reed and Ann Dalton
 7 Mar 1796 James Reid and Polly Griffin
 2 Jun 1796 Joseph Rincker [Rinker] and Susanna Good
25 Jun 1796 Gerard Roe and Mary Mehaul
21 Nov 1796 Charles Richter and Margaret Russell
18 Jul 1798 George Robinson and Barbara Allen
20 Sep 1798 Alexander Rodman and Sally Crump
14 Mar 1799 Robert Roberts and Biddy Casey
22 Mar 1799 Basil Ragan and Mary Watson
 8 May 1800 James Riddle and Arianna Steuart
14 Jun 1801 John Roach and Monica Drury
23 May 1803 John [Richter] and Mary Elser
 4 Jun 1803 Thomas Rustick and Elisabeth Pierce
24 Sep 1803 John Reynolds and Elisabeth Simpson
28 Dec 1803 William Reiley and Sabina Kent
 6 Dec 1804 David Ricketts and Elisabeth Ban
 2 Sep 1806 Anthony Reins and Elisabeth Tyler
19 Jan 1808 William Russell and Rhody Clark
19 Jan 1808 Andrew Rounsavel and Elisabeth West
28 Sep 1808 John Reynolds and Mary Lee
19 Jan 1811 John Rawlings and Jane Brooke
18 Jul 1811 Judson Richardson and Milley Richards
10 Dec 1812 Richard Rock and Margaret Spunaugle

Funerals
 4 Aug 1800 Riddle, Joseph, 1 yr., bowel complaint
13 Dec 1800 Riddle, ---, 6 wks
 7 May 1802 Ricketts, Mrs., 59 yrs., consumption
14 Oct 1804 Russell, Hannah Throgmorton, 1 yr. 2 mos., croup
 4 Nov 1804 Riddle, Bushrod Washington, 1 yr., croup
27 Mar 1807 Russell, Mrs. Nancy, 36 yrs., consumption
12 Feb 1808 Riddle, Joseph, 4 yrs. 1 mo 10 days, decline
31 Aug 1808 Riddle, ---, 1 yr., hives
30 Oct 1808 Russell, Jane, 38 yrs., fever
 5 Dec 1809 Riddle, of James, stillborn
25 Apr 1810 Riddle, Sarah, Mrs., 38 yrs., childbirth
 1 Sep 1810 Ramsay, Dennis, 56 yrs.
30 Dec 1810 Ricketts, E. of Benja., 25 yrs., childbirth
10 Aug 1811 Riddle, of Joshua, 6 mos., bowel complaint
 2 Sep 1811 Ramsay, Jane of John, 9 yrs., fever
16 Nov 1811 Reynolds, Mrs. Sarah, 39 yrs., short illness
30 Dec 1811 Ricketts, Charles, 28 yrs., pleurisy

7 Sep 1812 Ross, Mrs. (Episcopal Ground), 60 yrs.
18 Sep 1814 Ramsay, Anthony, 21 yrs., fever

pg. 35 Baptisms
20 Mar 1796 Stabler, Maria dau. of William Stabler and Margaret Cooper, b. 11 Feb
3 Apr 1796 Swann, Mary Ann dau. of Laurence Swann and Ann Watt, b. 12 Feb
1 Jun 1796 Simms, Emelia Jean Watson dau. of Charles Simms and Nancy Douglas, b. 6 Oct 1795
20 Jun 1796 Stewart, John son of William Stewart and Helena Kay
11 Sep 1796 Smith, Mary dau. of John Smith and Catherine Yost his wife, b. Jul
28 Mar 1797 Swift, Ann Selina dau. of Jonathan Swift and Ann his wife, b. 18 Feb
28 Jan 1798 Swann, John Watt son of Lau. Swann and Ann his wife, b. 1 Jan 1798
21 Feb 1798 Scott, Eliza dau. of John Scott and Mary his wife, b. 26 Oct 1797
9 May 1798 Stephen, Peter son of Peter Stephen and Sarah his wife, b. 23 Jan
19 Aug 1798 Stewart, Mary dau. of William Stewart and Helena his wife, b. 18 Aug 1798
29 Mar 1799 Smith, Louisa dau. of John Smith and Catherine his wife, b. 29 Dec 1798
22 Feb 1800 Swift, George Washington son of Jonathan Swift and Nancy his wife, b. 9 Feb 1800
28 Jun 1800 Simms, George Washington son of Charles Simms and Nancy his wife, b. 21 Oct 1799
16 Jun 1801 Smith, Sir Sidney son of John Smith and [Catherine] his wife, b. 10 Dec 1800
12 Jun 1803 Swift, Ann Foster dau. of Jonathan Swift and Ann his wife, b. 11 Oct 1802
27 Sep 1803 Smith, William Henry son of John Smith and Catherine his wife, b. Aug 1802
28 Oct 1803 Spooner, Jane Smith Scriger dau. of Holden Spooner and Mary his wife, b. May 1803
20 Nov 1803 Stevenson, David son of Robert Stevenson and --- his wife, b. Oct 1803
15 Sep 1804 Smith, George Archibald son of Hugh Smith and Jane his wife, b. 6 Nov 1802
15 Sep 1804 Smith, Hugh Charles son of Hugh Smith and Jane his wife, b. Jul 1804
21 May 1805 Swift, Mary Selina dau. of Jonathan Swift and Nancy his wife, b. 1805
12 Jul 1805 Simms, Phoebe Maria dau. of Charles Simms and Nancy his wife, b. 1805
15 Dec 1805 Stevenson, William son of Robert Stevenson and his wife, b. Sep 1805
27 Apr 1806 Smith, Rebecca dau. of John Smith and Catherine his wife, 3 mos.
5 Feb 1807 Smith, Mary dau. of Hugh Smith and Jane his wife, 11 mos.
29 Oct 1807 Stewart, William C. son of John Stewart and --- his wife, b. 17 Apr 1807
27 Jun 1808 Sanford, --- son of Thomas Sanford and--- his wife, 2 yrs.
27 Jun 1808 Sanford, Laurence son of Thomas Sanford and --- his wife, 9 mos.
14 Sep 1808 Simms, Nancy Neville dau. of William D. Simms and --- his wife, b. 13 Sep 1808
20 Sep 1808 Swift, William Taylor son of Jona. Swift and Nancy his wife, b. this morn.
19 Jan 1809 Smith, Thomas William son of Hugh Smith and Jane his wife, b. 21 Aug 1807
22 May 1809 Stewart, Charles Laurence son of John Stewart and Jane his wife, b. 25

First Presbyterian Church, Alexandria, Virginia   145

                    Nov 1808
20 Sep 1809   Sanford, Sarah Eveleth dau. of Thomas Sanford and --- his wife, 6
                    weeks
29 Jan 1810   Smith, Elisabeth dau. of Hugh Smith and Jane his wife, b. 5 Jul 1809
15 Apr 1811   Swift, Foster son of Jonathan Swift and Ann his wife, b. 20 May 1810
25 Oct 1811   Sanford, Esther Williams dau. of Thomas Sanford and --- his wife, 13
                    Aug 1811

pg. 37 Baptisms
5 Mar 1812   Smith, John Watson son of Hugh Smith and Jane his wife, b. Feb 1811
25 Apr 1812   Stewart, Elisabeth Mary, b. 21 Jul 1810
25 Apr 1812   Stewart, John Parks, b. 23 Dec 1811, above 2 children of Jo. Stewart
                    and Jane his wife
24 Aug 1812   Swann, --- son of William Swann and Fanny his wife, 8 days
9 May 1813   Smith, Ann M. dau. of Jo. Smith and--- his wife, b. Jan 1813
15 Jul 1813   Smith, James Pitts son of Hugh Smith and Jane his wife
3 Aug 1813   Stewart, Thomas R.M. son of James M. Stewart and Elisabeth Fletcher
                    his wife, 6 mos.
26 Mar 1815   Smith, Adeline A. dau. of John Smith and --- his wife, b. Aug 1814
29 May 1815   Smith, Richards son of Hugh Smith and Jane his wife
10 Sep 1815   Sanford, Frances A. dau. of Thomas Sanford and Catherine his wife, b.
                    1815

pg. 36 Marriages
5 Jul 1789   William Skinner and Valinda Sayre
26 Jan 1790   William Sullivan and Honoria Connors
27 Jan 1790   Thomas Steuart and Eleanor Key
18 Feb 1790   Adam Shurn and Kitty Fowler
3 Nov 1790   George Shuler and Jemima King
7 May 1791   Samuel Shreve and Peggy Bowling
7 May 1791   William Soley and Lenny Lightnem
8 Oct 1791   John Simpson and Decie Barker
  Feb 1792   Daniel Smith and Nelly Duvall
  Apr 1792   Adam Shurn [or Shinn] and Elizabeth Davis
  Oct 1792   Matthew Sexsmith and Elizabeth Lanphier
  Feb 1793   William Semple and Elisabeth St. George
  Dec 1793   Thomas Smith and Thesea Lewis
  Dec 1793   John Spencer and Elisabeth Boggess
  Feb 1794   John Spacey and Artley Taylor
  Jul 1794   Joseph Smith and Elisabeth Cradock
  Apr 1795   Barton Smoot and Polly Barton
28 Oct 1795   J.W. Smith and Mary Findley
23 Mar 1796   Augustine J. Smith and Susanna Taylor
12 May 1796   John Smith and Nancy Davis
2 Feb 1797   William Stetham and Alley Dove
31 Aug 1797   George Scott and Violet Morris
2 Sep 1797   George Savage and Frances Collins
21 Sep 1797   Willian Spencer and Elisabeth Edwards
2 Oct 1797   John Stewart and Polly Dougherty
7 Dec 1797   Lewis Simpson and Kitty [Uhler]

14 Jan 1798 William Simpson and Ann Lightfoot
1 Feb 1798 Christian Slimmer and Ann Trougantt
6 Mar 1798 Lewis Scisson and Frances Powell
23 Mar 1798 Alexander Shaw and Kitty Toupley
22 Aug 1798 Henry Selectman and Mary Fisher
18 Nov 1798 Thomas Simms and Peggy Fristoe
28 Feb 1799 Peter Sheares and Nancy Parker
7 Mar 1799 William Smith and Rebecca Walters
31 Aug 1799 Joseph Simpson and Elisabeth Stone
24 Jul 1800 Robert Shipley and Pernica Touch
29 Jul 1800 Job Sherwood and Elisabeth Day
9 Sep 1800 Russell Stephens and Catherine Shutz
4 Nov 1800 Charles Stephens and Polly Hamilton
13 Nov 1800 John Smith and Dolly Williams
4 Dec 1800 William Slater and Mary Ann Taylor
19 Feb 1801 Robert Smith and Ann Watson
5 Mar 1801 William Swallow and Elisabeth Moore
22 Jun 1801 John S. Sly and Susanna Curtan
15 Aug 1801 John C. Suremon and Elisabeth Devereux
17 Sep 1801 Robert Stewart and Elisabeth Ward
29 Oct 1801 Daniel Smith and Betsey Stitly
20 Nov 1801 James L. Scott and Mary Adgate
14 Jan 1802 Benjamin Shreve and Sarah Kitely
10 Jun 1802 Holden Spooner and Mary Ballard
19 Jul 1802 William Smith and Sarah Morgan
2 Sep 1802 Thomas Summers and Rachel Cooper
9 Jan 1803 James Simms and Betsey Lightfoot
3 Feb 1803 Gilbert Simpson and Susanna Zimmerman
21 Apr 1803 John Swann and Ann Batfford
11 Sep 1803 Daniel Strickland and Susanna Tracy
9 Oct 1803 James Sterrit and Polly Mills
19 Apr 1804 Geo. Stanley and Mary Church
2 Sep 1804 Joshua Sprague and Susanna Lee
14 Mar 1805 Frederick Shuck and Elisabeth Ragan
27 Jul 1805 Wm. C.R. Smith and Mary Morgan
8 Jan 1806 Joseph Swisler and Elisabeth McFaden
26 Feb 1806 Isaac Smith and Mary Walsh
23 Sep 1806 Charles Scott and Elisabeth Beedle
17 Dec 1807 John Stilwell and Sally Boswell
20 Dec 1808 Charles Stone and Hannah Marle
2 Nov 1809 Peter Syke and Esabella McFaden
10 Jul 1810 Thomas Scott and Mary Chaffline
19 Feb 1811 Joshua Sheriff and Mary Locker

pg. 38 Marriages
20 Jun 1811 John F. Smith and Martha Kent
26 Sep 1811 Richard Stanton and Harriet Perry
8 Jan 1812 Samuel Sheriff and Susanna Locker
23 Apr 1812 James M. Stewart and Elizabeth Trescher
25 Dec 1814 Charles Smith and Elisabeth Lloyd

2 May 1815 William B. Stewart and Catherine Reed
4 Jun 1815 Lewyllen Sherwood and Polly Robinson
1 Aug 1815 William R. Swift and Mary D. Harper

Funerals
13 Mar 1812 Shaw, Mrs., 30 yrs., consumption
22 Aug 1812 Simms, Maria, 18 yrs.
6 Mar 1813 Scull, William, 76 yrs., old age

pg. 36 Funerals
5 Nov 1796 Smith, Alexander, 19 mos., putrid ---
6 Jan 1797 Smith, Mrs., 28 yrs., childbirth
19 Jul 1797 Swift, Isaac Roberdeau, 3 yrs., cho. morb.
29 Dec 1797 Simms, Mrs., 30 yrs., childbirth
27 Apr 1798 Spooner, Capt., 40 yrs., dropsy
19 Jul 1798 Swift, Anne Selina, 1yr. 5 mos., flux
2 Oct 1798 Smith, Mary, 1 yr. 9 mos., teething
26 Aug 1799 Stewart, Mary, 1 yr.
24 Aug 1800 Simms, ---, 9 mos., smallpox
12 Sep 1800 Stewart, John, 54 yrs., cho. morb.
9 Jul 1802 Simms, ---, 2 yrs., measles
26 Sep 1802 Smith, of Thomas, stillborn
7 Sep 1803 Smith, Thomas, 45 yrs., stoppage
14 Sep 1803 Smith, Mrs., 44 yrs., fever
2 Oct 1803 Spear, ---, 29 yrs., fever
5 Oct 1803 Smith, Wm. Henry, 11 mos.
22 Oct 1804 Smith, Thomas W. of Hugh, 3 yrs., bowel complaint
12 Aug 1807 Smith, Mary of Hugh, 1 yr. 6 mos.
7 Apr 1808 Simms, Thomas, 46 yrs.
27 May 1808 Steele, Margaret, 67 yrs., comp. of disorders
29 Jun 1808 Sanford, Laurence, 9 mos., bowel complaint
15 Sep 1808 Simms, Nancy Neville, 2 days
21 Sep 1808 Swift, William Taylor, 1 day
12 Feb 1810 Smith, Mrs. of Alexr., 56 yrs.

pg. 39 Baptisms
24 Sep 1806 Taylor, Sarah dau. of --- Taylor and his wife Anne, b. 7 weeks ago, dying
17 Oct 1807 Taylor, John Rose son of Robert J. Taylor and Maria his wife, b. 1 Sep 1806
12 Nov 1808 Taylor, Maria Moore Rose dau. of Robert J. Taylor and Maria his wife, b. 1 Nov 1808
27 May 1812 Thomas, Wells Washington son of --- and ---, 5 mos.

pg. 40 Marriages
30 Mar 1790 Martin Toomey and Mary Murphy
5 Aug 1790 Charles Tucker and Catherine Bagnell
24 Aug 1790 Duke Taylor and Henny Johnston
2 Jan 1791 Sampson Talbot and Cassandra Jarber
6 Jul 1791 Charles Thompson and Henrietta A. Bladen

Oct 1792   Peter Toffler and Catherine Shuck
Jan 1794   Charles Todd and Elisabeth Pepper
Mar 1794   James Taylor and Susanna Combs
Aug 1794   Andrew Telifro and Polly Sullivan
Dec 1795   John Thompson and Polly McCarty
1 Jan 1797   John Tracey and Mary Ann Moony
12 Jun 1797   John Treackle and Barbara Allen
31 Aug 1797   Calby Taylor and Rebecca Humphreys
31 Jul 1798   Thomas Talbut and Mary Malony
4 Oct 1798   Thomas Tolbert and Penny Burgess
18 Oct 1798   John Taylor and Ann Kirk
22 Aug 1799   John Thompson and Francis [Avery]
3 Nov 1799   Henry Taylor and Sarah Gates
7 Nov 1799   James Tarbrer and Mary Harper
1 Dec 1799   Vincent Taylor and Margaret Reynolds
25 Jun 1801   George Taylor and Mary Eaton
3 Mar 1802   William Taylor and Sally Simpson
25 Aug 1802   John Thompson and Mattey Davis
28 Oct 1802   Thomas Taylor and Sarah Shuck
11 Aug 1803   Benja. Tait and Nelly Smallwood
4 Sep 1803   John Tutton and Ann Williams
12 Sep 1803   Geo. Thompson and Rebecca Gardner
2 Nov 1803   John Thompson and Jenny Manly
4 Dec 1803   Thomas Tattershell and Nancy Boyd
30 Jan 1806   Thomas Towers and Elisabeth Chattam
12 Jun 1806   Major Tignell and Louisa Wood
26 Jul 1811   John Turner and Mary Risby
16 Feb 1813   Evan P. Taylor and Rebecca Laurence
25 Apr 1815   William Thomas and Mary Hilton

Funerals
15 Oct 1800   Taylor, Jesse, 59 yrs., bilious fever
1 Dec 1802   Turner, Mrs., 73 yrs., decay
14 Dec 1807   Taylor, John Rose, 1 yr. 3 mos., inflammation of brain
22 Aug 1808   Tabor, ---, 6 mos.
6 Nov 1808   Taylor, Mrs. Maria of Robert, 22 yrs., childbirth
9 Oct 1812   Taylor, Jesse, 27 yrs.
24 Sep 1813   Tretcher, Mrs., 51 yrs., malign. fever
16 Oct 1813   Tretcher, Thomas, 53 yrs., consumption
8 Jun 1814   Toomey, Elisabeth, 30 yrs., consumption

pg. 41 Funerals
13 Sep 1803   Ular, of Mr. Sandford's family, 18 yrs., fever

pg. 42 Baptisms
28 Feb 1796   Verona, Sarah dau. of Joseph Verona and Mary Kelly, b. 29 Mar 1795
11 Mar 1796   Veitch, Louisa dau. of Richard Veitch and Betsey Black Crease, b. 27 Nov 1795
19 Mar 1797   Valdiney, Joseph son of Francis Valdiney and Margaret Parker, 6 weeks
7 Oct 1797   Vowell, Thomas in consequence of a public profession of his faith in

Christ
11 Nov 1797	Vowell, Sarah Wells dau. of Tho. Vowell and Polly his wife, b. Apr 1797
20 Oct 1798	Vowell, John C. in consequence of his profession of his faith in Christ
19 Feb 1799	Vowell, Mary Ann King dau. of John Vowell and Margaret his wife, b. 29 Feb 1797
19 Feb 1799	Vowell, John Goznell son of John Vowell and Margaret his wife, b. 22 Dec 1798
19 Feb 1799	Vowell, John son of Thomas Vowell and Mary his wife, b. 14 Jul 1795
19 Feb 1799	Vowell, Thomas son of Thomas Vowell and Mary his wife, b. 25 Nov 1798
7 Jan 1800	Veitch, Elisabeth dau. of Richard Veitch and Betsey Black his wife, b. 5 Jan 1799
6 Mar 1800	Vowell, James Craik son of Jno. Vowell and Marg. his wife, b. 9 Jan 1800
Aug 1801	Vowell, Eliza dau. of Jno. Vowell and Marg. his wife, b. 22 Jan 1801
7 Nov 1802	Vowell, Mary Ann dau. of Tho. Vowell and Mary his wife, b. 27 Jun 1802
23 May 1805	Vowell, Robert Harper son of Tho. Vowell and Mary his wife
21 Nov 1806	Vowell, Mary Moss dau. of John Vowell and Margaret his wife, 2 yrs.
23 Aug 1807	Vowell, Sarah dau. of Thomas Vowell and Charlotte his wife, b. 9 Jul 1807
4 Dec 1807	Veitch, James Anthony son of Richd. Veitch and Betsey Black his wife, 2 yrs. 9 mos.
7 Apr 1812	Vowell, Margaret Boyd dau. of J.C. Vowell and Mary his wife, born Oct 1811
26 Oct 1814	Vowell, Sarah Goznell dau. of J.C. Vowell and Mary his wife, b. 6 Oct 1813

pg. 43 Marriages
Sep 1794	Thomas Vowell and Mary Harper
28 Oct 1795	John C. Vowell and Peggy Harper
31 Jan 1796	Thomas Violett and Anne Groves
16 Feb 1796	Francis Valdinear and Margt. Barker
3 Apr 1806	Thomas Vowell and Charlotte Douglas
23 Jul 1807	George Vernell and Sally Purkis
6 Dec 1810	John C. Vowell and Mary J. Taylor
12 Oct 1813	Ebenezer Vowell and Eliza Orme

Funerals
13 Nov 1797	Vowell, Sarah Wells, 7 mos.
8 Apr 1799	Vowell, John G., 4 mos.
17 Oct 1799	Vowell, Thomas, 10 mos.
31 Mar 1800	Vowell, James Craik, 3 mos., dropsy
7 Jul 1801	Vowell, Charles, 1 yr., bowel compl.
3 Sep 1801	Vowell, Mary Ann King, 4 yrs. 6 mos.
27 Sep 1802	Vowell, son of John, 4 mos.
13 Aug 1805	Vowell, Mrs. Mary, 34 yrs., consumption
5 Dec 1807	Veitch, James Anthony, 2 yrs. 9 mos., fits
21 Apr 1808	Vowell, Sarah, 9 mos. 11 days, eped. cold

pg. 44 Baptisms
15 Mar 1796	Wilson, Eliza Johnston dau. of James Wilson and Elisabeth Taylor, b. 2 Jan 1794
15 Mar 1796	Wilson, Ann Campbell dau. of James Wilson and Elisabeth Taylor, b. 19 Jan 1796
12 Oct 1796	Wilson, Mary dau. of the Revd. James Wilson and Mary Clark, b. 21 Sep
4 May 1798	Wilson, Bruce son of James Wilson and Elisabeth his wife
8 Jan 1801	Watson, --- son of James Watson and --- his wife, 5 days
17 May 1801	Watters, John Galloway son of Robert Watters and --- his wife, 8 weeks
3 Sep 1801	Wilkes, Christian son of Peter Wilkes and --- his wife, 2 yrs.
11 Aug 1803	Wilkes, twins of Peter Wilkes and --- his wife, a few weeks
23 Apr 1805	Wilson, William Bruce
23 Apr 1805	Wilson, [Mason]
23 Apr 1805	Wilson, Ann Campbell
23 Apr 1805	Wilson, Melvina Allen
23 Apr 1805	Wilson, Robert Johnston Taylor, above 5 children of James Wilson and Elisabeth his wife
18 May 1805	Wise, John son of George Wise and Patty his wife, b. Feb 1805
3 Jun 1805	Woods, Thomas Irwin son of --- Woods and --- his wife, b. Oct 1804
23 Oct 1805	Wilkes, William son of Peter Wilkes and --- his wife, 6 mos.
2 Aug 1810	Wise, Francis
2 Aug 1810	Wise, Mary Ann, above 2 children of Geo. Wise and Patty his wife
10 Sep 1811	Washington, Thomas Turner son of --- Washington and his wife, 2 weeks
17 Jul 1814	Wallach, William Douglas son of Richd. Wallach and Nancy his wife, 6 mos.
24 Sep 1815	Wallach, Richard Simms son of Richd. Wallach and Nancy his wife, b. 1815

pg. 45 Marriages
24 Dec 1789	William Wilson and Sarah Smith
21 Jan 1790	James Wilson and Elisabeth Taylor
25 Apr 1790	Thomas White and Elisabeth Hawkes
16 Aug 1791	Michael Wise and Elisabeth Williams
Sep 1792	Samuel L. Warner and Lyzyan Clemons
Oct 1792	George Wise and Anna Mason
Feb 1793	Jesse Wherry and Ann Chapin
Jun 1794	William Willis and Nancy McManin
Sep 1794	Elijah Williams and Eliza. Duffey
Dec 1795	John White and Mary Gird
17 Oct 1796	Thomas White and Mary Marshall
24 Nov 1796	George Wyley and Mary Whaling
29 Dec 1796	John Wright and Jenny Sophy
14 Aug 1797	Peter Weltz and Caty Gowan
24 Dec 1797	Elijah Williams and Dolly Bedinger
20 Feb 1798	Horatio White and Tracey Ann Danley
10 Mar 1798	Nathaniel Wallace and Nancy Fergusson
28 Mar 1798	John White and Catherine Kenna
4 Oct 1798	John Webster and Elisabeth Pearson

First Presbyterian Church, Alexandria, Virginia 151

17 Dec 1798	Daniel Wright and Harriet Lee Marr
19 Dec 1798	William Woodcock and Elisabeth Hooper
24 Nov 1800	Levin Watson and Kitty Roberts
13 Jan 1801	George Wade and Sarah Williams
15 Jan 1801	Richard Wallace and Peggy Ballinger
19 Feb 1801	William W. Wood and Eleanor Dixon
21 May 1801	Martin Winsha and Elisabeth Kelly
23 Jul 1801	George Kerr Wise and Mary Ann Fulton
5 Dec 1801	John Wood and Elisabeth Fry
11 Mar 1802	William Windsor and Susanna Snell
22 Jul 1802	Ephraim Wiley and Phillis Hessen
9 Apr 1803	William Wright and Elisabeth Conner
30 Jun 1803	Littleton Wiley and Margaret Deakins
27 Oct 1803	Thomas Walden and Kitty Stintman
7 Jun 1804	William Wheat and Molly Feagen
23 Jul 1804	Joseph Wise and Elisabeth Fry
23 Dec 1804	John Williams and Catherine Goldsmith
16 Aug 1805	Samuel Wheeler and Winifred Winkfield
30 Jan 1806	Levin Walker and Margt. Williams
19 Aug 1806	William Wilson, Jr. and Ann Carson
30 Oct 1806	Henry Williams and Elisa. Boyer
20 Nov 1806	William Watson and Elisabeth [Uhler]
25 Dec 1806	Alexander Williams and Eliza Grisby
15 Jan 1807	Hugh Wiley and Anne Bladen
20 Jun 1807	Martin Winshear and Margaret Charles
29 Oct 1807	Andrew Wigart and Sally Davis
13 Oct 1808	Nathaniel Wise and Jane C. McKinney
22 Aug 1809	James C. West and Eliza Payne
29 Mar 1810	Oliver Wilson and Mary Heineman
31 Jul 1810	James Walker and Elisabeth Wilson
3 Nov 1810	Adam L. Webster and Sarah H. Hand
31 Dec 1811	John Wood and Jemima Hall
16 Feb 1812	James Whaley and Harriet Gooding
12 Dec 1812	Thomas Watkins and Mary Williams
2 Mar 1813	Richard Wallach and Nancy Simms
11 Nov 1813	James Walker and Kitty Wise
18 Jan 1816	James C. Wilson and A.L.B. Balch
8 Feb 1816	James C. White and Elisabeth Blufield

Funerals

3 Jan 1796	Wilbar, Sarah, 32 yrs., childbirth
3 Mar 1799	Wales, Mrs. Margt., 62 yrs., consumption
6 Aug 1799	Westcott, ---, 6 mos.
23 Nov 1799	Wales, Andrew, 62 yrs., decline
26 Apr 1800	[Westcott], ---, baptized as soon as b.
Nov 1800	Wilson, Anne C., 6 yrs., worms
9 Feb 1801	Watson, infant
1 Jul 1802	Wilson, Bruce, 5 yrs.
29 Jul 1802	Wilson, Campbell, 30 yrs., inflammation
4 Aug 1804	Wood, an infant

4 Dec 1804   Wise, of George, 4 yrs.
9 Jun 1805   Wilson, James, 38 yrs., fever
10 Aug 1805 Watson, Andrew, 19 yrs., consumption
1 Apr 1806   Williams, Mrs., 40 yrs., consumption
26 Aug 1806 Wood, an infant
16 Mar 1808 Wilson, Margaret, 56 yrs., consumption
25 Oct 1813 Westcott, John, 72 yrs., pleurisy

pg. 46 Baptisms
9 Apr 1797   Young, Frances dau. of James Young and Mary, b. 7 Nov 1796
9 Apr 1797   Young, William son of James Young and Mary, b. 16 Jan 1789
9 Apr 1797   Young, James son of James Young and Mary, b. 23 Dec 1787
14 Apr 1799 Young, Mary Ann dau. of James Young and Mary, b. Dec 1798
1 Nov 1801   Young, Andrew son of James Young and Mary
21 Oct 1804 Young, James son of Robert Young and B. Conrad his wife, 3 yrs.
14 Apr 1805 Young, Elisabeth Mary dau. of Robert Young and B. Conrad his wife, b. Nov 1804
15 Jul 1812 Young, William son of Robert Young and B. Conrad, his age 18 mos.
22 Jun 1814 Young, James son of Robert Young and B. Conrad his wife, 3 yrs.

pg. 47 Marriages
Aug 1794   William Young and Ann Farrell

Funerals
13 Jul 1798 Young, James, 8 mos., consumption
20 Oct 1804 Young, James, 17 yrs., lockjaw
21 Oct 1804 Young, James of Robt., 3 yrs., croup
8 Mar 1806   Youst, John, 70 yrs.
25 May 1813 Young, John, 35 yrs.
29 Jul 1803 Yeaton, Mrs., 32 yrs., consumption

pg. 48 Baptisms
10 Nov 1810 Zimmerman, Maria P. dau. of --- Zimmerman and his wife, 9 mos.

pg. 49 Marriages
10 Jan 1808 Jacob Zimmerman and Nelly Smith
22 Mar 1810 Jacob Zimmerman and Jane Smith

Funerals
22 May 1810 Mrs. [Mariana] Zeppernick, 80 yrs., old age

INDEX

Surname Unknown

()
Anthony 91; Delia 126; Jane 76; Peter 93; Prisey 92; Rebecca 29; Stephen 93; Ular 148; Zane 90

A

ACQUART
 Charles 76
ADAM
 Jane 125; John 118; Robert 62, 63, 66, 69; William 73
ADAMS
 Abednego 57, 64, 114; Anne 118; Francis 75, 78, 88, 101, 118; Gabriel 98, 115; James 118; John 77, 78; Leonard 118; Margaret 117; Mr. 74; Mrs. 118; Philip 74; Robert 63, 79, 117; Susanna 134; Sylvester 59, 62; William 54-59, 61, 62, 64, 70-72, 74-76, 88, 114; William G. 87
ADGATE
 Mary 146
ALEXANDER
 Alfred 117; Amos 117, 118; Ann 4; Charles 72-75, 77-79, 82, 88, 117; Dr. 63, 65; Gerrard 64; John 60, 89; Mary A. 117; Mary B. 117; Mrs. 118; Philip 79; Robert 57, 64, 66, 69; Samuel 108; W.T. 26; William 91; William F. 88
Alexandria Library:
 Lloyd House iv
Alexandria Monthly Meeting:
 Birth and Burial Records 3, 8, 26; Birth/Burial Records: 13, 18, 29; Marriage Records 3; Meeting Hours 2; Meeting House 9, 11-14, 18, 19, 25, 38; Meeting House Alterations 3; Membership Records 26; Properties 8, 12, 25, 28
Alexandria:
 Law on Interments 4; Military Presence in 16
ALLAN
 Marry 127
ALLEN
 Barbara 143, 148; Elizabeth 103; Henry 63; John 101; Mary J.
 122; Nathaniel 117; Rachel 133; Robert 101
ALLISON
 Amos 118; Bryan 117; Elias 118; Elisabeth 141; Mr. 93; Robert 75, 118; William 76, 90, 117
ALVERSON
 John 105, 106, 108
AMBROSE
 Sally 78
ANDERSON
 Ann 105; James 118; John 57, 64; John B. 115; Mrs. 90, 92; Ninian 90; William 77
ANDOL
 Bernard 117
ANDREW
 Benjamin 118; Jacob 118
ANDREWS
 () 118; John 109; Mr. 93
ANGELY
 Margaret 128
ANSLEY
 Henry 59
ANTRIM
 Parnell 118
APPLEBY
 Elisabeth 122
ARCHDEACON
 Richard 117
ARELL
 H. 118; Richard 79
ARMISTEAD
 Mr. 93
ARMSTRONG
 John 118; Tabitha 128
ASBERRY
 John 55
ASHBERRY
 Alice 65; Jane 63; Mary 62, 63
ASHFORD
 Ann 69; Anne 102; George 118; Michael 69, 98, 109; Tracey 130; William 114
ASHTON
 Rachel 120
ATCHISON
 Mary 74
ATHEY
 Samuel 105; Sarah 105
ATKINS
 Daniel 101; Nathaniel 117; Sarah 136
ATKINSON

Guy 82, 86, 88, 118; James 87, 88
AUBREY
 Eleanor 135
AUGUSTINE
 James 94
AULD
 Colin 84
AUSTIN
 () 118; Emily 117; Henrietta 117; John 117; Mary A. 117
AVERY
 Ann 122; Anthony 103; Francis 148
AWBREY
 Francis 98; John 100
AYRES
 John 109; William 91

B

BADEN
 () 120; Elizabeth 134
BAGGET
 Elisabeth 120
BAGGETT
 Mary 128; Robert 120
BAGGOTT
 Charles 120
BAGNELL
 Catherine 147
BAGNET
 William 119
BAGNETT
 Nancy 136
BAILEY
 Carr 120; Eleanor 92; G.W. 119; Robert 118
BAILLIE
 Robert 121
BAILY
 Mr. 74; Sarah 105; T. 91
BAIN
 Christian 105
BAINS
 Gilbert 59
BAIRERS
 Thomas 120
BAKER
 Elisabeth 133; James 119; Joshua 18, 44; Samuel 120
BALCH
 A.L. 151
BALDWIN
 () 121

BALEY
  Pierce 75
BALFOUR
  James 121; Mrs. 121
BALL
  () 121; Allan 120; Eliza 44;
  Eliza H. 42; Elizabeth 20;
  Elizabeth H. 26; John 20, 44,
  68-70; Joseph P. 20, 26, 35, 42;
  Moses 57, 62, 77; Susan 44;
  Susanna 20, 42; Susannah 26;
  William J. 20, 26, 42
BALLARD
  Ann 140; Liven 120; Martha
  133; Mary 146; Severon 120
BALLINGER
  Andrew 119; Frances 61;
  Francis 60; Henry 63; John 120;
  Milly 65; Peggy 151
BALMAIN
  William 62, 63
BALY
  Pierce 60
BAMBURG
  William 94
BANNENGER
  Conrod 75
BARBER
  () 120; Eliza 44; Eliza M. 29;
  Jonathan 29, 44; Joseph 28, 44;
  Mary 44
BARCLAY
  Francis 120; Mr. 90; Robert 87
BARCLOSS
  John 44
BARCROFT
  John 20, 32, 36
BARKER
  Decie 145; Eliza 54; Margaret
  149
BARNES
  Abraham 98, 114; Jesse 120;
  Joseph 103; Mr. 59, 75
BARNET
  Richard 90
BARNETT
  George 103, 120
BARNSBY
  Elinor 109
BARR
  Anne 117; Elisabeth 143;
  Elizabeth 123
BARRETT
  Isaac 120; John 103
BARRY
  Anne 102; Edward 98, 101,
  102; Elizabeth 102; John 101,
  103; Mary 102; William 120
BARTLE
  Samuel 120

BARTLEMAN
  Anne E. 119; George 121;
  Isabella 118; Margaret 118;
  Margaret D. 118; Rebecca L.
  119; William 78, 118, 119, 121
BARTLETT
  Andrew 82
BARTON
  Polly 145
BARWELL
  Mary 125
BASHAW
  Mr. 90; Pleasant 36
BASS
  Samuel 119
BATES
  Benjamin 40; Deborah 40;
  Edward 116; Fleming 3, 13, 40;
  Hannah 40; Lemuel 40; Peyton
  76; Spence 40; Thomas 71,
  Unity 4, 13, 40
BATFFORD
  Ann 146
BATTLE
  James 56
BAVERS
  Thomas 120
BAXTER
  James 98; John 98, 102; Polly
  118
BAYLEY
  Carr 121; Hannah 134
BAYLIE
  Henry 104
BAYLISS
  Robert 120; William 119
BAYLY
  Henry 109, 111; Peirce 109;
  Pierce 61, 62
BAYNE
  Edward 109
BEACH
  Thomas 65
BEACHER
  Edward 90
BEAKLEY
  Lucy 140
BEALE
  Isaac 41; John 120; William 103
BEALL
  Ann 127; Eleanor 119; Isaac B.
  22
BEALLE
  Thomas K. 86
BEAN
  Isaac B. 23
BEARD
  Margaret 105
BEDGOOD
  Samuel B. 40

BEDINGER
  Dolly 150; Hannah 128; Jacob
  119; Nancy 130
BEECH
  John 119; Thomas 119, 120;
  William 119
BEEDLE
  Elisabeth 146; Susanna 140
BEHIER
  Peter 119, 120
BELL
  B. 86; Ross 118
BELLMIRE
  Thomas 119
BELLONA
  Anne 125
BELTZ
  Elisabeth 128
BENCE
  Adam 75
BENDER
  Josiah 24, 44; Juliana 24, 44;
  Julianna 30; Margaret 43, 44;
  Mary 24
BENNET
  Charles 89, 95
BENNETT
  Elizabeth 123; Hannah 125; John
  120; Mary 100; Thomas 100,
  115
BENNIT
  John 105; Mary 109
BENSON
  Robert 119
BENT
  Elisabeth 118; Eliza L. 118;
  Nancy 120; Samuel 118
BENTLEY
  Caleb 39; Charles 39
BENTZ
  Mrs. 92
BERKELEY
  William 110
BERRY
  James 120; Tholemias 86
BERRYMAN
  Mr. 86
BERTRAM
  () 120
BEVAN
  Philip 105
BIDDLE
  Henry 54
BIDGOOD
  Samuel B. 4, 10
BIGGS
  Henry 78; James 120; Mary 105;
  Mrs. 93
BILLEY
  Peter 119

BIRCH
 Albina 118; Isaac 120; James 119; Joseph 75, 78
BIRD
 William 79
BIVINS
 Mary 105
BLACK
 Benjamin 90; Betsey 149; Capt. 118; Charles W. 119, 121; David 118; Eliza 118; Esther A. 118, 121; Helen A. 118; James 118; Margaret 118; Mrs. 90; Robert 121
BLACKBURN
 Edward 55, 56, 58, 60, 62, 88; Elisabeth 122; Richard 110; Thomas 119
BLACKFORD
 Henry 120
BLACKLOCK
 Eliza I. 119; Jean A. 119; Nicholas F. 119
BLADEN
 Anne 151; Henrietta A. 147
BLAGDEN
 George 119
BLINSTON/BLINSTONE
 John 76; Sarah 61; Thomas 61
BLOSS
 Adam 91
BLUE
 John 120
BLUFIELD
 Elisabeth 151
BLUMFIELD
 Joseph 102
BLUNT
 Elisabeth 136; Polly 121; Washer 75, 79, 91, 121
BOGGESS
 Elisabeth 145; Robert 71, 98, 104, 110, 114
BOGUE
 John 118; Judith 118, 120
BOID
 James 60, 62
BOILSTON
 James 105; John 105
BOLING
 Joseph 105
BOLLING
 Joseph 119; William 70
BOLTON
 Bartholomew 54; John 74
BOND
 Elizabeth 34; Elizabeth S. 35, 43; Joseph 34, 43, 52; Thomas M. 21, 30, 42, 44; William 120

BONNER
 Mrs. 93
BONSAL/BONSALL
 John 82, 83, 118
BONTEMPT
 Francis 119
BOONE
 Arnold 20; Elizabeth 20, 45; Hannah 20; Hannah J. 43; Hannah S. 20, 33, 35; Mary S. 20
BOOTH
 Sarah 123
BOSLEY
 Thomas 105, 110, 116
BOSWELL
 Benedicter 105; George 91; Henry 90; Mr. 92; Sally 146; Sarah 119; Thomas 105, William 59, 92
BOUCHER
 Miss 93
BOUCHIRE
 Charles 90
BOUTCHER
 Samuel 116
BOWEN
 () 121; Rosanna 130
BOWER
 Elisabeth 132
BOWIE
 Elizabeth 123; Forrest 118; James P. 86; John 101; Mary 118; William 92, 118
BOWLING
 Ann 77; Betsey 125; Elisabeth 141; George 120; Gerard 60; Gerrard 59, 62, 68; John 54, 63, 74; Peggy 145; Simon 71; William 73, 77
BOWMAN
 Kean 93
BOYAR
 Henry 95; John 94
BOYD
 () 121; Ann 119, 132; James 90; John 119; Nancy 148
BOYER
 Elias 120; Elisabeth 127, 151; Henry 91; Margaret 136; Mr. 91, 93
BRADDICK
 Thomas 86
BRADLEY
 John 58, 62, 63, 105; Matthew 54, 55, 58-60, 62, 63, 105, 110, 115
BRAITHWAIT
 William 120

BRAMMELL
 () 134; Isaac 119
BRANNER
 John 63
BRANSON
 Vincent 119
BRAUNER
 John 69
BRAWNER
 Henry 120
BRAY
 Richard 119
BRENAR
 Christian 91
BRENT
 Henry 96
BRIANT
 Philip 105
BRICKETS
 Mrs. 93
BRICKLES
 George 119
Bridges:
 Difficult 57, 58, 64
BRIGHT
 John 90, 119; Mrs. 92
BRIM
 Betsey 135
BRITTINGHAM
 Elisabeth 125; James 120
BRITTON
 Barbara 133
BROADBENT
 Eliza 62; Elizabeth 63
BROADWATER
 Charles 55-57, 59, 69, 70, 73, 88, 98, 110, 113; Col. 72; Elizabeth 105; Guy 114; Maj. 69; Martha 77; Mary 70
BROADY
 Elizabeth 60
BROCCHUS/BROCCUS
 George 73; Matilda 118; Thomas 75, 120
BROCHUS/BROECHUS
 () 121; Thomas 86
BROCKETT
 Robert 120; Walter B. 120
BRONAUGH
 Capt. 110; Jeremiah 98, 102; Margaret 105
BROOK
 Sarah A. 119; William 119
BROOKBANK
 Mr. 93
BROOKE
 Elizabeth 20; Ignatius 119; Jane 143; Roger 14; Samuel 20, 44; Thomas 120

156

BROOKES
  Capt. 92; George 119
BROOKS
  Agnes 62; Rachel 143
BROOKSHIRE
  Sarah 109; William 103
BROWN
  () 121; Anderton 94; David 119;
  Dr. 78; Helen B. 120; James
  110, 119; John 120; John D.
  120; Margaret 33, 43; Martha
  12, 24, 37; Mary 105; Mrs. 93;
  Nicholas 33, 43; Patty 134;
  Polly 120; Samuel M. 79;
  William 77-80, 88, 90; William
  H. 8, 11, 21, 22, 24, 41
BROWNE
  Archibald 119
BROWNING
  James 119
BROWNLY
  Thomas 60
BRUCE
  Aaron 120; Ann 120
BRUFFIELD
  Samuel 119; Sarah 119
BRUMLEY
  Joseph 120
BRUMMETT
  William 104
BRUNER
  Catharine 118
BRUNTON
  John 97
BRYAN
  Hanson 119; Mary 56, 58-60,
  62, 63, 65, 68-70, 72; Philip
  105-107; Zephaniah 56, 58, 60,
  62, 73, 74, 76-78
BRYANT
  Mr. 75
BRYCE
  Hannah 92
BUCHANAN
  John 83; Mary 12, 13; Thomas
  103
BUCHANNAN
  Mary 40
BUCKEY
  Elizabeth 52
BUCKHANAN
  James 71
BUCKLAND
  William 119
BUCKLEY
  William 68
BUCKLY
  James 63
BUFFIERE
  Eleanor 139

Buildings:
  Barn 67; Corn House 67; Court
  House 57, 64; Dairy 67; Falls
  Warehouse 57, 64; Glebe House
  66; Hen House 70; Kitchen 67;
  Meat House 67; Meeting House
  1; Meeting House, description 9;
  Mill 10; Office 67; Parish Hall
  89; Stable 67; Tavern 24, 32;
  Theatre 18, 97; Tobacco
  Warehouse 90
BURFORD
  John A. 120
BURGESS
  Joseph 77, 78; Lucy 120; Penny
  148; William 106, 119
BURK
  Mary 103
BURKE
  James 119
BURKETT
  Massie 134
BURNES
  John 91; Mary 130; Mrs. 91
BURNETT
  Mary 134
BURNS
  Mr. 92; Patrick 91
BURR
  Thomas W. 90
BUSHBY
  Edward 65; William 110
Businesses:
  Alexandria Library iv; Elisha
  Powell & Conn 74; Glasford &
  Henderson 68, 69; Library of
  Congress iv; Library of Virginia
  iv, v; Merchants Bank 20, 21;
  Robert Adam & Co. 69; William
  Lyles & Co. 78
BUTCHER
  Ann 32, 37, 44; Butcher 9;
  Catharine A. 44; John 1, 3, 44;
  Jonathan 1, 5, 7, 9, 25, 28, 44;
  Phebe 7, 35, 37, 44; Robert H.
  44
BUTLER
  Catherine 93; Mr. 91
BUTSFIELD
  William 110
BUTT/BUTTS
  Adam 91; Capt. 118; Margaret
  136; Mark 83, 86, 118, 119;
  Mr. 93; Mrs. 91, 92
BUTTERS
  Mary 110
BUZHARDT
  Abner M. 94
BYRILL
  Mrs. 92

BYRNE
  Elisabeth 120; Mary 128

C

CAITHER
  Samuel 122
CALLAHAN
  James 122
Cameron Parish: 108
CAMERSON
  Anne 125
CAMPBELL
  James 96; Leah 96; Mary 79
CANBY
  Amos G. 34; Ann 44; Beulah 30,
  44; Eliza 43, 44; Elizabeth 30,
  34, 44, 45; Joseph 24, 30, 41,
  44; Mary 30, 34, 45; Samuel 30,
  44, 45; Sarah 24, 41; Thomas
  22, 25, 30, 41; Thomas Y. 44;
  William 23, 24, 30, 44; Yardley
  30, 44
CANNON
  James N. 123; Mary 135;
  Nathaniel 122
CANTERBURY
  Samuel 115
CARD
  John 122
CAREY
  Ann H. 41; Benjamin 122;
  Catharine 122; John C. 41; John
  E. 23, 48; Mildred 123; Patrick
  122
CARLIN
  William 55, 56, 58-60, 62, 63,
  65
CARLISLE
  Daniel 122
CARLYLE
  John 54-56, 58, 62, 65, 66, 69,
  110, 115
CARNE
  Joseph 123; Rebecca 124
CARPENTER
  Richard 104
CARR
  Susan B. 46; Susannah 12;
  Susannah B. 12
CARROLL
  John 65; Nicholas 100, 106, 115;
  Polly 127; Sinclair 123
CARSON
  Ann 151; J. 86; John 123; N.
  86; Samuel 123
CARTER
  Catherine 55; Henny 59; John
  94; Mary 130

157

CARTRIGHT/CARTWRIGHT
  Seth 86, 122
CARVEL
  Peter 122
CARVILLE
  Mr. 90; Mrs. 90; Peter 90
CASEY
  Biddy 143; Hannah 93
CASH
  Joseph 114, 115
CASSGROVE
  Nancy 79
CASSO
  John J. 122
CASTELLO
  Bridget 110; William 70
CASTILE
  Rebecca 133
CASTLE
  John 103
CATHERBY
  Molly 128
CATHERS
  Henry 63
CATLETT
  Charles I. 123; Charles J. 86; Charles S. 89; Mr. 89
CATTERTON
  Lucretia 136
CAVENDER
  Mary 132
CAVERLY
  Joseph 73, 79
CAVIN
  Sarah 15
CAWOOD
  Benjamin 123
CAYTON
  Penelope 125
CAYWOOD
  Susan 118
CAZENOVE
  () 123; A.C. 121; Ann M. 121; Anne 121; Anthony C. 121; Charles 121; Charlotte B. 121; Juliana 125; Lewis A. 121; Octavius A. 121; Paul 121; Paulina 121
Cemeteries:
  Christ Church 64, 83, 84, 94; Christ Church, lot owners 86; Christ Church, plan 85; Protestant Episcopal 80; Quaker 1, 3, 4, 8, 15, 17, 19, 25, 26, 28; Quaker (Washington) 30; Soldier's 94
CHADWELL
  Franny 141
CHAFFLINE
  Mary 146

CHAMBERLAIN
  Hannah 90
CHAMBERS
  Margaret 74, 76; Thomas 111
CHAMPNEYS
  William 101
CHANDLEE
  Goldsmith 1
CHANDLER
  Benjamin 103; Mrs. 124; William 103
CHAPIN
  Ann 150; Gurden 83, 86, 122; Mrs. 91
CHAPMAN
  George 72, 75, 76, 79, 88
CHARLES
  Duncan 122; Margaret 151; Mary 123
CHARLTON
  Jane 110
CHASE
  A. 86
CHASSON
  Lewis 122
CHATTAM
  Elisabeth 148
CHATTHAM
  Jane 130
CHAVELIER
  Mrs. 93
CHEENEY
  Lemuel 94
CHENEY
  Mary 30, 31
CHESHER
  Dorothy 103, 106
CHEVALIER
  Jeremiah 90; Mrs. 90
CHEVERILL
  Catherine 128
CHEW
  Rodger 60, 63, 68-71; Roger 65, 74, 91, 94
CHICHESTER
  Mr. 71
CHICK
  Charles 122
CHISHOLM
  Elisabeth 122
CHISHOM
  John 122
Christ Church:
  Burial Permits 89; Painting 84; Repairs 54; Sale of Pews 82
CHRISTIE
  John 123
CHRISTMAN
  John 123

CHRISTMASS
  Charles 100; John 100
CHRISTOPHER
  Christian 123
CHUNN
  Mr. 93
CHURCH
  () 123, 124; Gilbert 123; Henry 123; Mary 146; Robert 108, 111; Sarah 141
Churches:
  Baptist 21; Christ Church iv, 54; Episcopal iv, 80; Falls Church 55, 56, 58, 59, 60, 62-64, 68-70, 74, 80, 100, 112; First Presbyterian 117; Goose Creek 101; Pohick Church iv, 100, 101, 110, 112; Presbyterian v; Protestant Episcopal 79, 83, 89; Quaker iv; Upper Church 100, 110, 111, 112
CHURCHMAN
  Hannah 45; Hannah J. 22, 29, 42
Cities:
  Arlington v; Baltimore 46, 48, 53, 97; Boston 96; Brooklyn 34, 53; Detroit 53; Dumfries 95, 96; Georgetown 97; Hanover 44; Hillsborough 48; Jarmney 95; London 2, 24, 29, 44; Lorton iv; Lynchburg 34; New London 97; New Orleans 49, 50, 53; Norfolk 95, 132; Petersburg 32, 38, 52; Philadelphia 4, 5, 11, 25, 26, 27, 44, 45, 47, 53, 97, 117; Richmond 80; Trenton 29; Waterford 49; Westminster v; Williamsburg 113
CLAGETT
  Horatio 88; Mr. 87; Richard H. 88
CLARK
  Benjamin 75; Hezekiah 122; Isaac 123; Jane 133; John 122; Margaret 122; Mary 136, 150; Michael 78; Rhody 143; Robert 122
CLEMENTS
  Hannah 58; Samuel 122; William 123
CLEMENTSON
  Mr. 93
CLEMONS
  Lyzyan 150
CLEMSTER
  Elisabeth 136
CLEVENGER
  Phebe 130
CLIFFORD
  Mr. 92; Mrs. 93, 123; Nehemiah

122
CLIFTON
 William 71, 115
CLINTON
 Samuel 122
COALE
 Amelia 33, 43; Lewis 47
COATES
 Ann 2, 39; Margaret 120
COBURN
 Premier 122; Primus 91
COCKBURN
 James 110; Martin 98, 110
COCKE
 Ben 82; Benj. 83; Catesby 110
COCKERILLE
 Joseph 58
COCKRILL
 Joseph 70; Nancy 122; Sampson 77; Susanna 122
COFFER
 Francis 98, 107, 110; Mary 104; Thomas W. 98, 110
COFFIN
 Daniel 123; John 123; Sarah 120
COHAGAN/COHAGEN
 Janey 63; Jeremiah 59; John 122, 123; Tony 62
COHEN
 William 122
COLBERT
 Thomas 122
COLE
 Elisabeth 121; Elizabeth 1; Lewis 31; Lydia 31, 119; Nelly 136; Samuel 31; Thomas 121, 123; Trephesa 121; William 36, 45
COLLARD
 Eliza S. 121; Ellen 121; James I. 121; Rachel 121; Samuel 121, 122
COLLIER
 Mrs. 92
COLLINS
 () 121; Ann 21; Frances 145; William 102; William A. 123
COLLUM
 Elizabeth 110
COLSTON
 () 121
COLTON
 Uriah 55
COLVILL
 John 98
COMB
 John 90
COMBS
 Susanna 148

COMPTON
 Mary 106; Susanna 118; William 123
CONDRAN
 Robert 68
CONDREN
 Richard 106
CONN
 Elizabeth 134; Gerrard T. 75; Thomas 122
CONNEL/CONNELL
 James 56, 59, 110; John 100; Simon 100; William 92
CONNELLY
 Clara 48; James 62
CONNER
 Edward 110; Elisabeth 151; Francis 122; Hannah 103, 106; Patrick 103; Richard 106; Samuel 104, 108
CONNEY
 Dennis 122
CONNOR
 James 92
CONNORS
 Honoria 145
CONRAD
 B. 152
CONWAY
 Capt. 74, 84; Joseph 122; Margaret 121; Peggy 121; Richard 72-76, 79, 82, 88, 121; Robert 121-123
COOK
 Cherity 76; Eliza 125; George 122; Giles 79; Jacob 90; Mary 120; Mrs. 91
COOKE
 Catharine E. 121; Julia E. 121, 123; Margaret 141; Stephen 121; Thomas 122
COOKSON
 Mrs. 91
COONES
 Mary 125
COOPER
 Athy 134; Elisabeth 128; Hayley 90; Joel 75; Margaret 144; Mary 32; Nancy 122; Rachel 146; Samuel 124
COPE
 Mr. 63
COPENS
 William 65, 68
COPPER
 Cyrus 63, 79; Mrs. 90; Thomas 91, 122
CORBETT
 Martha 23, 30, 42, 45; Mary 30, 31; Sarah 23, 30, 42, 45;

Zacheriah 78
CORNETADY
 Peter 122
CORNISH
 Charles 106
CORRY
 Elisabeth 120
CORYELL
 George 90
COUDER
 Jeremiah 90; Mrs. 90
Counties:
 Bucks 4, 35, 50; Cecil 96; Charles 95; Charles City 45; Chester 4, 30, 32, 45, 46; Clark 45; Columbiana 50; Fairfax iv, 1, 38, 46, 84, 103; Hanover 4; Isle of Wight 21; Loudoun 18, 38; Montgomery 52; Prince George's 7; Prince William iv, 102; St. Mary's 108; Stafford 60, 89
Countries:
 Bermuda 117; Canada 51; England 16, 24, 26-28, 30, 44, 45, 52, 97; Great Britain 6, 20, 23, 24, 50, 98; Ireland 1; Scotland 95; West Indies 4
COUPAR
 Margaret 138
COURTNEY
 Mercy 130
COURTS
 Daniel 122; John 88; William 116
Courts: 1, 102
COVERT
 John 123
COVES
 B. 87
COWAN
 John 122
COWMAN
 John 31, 45
COX
 Gambriel 94; Harriet 123; James 94; Jesse 122; Mr. 92; Presley 64, 72, 77, 88, 114
COYLE
 Michael 63
COZEEN
 John 122
COZZENS
 Mary 141
CRACROFT
 Eliza O. 86
CRADOCK
 Elisabeth 145
CRAFFTS
 Anne 124

159

CRAFORD
  Thomas 106
CRAIG
  Charles 74; Jeanna 123; Mary 123; Samuel 84, 123
CRAIK
  Ann 130; James 82, 149; Mr. 92
CRAMM
  Samuel 123
CRAMPTON
  Rebecca 132
CRANCH
  William 87
CRANDELL
  () 123; John 123; Joseph 123, 124; Mrs. 123; Samuel 123; Sarah 135
CRANDLE
  Thomas 123
CRANFORD
  William 110
CRANK
  () 123
CRANSTON
  () 123; John 122; Mary A. 120
CRAWFORD
  John 121, 122; Martha 121; Mr. 110; Mrs. 91; Thomas 92; William 54, 121
CRAWLEY
  James 116
CRAYCRAFT
  Mr. 59
CREAGOR
  Mrs. 93
CREASE
  Anthony 88; Betsey B. 148; John H. 88, 123
CREEK
  William 123
Creeks and Runs: 84
  Backlick Run 58, 64; Broad Lick Run 57; Cameron 64; Difficult Run iv; Dogue Creek iv; Goose Creek 100, 101; Great Hunting Creek 57, 58, 64; Little Hunting Creek 57, 64
CREIGHTON
  Robert 123
CREW
  John 79; Unity 3
Crimes:
  Mahlon S. Scott 30; Samuel Sutton 26
CRINLIN
  John 106
CRISPIN
  John 122
CROAK
  Richard 122

CROMWELL
  John 16
CROOKE
  Priscilla 121
CROSBY
  Lewis 123
CROSS
  John 74; William 122
CROTCH
  William 6
CROUCHER
  Thomas 96
CROWE
  Lanty 95; Mary 95; Mr. 92; Mrs. 92
CRUMP
  Sally 143
CRUSE
  James 121; Martha 121; Thomas 121
CULLISON
  William 104, 110
CUNNINGHAM
  Archibald 65
CURREY
  John 106, 115
CURRY
  John 104
CURTAN
  Susanna 146
CURTIS
  Joseph 122
CUSHAN
  Capt. 123
CUSTIS
  George W. 83; John P. 75, 77, 88; Mr. 92

D

DADE
  Baldwin 88, 115; Charles S. 125; Francis 125; Mr. 82, 83; Parthenia 91; Townshend 54, 55, 57-63, 65, 66, 69-72, 84, 87, 88
DAFFEN
  Joseph G. 125
DAGEN
  Henry B. 86
DAILY
  Elinor 74
DAINGERFIELD
  Bathurst 86, 124; John 124
DAINTY
  John W. 101
DALTON
  Ann 143; Daniel 125; John 54-58, 60-63, 65, 66, 68, 69-73, 88, 105, 110, 114; Rachel 130; Tristram 88

DALY
  Thomas 76
DANA
  Charles B. 87
DANE
  Jacob 61
DANIEL
  James 124
DANLEY
  Tracey A. 150
DARBY
  Elizabeth 75; John 55
DARLING
  George 125, 126
DARLY
  Mary 128
DARNE
  Henry 55-57, 60, 63, 64, 71, 72, 88; Thomas 112
DARNELL
  John 125
DARRELL
  Rachel 122; Sampson 58-61, 114
DAVEY
  Davey 125, 126
DAVID
  David 124
DAVIDSON
  Basil H. 125; Eliza 124, 126; James 124; Margaret 124; William 124
DAVIES
  Ann 119, 120; Eliza 118
DAVIS
  A. 134; Arnold B. 45; Benjamin 86; Catharine 45; Charles 86; Daniel 125; Delilah 120; Edward 86; Elijah 125; Elizabeth 97, 100, 145; Gideon 22, 29, 45; Herephila 22, 45; John C. 45; Levi 22, 45; Martha 22; Mary 37, 106, 135; Mary A. 34, 52, 130; Mattey 148; Morgan 22, 45; Mr. 82, 93; Nancy 22, 118, 134, 145; Neamiah 115; Patty 45; Rebecca 123; Robert 106, 108; Rodney 22, 45, 51; Sally 151; Sarah 130; Susanna 128; Thomas 69, 81, 87, 97; William 109
DAY
  Catherine 143; Elisabeth 146; Horatio 125
DAYLEY
  Ellender 76
DAYLY
  Thomas 76-78
DEAD
  Miss 93; Mr. 93; Mrs. 93

DEAKINS
() 126; Jane 124; Margaret 124, 140, 151; William 124
DEAN
Hannah 124; John 124; Joseph 124; William 124
DEBLOIS
Lewis 83
DeBUTTS
Richard 125
DEEBLE
Mary 125; William 59
DeKRAFFT
F.C. 125
DELAWHAN
Martha 122
DEMOVILL
Sampson 114
DENEAL
James 103
DENEALE
George 83, 86, 88, 125; William 98, 110
DENICK
Martha 125
DENNETT
John L. 126
DENNISON
Debby 130
DENNY
Edmund 82
DEREA
Catherine 127
DERRINGTON
Mr. 92
DETTERLY
Michael 125
DEVANN
Jonathan 125
DEVAUGHN
Samuel 125
DEVEREUX
Elisabeth 146
DEWITT
Aaron 125
DICK
David 124, 125; Elisabeth 124; Elisha C. 12-14, 19, 22, 23, 30, 45, 110; Margaret 124
DICKSON
Anne 102; Mary 103
DISKINS
Daniel 58
DIXON
() 126; Eleanor 151; George 86; John 86, 124, 125; Mary 124; Mary A. 124; Mr. 93
DOLPHIN
Swann 124

DONALDSON
James 114, 115; John 79; William 68, 101, 115, 116
DORCEY
Elizabeth 123, 133
DORING
James 125
DORSEY
Miles 125
DOUDILL
Thomas 60
DOUGHERTY
Arthur 125; James 125; Polly 145
DOUGLAS
Charlotte 149; John W. 125; Nancy 144; Thomas 108
DOUGLASS
Archibald O. 124; Charlotte 124; Daniel 124-126; Dr. 83; Eliza 124; James 124, 125; John L. 125; Louisa 124; Margaret 119; Martha 122; Mary 126; Robert 104, 115; Sarah 126
DOVE
Alley 145; John 125; Thomas 79
DOW
Peter 79
DOWDALL
Colin 125
DOWNES
B. 93
DOWNEY
Elizabeth 78
DOWNING
Miller 36
DOWNS
Sarah 122
DOYLE
Ann 93; C. 74; Conrad 74; Ganet 125; James 106; Mrs. 93
DOZIER
James I. 114
DRAKE
Edward 125
DREW
Charles 125
DRINKER
Elizabeth 34, 45; George 2, 3, 8, 9, 12, 13, 26, 45; Hannah 45; Joseph 34, 43, 45; Rebecca 45; Ruth 37; Samuel 45; Susanna 34; Susannah 45; William 45
DRINNAN
Thomas 125
DRURY
Monica 143
DUBIS
Mr. 92

DUCKET
Mr. 90
DUFF
James 90
DUFFEY
() 126; Elizabeth 150; John 125; Mr. 93; Mrs. 126
DUKE
John 68
DULANY
Benjamin 82; Louisa 125; Mary 86, 104; Walter 124; William 125
DULING
Edward 54-59, 65, 68, 71, 88
DUNBAR
Jesse 125; Silas 51, 126
DUNCAN
Andrew 125; George 76; Robert 125
DUNDAS
Edward 126; Edward B. 124; Henry T. 124; John 124, 126; Nancy 124; Nancy M. 133; Sophia M. 141; Thomas 124
DUNKIN
Blanch F. 63; Catherine 135
DUNLAP
() 126; Elisabeth 126; Esther A. 124; James 124; John 125, 126; Mary 118, 124; Mr. 92; Mrs. 126; William 124, 126
DUNMOOR
Mr. 110
DUNN
Elisabeth 127; James 125; Martha 133; William 90, 96
DUNNINGTON
Martha 125
DURINGTON/DURRINGTON
Ann 127
DUVALL
Catherine 140
DUVALL
Nelly 145; William 78
DYE
Elisabeth 124; Reuben 124, 125
DYER
Anthony 124; Caroline 124; Francis 125; Gideon 125; Harriet 124; Julia A. 124; Mary 124; Sarah 120
DYKES
Andrew 124; Elisabeth 126; Mungo 124, 125; Nancy L. 124
DYMEM
Philip 125
DYSON
() 126; Hannah 120

E

EACHES
  Ann 20, 37, 45; Nancy 19
EARLE
  Mr. 93
EARP
  Jane 122; Mary 77
EASTON
  John H. 49
EATON
  Mary 148
EDMUNSTON
  Mr. 93
EDWARDS
  Elisabeth 145; Eliza 77, 78; Elizabeth 77, 78; Polly 134; Sarah 90; Susan 70; Susannah 71, 74, 90
EGLING
  Amelia 130
ELDER
  James E. 94
ELGAR
  Ann 20, 28, 45; Eliza 28; Elizabeth 20, 45; Margaret 20, 28, 45
ELKINS
  Benjamin 116
ELLICOTT
  Andrew 18, 40; Ann 30, 33, 38, 45; Elizabeth 18, 37, 40; Hannah 19, 40; John 19, 47; John A. 19, 40; Jonathan 18, 40; Mary 18, 19, 40; Nathaniel 18, 40; Rachel 30, 45
ELLIOTT
  Ann 36; Eli 36; Elizabeth 36, 45; Elliott 45; Jesse H. 45; Margaret 36; Mary 36; Reuben 36; Sarah 36; Upton 36; William 36. 60
ELLIS
  Anne 136
ELLISON
  Martha 13, 21; Mary 77; William 23; William C. 45
ELLZEY
  Lewis 98, 102, 114; Mary 102; Patience 102; Sarah 102; Stacey 102; Thomazin 98, 110
ELSER
  Mary 143
ELTON
  John 78
EMBERSON
  Richard 110
EMBREE
  Daniel 26, 32, 45; David 42; Hannah M. 26, 45; Margaretta 26, 45; Rachel 26, 45; Sarah 26, 45; William 26; William L. 32, 42, 45
EMERY
  Peggy 136
EMMET
  Joseph 92; Josiah 91; Mr. 93
EMMETT
  Margaret 125
EMMIT/EMMITT
  Eve 63; Paul 63, 68-70
EMMONS/EMONS
  Edward 98, 105
ENDS
  Elisabeth 127
ENGLISH
  Walter 101
ESTEN
  Catharine 121
EVANS
  Catharine 120; Drucilla 86; Ephraim 91; Jane 106; John 91; Margaret 54, 110; Mr. 91-93; Mrs. 91; Nancy 135; Phillis 140; Sarah 139; Thomas 101, 104
EVEY
  Elizabeth 79

F

FAIRBROTHERS
  John 127
FAIRFAX
  Anne 123; Bryan 70, 80, 87, 88; Col. 115; George W. 98; Thomas 80, 88; William 98, 99, 115
Fairfax Parish: 97
  Boundaries 57, 64; Building a Vestry House 63; Building Glebe House 66; Building of Church 56; Building of Two Churches 56; Church Additions 79; Church Repairs 59, 60, 65, 68, 77, 78; Church Sold 60; Orphans 102; Pews Sold 69; Rectors of 87; Sale of Pews 65, 79, 82; Vestry House to be Built 55; Vestrymen of 88
FAIRFIELD
  Mr. 91; Reuben 127
FALKNER
  Richard 75
FARGUSON
  John 98
FARMER
  Mr. 93
FARNESTER
  Nancy 134
FARQUHAR
  Charles 30, 45; Margaret 46; Roger 49
FARR
  Margaret 22, 29, 42, 45
FARRELL
  Ann 152; Anne 124; Mary 126; Robert 127; Sarah 119; Thomas 126, 127
FAW
  Abraham 127; Mrs. 127
FAWCETT
  John 127; Lydia 2
FEAGAN
  James 101
FEAGANS
  Joseph 127
FEAGEN
  Molly 151
FEARSON
  Samuel S. 87
FEIZER
  Adam 91
FELSH
  Margaret 130
FENDALL
  Mr. 90; Philip R. 83, 88
FERGURSON
  Jermey 91
FERGUSON
  Anna 123; Zaccheus 127
FERGUSSON
  Jenny 122; Nancy 150
FERRELL
  James 71
Ferries: 62
  Johnson's 110; Rock Creek 57, 64
FERRIS
  Ann 14; John 14; Sarah 14
FIEGATE
  Patsey 135
FIELD
  Hannah 15; Horace 86; Horatio 127
FIELDON
  William 127
Fights: 33
FINDLAY
  Sarah 123
FINDLEY
  Mary 145
FINLAY
  Henry 127
FIRTICH
  Charles 94
FISHER
  Dawson 2, 3, 39; John 74; Mary 146; Rebecca 130

FITHEY
  David 106
FITZGERALD
  John 90
FITZHUGH
  Nathaniel 86; Nicholas 81, 83, 88; William 83; William F. 88
FITZPATRICK
  Thomas 127
FLANAGAN
  Cleary 130
FLATFORD
  Thomas 127
FLAX
  Francis 110
FLEET
  Lewis 98
FLEMING
  Andrew 126, 127; Andrew J. 126; Ann 127; Anna 126; Catherine S. 126; Elisabeth 126; H.L. 94; John 126; Kitty 132; Margaret 126; Mary 126; Peter 127; Peterson 126; Robert 126; Thomas 58, 66, 69
FLETCHER
  Elisabeth 145; George 88, 106; Sarah 92; Thomas 71; William 127
FLINN
  Michael 90
Flour: 21
FLOWER
  Samuel 127
FLOYD
  Mary 126; William 65
FLUDD
  Eleanor 119
FLYNN
  George 116
FOARD
  Mr. 93
FOLEY
  Dennis 127
FOOTE
  Ann 104
FORBES
  Hannah 106
FORD
  Andrew 127; Edward 98, 107; John 98; Thomas 98, 104, 109, 110, 114
FORGUSON
  Cumberland 70
FORSEY
  Winifred 130
FORSTER
  George 65; John 65, 127
FOSTER
  Peter 86

FOULKE/FOULKES
  Anthony 33, 34, 43, 45; Eleanor 33, 34, 43, 45; Phebe 33, 43, 45; Philip 34; Sarah P. 33, 34, 43, 45; William 31, 33, 45; William R. 21, 35, 43; William W. 34, 43, 45
FOUSHEE
  Mr. 93; Susanna G. 128
FOWLER
  Kitty 145
FOXTON
  William 127
FOXWOOD
  Daniel 127
FRANCE
  Charlotte 143
FRANCIS
  George 62; John G. 127; Matthew 127; Thomas 127
FRANKLAND
  Ralph 104
FRASIER
  Adam 91
FRAZIER
  Alexander 71, 73, 74, 76; Daniel V. 94; Edward 74; Joseph 90; Mr. 73-75; William 78, 79
FREDERICK
  Henry 127
FREEMAN
  Bennett 127; Samuel 127; Sarah 120
FRENCH
  Daniel 54-57, 59-62, 88, 98, 110, 114
FRISBY
  John 74
FRISTOE
  Peggy 146
FRIZBY
  John 74
FRIZZELL
  John 74
FROBELL
  J. 88
FROST
  Mr. 71
FRY
  Elisabeth 151; Leonard 127
FULFORD
  Joseph 127; Mary 128
FULLERTON
  Ann 136
FULMORE
  John 127
FULTON
  Mary A. 151; Mrs. 92

G

GABEL
  Mary 63
GADSBY
  Ann S. 140; John 83
GAHAGAN
  Thomas 104
GALAHAN
  Mrs. 92
GALE
  Nicholas 104
GALLIE
  Mary A. 127
GALLOWAY
  Jeremiah 128; Sophia 135
GALVIN
  Mr. 93
GAMMEL
  Mary 62
GAMON
  Mary 63
GARAT
  Jeanie 128
GARDINER
  William 98
GARDNER
  Merab 45; Rebecca 148; Silvester 104; William 98, 110
GARLICK
  Patience 130
GARNER
  Thomas 128; William 128
GARRET
  Nicholas 55
GARRETT
  Arthur 108; Eleanor 122; Nancy 141; Nicholas 58
GARROW
  John 128
GASCH
  Frederick 128
GATES
  Elizabeth 133; Isaac 105-107; Samuel 112, 128; Sarah 148; William 110, 128
GEIGER
  Anne 118
GEORGE
  Isaac 87; Martin 128
GESH
  Frederick 128
GIBBENS
  George 104
GIBORIE
  John 128
GIBSON
  Amos 3, 5, 39; Isaac 128; John 98, 99, 110; William L. 87

GIDDINGS
  Rebecca 78
GILBERT
  Amos 22, 24, 41
GILL
  James 128; John 128; Mr. 92
GILLIES
  Dr. 93; James 128
GILLINGHAM
  Catharine 27, 33, 43, 46; Eliza 43; Elizabeth 27, 33, 46; Esther 33, 43, 46; Isaac 27, 33, 43, 46; Jane 27, 38, 43, 46; Jehu 27, 46; William 27, 33, 43, 46
GILLIS
  J. 82
GILMAN
  () 129; Ann 127; Cornelia 127; Ephraim 127; Eugenia 127; Julia A. 127; Laura A. 127, 128; Lucy 127
GILPIN
  Ann 127; George 77, 79, 80, 82, 86, 88; Thomas 23, 24
GIRD
  () 128; Christopher 82; J. 128; Mary 150; Mr. 93
GLADDEN
  Susan 120
GLADDING
  John 106; William 107
GLADIN
  John 104; William 100
GLADING
  William 114, 115
GLADWIN
  Frances 103; John 103
GLANDERS
  John 128
GLANDES
  Anthony 128
GLASGOW
  Anna 125; Mary 119
GLASSELL
  Mrs. 92
GLOCESTER
  James 103, 106
GLOVER
  Mr. 93; Thomas R. 128
GOAD
  Joseph 110
GODFREY
  William 98
GOHEGAN
  Michael 91
GOLDSMITH
  Catherine 151; Mary 118
GOLIER
  Dorcas 141

GONSALVES
  Francis 128
GOOD
  Mr. 91, 92; Susanna 143
GOODE
  Samuel 92
GOODES
  George 93; Mr. 93
GOODIN
  James 54
GOODING
  Eleanor 122; Harriet 151; John 128
GOODWIN
  Hepsiba 136
GOOSLEN
  Isaac 75
GORBELL
  Amelia 78
GORDON
  Alexander 86; David 65
GORE
  John 116; William 5, 6
GOSBEL
  John 76
GOSS
  Andrew 128
GOSSAM/GOSSOM
  William 105, 106
GOUGH
  Thomas 71
GOURD
  Joseph 65, 68
GOVER
  Anthony 9; Anthony P. 17, 46; Caroline 46; Cornelia 46; Jane 46; Mary A. 46; Robert 5, 12, 40; Sarah 18, 37
GOWAN
  Caty 150; Joseph 128
GOWEN
  William 102
GRACE
  Pat 116
GRADY
  Grigsby 128
GRAFFORT
  Thomas 128
GRAHAM
  David 128; John 69, 101, 111, 115; William 73, 76, 77
GRANT
  Mary 111; Nancy 125
GRAY
  Ann 130, 141; Edward 128; Emma 127; Hester 130; James 128; John 73, 115; Levy 128; Mary 104, 106; Priscilla 128; Robert 127, 128; William 73

GRAYSON
  Spence 73; William 58, 69, 111
GREEN
  Caleb 128; Charles 98, 111, 115; Elisabeth 128; Frederick 128; George 128; James 64, 128; Lydia 2, 6, 39; Priscy 119; Sarah 117; Shadrack 104, 108; Susanna 120; Thomas 128; William 92
GREENAWAY
  Rebecca 128
GREENE
  Elisabeth 119
GREENWAY
  Joseph 90
GREENWOOD
  John 128
GREGG
  Albinah 46
GRETTER
  Elias T. 128; Elizabeth 68; Mary 128; Mary G. 120; Michael 60, 62, 63
GREY
  Martha 111
GRIFFIN
  Charles 105, 106, 109, 111; Elisabeth 125; Polly 143
GRIFFIS
  Richard 55
GRIFFITH
  Amos 23; Camillus 86; Child 90; David 73, 76, 77, 79, 87; Esther 15; Mr. 75, 91
GRIGSBY
  Ann 106; James 106; Mary A. 122; Witherson 68
GRIMES
  Frances 125; John 128; Robert 128; William 60
GRIMSLEY
  James 103
GRINNEL
  Mockey 135
GRISBY
  Eliza 151
GRISWOLD
  George 87
GROVE
  William 100
GROVES
  Anne 149
GRUBB
  John 88; Mary 13, 20, 37, 41
GRYMES
  John 92, 106; William 128
GUEST
  Joshua 128
GULLATT
  Betsey 128; James 128; William

128
GUNN
  Obediah 128
GUNNELL
  Allen 76; Henry 58, 62, 65, 69-72, 78, 88, 98; John 62, 64, 128; William 62, 63, 71
GUNSTON
  Mary 111
GUY
  Miranda 25, 46
GUZMAN
  Peggy 127

H

HADEN
  Garret 130; Stephen 130
HAGAN
  Mary 78
HAGERTY
  Patrick 91
HAGGIN
  Joseph 78
HAHN
  John 74
HAINES
  Beulah 20, 37; Daniel 20, 23, 24, 41; John 1; Maria 20, 24; Rebecca 20, 24; Susan 20, 24
HAINS
  Mr. 92
HAIRBOTTLE
  Elizabeth 106
HALBERT
  Isaac 61, 106; Mary 76; Sarah 76
HALE
  Michael 111; Mrs. 93
HALL
  Elisabeth 129; Elisabeth B. 135; Elizabeth 122; Grace 129, 131; James 129, 130; Jemima 151; John S. 129, 131; Lawrence 130; Letty 128; Mary G. 129; Mr. 83, 93; Robert C. 130; Sarah 20; Sarah O. 20; Thomas S. 20; William 104, 129; William J. 129, 131
HALLEY
  Benoni 109, 111; James 114
HALLOCK
  James 23
HALLOWELL
  Benjamin 30, 46, 49; Caleb S. 35, 46; Caroline 46, 49; Charles 46; H.C. 49; Henry C. 46; James 46; John E. 46; Margaret 30, 37, 49; Mary J. 46; Mary S. 32, 33, 43, 46

HALLWOOD
  Charles 131
HAME
  Mary 68
HAMILTON
  Ann 46, 106; Arrabella 106; David 46, 130; Eliza 133; James 98, 115; Jane 123; Polly 146; Robert 111, 130; Susanna 131
HAMMOND
  James 130; Mr. 68
HAMON
  Samuel 54
HAMPSON
  Bryan 82, 129; Leonora 129; Paul 129
HAMPTON
  John 114
HAND
  Sarah H. 151; Tryphesia 123
HANLEY
  John 77
HANNA
  Elisabeth 125
HANNAH
  Alexander 131; Hannah 41; Jane 128; John 131
HANNON
  William H. 131
HANSON
  Elizabeth 106; Miss 92; Samuel 90
HARDEN
  Elisabeth 130
HARDGROVE
  Pollard 130
HARDIN
  William 57, 64
HARDING
  Lettice 132; Mary 131
HARDY
  Ann 133; Charles 130; John 130; Letitia 135; Margaret 78
HARDYMAN
  Thomas 130
HARGIS
  Abraham 111
HARLE
  Robert 92; William 111, 112
HARLEY
  Enoch 130
HARMAN
  Henry 107; Mary 133
HARPER
  () 131; Ann 33; Charles 129; Dorothy 96; Edward 131; Elizabeth 133; Fanny R. 143; James 130; Joel 129; John 91, 129-131; John W. 96; Joseph 129, 131; Joshua R. 129; Julia

129; Leonard 112; Mary 129, 148, 149; Mary A. 129; Mary D. 147; Mrs. 129; Peggy 149; Robert 129-131; Rosa 131; Sarah 129, 135; Sophia 131; Washington T. 129; William 129; William W. 130
HARRIS
  () 131; Benjamin 88; James 131; Joseph 130; Mr. 91; Nancy 122; S. 93
HARRISON
  George 131; Mary 93; Richard 93, 130; Robert 63; Robert H. 68; Sally 119; Thomas 114
HARRISS
  Anne 141
HARROWER
  Hynam 131
HART
  Daniel 111; Thomas 77
HARTER
  Joseph 27
HARTLOVE
  John 75
HARTSHORNE
  Anna E. 52; Hannah 46; Hugh 46; Mary 9, 38, 52, 129; Pattison 10, 40; Peter 16; Robert 6, 7, 39; Sarah 12; Sarah S. 46, 48; Saunders W. 129; Susannah 37, 38; William 1-3, 8, 11, 17, 26, 38, 46, 48, 75, 79, 129
HASKINGS
  Mary 106
HASLIP
  Margaret 106
HASSEL
  Mrs. 91
HATTON
  Hatty 129
HAWKE
  Mr. 91
HAWKES
  Elisabeth 150
HAWKINS
  Benjamin 130; John 79; Mary 65; Sarah 65
HAWLEY
  James 114
HAYCOCK
  Mr. 93; William 130
HAYES
  Andrew 90, 92; Fielder 130; Mr. 93; Sarah 123
HAYLEY
  James 90; Mrs. 90
HAYNE
  Susanna 133

HAYS
　Erastus W. 94
HEADRICK
　Robert 75
HEARTELY
　Mr. 93
HEATH
　Charles 130; Margaret 122
HEDRICK
　Ann 91; Mr. 91; Thomas 91
HEINEMAN
　Margaret 140; Mary 151; Sarah 139
HELM
　John 90, 91
HENDERSON
　Alexander 99, 106-109, 111; Mr. 69
HENGARTY
　William 130
HENLY
　John 78
HENNIKEN
　Ann 119
HEPBURN
　Agnes 131
HERBERT
　Fanny 95; Mr. 68; Noblet 88; Thomas 79, 95; William 75-80, 83, 86, 88, 90
HEREFORD
　John 114
HERLIHY
　David 95
HERRON
　G.S. 94
HERYFORD
　Frances 102; George 102; Jane 102; John 99, 102, 111
HESS
　Jacob 90, 97
HESSEE
　John 76
HESSEN
　Phillis 151
HESTON
　Ann 16; Charles 16, 25, 41; Jane 16, 25, 41; Joseph 16, 26, 42, 46; Letitia 16; Letitia M. 28, 42, 46; Samuel 2, 8, 39; William 16, 26, 42, 46
HEWES
　Aaron 1, 2, 6, 10, 11, 13, 16, 17, 26, 39, 40, 79; Abram 46; Deborah 16, 21, 22, 40, 52; Eliza 46; James A. 32, 43, 46; John 18; Mary 16, 37, 40; Mary A. 17, 40, 46; Mr. 93; Rachel 37, 46; Sarah A. 16, 40; Sarah P. 17, 40; Susan 37

HEWETT
　Mrs. 93
HIBBARD
　Jane 14
HICKMAN
　Mary 123
HIGGINSON
　John 111, 115
HILL
　Barton 130; Elisabeth 141; George 90; Jane 129; John 130; John B. 130; Lawrence 129; Mary 141; Mr. 91; Mrs. 93; Samuel 75; Sarah 127; Shadrack 59, 62, 69, 76; Silvam 129
HILTON
　Mary 148
HINDMAN
　Mr. 90
HINSHAW
　William W. 44, 53
HIPKINS
　Lewis 80, 88
HIRST (see "Hurst")
　John 1
HOATZ
　Peter 130
HODGES
　William 91
HODGESON
　William 83, 86, 88, 91
HODGKIN
　Mary 131
HODGKINS
　John 130; Mary 132
HODGSON
　Charles H. 131
HOGARTHY
　Dr. 90
HOGARTY
　Mr. 93
HOGNER
　Martin 130
HOGUE
　Charles 130
HOIT
　Reuben 130
HOLBERT
　Thomas 76
HOLDSWORTH
　Joseph 104
HOLLINDUFF
　Henry 130
HOLLINSBURY
　Richard 58
HOLLIS
　John 104, 106, 115
HOLLISS
　John 111

HOLMES
　Hannah J. 43; Isaac 33, 43, 51, 129; Lot 31, 35, 43, 46; Margaret 129; Sarah 104
HOLT
　Edward 58
HONEST
　Jean 75; John 76
HOOD
　Benjamin 130
HOOE
　Bernard 88; Col. 79; James H. 88; Robert T. 76-80, 82, 88
HOOFF
　Lawrence 79, 82, 90, 91
HOOKES
　John 130
HOOPER
　Elisabeth 151; James 61; Mary 59, 60; Robert 130; Thomas 60
HOPKINS
　Basil B. 33, 46; Deborah 20, 38, 46; Elizabeth 13, 47; Hannah 25, 48; Hannah H. 20; Hannah S. 35; Isaiah 13, 17, 40; John 35, 46; Richard 107; Richard S. 33, 46; Samuel 48; Sarah J. 35; William 7-9
HORNER
　Elizabeth 15, 24; Isaac 15, 24; John 15, 24, 41, 90, 130; Lydia 2, 4, 15, 24, 37, 41; Lydia A. 15, 24; Martha B. 15, 23, 41; Mr. 91, 92; Phebe 27, 31, 38, 46; Thomas F. 15, 16, 40
Horse Races: 36
HORSEMAN/HORSMAN
　William 58, 63, 77
HORWELL
　Charles 130
HOSKINS
　Sarah 117
HOUGH
　Amelia 26, 31, 38, 46, 47; Catharine 47; David C. 96; Edward S. 46; George S. 11, 12, 15, 19, 24, 25, 28, 46; Harrison 46; Mahlon 26, 31, 47; Mary 38, 47; Robinson 21, 47; Sophia 47
HOUSE
　David 130
HOUSLEY
　Joseph 102
HOUSMAN (see "Horsman")
　William 62
HOVERMAN
　Martin 130
HOWARD
　Ann 86; Elisabeth 136; Elizabeth

139; Mary 68, 69; Mr. 91; Mrs. 93; Rosetta 140; Thomas 70, 72
HOWEL
  Philip 107
HOWELL
  David 34, 47; Hannah M. 34, 43; James 34; Philip 100, 111; Sarah 34
HOWLAND
  Abraham 27, 42; Abram 19, 27, 47; Thomas H. 14, 28, 29, 47
HOY
  () 129; Charlotte 129; Nancy 129
HOZIER
  Hannah 30, 35, 47; James M. 30, 32, 47; Maria 30, 35, 47
HUBBOLD
  John 131
HUBBUT
  Jacob 71
HUBLE
  Polly 125
HUCK
  Joseph N. 47; Mary 32, 38, 42; Rebecca 32; Rebecca N. 43, 47; Richard 32, 43; Richard S. 47, 52; Thomas V. 16, 21, 22, 28, 29, 32, 42, 47, 50
HUDSON
  Esther H. 128
HUGH
  Susan 37
HUGHES
  Isaiah B. 21, 47; John 20, 40, 68, 87; Mary 65; Mr. 62, 94; Nancy 22, 45; Thomas 130
HUGHS
  John 14
HULL
  Samuel 101, 102
HUMPHREYS
  Rebecca 148
HUNN
  Jonathan 11
HUNT
  Philip 131; Priscilla 26; Richard 60, 62, 63, 68; William 78
HUNTER
  () 131; Alexander 131; Catharine A. 120; Colin 129; Cordelia M. 131; Eliza 125; George 131; Hatty H. 129; Henrietta 130; Henrietta H. 130; Janet 129; John 57, 59, 71, 72, 77, 78, 88, 105, 111, 114, 129; John C. 88; Margaret 125; Martha A. 130; Mrs. 131; Robert 131; Samuel E. 129; William 129, 131; William F. 129

HUNTINGTON
  William 130
HUNTLEY
  George 130
HURDLE
  Susanna 20; Susanna H. 21, 23, 41, 42; Susannah H. 22, 26, 47
HURLEY
  Daniel 130; John 106; Morris 130
HURST
  James 70, 73; John 58, 62, 64, 70, 111
HUSSEY
  Henry 104
HUTCHERSON;
  Ann 75, 76
HUTCHINGS
  Ann 95; John 95
HUTCHINSON
  Andrew 99, 111; John 24, 47; Mary 75; Mr. 112; Samuel 1, 20, 24, 26, 29, 47; Thomas 24, 47
HUTCHISON
  Mary 74
HUTTON
  Rebecca 107

I

IAMS
  Becca 125
Indians: 2, 3, 7
INGLE
  Joseph 86, 131
INGLIS
  James 131
INGRAM
  Hannah 139
INSLEY
  Peggy 127
IRONMONGER
  Lucy 136
IRVINE
  James 90
IRWIN
  Ann H. 23, 41; Elizabeth 37; Hannah 13, 14, 53; James 30, 31, 88; Thomas 18, 19, 42, 131
ISLER
  George 97; Mary 125
ISRALEAN
  Jasper 131

J

JACKSON
  Hannah 1, 4, 39; Isaac 4, 39; Jane 123, 141; John 64, 88; Mr. 92; Nancy 135; Sarah 107;

William 132
JACOB
  Mrs. 92; Thomas 86
JACOBS
  Edward H. 132; Joseph 107; Mrs. 91
JAMES
  Dr. 108; Henry 132; Ruth 27, 49; William 132
JAMESSON
  R.B. 82
JAMIESON
  Andrew 132; Charles 133; George 132, 133; Mary 132, 133; Robert 132
JANNEY
  Abel 133; Abijah 14, 15, 18, 19, 31, 33, 34, 47; Albina 10; Albinah 40; Ann 38, 41; Ann S. 33, 43; Anna 10, 15, 18, 27, 31, 32, 40, 47-49; Anthony B. 48; Aquila 1, 4, 10, 39, 40; Asa M. 18, 30, 35, 42, 47; Benjamin 6, 7, 39; Caroline 47; Caroline W. 25, 41; Charles W. 25, 41; Cornelia 10, 40, 48; Cosmelia 37, 47; Daniel 39; David 49; E. 37; Edward A. 47, 48; Edward H. 47; Eleanor 28, 47; Elisha 1, 2, 10, 40, 46, 49; Eliza 35, 47; Elizabeth 6, 7, 13, 15, 25, 28, 31, 32, 37, 38, 39, 41, 47-49; Elizabeth W. 22, 38; Ellen 48; Ellen E. 47; Ellen H. 47; Emma 48; Esther 22, 25, 42; Francis H. 47; George 22, 25, 41; Hannah 8, 17, 18, 20-22, 25, 27, 39, 42, 47; Hannah A. 48; Hannah M. 18, 34, 43, 47; Hannah S. 34; Henry 20, 28, 41, 47, 51; Hugh S. 47; Isaac 9, 15, 40; Isaac M. 48; Isaac R. 11; Isaiah 22, 25, 42; Isaiah B. 47; Israel 1, 19, 21, 25, 39, 41; Israel H. 29, 47; Jacob 3, 7, 8, 15, 20, 22, 25, 28, 41, 42, 47; Jacob F. 47; James 10, 40; James M. 29, 47; Jane 18, 29, 31, 34, 38, 47; Jane E. 48; Janney 13, 50; John 1, 3, 5-10, 12, 17, 19, 26, 28, 31, 40, 47, 48; John H. 48; John T. 48; Jonathan 15, 19, 28, 48; Joseph 8, 13-15, 25, 48; Judith 9, 11, 37, 40; Levis 6, 7, 39; Lewis 20, 28, 41, 47; Lydia 35, 47; Lydia N. 47; Margaret 48; Mary 6, 7, 10, 19, 20, 28, 37, 39-41, 47, 49; Mary A. 39, 48; Mary J. 47; Moses 3, 5, 6, 9, 11, 12, 40, 132; Mrs. 133; Oliver 11, 29,

40, 48; Phebe A. 27, 48, 49;
Philip 20, 28, 41; Philip H. 47;
Phineas iv, 4, 7, 9, 12, 15, 17,
19, 28, 46, 48; Pleasant 29, 38,
48; Rachel 47; Rebecca 39, 47;
Richard 26, 42; Richard F. 15;
Richard M. 18, 34, 35, 47, 48;
Richard T. 48; Ruth 7, 10, 22,
37, 39, 40; Ruth H. 25, 41;
Samuel 32; Samuel M. 18, 31,
32, 47, 48; Sarah 16-18, 23-25,
37, 40, 42, 46; Sarah J. 29, 38,
48; Susan 25, 42; Susanna 22;
Susannah 25, 41; Tacey M. 47;
Tamsin 47; Tamson 18; Thamsin
47; William 39
JARBER
Cassandra 147
JAWIN
Ann 48; Elizabeth 48; Hannah
48; James 48; Mary 48; Thomas
48; William H. 48
JENKINS
Charles 74; James 57, 76;
Jemima 86; Johnston 132;
Keziah 59; Mary 119; Sarah
134; Thomas 76
JENNINGS
Alexander 100; Anne 84; Daniel
61-63, 84
JENNISON
Priscilla 91
JEROME
Elisabeth 123
JOACHIM
Henry C. 132
JOBBIN
Mr. 93
JOBSON
David 132
JOHNS
George 132; Peter 132
JOHNSON
Joseph 101, 102; Massey 107;
Rachel 26; William 74, 111
JOHNSTON
Agnes 123; Alexander M. 132;
Anne 133; Charles 132; Charles
A. 132; Dennis M. 133; George
111; Henny 147; Hezekiah 132;
James 132; James H. 132; Jane
132, 133; Jane S. 131; Jean 132;
John 132, 133; John D. 132;
Margaret M. 132; Mary 132;
Mary A. 133; Mary M. 132;
Samuel 61, 132; Sarah 122;
Sarah C. 132; Susanna 119;
William 132
JOLLIFFE
Elizabeth 8, 17, 40; John 8, 17,
40; Joseph 17, 40; Mary 8, 17,
40; Rebecca 8, 17, 37, 40;
William 8, 13, 17, 40
JOLLY
John 90
JONES
Ann 132; Catesby 132; Charles
132; David 111; Jonathan 132;
Martha 6-8; Mrs. 93; Robert 58,
59; Sarah 132; Thomas 132;
Winefred 103
JORDAN
Jesse 132; Joshua 132; Mr. 93
JOURDAN
Angel J. 111
JUDGE
Andrew 76; Margaret 31-33, 37,
43, 48; Rachel 13, 14
JURA
Mary 125

K

KAY
Helena 144
KEACH
Samuel 133
KEAN
John 90; Mr. 91
KEARSLEY
Sarah 142
KEATING
Ann 138; Edward 133; Sarah
132
KEATON
Lucy 138; Mary 91
KEEN
John 105; William 114
KEENE
Elisabeth 141; James 133;
Newton 88, 133
KEETH
Joseph 69
KEITCH
Samuel 82
KEITH
Alexander 90; James 79, 82, 86,
88, 102, 133; Mary 124; Reuel
87
KELLY
Elisabeth 151; James 133; John
133; Katherine 92; Martha 140;
Mary 143, 148; Mary A. 133;
Rebecca 133; Samuel 107
KENNA
Catherine 150
KENNEDY
James 133, 134; Letty 133;
Sarah 91; Timothy 69; William
133
KENNON
Michael 104
KENNY
Moses 133
KENT
Absolom 107; Benonie 105; Jane
105; Jean 105; John 133; Martha
146; Melinda 130; Nancy 118;
Prise 107; Sabina 143; Samuel
104
KENWORTHY
Rebecca 6, 14, 17, 37, 39, 40;
William 2-6, 14, 15, 17, 39, 40
KERR
Alexander 133; John 107
KEY
Eleanor 145; F.S. 30
KEYLING
James 86
KIBBY
Alexander 133
KIDD
Mr. 93
KIDWEL
William 104
KIDWELL
Benjamin 133; Elisabeth 133;
John 133
KILMASTER
John 58
KILTON
() 133
KIMBER
Joseph 91; Mrs. 92
KINCAID
() 133; Eliza 125; Isabel 133;
John 133
KING
() 105; Aminta 132; Ann 120;
Anna 138; Benjamin 107, 133;
Elisabeth 141; James 133;
Jemima 145; John 115; Rebecca
141; Sampson 107; Samuel 133;
Stephen 106, 107; Susanna 122,
134; William 133
KINGSBURY
Damulian 133; James 133
KINSELL
Mary 125
KINSEY
Elizabeth 34; Ezra 48; Rebecca
135; Ulysses 10
KIRBY
William 133
KIRK
Ann 148; Grafton 105, 107, 111;
Samuel 133
KIRKLAND
Richard 103

KITCHEN
  William 109
KITELY
  Rachel 130; Sarah 146
KLINE
  Catherine 128
KNOWLES
  John 133
KOONES
  Freiderick 82
KORN
  John 86, 90
KURTZ
  Daniel 35, 48

L

LADD
  () 135; Elisabeth A. 134; Joseph 134; Samuel 134; Sarah 135; William 134, 135
LAGETON
  Benjamin 90
LAKE
  Cassina 122
LAMMOND
  Alexander 134
LANDRES/LANDRESS
  Henry W. 134, 135
LANE
  Elisabeth 141; Henry S. 101; Richard 134; Sarah 11; Thomas 75
LANGHAM
  Ann 62
LANGTON
  Judie 111
LANHAM
  John 134, 135; Letty 128; Susan 128
LANPHIER
  Elizabeth 145
LARKIN
  Joseph 92
LASWELL
  Jacob 103
LATHAM
  Edward 87, 88
LATIMER
  Alexander 95, 134
LAURANCE
  Benjamin 2; Jadedah 2; James C. 2; Sally 2
LAURENCE
  Charles S. 8; George 1; James 135; James C. 5; Joseph 135; Judith 1; Rebecca 148; William 1, 3, 135
LAVAZON
  Elisabeth 119

LAWRANCE
  Charles S. 2
LAWRASON
  J. 83; James 90; Joseph T. 86
LAWRENCE
  Benjamin 39; Charles S. 39; George 2, 9; James 76; James C. 39, 40; Jedidah 39; Judith 37, 132; Lawrence 13; Lydia 39; Mary 2; Noble 104, 107; Sally 39; William 4
LAWRIE
  James 106, 108, 109, 111, 135
LAWSON
  Martha 107; William 135
LEACH
  James 109
LEAKE
  Richard 63
LEAP
  Ann 97, 136; Jacob 97; Thomas 97
LEATHERLAND
  Ann 100
LEE
  Cassius F. 86, 88; Charles 82; Edmund 82; Edmund F. 86; Edmund J. 88; Ludwell 88; Mary 143; Susanna 146
LEHON
  John 134
LEIP
  Mr. 92
LEMOINE
  John 134; John E. 134; Susanna 134
LENNOX
  Margaret 117
LEONARD
  Benjamin 77
LESLIE
  Benjamin 135; Rebecca 16, 18, 40
LESTER
  Mary 127
LETHUE
  Jane 136
LeTRAIT
  Mary 132
LEVAN
  John 91
LEVENSTON
  John 134
LEVERING
  Griffith 48; Joseph 48; Mary 48, 122; Rachel A. 20, 48; Samuel 48; Thomas 20, 32, 48
LEWIS
  () 134; David 134; Edward 95; Eleanor 134; Jane 100, 111;

John 74, 82, 99; Laurence 134; Mrs. 115; Richard 100; Sally 133; Samuel 134; Thesea 145; Thomas 74, 99, 101, 102, 103, 135; William 135
LIGHTFOOT
  Ann 146; Betsey 146; Elizabeth 141; George 135; John M. 135; Mrs. 92; Richard 107; Sarah 132; William 134
LIGHTNEM
  Lenny 145
LIMERICK
  Ann 130; Hannah 95; John 95, 134; Mr. 91, 93
LIMMERMAN
  George 135
LINAS
  Thomas 116
LINCH
  Barton 134
LINDSAY
  Benjamin 134; Charlotte 107; George 74; John 134; Michael 74; Robert 62, 63, 69, 70, 76, 78, 108, 111; Susanna 122; Susannah 78
LINDSEY
  Dr. 74; Opie 74; Robert 72-74, 76, 77
LINTER
  William 135
LINTON
  George 135; Lilly 86; Mary 111; William 99
Liquors: 5, 6, 10, 16, 24, 30, 31, 34, 36
LISTER
  John 59; Susannah 77, 78; Thomas 58
LITE
  Nathan P. 49
LITHCOE
  Jane 136
LITLE
  Charles 13, 17, 33, 40, 48; Charles W. 33, 49; Elizabeth 12, 37; Hannah 9, 17, 21, 49; Isaac P. 33, 49; John 21, 26, 35, 49; John J. 43, 49; Lydia 33; Rebecca 49; Richard 49, 53; Richard H. 7, 11, 13-15, 17, 19, 26, 27, 30, 49; Robert S. 21, 49; Ruth 27, 35, 38, 43; Samuel B. 49; Sarah 21, 49; Sarah A. 49; Sidney 49; William 49
LITTLE
  Charles 76, 88; Mary 132; Mrs. 91; Webster 111

LITTLEJOHN
  Marielles 114; Samuel 100, 102,
  111
LIVINGSTON
  Mr. 93
LIZURM
  William 134
LLOYD
  Elisabeth 146; John 87, 88;
  Mary 107; Rebecca 10, 37;
  Robert 107
LOCK
  John W. 60
LOCKE
  Catherine 134; Joseph 134;
  Thomas 134
LOCKER
  Amelia 132; James 134, 135;
  Mary 146; Susanna 146
LOGAN
  () 134; Anna M 134; Elizabeth
  134; Fanny 134; Mrs. 135;
  Randolph 134; Samuel 134
LOMAX
  John 60, 135
LONG
  Elizabeth 75; Frances M. 48;
  Jane B. 134; Margaret 63; Mary
  D. 134; Polly 136; Rebecca 135;
  Samuel 135; Sarah 134; Seth
  134, 135; Susanna 134; William
  134, 135; William H. 134
LONGDEN
  Elias 134; Elisabeth 120; George
  C. 135; John 55, 69, 91; Lucy
  131; Olpha 135
LONGDON
  Judith 107
LONGWORTH
  James 63
LOTT
  Betsey 91
LOTZ
  J. 134; John C. 134; Rosanna E.
  134; Susanna 134; Susanna H.
  134
LOVE
  Mr. 91, 93
LOW
  Mrs. 135
LOWDEN
  Mary 127
LOWE
  Catherine 122; Henry 134; John
  134; Thomas 135
LOWNDES
  Mrs. 91
LOWNES
  James 2; William 2, 8

LOWREY
  Esther 128
LOWRY
  Olivia 135
LOWTHER
  Mrs. 92
LUCAS
  Rachel 75
LUCKETT
  Cloughley 122
LUDBERG
  John G. 135
LUDWELL
  Martha 107
LUKE
  John 69
LUKENS
  Elizabeth 25, 26, 32, 51; Rachel
  49; Samuel 26
LUMLEY
  John 101
LUMPKIN
  Mr. 92
LUMSDEN
  () 135; John 134, 135; Margery
  134; Mr. 84
LUPTON
  Ann 12, 29, 37, 42, 49; Anna
  32, 42; David 1, 12, 15, 16, 49;
  Esther 31; Jane 29, 42, 49; John
  29, 42, 49; Joseph 31; Mary 29,
  42, 49; Rachel 12, 29, 42, 49;
  Richard R. 31, 32; Ruth 48
LUSTRE
  Emma 136
LUTZ
  Catherine 122; Mr. 93
LYLE
  () 135; Henry 77; Zachariah 134
LYLES
  Alexander 94; Henry 135; John
  N. 82; Margaret 97; Mrs. 93;
  William 78, 79, 88, 134;
  Zachariah 97
LYMBURN
  Ann 138
LYNN
  Adam 72; Ann 119; J. 93
LYON
  Andrew 135; Michael 71;
  Timothy 111
LYONS
  Grace 74; Timothy 104

M

MacALISTER
  Mr. 75
MacFARLANE
  B. 133

MacGILL
  Robert 79
MacMANNIN
  Elisabeth 119; Sarah 127
MADDEN
  Mary F. 141; Michael 79; Nancy
  137
MAFFITT
  William 136
MAGNESS
  George 58; Sarah 130
MAGRATH
  Owen 86
MAKIN
  John 92
MALONE
  Mary 77
MALONY
  Mary 148
MANDELL
  Daniel 136
MANDEVILLE
  James 86; Jonathan 83, 86; Miss
  93
MANDLEY
  Elisabeth 141
MANKIN
  Charles 136; David 86
MANLEY
  John 107; Sarah 118
MANLY
  Jenny 148
MANN
  Charles 87; Mr. 91
MAR/MARR
  Harriet L. 151; Mrs. 90
MARCLAY
  () 137
MARK
  Eliza 125; Elizabeth 48; John L.
  137; Mr. 92
MARLE
  David 136; Elisabeth 141;
  Hannah 146; Joseph 71, 73, 74;
  Rebecca 135
MARSH
  Susan 27, 49; Susannah 32
MARSHALL
  Mary 150
MARSTELLER
  Col. 91; P. 137; P.G. 84, 93;
  Philip 82
MARTIN
  Barton 105; James 135; John
  108, 111; Mary 6; Nicholas 109;
  Sarah 105; William 136
MARVEL
  Sarah 63
MASON
  Ann 90; Anna 150; Benjamin 5,

136; Col. 74; George 93, 95, 99, 111; John 62, 63, 88, 136; Philip 74; Richard C. 88; Samuel 75; Sarah 72, 76-78, 130; Susanna 20; Thomson F. 86

MASSEY
Lee 99, 101; Mary 135; Thomas 136; William 116

MASSIE
Mr. 87

MASTERS
Solomon 88

MASTERSON
Edward 114; Mrs. 109; Sarah 137

MATCHEN
Mrs. 92

MATCHUM
Mr. 90

MATHESON
() 137; Kenneth 137

MATTHEWS
Caleb B. 6; Charles 6; Jabez 136; Martha 8; Matthews 6; Sarah 5, 6, 37, 39; Thomas 1, 3, 5-7, 39; William 4, 6, 39

MATTINGLY
Elizabeth 20, 21, 53

MATTOX
James 74

MAXWELL
Arthur 90

MAY
Frederick 83; Mr. 92

MAYHALL
Eleanor 136; James 136; Mr. 92

MAYS
Jane 127

MAZINGO
William 86

McBRIDE
John 138

McCALLISTER
Margaret 123

McCARTY
Catherine 104, 107; Daniel 99, 106, 111; Dennis 99; Patrick 138; Polly 148

McCAUGHLIN
Thomas 138

McCLEAN (see "McLean")
Daniel 86

McCLEISH
Archibald 137; Elisabeth 137; George 137; James 139; Jane 139; William 137

McCLELLAN
Mary 137

McCLOSSES
Thomas 69

McCOBB
John 138

McCORMACK
Bernard 138

McCREA
Ann A. 138; Catherine 138; Henry 138; James 137-139; James M. 138; John 139; Kitty 120, 137; Nancy 139; Peter 138; Rebecca 138, 139; William A. 138

McCRETY
July 130

McCUE
Fanny 96; Henry 96; Mr. 91; Mrs. 86; Rebecca 96

McCULLOCH
Mrs. 139

McCUTCHEON
Patrick 138

McDANIEL
Mrs. 91

McDERMOT/McDERMOTT
M. 74; Martin 92

McDIMMICK
James 138

McDONALD
Ann 138; Archibald 56; Elizabeth 131; John 138, 139; Margaret 56; Mr. 91; Nelly 91, 127; William K. 138

McDORMANTO
David 73

McDOUGALL
() 139; Daniel 138

McDOWELL
Mary 100

McFADDEN
James 138

McFADEN
Ann 135, 137; Elisabeth 146; Esabella 146; James 137, 139; Nancy 137

McFALL
Margaret 54, 111

McFARLANE
Elizabeth 73; George 138

McFARLIN
Ignatius 76, 77; Mary 76, 77

McFARLING
Elizabeth 74; Ignatius 77; Mary 77

McGAHAN
Fanny 134

McGARR
James 137; Margaret 137

McGAUGHAN
Hugh 138

McGEHANNY
A. 137; Margaret 137, 139

McGREGOR
Christian 129

McGUIRE
John P. 87; Margaret 78

McHENRY
Ann 141; James 95

McILHENNY
William 139

McINTYRE
Catherine O. 138; Charles 138, 139; Margaret A. 138; Sarah 138

McIVER
Colin/Coilin 78, 90; Evander 137; John 137, 138; Margaret 137; Mary G. 137

McKABOY
Mary 107

McKAY
Elisabeth 139; Jacob 1

McKEAY
John 82

McKECKNIE
() 139

McKEIVOR
Mary 120

McKENNA
J.L. 86

McKENNEY
Alexander 103; Anne 103; John 103

McKENZIE
Alexander 137, 138; Andrew J. 138; Ann 139; George 138; Harriet R. 138; James 137, 138; John 137, 139; Louis 138; Margaret 137, 138; Peggy 138

McKINNEY
Helen 137; Henrietta 135; Jane C. 151; Mary A. 137; S. 139

McKNIGHT
Catherine 137, 138; Catherine A. 138; Ch. 139; Charles A. 137; Christiana P. 138; John 137; Kitty 138; Margaret 138; Martha B. 137; Mary E. 138; Susanna 138; William 139; William H. 137

McLEA
Elisabeth 135

McLEAN
Bethanath 96; Daniel 83, 88, 96; Isaac 138; Lucretia 96; Mary 137; Thomas 138

McLEOD
() 139; Daniel 137; Helen 137; John 137, 139; Mary 137; Mary A. 137; Mr. 84; Philip 137

McMAHAN
  Michael 95
McMAHON
  Elisabeth 133; Esabella 133; Mrs. 90
McMAKEN
  Mr. 91
McMANIN
  Nancy 150
McMANING
  Margaret 136
McMASTERS
  Mrs. 92
McNAMER
  Mary 143
McNEIL
  Patrick 139
McNEMARA
  John 138; John H. 138
McPHERSON
  Ann 49; Charles 49; Daniel 10, 13, 15, 20-22, 34, 49; Elizabeth 2, 10, 34, 37, 39, 48, 49; Emily 49; Esther 39, Hannah 10, 20, 24, 41, 51; Hesther 2; Isaac 2, 39, 48; Jane 2, 18, 39, 47, 49; Jean 78; Jessie 78; John 1, 20, 23, 24, 27, 32, 35, 41-43, 49; John D. 49; Joseph G. 49; Mary 2, 15, 37, 41; Mary A. 39, 49; Mary-Ann 10; Rebecca 10, 20, 24, 34, 35, 41, 50; Rebecca N. 34, 43, 49; Samuel 10, 15, 19, 41, 48, 49; Sarah 136; Tacy 2, 3, 39; William 2, 39
MEAD
  Mr. 112
MEADE
  William 87
MEARECHTREE
  John 136
MEARSHEIMER
  Mary 122
MEASE
  Eliza 136; Robert 135, 137
Medicines: 73, 106, 108
MEEKS
  Edward 96; Hetty 96; Mr. 92
MEHAUL
  Mary 143
MELANCE
  Timothy 76
MENDENHALL
  James 1
MERCY
  Robert 136
MERICK
  Sarah 134
MERTLAND (see "Murtland")
  Susanna 136

MEYERS
  John 136
MEZARVEY
  Thomas 136
MIDDLETON
  Honor 111; Hugh 78; Luther 111; Mary 77; William 62, 136
MIFFLIN
  Ann 11
MILBURN
  Joseph 136
MILES
  James 79
Military: 5, 6, 8, 13, 14, 17, 18, 19, 30, 31, 95, 118, 121; Civil War 38, 89, 94
MILLER
  Amy A. 24, 38; Anna 28, 38, 52; Arthur 49; Caroline 49, 136; Caroline S. 49; Charles 49, 50; Cornelia J. 49, 52; Edgar 49; Elisha 49; Eliza H. 49; Francis 46, 49; John S. 32, 33, 49; Joseph H. 48, 49; Llewellyn 49; Martha 104; Mary A. 49; Mary H. 49; Mordecai 1, 9, 12, 13, 49; Mrs. 136; Rebecca 49; Rebeckah 7, 37; Robert 52, 136, 139; Robert H. iv, 27, 34, 49; Ruth 45; Samuel 49, 50; Sarah 46, 49; Sarah P. 49; Susan 49; Thomas P. 49; Warwick P. 13, 40, 49; William 78; William H. 23, 49
MILLS
  Daniel 62, 68; Isaac 107; James 135; John M. 136; Polly 146; Robert 60, 107; Sarah 104, 106, 107; William 112, 136; William N. 136
MINOR
  Daniel 86, 88; George 76-78; John 54, 55, 62, 63, 65, 68, 69-71, 99
MITCHEL
  James 61; Mary 8
MITCHELL
  Elizabeth 33, 50; Hannah 33, 50; Janet 127; Mary 19, 47; Matthew 33, 50; Pleasant 33, 36, 50; W. 84; William 137
MOBBS
  Mary 107
MOCKLAR
  Samuel 136
MOLAN
  Sina 125
MONDAY
  Crittendon 110

MONROE
  Eley 74; Lawrence 74; Mrs. 137; Thomas 26, 62
MONTGOMERY
  Mrs. 91; Nancy 122; P. 92; Thomas W. 94
Monthly Meetings:
  12th Street 27, 51; Abington 35, 46; Alum Creek 36, 45; Baltimore 2, 3, 5-11, 13, 14, 15-23, 25-30, 32, 33, 35, 44-50, 52, 53; Bradford 26, 45; Buckingham 4, 18, 22, 34, 52; Burlington 23, 52; Cedar Creek 3, 4, 11, 13; Chattens 24; Cherry Street 44, 45, 48, 49, 51, 53; Chesterfield 2, 21-23, 25, 27, 52, 53; Cincinnati 29, 45, 50; Clear Creek 29; Concord 3, 14, 17, 22, 26, 30-32, 35, 45, 46, 49, 50, 51; Crooked Run 2, 4; Crosswicks 16; Deer Creek 47; Dunnings Creek 6; Fairfax 2-12, 15-35, 44, 46, 47-53; Frankford 19, 25; Goose Creek 3, 6, 7, 14, 17, 18, 21, 22, 24, 29, 33, 35, 44-48, 51; Goshen 30, 46; Grace Church Street 24, 29, 44; Gravelly Run 27, 51; Green Plain 51; Green Street 25, 44, 46, 51; Gun Powder 26, 46, 50; Gwynedd 33, 25, 26, 49, 51; Hardshaw East 23, 30, 45; Honey Creek 51; Hopewell 1, 3, 7-13, 15, 17-20, 22-24, 26, 27, 29, 30, 31-34, 44, 45, 47, 48-51, 53; Horsham 22, 52; Indian Spring 2, 4, 7-14, 16-35, 44-48, 51, 52; Kennet/t 32, 45; Little Falls 20, 21, 36, 45, 49; Lombard Street 48; Makefield 44, 45; Marlborough 23; Miami 23; Middletown 35, 50; Milford 51; Mother Kiln 11; Nantucket 1, 2, 5, 8, 9, 45; New Bedford 14, 19, 27, 47; New Garden 4, 12, 45, 47, 50, 51; New York 6, 10, 53; Newtown 51; Philadelphia 2, 4, 6-8, 12, 13, 16, 17, 20-25, 27, 32, 33, 35, 46, 49, 51; Pipe Creek 10, 14, 21, 35, 36, 45; Plainfield 16, 23, 24, 29, 34, 45, 51; Purchase 15; Radnor 23; Rahway & Plainfield 32, 49; Redstone 31; Rensselaerville 33, 46; Sadsbury 22; Salem 24, 30, 47; Sandy Spring 2, 10, 46, 49; Short Creek 13, 20, 24, 31; South River 34, 52;

Spalding and Wainfleet 27, 28, 44, 52; Springborough 51; Spruce Street 52; Still Water 32, 51; Upper Springfield 11, 46; Uwchlan/d 28, 36; Waterford 1; Wayne Oak 26, 34; Waynesville 44; Westland 23; Weyanoke 10, 11, 45; White Oak Swamp 2, 3, 6, 8; Wilmington 8, 14, 23; Wythan 20, 26, 27, 50; Yonge Street 33, 48, 51; York 35, 53

MOODY
Benjamin 64, 136; Elisabeth 137; Jane 122; Mr. 93; Sarah 127

MOON
Catharine 18; Elisabeth 119; James 62

MOONEY
Mrs. 92

MOONY
Mary A. 148; Neil 136; William 135

MOORE
Alexander 86; Cleon 99; Elisabeth 146; Esther 29, 30, 42, 50; James 22, 28-30, 42, 50, 100, 106, 112; John 94, 106; John M. 136; Margaret 103, 108; Mary 42, 94; Miss 93; Stephen 136; Thomas 30, 42, 50; William 115; William S. 88

MORELAND
Hanson 136

MORGAN
Deborah 19, 31, 42, 50; Elisabeth 119; Eliza 18, 38, 50; Elizabeth 50; Ellen 49; Ellen M. 50; Hannah 50; Jane 20, 50; John 12, 18, 31, 32, 40, 50; Joseph 18, 50; Mary 146; Mary A. 50; Miranda 20, 25, 46; Sarah 20, 146; Thomas 20, 25, 41, 50; Thomas P. 50; William 20, 22, 25, 26, 30, 31, 41, 50, 86, 88, 136

MORRIS
Capt. 92; Lee 136; Levin 136; Rev. 69; Richard 60, 62, 68, 69; Robert J. 94; Violet 145; William 76

MORRISON
() 136; Hugh 86

MORROW
Mr. 92

MOSLEY
Joseph 101

MOSS
Thomas 104, 136

MOXLEY
John 58, 59, 79; Joseph 100; Mary 119, 125; Nancy 119; Patty 73, 74; Thomas 68, 79, 115

MOYER
John 136

MUIR
Elisabeth 136; Hugh 95; James v, 62, 68, 117; John 54, 58, 60, 62, 63, 65, 66, 68-72, 91, 95, 112, 136; Robert 89, 91, 95; Samuel 79

MULEY
Jane 127

MULLON
John 135

MUMFORD
Capt. 97

MUNCASTER
John 82, 86, 88

MUNROE
Andrew 80

MURPHEY
Christian 65, 68-70, 72, 73, 74; George 60, 62, 63

MURPHY
Christian 74; John 136; Lucy 138; Mary 108, 147

MURRAH
John 108

MURRAY
Edward 136; Francis 136; George 90; George W. 135; James 93, 135, 136; John 136; Thomas 86, 136

MURRY
Mary 55, 60

MURTLAND (see "Mertland")
John 90; Mr. 91, 93

MUSGROVE
Israel 136

MYERS
Fanny 128; Hannah 24, 50; Jane 50; John 95; Joseph 50, 86; Julia A. 50; Mary 24, 50; Paulina 24, 50; Rachel 50; Samuel 24, 30, 50; Sarah 24, 35, 43; Sarah H. 50; William M. 50

N

NAINBY
Joseph 139

NASH
George 139; Jane 139; Jane A. 139; John 77; Mary M. 139; Sarah 79

NEALE
Rodham 102

NEBTON
James 140

NEIL
Rosanna 119

NEILL
Ann 7; Jane C. 139; John 139, 140; Joseph 50; Lewis 7, 13, 17, 50; Lydia 17, 26, 42, 50; Mary 15, 21-23, 37, 41, 47, 50; Rachel 7; Rebecca 17, 26, 37, 42, 50; Thomas 15, 23, 24

NELSON
Andrew 56; Mrs. 140; Polly K. 128; Richard 103, 115

NELVILLE
Catherine 136

NESBETT
James 108, 110, 112

NEVITT
John 140

NEWMAN
Michael 108; Mr. 92; Nancy 136

NEWSON
James 104

Newspapers:
Maryland Gazette 56, 73; Virginia Gazette 56, 73

NEWTON
Albert O. 139; Augustine 86, 140; Augustine W. 139; Jane 123; Jane B. 139, 140; Joseph M. 139; Margaret 74, 75; Mary R. 118; Mr. 74; Sinah 139; William 83, 139, 140

NICHOLAS
Lewis 140

NICHOLLS
James B. 88; Mr. 83

NICHOLSON
Henry 139, 140; Margaret 139; Mary A. 139; Rebecca 76

NICKOLLS
Scudamore 140

NIGHT
Maria 139

NISBETT
James 110

NIVIN
Duncan 140

NOBBS
Mary 108

NOBLE
Mary 108

NOEL
William 90

NOLAND
Barnaby 55

NORMAN
George 116

NORRIS
  Oliver 87; William 139
NORTH
  Mary 141
NOSE
  Andrew 91
NOTTINGHAM
  Eleanor 130
NOWLAND
  John 140

O

O'CONNER/O'CONNOR
  William 86, 140
O'NEAL
  Henry 140
OAKLEY/OAKLY
  John 140; Mary 63
OATES
  Margery 134
Occupations:
  Attorney 111, 113; Baker 86;
  Blacksmith 79; Brewer 63;
  Carpenter 102, 103; Clerk 101;
  Cooper 62, 65, 68, 103;
  Cordwainer 58; Distiller 96;
  Doctor 54, 62, 63, 65, 68,
  71-75, 78, 83, 86, 88, 93, 105,
  106, 108, 110, 111, 121, 128,
  133, 140; Gauger 90; Historian
  94; House Builder 89; Joiner 60;
  Justice of the Peace 72; Marshal
  17; Mayor 95; Merchant 31, 38,
  95, 96; Minister 17, 21, 25-27,
  30-32, 41, 54, 55, 60, 72, 73,
  76, 77, 80, 87, 98, 101, 102,
  109, 120, 131, 135, 136, 150;
  Reader 102; Rector 72, 97;
  Sadler 61; Sexton 100; Sheriff
  113; Ship Carpenter 68;
  Shoemaker 58, 61, 102, 103;
  Surveyor 61; Tanner 102; Taylor
  59, 61, 65, 68, 71; Teacher 16,
  17; Tile Cooper 60; Vestryman
  88, 98
OFFUTT
  Rebecca 139, 140
OLISTER
  Ann 73
OLNEY
  Anstis 142
ORME
  Charlotte 125; Eliza 149
ORR
  Dr. 140; Eleanor 140; Lucinda
  140
OSBORN(E)/OSBURN
  Ann 128; Richard 99, 112;
  Thomas 140

OSTAND
  Mr. 92
OSWALD
  Henry 140
OUTTEN
  John 140
OVERMAN
  John A. 140
OXLEY
  William 83

P

PAGE
  Bernard 80, 81; Charles 86, 140;
  John 90; Mr. 91; Washington C.
  88, 140
PAINTER
  Rachel 17, 37, 38, 50
PALMER
  Elizabeth 54, 56, 59, 60, 62, 63,
  65, 68, 105, 108, 112; George
  56; Hannah 34; James 100; John
  100; Moses 34; Pennell 26, 34,
  35, 43, 49, 50; Rebecca 43;
  Rebecca N. 35
PAN
  Rebecca 93
PANCOAST
  David 53; Mary 53; Sarah 37,
  53
PARKER
  Ann 21; James 141; John 54, 63,
  141; Nancy 146
PARKERSON
  William 68
PARKHOUSE
  William 141
PARKINS
  Joseph 44; Lydia 48; Maria 20,
  21, 41, 50; William J. 44
PARKS
  George 141; William G. 136
PARSONS
  Catherine 63; James 56, 57, 62,
  63, 68, 74; John 141; Sarah 120;
  Thomas 59; Walter 141
PATERSON
  Catharine 119
PATON
  Rebecca 9, 37
PATTEN
  Elisabeth C. 140, 141; Isaac R.
  140; James 83; Joseph M. 140;
  Mary 125, 142; Mr. 126; Selina
  B. 140; Susan 140, 141; Thomas
  140, 141; Thomas B. 140
PATTERSON
  Beulah 20, 29, 42, 50; Catherine
  128; Ellwood 27, 42, 50;

Elwood 29; Esabella 76; Hannah
46; James 141; Jared 32; John
104; Joseph 141; Matthew 68;
Mrs. 92, 93; Samuel N. 29, 50;
Samuel W. 42; Sarah M. 141;
William 20, 27-29, 42, 50, 141
PATTON
  James 21; Mr. 91-93; Mrs. 90;
  Rebecca 37; William 68
PAUL
  Zachariah 141
PAYNE
  Anenias 78; Edward 99, 112;
  Elija 74; Eliza 77, 151; Elizabeth
  70, 72, 74, 78; Hezekiah 141;
  John 74; Margaret 71, 73, 74;
  Mary 102; William 54-57, 59,
  60, 63, 64, 71-79, 88, 99, 109
PEACH
  Elizabeth 12; Mary 14, 37, 38,
  50; Samuel 18, 28, 50; Sarah 12
PEAKE
  Humphrey 57, 64, 102; John
  114; Sarah 102; William 99,
  102, 103, 115
PEARCE
  Simon 114
PEARSON
  Elisabeth 150; Margaret 122;
  Sarah 128
PEASE
  Mr. 93
PEESCH
  John 71; Joshua 71
PELTON
  Enoch 141
PENNY
  John 141; Thomas 141
PEPPER
  Elisabeth 148; Eliza 119;
  Michael 92; Sarah 130
PERKINS
  Eli 74; Francis 141; John 58,
  141; Maria 18; S. 74
PERRIN
  Joseph M. 91
PERRY
  Anne 120; Charlotte 140; Daniel
  C. 140, 142; Frances 141;
  Harriet 146; Jane 130; Mary
  130; Mary A. 117; Matilda 140;
  Peter 54, 56, 63-65, 69, 70, 71,
  74, 112; William 140; William
  H. 141
PETERS
  John 109, 141
PETTIT
  Mary 140
PEYTON
  Francis 92; Thomas W. 141;

Valentine 115
PHARR
 Elizabeth 18; James 18
PHENIX
 Ann 130
PHILIPS
 Amy A. 23, 49; Amy Ann 49
PICKERILL
 Isaac 141; Richard 141
PICKERING
 Mrs. 92
PIERCE
 Elisabeth 143; Elizabeth 100; Isaac 96; Peter 74; Thomas 141
PIERCY
 () 142; C. McKnight 141; George 140; George A. 140; Henry 86
PIERPOINT
 John R. 30, 50, 53
PILE
 Mr. 91
PILES
 Frances 136; Lewis 141
PINDALL
 Ann 133; Mary 136; Mr. 92
PIPER
 David 114; Harry 63, 64; Henry 63; John 103; Margaret 62, 65, 68, 69, 103; Sarah 103
PIPPENGER
 Wesley E. v
PIPSECOE
 Priscilla 104
PITTMAN
 () 142; Nancy 135; R. 94
Places:
 Belhaven 101; Occoquan 44; Owl Creek 36, 45; Rock Creek Ferry 57; Sandy Spring 2; Upper Ridge Meeting House 48
PLATT
 George 100
PLEAR
 Peter 141
PLEASANTS
 Mary 52; William H. 47
PLUMB
 Joseph 141
PLUMMER
 Gerard 12, 50; Mary 12, 37, 50; Mary A. 50; Philip 12; Rebecca 50; Richard H. 50; Thomas 50
POLLARD
 Thomas 99
POMERY
 () 141; Francis D. 141; William 141
POOLE
 Dennis 141; Edmund 141;

Henry 141
POPE
 Abner 20, 21, 25, 33, 43, 50; Abner J. 33, 43; Edward 25, 33, 43, 50; Hannah 20, 22; Joseph D. 50; Joseph P. 33, 43; Maria 21, 25, 33, 41, 43; Mary A. 25, 33, 43, 50
PORTER
 Elias 68; James 141; Mackenzie 62; Maria M. 140; Reuben 141; Sarah 140; Sarah R. 140; Thomas 140, 141
PORTLOCK
 Gustavus W. 94
POSEY
 Henry 141; John 99, 112, 114, 116; Sarah A. 125
Potomac River: 57, 64
POTTER
 Kitty 122
POTTS
 Eliza 86; J. 83; John 79, 141; Thomas 82
POWELL
 () 141; Benjamin W. 20, 30, 42, 50; Burr 79; C. 82; Cuthbert 86, 88; Edward 141; Elisha 70-72, 74; Frances 146; Mary 91; Mary G. iv, 89, 94; Robert 88
POWER
 Ann 119; Peggy 120
POWERS
 Mr. 93
PRATHER
 John S. 76
PRATT
 Elisabeth 140; Levin 140; Mary S. 140
PRESTON
 Thomas 78, 141
PRICE
 David 64; John 104; Oliver 79, 80, 91, 92; Sarah 50; Thomas 56, 112
PROCTOR
 Henry G. 94
Properties:
 Cameron 55, 64; Mount Vernon iv; Red Oak 60; Spring Garden 84
Property Deeds: 63
 Christ Church 60; Glebe Land 61; Quaker 1, 26; Truro Parish 112
PUGH
 Catharine 4, 39; Catherine 37; Isaac 4, 39; Sarah 4, 39
PUMPHREY
 Samuel 141

PUPPO
 () 142; Daniel C. 141
PURKIS
 Sally 149
PURSLEY
 Miss 92
PUSEY
 Stephen 58
PUTNEY
 Elena 133; J.G. 96

R

RAGAN
 Basil 143; Elisabeth 146; Michael 59
RAILEY
 Sarah 108
RALY
 John 108
RAMSAY
 Amelia 142; Ann M. 142; Anthony 144; Betty 55; Dennis 142, 143; Edward 70, 76, 79; Elizabeth 68, 70; George W. 142; Jane 142, 143; Jane A. 142; John 63, 143; Mr. 69, 93; Nomy 57; Robert J. 142; Thomas 76; William 54, 66, 69, 93, 104, 112, 115
RANDALL
 Mr. 91
RANDOLPH
 Mr. 91
RANKIN
 Robert 78
RANSOM
 Joseph 108; Richard 108
RANTOR
 Mrs. 92
RATCLIFF
 John 58, 68-70, 77, 114; Richard 78
RAWLINGS
 James 24, 50; John 20, 24, 26, 27, 30, 42, 50, 143; Mary 24, 32, 50; Robert 24, 50; Samuel 24, 50
RAWLINS
 Priscilla 138
RAY
 Benjamin 70, 71; Mr. 69
READ
 John 68, 74
REAGAN
 Michael 58, 102, 110
REARDON
 John 143; Michael 143; Mrs. 92; William 104, 108, 111, 112, 114

REDMAN
    Henry 92, 143; Thomas 91
REDMON
    Jacob 94; Mr. 90
REED
    Alexander 143; Catherine 147;
    James 76, 77, 143; Jane 122;
    John 143; Mr. 92; Nelson
    75-78; Sarah 107; Thomas 75
REEDER
    Alexander 142; John 142;
    Margaret 122; Rebecca 142
REEDY
    William 60, 74
REESE
    Gerard H. 48; H. 49
REID
    Absalom 108; James 143; Mr. 93
REIDER
    Thomas 91
REILEY
    Phillis 104; William 82, 143
REINS
    Anthony 143
REINTZEL/REINTZELL
    Catherine 128; Mr. 92
REISCH
    Maria J. 136
REMY
    Jacob 112; Sandford 58, 59
RENOLDS
    Mr. 92
RENWICK
    John W. 94
RESLER
    Jacob 83, 96
REYNOLDS
    () 142; George 79; John 143;
    Margaret 148; Mary 138; Mr.
    93; Sarah 142, 143; William 75
REZIN
    Mary 132
RHOADES
    William 76
RHODES
    John 54, 55, 58-60, 62, 63, 65,
    68-70, 100, 112, 114; Joshua
    68; Mary 104; Susan 120
RHOE (see "Roe," "Wroe")
    Sarah 119
RICE
    Anna 130; Capt. 92
RICH
    Christiana 130
RICHARDS
    Elizabeth 136; George 90; James
    76, 77; John 112; Kitty 138;
    Mary A. 132; Milley 143;
    Thomas 56, 59, 60; William 65,
    76
RICHARDSON
    Capt. 142; Daniel 142; Forrest
    82; Foster 142; John 101, 115;
    Judson 143; Widow 108;
    William P. 5-7
RICHETER
    John 82
RICHTER
    Charles 143; John 143
RICK
    Mrs. 91
RICKETTS
    Ann 117; Benjamin 143; Charles
    143; David 142, 143; E. 143;
    Elisabeth 142; John T. 142;
    Mary E. 142; Mrs. 143
RICKS
    Hannah 127
RIDDELL
    Henry 59
RIDDLE
    () 143; Anna M. 142; Bushrod
    W. 142, 143; Charlotte V. 142;
    Eliza M. 142; Frances 142;
    Henry 56, 58-60, 69; James 143;
    James D. 142; Jane 142; John A.
    142; John H. 142; Joseph 142,
    143; Joshua 142, 143; Julia M.
    142; Robert 142; Sarah 142, 143
RIGBE
    George 112
RIGDON
    Edward 60, 63; Mary 60
RILEY
    Joshua 22, 32, 34, 50; Margaret
    119
RIND
    Mrs. 68
RINKER
    Joseph 50, 143
RIPTON
    Ann 139
RISBY
    Mary 148
RISTON
    Hannah 76
ROACH
    John 143
Roads: 110
    Avery's 57, 64; Cameron 58,
    64; Difficult Bridge 57
ROBERDEAU
    Mary 140, 141; Selina 140
ROBERTS
    Bridget 95; Bridgett 132; Capt.
    82; James B. 95; John 83, 86,
    88; Kitty 151; Robert 95, 143
ROBERTSON
    Andrew 56, 59; Elinor 60;
    Elisabeth 130; James 64, 77,
    114; John 112, 143; Mary 20, 50
ROBINSON
    Amelia 134; Andrew 108; Dr.
    105, 109; George 75, 143;
    Hannah 128; Joseph 75; Mary
    108; Mr. 74; Nancy 119; Polly
    147; Thomas 104
ROCK
    Richard 86, 143
RODMAN
    Alexander 143
ROE (see "Rhoe," "Wroe")
    Alexander 103; Gerard 143;
    Oliver 100, 108
ROGERS
    David 94; William 77, 78
ROGERSON
    Robert 142; Thomas 142
ROLINGS
    Sepr. 58
ROLLINGS
    John 76
ROLLINS
    James 74; John 74, 76; Martha
    119
ROSE
    H. 82; Mr. 112
ROSS
    Charles 51; David 10, 24, 50;
    Edward 96; George 104; Hannah
    22, 29, 42, 51; Hector 62, 112;
    Isaac 58, 62; Isabella 96; James
    51; John C. 51; Jonathan 9, 14;
    Katherine 51; Mary 10, 37, 50;
    Mary S. 51; Mrs. 144; Phebe 7;
    Samuel 51; William D. 96
ROUNSAVEL
    Andrew 143
ROUNTER
    Mr. 93
ROYAL
    Thomas 94
RUKSBY
    Edward 65, 68-70, 72, 73,
    74-76; Mrs. 77
RUMNEY
    Dr. 74; William 54, 56, 58, 59,
    63, 65, 68-70, 75, 76, 112
RUNNALDS
    Harrison P. 79
RUSSELL
    Charles 51, 108; Hannah A. 17,
    51; Hannah T. 142, 143; James
    17, 51, 56, 142; James B. 142;
    Jane 74, 143; Jean 75, 76; John
    T. 17, 51; Joseph J. 17, 51;
    Margaret 143; Mary 20; Mary A.
    142; Nancy 142, 143; Rebecca
    17, 23, 42, 51; Rosley 131;

Samuel 104, 108; Sarah A. 123;
Susan 17, 37, 38; Susannah 51;
William 143
RUSTICK
  Thomas 143
RUTLEDGE
  John 76
RUTTER
  Thomas 20, 27, 42, 51
RYAN
  Thomas 91
RYLEY
  Terence 104

S

SAD
  Benjamin 104
SAILER
  Mr. 93
SANDERS
  James 112; Thomas 107;
  William 112
SANDFORD
  Mr. 148; Richard 54-57, 75
SANDS
  Eliza 29, 51; Samuel B. 35, 51
SANFORD
  Ann 135; Catherine 145; E. 135;
  Esther W. 145; Frances A. 145;
  Laurence 144, 147; Mrs. 91;
  Richard 88; Robert 91; Sarah E.
  145; Thomas 144, 145
SANGSTER
  Jean 91; Mary 90; Mr. 90;
  Thomas 90
SAUNDERS
  David 15, 40; Hannah 11, 37;
  John 1, 38; John M. 27, 51;
  Joseph 27, 46, 51; Lewis 115;
  Mary 38, 51, 53; McPherson
  51; Peter 10, 15, 20, 21, 27,
  42, 51; Samuel C. 27, 51; Sarah
  7, 27, 38, 52; Sarah P. 51;
  Susanna 48; Susannah 46;
  Thomas 104; Thomas H. 27, 51;
  William 107
SAVAGE
  George 145
SAYRE
  Valinda 145
SCANDLAND
  Michael 108
SCANLIN
  Michael 115
SCHOLFIELD
  Andrew 8, 9, 11, 12, 15, 16-18,
  35, 51; Ann 8, 14, 29, 37, 42,
  51; Betsy 35; David B. 51;
  Edith 3, 4, 14, 39; Eleanor 8,
51; Elizabeth 9, 29, 37, 42, 51;
Ellen 37; Hannah 20; Hannah R.
51; Isachar 2, 4; Issachar 39;
John 7; Jonathan 7, 15, 19, 33,
51; Joseph 20, 29, 42, 51;
Joseph L. 20, 51; Lewis 29, 42,
51; Mahlon 7, 13, 15, 29, 42,
51; Margaret A. 51; Maria P.
51; Mary 20, 51; Mary E. 51;
Phebe E. 51; Rachel 7, 20, 29,
42, 51; Samuel W. 51; Sarah 51;
Sarah A. 51; Susanna 51;
Thomas 4, 39; Thomas M. 31,
51; William 29, 42, 51; William
A. 51
SCHOOLEY
  Reuben 1
Schools: 16-18, 20-23, 25
  Fair Hill Boarding 25, 28
SCISSON
  Lewis 146
SCOTT
  Ann 20, 51; Charles 146; E.A.
  135; Eliza 144; George 20, 51,
  145; Harriet 125; Horatio 14,
  17; James 112; James L. 146;
  John 144; Mahlen 24; Mahlon S.
  30, 31, 51; Mary 144; Mary M.
  28, 32, 43, 51; Mr. 82; Rev.
  54; Richard M. 88; Thomas 146;
  William A. 20, 51
SCULL
  William 147
SEALE
  Capt. 74; John 71, 73, 74, 76
SEBASTIAN
  Ann 116; Benjamin 54, 59, 60,
  112, 114; Mr. 112; William 92
SELDEN
  Jane 96
SELECTMAN
  Henry 146
SELLERS
  John 86
SEMMES
  Thomas 88
SEMPLE
  Mr. 93; William 145
SERTAR
  John 108
SEXSMITH
  George 96; Matthew 96, 145
SEYMOUR
  Mr. 92
SHAKESPEARE
  William 77, 78
SHAW
  Alexander 146; Elizabeth 22, 41;
  James 22, 91; Mrs. 92, 147;
  Thomas 54-60, 62, 65, 68, 72,
88, 114
SHEARES
  Peter 146
SHELTON
  Sarah 106, 108
SHELVIN
  Edward 107
SHEPHARD
  Ann 138; Harriet 125
SHEPHERD
  Mr. 93
SHERIFF
  Joshua 146; Samuel 146
SHERRON
  Mary 128
SHERWOOD
  Job 146; Lewyllen 147
SHIESE
  Mr. 92
SHILMAN
  William C. 87
SHINBANK
  Ann 104; Peter 104
SHINN (see "Shurn")
  Adam 145
SHIPLEY
  Robert 146
SHOEMAKER
  Abagail 25; Abigail 33, 38, 43,
  51; Ann 19, 48; Anna 51;
  Arnold 51; Charles 52; David L.
  52; Edward 52; Elizabeth 26, 51;
  Elizabeth L. 52; Ellen 51;
  Francis D. 52; George 22, 25,
  26, 51, 52; Hannah 51; Isaiah
  51; Jonathan 26; Mary A. 52;
  Mary S. 51; Peter 116; Rebecca
  A. 52; Samuel S. 51; Susan 51;
  Tace 22; Tacey 52; William L.
  51
SHORTBRIDGE
  George 75; John 73
SHORTEN
  Betty 103
SHOTWELL
  Mary 7, 12, 40
SHREVE
  Ann 2, 12, 37; Benjamin 1, 4, 5,
  46, 52, 146; Elizabeth 25, 41;
  Grace 11, 25, 37, 41; Hannah
  52; John 7, 9, 14, 39; Margaret
  25, 41; Mary 25, 41; Rachel 37;
  Samuel 14, 15, 145; Samuel B.
  34, 52; Susannah 2, 3, 38, 46;
  Thomas 2, 7, 8, 10, 14, 15, 25,
  41
SHUBBORD
  John 115
SHUCK
  Catherine 148; Frederick 146;

Jacob 91; Mrs. 92; Sarah 148
SHUEN
 Prudence 132
SHULER
 George 145
SHULTZ
 Becky 130
SHURN
 Adam 91, 145; Mr. 93
SHUTZ
 Catherine 146
SIMMON
 Mary 131
SIMMONS
 Mrs. 92; Simon 108; Thomas 105; William 92
SIMMS
 () 147; Ann 125; Charles 79, 82, 88, 95, 144; Emelia J. 144; George W. 144; James 146; John D. 86; Margaret 128; Maria 147; Mrs. 147; Nancy 144, 151; Nancy N. 144, 147; Phoebe M. 144; Thomas 146, 147; William D. 144
SIMPSON
 Ann 135; Elisabeth 143; George 106, 114, 116; Gilbert 146; John 145; Joseph 112, 146; Lewis 145; Mary 119; Mimay 135; Moses 114; Richard 114; Sally 148; Thomas 108; William 106, 112, 146
SINCLAIR
 Esther 28, 29, 50; Jacob 35, 43; Jacob L. 34, 52; Sarah 34, 52
SISSON
 Mary 141; Sarah 119
SKELTON
 John 74
SKIDMORE
 Samuel 76
SKINNER
 Mary 136; William 145
SKIPPER
 Wesley W. 94
SLACUM
 George 86; Mr. 83
SLADE
 Mr. 93; William 95
SLATER
 William 146
SLAUGHTER
 Mrs. 74; Philip iv
Slaves: 6, 18, 31
SLIMMER
 Christian 146
SLOANE
 Mrs. 93

SLUSE
 Mr. 93
SLY
 John S. 146
SMALL
 Elisabeth 128
SMALLWOOD
 Nelly 148
SMEDLEY
 David 3, 4, 29, 52; Rachel 14, 52
SMITH
 Adeline A. 145; Alban G. 17, 20; Alexander 73, 147; Ann M. 145; Anne 141; Augustine J. 88, 145; Caleb 96; Catherine 144; Charles 146; Cordelia 120; Daniel 145, 146; Dr. 69, 71, 73; Elisabeth 145; Elizabeth H. 136; George A. 144; Hugh 144, 145, 147; Hugh C. 144; Isaac 146; J.W. 145; James P. 145; Jane 144, 145, 152; John 74, 91, 144-146; John F. 146; John W. 86, 145; Joseph 54, 58, 63, 112, 145; Louisa 144; Margaret 127; Mary 120, 123, 132, 144, 147; Mr. 92, 93; Mrs. 147; Nancy 120; Nathaniel 114; Nelly 152; Rebecca 125, 144; Richard 112; Richards 145; Robert 146; Samuel 79; Samuel E. 34, 52; Sarah 150; Sir S. 144; Susanna 34; Thomas 114, 145, 147; Thomas W. 144, 147; Walter 72; William 146; William C. 146; William H. 144, 147
SMITHERMAN
 Elisabeth 130
SMOOT
 Barton 145; Hezekiah 83, 88
SMYTH
 Hannah 26
SNAFORD
 Richard 72
SNALUM
 Elisabeth 143
SNELL
 Catherine 135; Stephen 78; Susanna 151
SNIDER
 Matthias 82
SNYDER
 Polly 131
SOLEY
 William 145
SOLLAR
 Patrick 90
SOLOMON
 John 104, 108

SOPHY
 Jenny 150
SOULBY
 Harper 27, 28, 52; Henry 27, 28; Sarah A. 27, 28, 52
SPACEY
 John 145
SPANGENBURG
 Mr. 91
SPARROW
 Mr. 108
SPEAR
 () 147
SPENCE
 William 90
SPENCER
 Alice 20, 27, 52; John, 145; Mary A. 20, 52; Rebecca 52; Thomas 20, 30, 31, 52; William 145
SPICKETT
 Catharine 92; Polly 122
SPICOTT
 Polly 127
SPINKS
 Enoch 75
SPONNIGIL
 Mr. 93
SPOONER
 Capt. 147; Holden 144, 146; Jane S. 144; Mary 144
SPRAGUE
 Joshua 146
SPUNAUGLE
 Margaret 143
SPURLING
 Ann 58
ST. GEORGE
 Elisabeth 145; Nelly 125
STABLER
 Anna 29, 32, 42, 52; Anna E. 52; Caleb 8, 20, 25, 27, 29, 39, 42, 52; Caroline H. 52; Deborah 8, 11, 38; Deborah H. 22; Edward 1, 2, 4-13, 15, 18, 19, 21, 28, 32, 34, 38, 40, 52; Edward H. 52; Elizabeth 29, 32, 34, 35, 42, 43, 52; Francis 52; Harriet 52; Henry 8, 39, 52; Maria 144; Mary 2, 3, 34, 37, 38, 52; Mary P. 52; Rebecca 52; Richard H. 47, 52; Robinson 34, 52; Sarah 47, 52; Sarah Z. 52; Susan 52; Thomas 52; Thomas S. 27, 32, 52; William 21, 22, 26, 31, 33, 52, 144; William D. 52
STANLEY
 George 146
STANTON
 Richard 146

STAPLES
  Sarah 120
States:
  Connecticut 97; Delaware 8, 11;
  Florida 94; Georgia 94; Illinois
  44, 51; Indiana 26, 49, 51;
  Maryland 22, 47, 49, 50, 95,
  96, 97, 105, 108; Massachusetts
  19, 27, 30, 47; Mississippi 94;
  New Jersey 11, 16, 21, 22, 25,
  27-29, 32, 46, 53; New York
  15, 23, 28, 32, 33, 53, 96;
  North Carolina 4, 94; Ohio 13,
  16, 20, 23, 24, 29, 31, 32, 34,
  36, 45, 47, 50, 51; Pennsylvania
  4, 6, 12, 17, 18, 19, 22, 23, 25,
  26, 28, 30-32, 34-36, 44-46,
  49-51, 53; Rhode Island 124;
  South Carolina 94; Tennessee 94
STATFORD
  Sarah 123
STEELE
  Catharine 127; Catherine 126;
  Margaret 147
STEER
  Benjamin 3, 39; Isaac 1; Isaac
  H. 25, 28, 42, 52; James M. 25,
  28, 42, 52; Joseph 25, 28, 42,
  52; Lydia A. 25, 28, 42, 52;
  Mary 42; Mary M. 25, 28, 29,
  52; Phebe M. 28, 42, 52;
  Phineas J. 25, 52; Phoebe M.
  25; Sarah 25, 28, 42, 52
STEPHEN
  Peter 144; Sarah 144
STEPHENS
  Charles 146; Cloe 57; Joseph
  114; Richard 103, 106, 108;
  Russel 86; Russell 146
STERRIT
  James 146
STETHAM
  William 145
STEUART
  Arianna 143; Catharine 119;
  Jane 139; Thomas 145
STEVENSON
  David 144; Hannah 104; Robert
  144; William 144
STEWARD
  Elisabeth 128
STEWART
  Betty 135; Charles L. 144;
  Elisabeth M. 145; Helena 144;
  James 63; James M. 145, 146;
  Jane 144; John 144, 145, 147;
  John P. 145; Mary 144, 147;
  Polly 128; Robert 146; Susanna
  135; Thomas R. 145; William
  144; William B. 147; William

C. 144
STICHBORNE
  Elizabeth 59
STIDOLPH
  Sophia A. 135
STIEBBY
  Nancy 141
STIEBER
  Michael 79
STILWELL
  John 146
STINTMAN
  Kitty 151
STITLY
  Betsey 146
STOKELY
  Margaret 125
STONE
  Catherine 141; Charles 146;
  Eleanor 117; Elisabeth 146; John
  59, 60, 62, 63; Jonathan 112;
  Margaret 122; Mary 136; Mary
  A. 136
STOOPS
  Elizabeth 97; William 97
STRAIT
  Sarah 123
STRAUGHAN
  John 102; Mary 104, 109, 110
Streets:
  Cameron 89; Cherry 35; Duke
  82; Franklin 3; Green 22; Queen
  1; Royal v; St. Asaph 1, 3, 28;
  Washington iv, 83; Wilkes 86;
  Wolfe 1, 28
STRICKLAND
  Daniel 146
STRICKLEN
  Sarah 125
STROM
  Henry A. 94
STROMAN
  Elisabeth 141
STUART
  David 88; James M. 94
STURMAN
  John 99
Suits: 23, 61, 75, 110, 112, 113
SULLIVAN
  Mary 79; Polly 148; William
  145
SUMMERS
  Daniel 64, 116; Francis 56, 58,
  64, 65, 68, 69-74, 76-78; John
  58-65, 68, 105, 106, 112, 115;
  Mr. 92; Thomas 146; William
  58, 64, 76
SUMMERSET/SUMMERSETT
  Henry 58, 59, 62

SUREMON
  John C. 146
SUTTON
  James 23, 52; John 1, 79; Mary
  23, 41; Phoebe 23; Rebecca 23;
  Samuel 23, 26; Thomas 63
SWAIN
  Charles W. 51
SWALLOW
  John 106; William 146; Zepha.
  112
SWANN
  Ann 96; Fanny 145; John 146;
  John W. 144; Laurence 144;
  Mary A. 144; Mr. 82; Thomas
  86, 88; William 96, 145; Wilson
  96
SWAYNE
  John 17, 18, 52; John T. 52;
  Joshua 19, 24, 41; Mary A. 52;
  Noah 19, 27, 52; Rebecca 19,
  24, 41; Sarah 17, 37, 52;
  Thomas 19, 24, 41
SWEET
  John 103, 104, 107; Margaret
  123; Mary 132
SWIFT
  Ann 144; Ann F. 144; Ann S.
  144; Anne S. 147; Foster 145;
  George W. 144; Isaac R. 147;
  Jonathan 117, 144; Mary S. 144;
  Nancy 144; William R. 147;
  William T. 144, 147
SWISLER
  Joseph 146
SYKE
  Peter 146

T

TABOR
  () 148
TAIT
  Benjamin 148
TALBERT
  David 64; Mr. 92; O. 74;
  Osburn 74
TALBOT
  Nancy 132; Pretius 78; Sampson
  147
TALBOTT
  Ann 49; Anna 38; Elisha 5, 7-9,
  11, 13, 18, 32, 38, 52; Elizabeth
  11, 49; Hannah 9, 11, 40; Jane
  123; Jesse 9, 11, 40; John L. 11,
  32, 40, 53; John S. 52; Joseph
  38, 49; Joseph C. 52; Mary A.
  52; Precious 140; Rebecca 52;
  Sarah 37; William W. 53

TALBUT
  Betty 91; Thomas 148
TALBUTT
  Elisabeth 134; Lydia 138; Mary 138; Rebecca 120
TARBRER
  James 148
TARLETON
  Mrs. 91
TARPLEY
  Ashbury 94
TASKER
  George 109
TATESPAUGH (sp.)
  Adam 90, 92
TATTERSHELL
  Thomas 148
TAYLOE
  Anne 147; Duke 147
TAYLOR
  Ann 91; Artley 145; Calby 148; Capt. 76; Elisabeth 150; Elizabeth 128, 131; Evan 8; Evan P. 14, 15, 24, 148; George 83, 86, 88, 115, 148; Henry 148; James 109, 148; Jesse 90, 148; John 79, 148; John R. 147, 148; Mahlon 1; Maria 147, 148; Maria M. 147; Mary 125, 138; Mary A. 146; Mary J. 149; Mr. 71; Nancy 120; Rhodey 125; Richard 75; Robert 148; Robert J. 147; Robert M. 79; Sarah 147; Susanna 132, 145; Thomas 148; Vincent 148; Walter 108, 112; William 74, 148; William W. 94
TELIFRO
  Andrew 148
TEMPLE
  William 21, 22, 41
TENISON
  Lucretia 130
TERRETT
  William H. 88, 101, 112
THOM
  Cassa 134
THOMAS
  Hugh 111, 112; Jemima 128; Joseph 80, 86; Katherine 51; Mary 96; Mr. 92; Priscilla 72, 74; Richard 96; Wells W. 147; William 12, 13, 40, 96, 148
THOMPSON
  Charles 147; Craven P. 88; George 148; Israel P. 88; J. 86; John 148; Jonah 82; Maria 135; Miss 92; Sarah 63
THOMSON
  Nelly 119

THORN
  Michael 74
THORNTON
  Joseph 82, 86; Mary A. 96; Mr. 93; William 96
THRIFT
  Ann 78; Charles 57, 64; George 57, 64, 100; James 78; Jeremiah 74, 78; Tony 62
TIGNELL
  Major 148
TILLET
  James 115
TILLETT
  Giles 99
TODD
  Charles 148
TOFFLER
  Cyrus 95; Jonathan 95; Peter 148
TOLBERT
  Thomas 148
TOLSON
  Elisabeth 136
TOMLIN
  John 54; Mr. 112
TOOMEY
  Elisabeth 148; Martin 147
TOUCH
  Pernica 146
TOUGH
  Arthur 107, 109
TOUPLEY
  Kitty 146
TOWERS
  Thomas 86, 148
TOWNSHEND
  Dr. 62
TRACEY
  John 148
TRACY
  Susanna 146
TRAMMELL
  Edward 54; Gerard 74; Gerrard 54, 55, 58-60, 62, 63, 65, 68-78, 100, 103, 116; John 112; William 105, 109
TRAYHERN
  James 1
TREACKLE
  John 148
TRESCHER
  Elizabeth 146
TRETCHER
  Mrs. 148; Thomas 148
TREU
  Henry 104
TRIPLETT
  Sarah 76; Thomas 57, 71, 75, 88; William 99, 114

TROSSEL
  William 56
TROTTER
  Sarah 122
TROUGANTT
  Ann 146
TROUT
  Margaret 119
TRUMAN
  Ann 122
Truro Parish:
  Accounts 109; Adjustments in Levies 115; Birth Records 102; Burials 103; Church Painting 112; Church Repairs 111, 112; Clerks 101; Needy Persons 105; Processioners 114; Readers 102; Sextons 100; Vestrymen 98
TUCKER
  Charles 147; J. 86; John 83, 88; Mr. 93; Thomas 83
TULL
  Charlotte 134
TURBERVILLE
  Harriet 136
TURLEY
  John 99, 103
TURNER
  Elisabeth 125; John 148; Joseph 1; Mary 138; Mrs. 148; William 116
TUTTLE
  Baptist 74
TUTTON
  John 148
TYLER
  Elisabeth 143
TYSON
  Margaret 48

U

UHLER
  Elisabeth 151; Kitty 145; Valentine 78, 93
UNDERHILL
  Daniel 53; Elizabeth 53; Levi 20, 21, 53; Levi A. 53; Sarah 53; William F. 53
UNDERWOOD
  Mary 130
URTON
  John 60

V

VALDINEAR
  Francis 149
VALDINEY
  Joseph 148

179

VALIENT
　Henry 79; Mary 119
VANDIVER
　Ann 109
VASSE
　Sarah 2, 37, 53
VAUGHAN
　Jane 125
VEITCH
　Elisabeth 120, 149; James A. 149; Louisa 148; Richard 148, 149
VERMILLION
　Elenor 130
VERNELL
　George 149
VERNON
　John 75
VERONA
　Joseph 148; Sarah 148
VILNER
　Priscilla 90
VINARA/VINNARD
　Wineford 63, 74
VIOLET/VIOLETT
　Edward 109, 112, 114; Thomas 149
VORE
　Isaac 35, 53
VOWELL
　Charles 149; Charlotte 149; Ebenezer 149; Eliza 149; J.C. 149; James C. 149; John 149; John C. 149; John G. 149; Margaret 149; Margaret B. 149; Mary 149; Mary A. 149; Mary M. 149; Polly 136, 149; Robert H. 149; Sarah 149; Sarah G. 149; Sarah W. 149; Thomas 148, 149

W

WADE
　Ann 124; Anne 125; George 151; Valinda 104, 115; Zephaniah 104, 105
WAGENER
　Mary 104; Mr. 93; Peter 54, 56, 58-62, 65, 68, 69, 70, 72-75, 99, 101, 112
WAHL
　Mary A. 29
WAITE
　Thomas 113
WAITMAN
　Mr. 91
WAITS
　Andrew 63

WALDEN
　Thomas 151
WALES
　Andrew 90, 151; Margaret 151
WALKER
　Elisabeth 120; Fanny 125; James 151; Levin 151; Mr. 110; Rosanna 53; Sarah 136; Susanna 29
WALL
　Mary A. 53; Mr. 90; Mrs. 90
WALLACE
　Nathaniel 150; Richard 151; Susanna 127
WALLACH
　Nancy 150; Richard 150, 151; Richard S. 150; William D. 150
WALLHOUSE
　Rebecca 122
WALLIS
　Elizabeth 134
WALSH
　Mary 146
WALTERS
　Rebecca 146
WALTON
　Fanny B. 52; Mary A. 52
WANTON
　Hannah 53; Mary 37, 53; Mary H. 53; Philip 1-3, 5, 6, 8, 53; William R. 13, 16, 17, 40, 53
WAPER
　Elisabeth 130
WARD
　Elisabeth 146; Elizabeth 104; William 74, 79
WARDER
　Ann 21; Elizabeth 21; John 21
WARNER
　Samuel L. 150
WARREN
　Anne 97; William 97
WASHINGTON
　Augustine 99; Col. 69; Edward 99, 109, 113; George 66, 69, 79, 95, 99, 113; Henry 86; Lawrence 115; Lund 99; Thomas T. 150; William 86
WASS
　Mr. 92
WATERS (see "Watters")
　Ann 77; Mary 109
WATKINS
　Thomas 86, 151
WATSON
　() 150, 151; Andrew 152; Ann 146; B. 74; Benjamin 71, 73, 75; James 150; Josias 72; Levin 151; Mary 78, 143; Mr. 74; William 151

WATT
　Ann 144
WATTERS (see "Waters")
　Ann 78; John G. 150; Robert 150
WATTLES
　Ann 123; Nathaniel 86
WATTS
　Elizabeth B. 65; James 74; John 83; Mary 65; Polly 138
WAUGH
　James 99; Rachel 14, 22
WAY
　Salome 135
WEBB
　James 71, 73; T.W. 96
WEBSTER
　Adam L. 151; John 150
WEDGWORTH
　Kitty 122
WEEDS
　Priscilla 128
WEIGHTMAN
　Mr. 93; Richard 86; Sarah 138
WEILEY (see "Wiley")
　Alexander 92; Ephraim 80, 89
WELCH
　Alice 132; Susanna 141
WELDING
　Mecajah 41; Micajah 16, 19
WELL
　Mr. 93
WELLMAN
　Elizabeth 117
WELSH
　Elizabeth 109; Erasmus 91
WELTZ
　Peter 150
WEST
　Benjamin 58-60, 62, 63, 65; Benjamin H. 101; Elisabeth 143; George 56, 61, 113; Hugh 99, 104, 109, 113; James C. 151; John 54-57, 60-66, 68, 69, 70, 71, 88, 99, 101, 113; Margaret 63; Mr. 93; Pierce B. 68; Roger 80, 88; Sarah 107, 109; Sibyl 113; Susanna 68; Sybil 54; Thomas 1, 79, 88, 104, 106, 109; William 68, 73, 87
WESTCOTT
　() 151; John 152; Mary A. 133
WESTLEY
　Richard 90
WESTON
　Ann 127; Lewin 92; Mary 117; Mr. 91; Sarah 138
WETHERALD
　Ann 27, 35, 53; Esther 27, 35, 53; Joseph E. 27, 35, 53; Mary

27, 53; Samuel B. 35, 53;
Thomas 27, 28, 32, 35, 53
WETHERALL
  Sarah E. 32, 53
WEYLEY
  Nelly 118
WHALEY
  James 151
WHALING
  Mary 150
WHEAT
  Charity 141; William 151
WHEELER
  Drummond 76, 109, 113; Samuel 151; William 93
WHERRY
  Jesse 150; Mr. 92
WHITE
  Ann 128; Horatio 150; James C. 151; John 150; Mr. 92; Polly 91; Sarah 134; Thomas 150; William T. 94
WHITEHEAD
  Benjamin 104
WHITMORE
  Charles 71; Mr. 71
WICKLIFF
  Nathaniel 71
WICKLIFFE
  Benjamin 116
WIGART
  Andrew 151
WILBAR
  Sarah 151
WILCOCK
  Elizabeth 136
WILEY (see "Weiley")
  Anne 120; Ephraim 151; Hugh 151; Littleton 151; Martha 128; Mary 13; Sarah 127; Susanna 141
WILK
  Mrs. 93
WILKERSON
  Thomas 91
WILKES
  Christian 150; Peter 150; William 150
WILKINSON
  Ann 127; Thomas 75, 109
WILKISON
  Thomas 109
WILKS
  Margaret 109
WILLIAMS
  A. 93; Alexander 56, 151; Amelia 75; Ann 74, 148; Catherine 109; David 109; Elijah 101, 102, 106, 113, 150; Elisabeth 150; George 58, 74;
Henry 151; Jean 109; Jeremiah 70; John 58-60, 62, 63, 71, 73, 76, 151; Joseph 109; Kizzia 60; Margaret 151; Mary 151; Mr. 92; Mrs. 152; Owen 60-62, 69, 70, 113; Samuel 58; Sarah 134, 141, 151; Sophia G. 140; Susanna 109; Sybil 119; Thomas 83, 109, 113; Williams 146
WILLING
  Priscilla 141
WILLIS
  Dulick 71; Nancy 130; William 150
WILSON
  () 37; Ann C. 150; Anne C. 151; Bruce 150, 151; Campbell 151; Catharina 35; Catharine 13, 38, 53; Daniel 76; David 13, 14, 27, 29, 42, 48, 53; Elisabeth 151; Eliza J. 150; Enoch 13, 36, 53; Hannah 22, 29, 37, 41, 42; James 113, 150, 152; James C. 151; Jesse S. 24, 41; John 6, 8, 40; John W. 27, 29, 42, 53; Joseph 104, 109, 115; Julianna 30; Margaret 152; Martha 11; Mary 13, 16, 95, 150; Mason 150; Melvina A. 150; Mr. 90; Oliver 10, 11, 15, 151; Rebecca 13, Robert 54, 113; Robert J. 150; Samuel 13, 26, 53, 107; Stephen 22; Thomas 13, 31, 53; Thomas I. 27, 29, 53; William 70, 71, 83, 84, 150, 151; William B. 150
WIN/WINN
  Eliza 58; John 58
WINDSOR
  Susanna 140; William 151
WINKFIELD
  Winifred 151
WINSHA/WINSHEAR
  Martin 151
WINSLOW
  William 76
WINTERBERRY
  Elisabeth 119; John 83
WISE
  Catherine 138; Francis 150; George 150, 152; George K. 151; John 78, 86, 150; Joseph 151; Kitty 151; Mary A. 150; Michael 150; Nathaniel 151; Patty 150; Peter 59, 60, 68, 75, 89
WITHERINGTON
  Mary 113
WITTON
  John 76
WOOD
  () 151; Eleanor 130; John 151; Louisa 148; Margaret 18, 19, 22, 41; Susannah 46; Thomas 14; William W. 151
WOODCOCK
  William 151
WOODROW
  Grace 136; Henry 5; Mary 6, 37, 136
WOODS
  Thomas I. 150
WOODWARD
  James 90; Joseph 74
WOOLS
  William 78
WOOTEN
  Mr. 90
WORTHEN
  Henry 107
WREN
  Daniel 94; Dinah E. 94; Eleanor 94; J. 74; James 56, 57, 59-63, 68, 70, 71, 72, 77, 78, 81, 84, 88, 113; John 94; Maj. 74; Sarah 94; Thomas 54-58, 65, 88, 99, 115, 116
WRIGHT
  Abraham 63; Anne 122; Catherine 127; Charles 100, 109, 113; Daniel 151; Elisabeth 141; F. Edward v; Joel 18, 25, 29, 41, 53; John 150; Joseph H. 16; Mr. 92; Sarah 124; Thomas 75, 76; William 151
WROE (see "Roe")
  Elisabeth 118
WYAT
  Thomas 116
WYLEY
  George 150
WYN
  George 116

Y

YATES
  William 3, 5
YEATES
  Ann 53; Elizabeth 20, 37, 53; Hannah 20, 38, 53; Henry 20, 53; Rachel 53; Sarah 16, 37, 38, 53; William 7, 9, 10, 12, 15, 20, 26, 39, 40, 53
YEATON
  Mrs. 152
YOEN
  Ann 103
YOST
  Catherine 144; John 90; Rebecca

131
YOUNG
Alexander 104; Andrew 152; Elisabeth M. 152; Elizabeth 56, 63, 107, 113; Frances 152; James 152; John 75-78, 96, 113, 152; Joseph 73; Mary 152; Mary A. 152; Mrs. 92; Rebecca 96; Robert 152; Thomas 79; William 78, 152
YOUST
John 152

Z

ZANE
Mrs. 91
ZEPPERNICK
Mariana 152
ZIMMERMAN
Henry 96; Jacob 152; John 86; Maria P. 152; Mr. 92; Susanna 146

Other Heritage Books by Wesley E. Pippenger:

Alexandria (Arlington) County, Virginia Death Records, 1853–1896

Alexandria City and Arlington County, Virginia Records Index: Vol. 1

Alexandria City and Arlington County, Virginia Records Index: Vol. 2

Alexandria County, Virginia Marriage Records, 1853–1895

Alexandria Virginia Marriage Index, January 10, 1893 to August 31, 1905

Alexandria, Virginia Marriages, 1870–1892

*Alexandria, Virginia Town Lots, 1749–1801
Together with the Proceedings of the Board of Trustees, 1749–1780*

Alexandria, Virginia Wills, Administrations and Guardianships, 1786–1800

Alexandria, Virginia 1808 Census (Wards 1, 2, 3, and 4)

Alexandria, Virginia Death Records, 1863–1896

Alexandria, Virginia Hustings Court Orders, Volume 1, 1780–1787

Connections and Separations: Divorce, Name Change and Other Genealogical Tidbits from the Acts of the Virginia General Assembly

Daily National Intelligencer *Index to Deaths, 1855–1870*

Daily National Intelligencer, *Washington, District of Columbia Marriages and Deaths Notices (January 1, 1851 to December 30, 1854)*

Dead People on the Move: Reconstruction of the Georgetown Presbyterian Burying Ground, Holmead's (Western) Burying Ground, and Other Removals in the District of Columbia

Death Notices from Richmond, Virginia Newspapers, 1841–1853

District of Columbia Ancestors, A Guide to Records of the District of Columbia

District of Columbia Death Records: August 1, 1874–July 31, 1879

District of Columbia Foreign Deaths, 1888–1923

District of Columbia Guardianship Index, 1802–1928

*District of Columbia Interments (Index to Deaths)
January 1, 1855 to July 31, 1874*

District of Columbia Marriage Licenses, Register 1: 1811–1858

District of Columbia Marriage Licenses, Register 2: 1858–1870

*District of Columbia Marriage Records Index
June 28, 1877 to October 19, 1885: Marriage Record Books 11 to 20*
Wesley E. Pippenger and Dorothy S. Provine

*District of Columbia Marriage Records Index
October 20, 1885 to January 20, 1892: Marriage Record Books 21 to 30*

*District of Columbia Marriage Records Index
January 20, 1892 to August 30, 1896: Marriage Record Books 31 to 40*

*District of Columbia Marriage Records Index
August 31, 1896 to December 17, 1900: Marriage Record Books 41 to 65*

District of Columbia Probate Records, 1801–1852

District of Columbia: Original Land Owners, 1791–1800

Early Church Records of Alexandria City and Fairfax County, Virginia

Georgetown, District of Columbia 1850 Federal Population Census (Schedule I) and 1853 Directory of Residents of Georgetown

Georgetown, District of Columbia Marriage and Death Notices, 1801–1838

Husbands and Wives Associated with Early Alexandria, Virginia (and the Surrounding Area), 3rd Edition, Revised

Index to District of Columbia Estates, 1801–1929

Index to District of Columbia Land Records, 1792–1817

Index to Virginia Estates, 1800–1865 Volumes 4, 5 and 6

John Alexander, a Northern Neck Proprietor, His Family, Friends and Kin

Legislative Petitions of Alexandria, 1778–1861

Pippenger and Pittenger Families

Proceedings of the Orphan's Court, Washington County, District of Columbia, 1801–1808

The Georgetown Courier Marriage and Death Notices: Georgetown, District of Columbia, November 18, 1865 to May 6, 1876

The Georgetown Directory for the Year 1830: to which is appended, a Short Description of the Churches, Public Institutions, and the Original Charter of Georgetown, and Extracts of the Laws Pertaining to the Chesapeake and Ohio Canal Company

The Virginia Gazette and Alexandria Advertiser: Volume 1, September 3, 1789 to November 11, 1790

The Virginia Journal and Alexandria Advertiser: Volume I (February 5, 1784 to January 27, 1785)

Volume II (February 3, 1785 to January 26, 1786)

Volume III (March 2, 1786 to January 25, 1787)

Volume IV (February 8, 1787 to May 21, 1789)

The Washington and Georgetown Directory of 1853

Tombstone Inscriptions of Alexandria, Volumes 1–4

Other Heritage Books by F. Edward Wright:

Abstracts of Bucks County, Pennsylvania Wills, 1685–1785

Abstracts of Cumberland County, Pennsylvania Wills, 1750–1785

Abstracts of Cumberland County, Pennsylvania Wills, 1785–1825

Abstracts of Philadelphia County Wills, 1726–1747

Abstracts of Philadelphia County Wills, 1748–1763

Abstracts of Philadelphia County Wills, 1763–1784

Abstracts of Philadelphia County Wills, 1777–1790

Abstracts of Philadelphia County Wills, 1790–1802

Abstracts of Philadelphia County Wills, 1802–1809

Abstracts of Philadelphia County Wills, 1810–1815

Abstracts of Philadelphia County Wills, 1815–1819

Abstracts of Philadelphia County Wills, 1820–1825

Abstracts of Philadelphia County, Pennsylvania Wills, 1682–1726

Abstracts of South Central Pennsylvania Newspapers, Volume 1, 1785–1790

Abstracts of South Central Pennsylvania Newspapers, Volume 3, 1796–1800

Abstracts of the Newspapers of Georgetown and the Federal City, 1789–99

Abstracts of York County, Pennsylvania Wills, 1749–1819

Bucks County, Pennsylvania Church Records of the 17th and 18th Centuries Volume 2: Quaker Records: Falls and Middletown Monthly Meetings
Anna Miller Watring and F. Edward Wright

Caroline County, Maryland Marriages, Births and Deaths, 1850–1880

Citizens of the Eastern Shore of Maryland, 1659–1750

Cumberland County, Pennsylvania Church Records of the 18th Century

Delaware Newspaper Abstracts, Volume 1: 1786–1795

Early Charles County, Maryland Settlers, 1658–1745
Marlene Strawser Bates and F. Edward Wright

Early Church Records of Alexandria City and Fairfax County, Virginia
F. Edward Wright and Wesley E. Pippenger

Early Church Records of New Castle County, Delaware, Volume 1, 1701–1800

Frederick County Militia in the War of 1812
Sallie A. Mallick and F. Edward Wright

Inhabitants of Baltimore County, 1692–1763

Land Records of Sussex County, Delaware, 1769–1782

Land Records of Sussex County, Delaware, 1782–1789
Elaine Hastings Mason and F. Edward Wright

Marriage Licenses of Washington, District of Columbia, 1811–1830

Marriages and Deaths from the Newspapers of Allegany and Washington Counties, Maryland, 1820–1830

Marriages and Deaths from The York Recorder, 1821–1830

Marriages and Deaths in the Newspapers of Frederick and Montgomery Counties, Maryland, 1820–1830

Marriages and Deaths in the Newspapers of Lancaster County, Pennsylvania, 1821–1830
Marriages and Deaths in the Newspapers of Lancaster County, Pennsylvania, 1831–1840
Marriages and Deaths of Cumberland County, [Pennsylvania], 1821–1830
Maryland Calendar of Wills Volume 9: 1744–1749
Maryland Calendar of Wills Volume 10: 1748–1753
Maryland Calendar of Wills Volume 11: 1753–1760
Maryland Calendar of Wills Volume 12: 1759–1764
Maryland Calendar of Wills Volume 13: 1764–1767
Maryland Calendar of Wills Volume 14: 1767–1772
Maryland Calendar of Wills Volume 15: 1772–1774
Maryland Calendar of Wills Volume 16: 1774–1777
Maryland Eastern Shore Newspaper Abstracts, Volume 1: 1790–1805
Maryland Eastern Shore Newspaper Abstracts, Volume 2: 1806–1812
Maryland Eastern Shore Newspaper Abstracts, Volume 3: 1813–1818
Maryland Eastern Shore Newspaper Abstracts, Volume 4: 1819–1824
Maryland Eastern Shore Newspaper Abstracts, Volume 5: Northern Counties, 1825–1829
F. Edward Wright and Irma Harper
Maryland Eastern Shore Newspaper Abstracts, Volume 6: Southern Counties, 1825–1829
Maryland Eastern Shore Newspaper Abstracts, Volume 7: Northern Counties, 1830–1834
Irma Harper and F. Edward Wright
Maryland Eastern Shore Newspaper Abstracts, Volume 8: Southern Counties, 1830–1834
Maryland Militia in the Revolutionary War
S. Eugene Clements and F. Edward Wright
Newspaper Abstracts of Allegany and Washington Counties, Maryland, 1811–1815
Newspaper Abstracts of Cecil and Harford Counties, Maryland, 1822–1830
Newspaper Abstracts of Frederick County, Maryland, 1816–1819
Newspaper Abstracts of Frederick County, Maryland, 1811–1815
Sketches of Maryland Eastern Shoremen
Tax List of Chester County, Pennsylvania 1768
Tax List of York County, Pennsylvania 1779
Washington County Church Records of the 18th Century, 1768–1800
Western Maryland Newspaper Abstracts, Volume 1: 1786–1798
Western Maryland Newspaper Abstracts, Volume 2: 1799–1805
Western Maryland Newspaper Abstracts, Volume 3: 1806–1810
Wills of Chester County, Pennsylvania, 1766–1778

www.ingramcontent.com/pod-product-compliance
Lightning Source LLC
Chambersburg PA
CBHW070658100426
42735CB00039B/2264